Contents

Introduction

Introduction   v
Studying A2 physics   vii
How science works   viii

Unit 4
Physics inside and out   2

1   Attracted to the Earth

1.1   Feeling the force   4
1.2   Effect of atmosphere   6
1.3   Pulling together   8
1.4   Circling the Earth   11
      Examination-style questions   14

2   Leaving the Earth

2.1   Going up   16
2.2   Energy changes   19
2.3   Conservation rules   21
2.4   It is rocket science!   25
2.5   Rocket propulsion   29
      Examination-style questions   32

3   What goes around comes around

3.1   Moving harmonically   34
3.2   Back and forth   39
3.3   Up and down   41
3.4   Gaining and losing height   44
3.5   Round and round   47
3.6   Spinning faster and faster   50
      Examination-style questions   54

4   Imaging the invisible

4.1   Beneath the Earth   58
4.2   Gravity surveying   61
4.3   Magnetic field surveying   64
4.4   Measuring magnetic fields   67

4.5   Using electromagnetic induction   71
4.6   Eddy currents   74
4.7   Resistivity surveying   77
4.8   Seismology   80
      Examination-style questions   83

5   Inside the body

5.1   Using X-Rays   86
5.2   Production and properties of X-rays   89
5.3   Using ultrasound   92
5.4   Magnetic resonance imaging   95
5.5   Endoscopy   97
5.6   Charge coupled device cameras   99
      Examination-style questions   101

Unit 4 examination-style questions   103

Unit 5
Energy under the microscope   108

6   Matter under the microscope

6.1   Molecules in motion   110
6.2   Energy in gases   113
6.3   Heat engines and cycles   116
6.4   Cooling the engine   120
6.5   The arrow of time   124
      Examination-style questions   127

7   Breaking matter down

7.1   Accelerating charged particles   130
7.2   Deflecting particles   133
7.3   Mass spectrometers   137
7.4   Linear accelerators   140
7.5   Cyclotrons   144
7.6   From the first synchrotron to the LHC   146
      Examination-style questions   150

8 Nuclear radiation and its uses

8.1	Radiated energy	154
8.2	Radiation through matter	157
8.3	Radioactive decay rate	160
8.4	Radiation in medicine	164
8.5	Atomic batteries	166
8.6	Keeping a regular heartbeat	169
	Examination-style questions	174

9 Energy from the nucleus

9.1	Nuclear reactions and mass–energy equivalence	178
9.2	Nuclear binding energy	182
9.3	Energy from nuclear fission	185
9.4	Energy from nuclear fusion	190
9.5	What's the risk?	194
	Examination-style questions	198

Unit 5 examination-style questions 201

Unit 6
Investigative and practical skills 206

10 Practical work in A2 physics

10.1	Comparison of physics practical work at A2 and AS level	208
10.2	More about measurements	211

11 Internal assessment in A2 physics

11.1	The EMPA/PSV scheme at A2 (scheme T)	214
11.2	The AQA-marked scheme at A2 (scheme X)	217

12 Mathematical skills for A2 physics

12.1	Trigonometry	220
12.2	Logarithms	223

13 Extension mathematics

13.1	Simultaneous and quadratic equations	226
13.2	Differentiation and exponential change	228
13.3	Areas and integration	231

For reference

1.	Useful data for AS physics	234
2.	Useful data for A2 physics	236
3.	Glossary	238
4.	Answers to numerical questions	246
5.	Index	249

AQA Physics B:

Physics in Context

A2

Exclusively endorsed by AQA

Ken Price
Mike Bowen-Jones

rnes

Published in 2008 by:
Nelson Thornes Ltd
Delta Place
27 Bath Road
CHELTENHAM
GL53 7TH
United Kingdom

09 10 11 12 / 10 9 8 7 6 5 4 3 2

A catalogue record for this book is available from the British Library

ISBN 978 0 7487 8284 0

Cover photograph by Alamy / Jupiter Images / Ablestock

Illustrations include artwork drawn by GreenGate Publishing

Page make-up by GreenGate Publishing, Kent

Printed and bound in Croatia by Zrinski

Introduction

Nelson Thornes has worked in partnership with AQA to ensure this book and the accompanying online resources offer you the best support for your A Level course.

All resources have been approved by senior AQA examiners so you can feel assured that they closely match the specification for this subject and provide you with everything you need to prepare successfully for your exams.

These print and online resources together **unlock blended learning**; this means that the links between the activities in the book and the activities online blend together to maximise your understanding of a topic and help you achieve your potential. These online resources are available on kerboodle! which can be accessed via the internet at **http://www.kerboodle.com/live**, anytime, anywhere. If your school or college subscribes to this service you will be provided with your own personal login details. Once logged in, access your course and locate the required activity.

For more information and help visit **http://www.kerboodle.com**

Icons in this book indicate where there is material online related to that topic. The following icons are used:

💡 Learning activity

These resources include a variety of interactive and non-interactive activities to support your learning:

■ Animations   ■ Simulations   ■ Maths skills
■ Key diagrams   ■ Glossary

☑ Progress tracking

These resources include a variety of tests that you can use to check your knowledge on particular topics (Test yourself) and a range of resources that enable you to analyse and understand examination questions (On your marks...). You will also find the answers to examination-style questions online.

⚡ Research support

These resources include WebQuests, in which you are assigned a task and provided with a range of web links to use as source material for research.

These are designed as Extension resources to stretch you and broaden your learning, in order for you to attain the highest possible marks in your exams.

Web links

Our online resources feature a list of recommended weblinks, split by chapter. This will give you a head start, helping you to navigate to the best websites that will aid your learning and understanding of the topics in your course.

🔬 How science works

These resources are a mixtures of interactive and non-interactive activities to help you learn the skills required for success in this new area of the specification.

🧪 Practical

This icon signals where there is a relevant practical activity to be undertaken, and support is provided online.

When you see an icon, go to Nelson Thornes *learning space* at www.nelsonthornes.com/aqagce, enter your access details and select your course. The materials are arranged in the same order as the topics in the book, so you can easily find the resources you need.

How to use this book

This book covers the specification for your course and is arranged in a sequence approved by AQA.

The book is divided into two theory units and a practical unit.

Unit 4 Physics inside and out is divided into three modules:

> 'Experiences out of this world', 'What goes around comes around' and 'Imaging the invisible'.

Unit 5 Energy under the microscope is also made up from three modules:

> 'Matter under the microscope', 'Breaking matter down' and 'Energy from the nucleus'.

Unit 6 includes information and advice about practical assessment and the essential additional mathematical skills required for the A2 course.

The modules are further subdivided into chapters and then topics that make the content clear and easy to use.

The Unit openers for the theory units give you a summary of the content you will be covering and a recap of the principles and ideas from the AS course that are needed when studying the A2 content.

The features in this book include:

Learning objectives

At the beginning of each section you will find a list of learning objectives that contain targets linked to the requirements of the specification. The relevant specification reference is also provided.

Key terms

Terms that you will need to be able to define and understand are highlighted in bold blue type within the text, e.g. **superconducting**. You can look up these terms in the Glossary (page 226).

■ Hint

Hints to aid your understanding of the content.

■ Link

Links highlight any key areas where sections relate to one another.

■ How science works

'How science works' is a key part of the new A Level Physics specifications. As with the specification, 'How science works' is integrated throughout the content of the book. This feature highlights 'How science works' as it occurs within topics, so that it is always relevant to what you are studying. The ideas provided in these features are intended to teach you the skills you will need to tackle this part of the course, and give you experience when dealing with applying your knowledge to different contexts.

See the 'How science works' spread on page viii for more detail.

■ Summary questions

Short questions that test your understanding of the subject and allow you to apply the knowledge and skills you have acquired to different scenarios. Answers are supplied at the back of the book (page 234).

AQA Examiner's tip

Hints from AQA examiners to help you with your studies and to prepare you for your exam.

AQA Examination-style questions

Questions from past AQA papers that are in the general style that you can expect in your exam, including the new 'How science works' strand. These occur at the end of each chapter to give practice in examination-style questions for a particular topic. They also occur at the end of each unit; the questions here may cover any of the content of the unit.

When you answer the examination-style questions, remember that quality of written communication (QWC) will be assessed in any question or part-question in the Unit 4 and 5 examination papers where extended descriptions or explanations are required. So as well as making sure that you include correct and relevant physics, make sure that your answers are coherent, that spelling is correct and that your sentence structure is grammatically correct. The answers to these questions are supplied online.

AQA examination questions are reproduced by permission of the Assessment and Qualifications Alliance.

Nelson Thornes is responsible for the solution(s) given and they may not constitute the only possible solution(s).

■ Web links in the book

As Nelson Thornes is not responsible for third party content online, there may be some changes to this material that are beyond our control. In order for us to ensure that the links referred to in the book are as up-to-date and stable as possible, the websites are usually homepages with supporting instructions on how to reach the relevant pages if necessary.

Please let us know at **kerboodle@nelsonthornes.com.** if you find a link that doesn't work and we will do our best to redirect the link, or to find an alternative site.

Synopticity

Many of the topics that you will study at A2 require the application of ideas that you have learned in AS. It is important therefore that as you study the A2 topics you refer back to the essential AS topics when necessary. The ability to use ideas that have been previously met when analysing and learning new ideas, such as those you meet in the A2 course, is an important aspect of physics. Therefore, when answering a question in an A2 examination, you may need to draw on knowledge, understanding and skills from AS level.

Synoptic links are highlighted in the margin near the relevant text using the links icon accompanied by brief notes which include page references to where the linked topics are to be found in this book or the AS book.

Stretch and challenge

Some of the questions in the A2 examination will require you to solve a problem where you have to decide on a suitable strategy and appropriate methods. You may have to link different ideas from within a Unit or discuss, in an extended written answer, a controversial issue involving physics, perhaps in terms of advantages and disadvantages of an application that affects people or society at large.

The questions test your ability to think deeply and clearly about physics and to provide solutions and answers that are coherent and clear.

Studying A2 Physics

A2 Physics for AQA specification B

This book covers the entire content of the A2 course AQA Physics B: Physics in Context. The course builds on knowledge, understanding and skills from the AS course. The topics will deepen your knowledge and understanding of physics and your awareness of its many applications. The course provides a solid foundation for those who intend to proceed to university to study physics, a physics-based subject such as astrophysics or geophysics, one of the engineering disciplines, or subjects such as medicine, dentistry or veterinary science.

About A2 physics

At AS level you will have studied particle physics, cosmology and aspects of engineering linked with energy production using renewable resources. You will have an appreciation of what is involved in communications and the basic ideas necessary for further studies in electrical or electronic engineering.

In the A2 course you will have further opportunities to find out which aspects of physics interest you most. You will be introduced to the physics of satellites and how physics is used in the work of geophysicists and archaeologists. You will find out about some of the techniques used in medical diagnosis and treatment including scanners and the use of radioisotopes. The work on particle physics is extended to discuss how accelerators work and you will learn how energy is obtained from fission and fusion.

This course therefore provides a sound base whether you are interested in a study of physics itself or whether an understanding of physics techniques and principles is necessary for another career choice.

The physics content

Through a study of the contexts outlined above you will learn the important principles that are essential at this level. In mechanics, you will learn about momentum, circular and oscillatory motion. You will study the basic ideas of the three types of field: electric, gravitational and magnetic. In thermal physics you will study gases and how their behaviour can be described by the kinetic theory. You will develop further your understanding of nuclear physics by a study of radioactive decay and learn how concepts like mass–energy equivalence and binding energy are used to predict the energy release in nuclear fission and fusion.

A2 course structure

The following summarises the course structure, the examinations you will have to sit, their weighting in the A2 examination and the chapters that relate to them.

Unit 4 Physics inside out (40%)
Chapters 1–5

Unit 5 Energy under the microscope (40%)
Chapters 6–9

Unit 6 Investigative and practical skills (A2) (20%)
Chapters 10–11

Each unit starts with two opening pages that outline the key topics. In addition, a list of key elements from the AS course that underpin the unit are provided. Examinations in both the theory units (Unit 4 and Unit 5) may be sat in January or in June.

Chapters 10 and 11 describe the practical skills that are assessed in Unit 6. There are plenty of opportunities for you to develop these skills as you progress through Units 4 and 5.

In a similar way to the AS course, the practical test of the skills will be either:

- an assessment of your practical skills marked by your teacher(s) (route T) consisting of a practical skills assessment (PSA) and an investigative skills assignment (ISA)

or

- an assessment of your practical skill marked by an external examiner (route X) consisting of a practical skills verification (PSV) and an externally-marked practical assessment (EMPA)

Your teacher will decide which one of these tests will be used to assess your practical skills.

Chapter 12 Mathematical skills for A2 Physics covers the essential mathematics that is additional to that in AS and you should refer to this when necessary.

Chapter 13, Extension mathematics is not a requirement of the course but is included to give interested students a greater insight into the essential mathematics.

The reference section

This provides useful data, a glossary, answers to numerical questions, and a comprehensive index. A full list of the formulae and data that you will be provided with in your A2 examination papers is included at the end of the book.

How science works

The skills involved in 'How science works' will not be new to you. You will have gained some of the skills associated with 'How science works' during your GCSE and AS courses. Understanding and developing the skills in 'How science works' are important to scientists in all disciplines. Scientists use them to probe and test new theories and applications in whatever field of science they are working in.

During the A2 course you will develop these skills further by learning new practical and analytical skills. The topics you will study will increase in complexity and you will study how these ideas have developed, learn how they can be applied and consider the advantages and disadvantages to society of these applications.

'How science works' at A level (and at GCSE) has several different strands summarised in Table 1 and these are brought out in your course as appropriate in different topics. These strands include practical and investigative skills in science. They also consider the implications of scientific work in terms of how science is used not just by scientists and engineers but also by society at large. Science is often in the headlines, not only as a result of 'good news' such as major new discoveries but also through issues that concern us all, for example 'climate change' and 'depleting energy resources'.

Most of the strands in the table relate to practical work and the ability to communicate scientific ideas. The practical aspects are assessed in Unit 6. Other strands deal with the way scientific discoveries are made, how they change our understanding of the world we live in and the use we make of the discoveries, for example the development of MRI scanners.

The strands relating to the implications of science are important because what scientists do affects us all, and ethical issues are often associated with their work. For example:

- Should children be banned from using mobile phones because of concerns about the effects of mobile phone radiation?

How science works

Medical imaging

Discoveries in physics have led to a wide range of scanning techniques and the development of fast computers with large capacity memory. The ability to produce high quality images of the inside of the human body has produced a revolution in medical diagnosis.

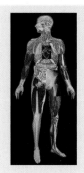

- Should scientists working on the use of radiation to treat cancer use patients to test the effectiveness of new treatments?

These strands will be tested in your AS and A level examinations; so you need to be able to discuss in depth a scientific issue by considering the benefits and the risks or the advantages and disadvantages. You will develop the necessary skills for these strands as you progress through your course and meet topics that touch on issues that show how and why science affects us all.

A major feature of this course is that you will learn the physics laws and principles through a study of their application in defined contexts that are particularly relevant in today's world. The topics also include consideration of many of the ethical issues brought about by scientific and technological developments where this is appropriate. This means that you will be learning 'How science works' throughout the course. Some particular examples are also highlighted in margin features where appropriate.

All the 'How science works' strands of AQA's Advanced level science specifications are the same. A study of the topics in this book and the 'How science works' features will help you to develop the relevant skills necessary for examination purposes. More importantly, it should give you a thorough grasp of how scientists work and what they do as well as a deeper awareness of how science is used to improve the quality life for everyone.

Table 1 *How science works specification summary*

Strands	Skills
A Theories, models and ideas are used to develop and modify scientific explanations.	Scientists make progress when validated evidence is found that supports a new theory or model.
B Predictions from a hypothesis (i.e. untested idea) or a theory need to be tested by experiment. If a reliable experiment does not support a hypothesis or theory, the hypothesis or theory must be changed.	Scientists use their knowledge and understanding in forming a hypothesis and when questioning the explanations of themselves or of other scientists.
	continued

Strands	Skills
C Appropriate methodology, including ICT, is used to make observations and measurements. Experiments are the key links between the 'real world' and the abstract ideas of science.	When scientists plan and carry out investigations, they need to: • identify the dependent and independent variables in the investigation and the control variables, • select appropriate apparatus and methods, including ICT, • choose measuring instruments according to their sensitivity and precision and carry out reliable measurements.
D The range of experimental skills needed to carry out scientific investigations include manual and data skills (tabulation, graphical skills, etc.).	Scientists have to follow appropriate experimental procedures in a sensible order, use appropriate apparatus and methods to make accurate and reliable measurements, identify and minimise significant sources of experimental error and identify and take account of risks in carrying out practical work.
E Data must be analysed and interpreted to provide evidence, recognising correlations and causal relationships. When experimental data confirm predictions from a theoretical model, scientists become more confident in the theory.	Scientists look for patterns and trends in data as a first step in providing explanations of phenomena. They need to know how to: • process measurement data, • use equations and carry out appropriate calculations, • plot and use appropriate graphs to establish or verify relationships between variables, • relate the gradient and the intercepts of straight line graphs to appropriate linear equations.
F The methodology used, evidence and data must be evaluated and conflicting evidence resolved. The validity of new evidence is a stimulus for further scientific investigation, which involves refinements of experimental technique or development of new hypotheses.	Scientists need to be able to distinguish between systematic and random errors, make reasonable estimates of the errors in all measurements, use data, graphs and other evidence from experiments to draw conclusions and to use the most significant error estimates to assess the reliability of conclusions drawn.
G The tentative nature of scientific knowledge needs to be considered. Scientific knowledge changes when new experimental evidence provides a better explanation of scientific observations.	Scientists need to know that if evidence that is reliable and reproducible does not support a theory, the theory must be modified or replaced with a different theory.
H Research findings need to be communicated to the scientific community to see if they can be replicated, thus either confirming new explanations or refuting them.	Scientists need to provide explanations using correct scientific terms, and support arguments with equations, diagrams and clear sketch graphs when appropriate.
I The applications and implications of science and their associated benefits and risks need to be considered.	Scientists apply their scientific knowledge to develop technologies that improve our lives. We all need to appreciate that the technologies themselves may pose significant risks that have to be balanced against the benefits.
J The ethical issues associated with scientific developments need to be considered.	Scientists have a duty to consider ethical issues associated with their findings. Scientists provide solutions to problems but the solutions often require society to form judgements as to whether the solution is acceptable in view of moral issues that result. Issues such as the effects on the planet, and the economic and physical well being of the living things on it should be considered.
K The scientific community itself validates new knowledge and ensures integrity.	Scientists need a common set of values and responsibilities. They should know that scientists undertake a peer-review of the work of others. They should know that scientists work with a common aim to progress scientific knowledge and understanding in a valid way and that accurate reporting of findings takes precedence over recognition of success of an individual.
L Decision makers are influenced in many ways, including their prior beliefs, their vested interests, special interest groups, public opinion and the media, as well as by expert scientific evidence.	Scientific evidence should be considered as a whole. Media and pressure groups often select parts of scientific evidence that supports a particular viewpoint and that this can influence public opinion which in turn may influences decision makers. Consequently, decision makers may make socially and politically acceptable decisions based on incomplete evidence.

Chapters in this unit

1 **Attracted to the Earth**

2 **Leaving the Earth**

3 **What goes around comes around**

4 **Imaging the invisible**

5 **Inside the body**

This unit looks at how physics is applied in three quite different contexts. The first involves space travel and orbiting satellites. The second is more down to earth and shows how physics is important in the construction of leisure parks. Finally there is a study of the science behind the methods used to investigate inside the Earth and inside the human body.

Experiences out of this world

Satellites are now taken for granted in many parts of our everyday lives. They enable us to communicate over long distances by telephone, to receive television signals from around the world, to operate 'satnav' systems and to forecast the weather accurately. Scientists now also work continuously in the International Space Station conducting experiments in conditions of 'weightlessness' and making astronomical observations that are not influenced by the Earth's atmosphere. This section includes a study of **Newton's gravitational law, momentum conservation** and the **laws of thermodynamics**. These laws are used to gain an understanding of the physics used in the launching of satellites and rockets and the positioning of satellites into suitable orbits around the Earth.

What goes around comes around

Theme parks are becoming ever more sophisticated in providing thrills. To construct safe but exciting rides, such as roller coasters and swing boats, designers need to understand the physics of the motion so that the structure can account for all the forces involved. This section looks at how **centripetal forces** produce the **accelerations** when bodies move in circular paths, and the way acceleration and force changes when bodies undergo natural or forced **simple harmonic motion**.

Imaging the invisible

How can we examine what is inside the Earth without digging or inside the human body without surgery? As the world's population increases and resources become scarcer, the discovery of new mineral deposits becomes increasingly important to satisfy our needs. The first part of this section looks at the ways in which geophysicists can use **gravitational forces, magnetism, electrical resistance** and **sound waves** to probe beneath the surface of the Earth in the search for new deposits. Non-invasive diagnosis of disease using physical methods is now commonplace in medicine. To make tests on the human body doctors have at their disposal techniques including using **X-rays, ultrasound scanners, endoscopes** or **MRI scanners**. The second part of this section looks at the physics of each of these procedures.

What you should already know:

From your studies at AS level on mechanics you should know that:

- a scalar quantity has magnitude only whereas a vector quantity has magnitude and direction
- a force is necessary to produce an acceleration; the magnitude of the force is proportional to the acceleration $F = ma$
- change in momentum = impulse
- motion with constant acceleration is described by the equations of motion and momentum is the product of mass and velocity
- motion is affected by friction and air resistance
- kinetic energy $E_k = \frac{1}{2}mv^2$
- change in gravitational potential energy close to the Earth's surface $\Delta E_p = mg\Delta h$
- total energy is conserved
- work done is force × distance moved in the direction of the force
- power is the rate of doing work
- stored elastic potential energy $= \frac{1}{2}F\Delta L$ if $F \propto \Delta L$

From your studies at AS level on electricity you should know that

- resistance = potential difference ÷ current
- resistance of liquids depends on the concentration of mobile ions that they contain
- resistivity is given by $\rho = \dfrac{RA}{L}$
- a potential divider enables a variable voltage to be produced from a constant voltage supply
- potential difference across each component in a series circuit is proportional to the resistance of the component

From your studies at AS level on waves you should know that

- the relationship between speed v, frequency f, and wavelength λ is $v = f\lambda$
- the intensity of waves from a point source varies with distance according to an inverse square law
- light energy can be transmitted along optical fibres
- total internal reflection occurs when the angle of incidence exceeds the critical angle
- the equation relating angles of incidence and refraction at a boundary is given by $n_1 \sin i_1 = n_2 \sin i_2$
- ultrasound waves are high frequency sound waves
- X-rays are part of the electromagnetic spectrum
- a photon of e-m radiation is emitted when electrons in an atom fall from a high energy level to a lower energy level
- the frequency of the radiation emitted is higher for larger differences between the energy levels
- photon energy $= hf$

1 Attracted to the Earth

1.1 Feeling the force

Learning objectives:

- What is weight?
- How can we be weightless?

Specification reference: 3.4.1A

Weight

Weight was considered at AS where it was demonstrated that it is related to gravity. People often refer to their mass as being their weight and statements such as 'I weigh 70 kg (or 11 stone)' are commonplace. Weight is the force of gravity acting on a body. The **gravitational field strength, g**, is defined as being the force per unit mass and is measured in $N\,kg^{-1}$. Thus the weight (w) of a body must be equal to the mass (m) of the body multiplied by the gravitational field strength:

$$w = mg$$

This equation is a special case of the familiar $F = ma$. So g can also be viewed as an acceleration meaning that $N\,kg^{-1} \equiv m\,s^{-2}$.

As the acceleration due to gravity is reasonably constant over the surface of the Earth, weight is calculated by multiplying the mass in kg by 9.81. This gives the weight in N.

Experiencing weight

You experience the sensation of weight from the reaction force of whatever you are standing or sitting on. When objects are not moving vertically in any way the reaction acting on the object is equal to the weight of the object (see Figure 1). When the object is a human body, it is the reaction that is felt not the pull of gravity. When a person free-falls out of an aircraft they would not experience their weight since there would be no reaction force (They would, of course, experience the drag force of the air). When in freefall the gravitational attraction of the Earth is present but since there is no reaction force there is a sensation of weightlessness.

AQA Examiner's tip

Which unit should be chosen?

It is usual to use $m\,s^{-2}$ when dealing with the motion of an object acting under the influence of gravity, however when dealing with the forces on an object it is preferable to use $N\,kg^{-1}$. However, since the two units are equivalent it really does not matter.

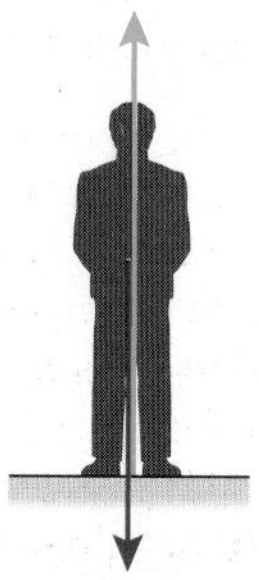

Figure 1 *Experiencing weight*

Weightlessness

There are only two possible reasons why an object should be weightless: either there can be no mass or no net gravitational field. Everywhere in the Universe is subject to some gravitational field, even if practically it is zero. This means that true weightlessness can only be achieved when two identical gravitational forces act on an object and cancel the effect of each other out (but even then there will still be other gravitational fields acting from everywhere else in the Universe). A point at which gravitational fields cancel is called a *neutral point*.

Rides and lifts

Fairground and theme park rides give some of their thrills from the sensation of weightlessness. To a far lesser extent it is possible to get the same sensation from a ride in a lift as shown in Figure 2. Figure 2(a) shows the occupant of a lift which is accelerating upwards; the occupant has a mass m. The two vertical forces acting on this person are the weight (w) and normal reaction (R). Since the lift is accelerating upwards we should choose up as positive and so the difference between the reaction and the weight must provide the upward accelerating force on the person.

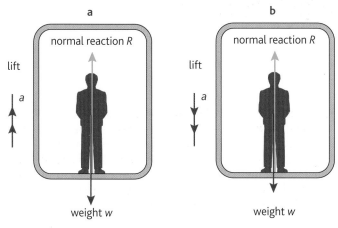

Figure 2 *The occupant of a lift*

$$R - w = ma$$

or

$$R - mg = ma$$

and this means that
$$R = ma + mg = m(a + g)$$

In other words the person feels heavier than normal by an amount ma.

Figure 2b shows the lift accelerating downwards. In this case let us choose down as positive and we can write: $w - R = ma$

or

$$mg - R = ma$$

this means that
$$R = mg - ma = m(g - a)$$

In other words the occupant of the lift feels lighter than normal by an amount ma. In an extreme case such as in the controlled condition of a theme park ride the vehicle in which a rider is strapped may accelerate so that $a = g$. The rider then feels weightless. When the car accelerates upwards at, say, $2g$ the rider feels three times as heavy as normal because the reaction will equal $3mg$.

Application and How science works

Maximum *g*-force

Human tolerances to acceleration depend not only on the acceleration but also on factors such as how fit the person is, the direction of motion, the length of time for which the acceleration acts and the position that the body is in when accelerated. Typically people can cope with vertical accelerations of about $5g$ before losing consciousness whereas military pilots are trained to cope with upward accelerations in excess of $9g$ for a sustained period. Downward acceleration which drives blood to the head is harder to tolerate and is typically $2g$ to $3g$.

Link

If you are unsure of this material you should review your understanding of free-body diagrams from the AS course, Topic 6.3.

Summary questions

1 Explain the role of the normal reaction force in the sensation of weight.

2 Explain how the **sensation** of weightlessness differs from true weightlessness.

3 In a fairground ride the peak resultant upward acceleration is $25\,\text{m s}^{-2}$ whereas that downward is $5\,\text{m s}^{-2}$. Calculate the maximum and minimum reaction force acting on a girl of mass $45\,\text{kg}$ under these circumstances. $g = 9.81\,\text{N kg}^{-1}$

4 Show that m s^{-2} and N kg^{-1} are equivalent units for g.

1.2 Effect of atmosphere

Learning objectives:

- What determines the resistance to motion through a fluid?

- How does Stokes' law apply to an object falling at its terminal velocity?

Specification reference: 3.4.1A

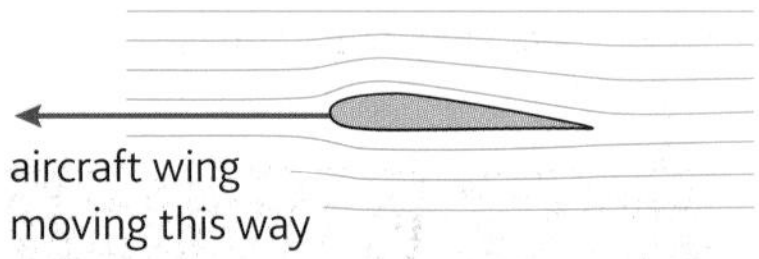

molecules stay in their layers

aircraft wing moving this way

Figure 1 *Streamline flow around the wing of an aircraft*

molecules move between layers in unpredictable ways

aircraft wing moving this way

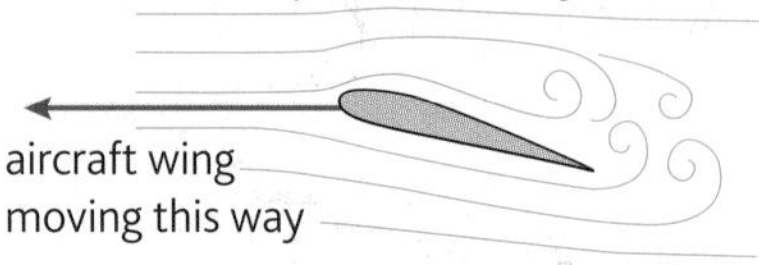

Figure 2 *Turbulent flow around the wing of an aircraft*

Viscosity

A fluid is a gas or a liquid. All fluids have a property called viscosity which is a measurement of a fluid's resistance to flow or its 'stickiness'. Oil has a high viscosity whereas air has a low viscosity. When a fluid flows or an object moves through a fluid the layers in the fluid exert resistive forces on each other (producing a stress across the fluid). A quantity called the coefficient of viscosity (η, the Greek letter eta) is used to compare viscosities of fluids. It is unnecessary to go into the details of how this is defined, for the purposes of this course, but you should know that its SI unit is pascal seconds (Pa s). Viscosity in gases arises from the molecular diffusion that carries momentum between the different layers in a moving gas. Surprisingly it is independent of pressure (except at very high or very low pressures) but it does increase with increasing temperature.

There are two types of flow in fluids:

Streamline flow is when the molecules of the fluid remain in layers and do not cross over into other layers. This is important for the wings of aircraft in normal flight where any turbulence in the flow is undesirable (see Figure 1).

Turbulent flow is when molecules move from layer to layer in a chaotic manner. When an aircraft wing is pitched at too large an angle, turbulence is produced and this can cause the aircraft to rise and sink in an unpredictable way. (see Figure 2).

Stokes' law

In the AS course it was shown that the viscous drag of the air caused objects in free fall to reach a terminal velocity. As the object accelerates the drag force increases and eventually equals the weight of the object which is then in equilibrium. Stokes' law is an equation which applies to small spherical objects moving through a viscous fluid. When a ball is at its terminal velocity the drag is given by the equation:

$$F_d = 6\pi\eta r v_t$$

where F_d is the drag force, η is the coefficient of viscosity, r is the radius of the ball and v_t is its terminal velocity. At the terminal velocity the drag force must equal the weight of the ball (ignoring any upthrust due to fluid displaced by the ball) so

$$mg = 6\pi\eta r v_t$$

For a ball the mass is given by the volume multiplied by the density of the material from which it is made. Thus $mg = \frac{4}{3}\pi r^3 \rho g$, where ρ is the density of the ball material. From this we can see that

$$6\pi\eta r v_t = \frac{4}{3}\pi r^3 \rho g$$

or

$$v_t = \text{constant} \times r^2$$

As the surface area of a sphere is given by $4\pi r^2$, the terminal velocity can be thought of as being equal to a (different) constant multiplied by the surface area of the ball.

Investigation

Figure 3 shows the apparatus that can be used to investigate how the terminal velocity depends upon the radius of a series of ball bearings dropped into a viscous liquid such as oil or glycerol.

A large transparent tube is filled with glycerol or fresh oil. Two rubber bands are placed round the tube at a separation of 20.0 cm. The radius of the ball bearings is measured using a micrometer screw gauge. The terminal velocity is calculated for each ball bearing by timing the fall between the rubber bands and then dividing the distance between the bands by the measured time. This should be repeated and averaged for each of the ball bearings. The larger the tube the more reliable the experiment, since the effect of drag at the edges of the tube will be reduced. A graph of terminal velocity against the square of the radius should be linear and pass through the origin. By using very viscous liquid and relatively small ball bearings, it is reasonable to assume that these bearings have achieved their terminal velocity before reaching the first of the rubber bands.

◼ The problem with the air

The drag produced by the air is present whether an object is moving upwards or downward towards the Earth. Gravity is always attractive and pulls objects towards the Earth but the drag of the atmosphere always opposes the motion of an object. This means that spacecraft leaving the Earth must overcome both gravity and air resistance; this limits the maximum speed which the craft can achieve. On re-entry air resistance again opposes the motion of a space capsule as it passes through the atmosphere; the space capsule compresses the air in front of it which heats up to very high temperatures. This is similar to a meteorite which, although usually tiny, gains so much **internal energy** whilst coming through the atmosphere that it becomes white hot. This effect is even more significant with a space capsule which is much larger than a meteorite. The surface of a space capsule can reach 1600 °C so they are typically coated with a material that melts then vaporises, a process called **ablation**. The process of vaporising the surface material requires latent heat which therefore removes heat from the structure of the space capsule.

The Space Shuttle is coated with ceramic tiles which are less effective than ablation but still suitable due to its much lower re-entry speed. When the Shuttle initially begins to re-enter, it is travelling at over 30 000 km h^{-1} (see Figure 4). This is far too fast to land safely and so kinetic energy must be converted into the Shuttle's internal energy. The stages in making a safe landing are listed below:

◼ The Shuttle inverts to gain protection from solar radiation.

◼ The rear thrusters fire to move the Shuttle into a tail-first position to help slow it down.

◼ The Shuttle slows before returning to a nose-first position.

◼ Any leftover fuel is burned to avoid it igniting.

◼ With the air resistance raising the temperature of the outside of the Shuttle, the astronauts lose communication for about 12 min. At this time the Shuttle slows further by making a series of wide S turns similar to those made by a slalom skier.

◼ At 600 m above the land the Shuttle is brought down at a very steep angle and the landing gear is deployed.

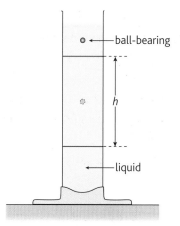

Figure 3 Stokes' law apparatus

ball-bearing

h

liquid

Figure 4 The Space Shuttle landing sequence

◼ Summary questions

1 Explain how the viscosity experiment, described above, could be developed to calculate the coefficient of viscosity of the liquid through which it falls.

2 By using the equation $mg = 6\pi\eta r v_t$ show that the unit of viscosity (Pa s) is equivalent to kg m^{-1} s^{-1}.

3 Calculate the terminal velocity of a ball of mass 50.0 g and radius 4.50 mm when if falls through a liquid of viscosity 0.985 Pa s. Use $g = 9.81$ N kg^{-1}.

1.3 Pulling together

Figure 1 *Newton's cannon ball*

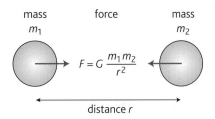

Figure 2 *Newton's law*

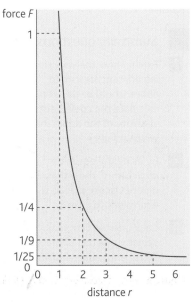

Figure 3 *Inverse square law for force*

Newton's brilliant idea

It is unlikely that Newton 'discovered' gravity by an apple striking him on the head, although it is perfectly feasible that a falling apple was the stimulus for his explanation of gravity. The steps in his argument are logical: apples fall from trees, no matter how tall the tree is, this will require a force, which we call gravity. If we fire a cannon ball from the top of a tall tower the cannon ball will eventually fall to the ground but if we choose taller and taller towers the distance that the cannon ball travels, before hitting the ground, will increase and the curvature of the Earth will mean that the cannon ball will eventually fall below the horizon (Figure 1). Eventually the curvature of the Earth will match the ball's trajectory and the ball will be in a fixed orbit around the Earth. This seems to be the case with the Moon and so it is sensible to suggest that the Moon is also held in its orbit around the Earth by gravity. The even more brilliant inference that Newton made is that if this happens to a distant object such as the Moon, then this will happen to even more distant objects; in other words all objects will attract all other objects.

Using Kepler's experimental laws of planetary motion (not required for this course), Newton concluded that gravity was an inverse-square law which takes the form:

$$F = G\frac{m_1 m_2}{r^2}$$

In other words: every particle of matter in the Universe attracts every other particle of matter with a force directly proportional to the product of their masses $(m_1 m_2)$ and inversely proportional to the square of the distance between them (r). This is known as Newton's Universal law of Gravitation. Figure 2 shows that the distance between the objects is measured from each of their centres of mass.

A graph of this relationship is a typical inverse-square law graph (see Figure 3) in which doubling the distance reduces the force to a quarter, tripling the distance reduces the force to a ninth, etc.

Big *G* and little *g*

You have met g, the gravitational field strength or acceleration due to gravity already. Newton's law contains one more quantity: G. This is known as the (universal) gravitational constant. It is not the same as g the gravitational field strength. G has a value of $6.67 \times 10^{-11}\,\mathrm{N\,m^2\,kg^{-2}}$. This is such a small constant that in order to have significant forces between objects the masses of the objects need to be very large. When an object of mass m is on the Earth's surface the force on the object is its weight (mg). The Earth behaves as if all its mass were at its centre of mass and so the separation of the object and the Earth is equal to the radius of the Earth (R_E). Using M_E to represent the mass of the Earth itself gives:

$$mg = G\frac{M_E m}{R_E^2}$$

$$\cancel{m}g = G\frac{M_E \cancel{m}}{R_E^2}$$

SO

$$g = G\frac{M_E}{R_E^2}$$

This shows that from the Earth's surface g falls off with distance from the centre of the Earth as an inverse-square relationship.

Although **you will not be examined on this concept**, it is interesting to note that inside the Earth the gravitational field strength would be linear, if we assume the Earth to be made up of material of uniform density. The mass of the Earth is $\frac{4}{3}\pi R_E^3 \rho$, where ρ is the density of the material making the Earth. This means that

$$g = G\frac{\frac{4}{3}\pi R_E^3 \rho}{R_E^2} \quad \text{or} \quad g \propto R_E$$

The Earth can be imagined to be constructed of layers where successive outer layers have no gravitational effect on the inner ones. This gives a graph for g from the centre of the Earth as shown in Figure 4.

Why do we consider *g* to be constant?

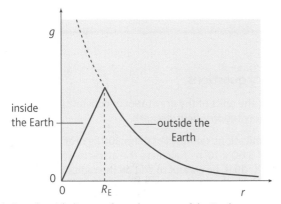

Figure 4 *Variation of g with distance from the centre of the Earth*

Close to the Earth's surface the Earth's gravitational field strength is very nearly constant but further away it falls in the way described above. Another way to think of this is by saying that the Earth's field is uniform close to the surface but radial further away (see Figures 5 and 6). Close to the surface the field lines are very close to being parallel so that for normal life near to the Earth they can be treated as being a constant distance apart.

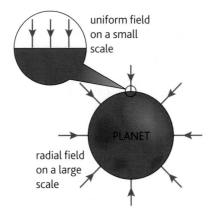

Figure 5 *Earth's uniform gravitational field*

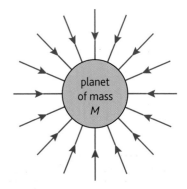

Figure 6 *Earth's radial gravitational field*

Application and How science works

Field lines

Lines of force (or field lines) are one model that physicists use to help understand fields. The lines themselves represent the direction in which objects move if they were placed on the line. The number of lines of force passing through equal areas (the density of the lines) gives an indication of the relative strengths of the fields. So in the case of gravitational fields, the direction of the arrow shows the direction in which a small mass would move from rest. Unlike other fields, gravitational fields are believed to only be attractive. This fact should be recognised by putting a minus sign in Newton's law equation:

meaning that $$F = G\frac{m_1 m_2}{r^2}$$

is sometimes written as $F = -G\dfrac{m_1 m_2}{r^2}$

This indicates that F acts in the opposite direction to r.

Summary questions

1 Show that the units of the gravitational constant are **not** equivalent to those of gravitational field strength.

2   A communications satellites of mass 300 kg orbits the Earth at an altitude of 3.60×10^7 m. Calculate the attractive force from the Earth acting on it. [hint; be careful to add on the radius of the Earth]
$G = 6.67 \times 10^{-11}$ N m² kg⁻², mass of the Earth = 5.97×10^{24} kg, radius of the Earth = 6.38×10^6 m.

3 Find the altitude above the Earth's surface where the Earth's gravitational field strength would be 20% of its value at the surface.

4 The graph in **Figure** 3 and the portion of the graph outside the Earth in **Figure 4** do not appear to be the same. Explain why these two graphs are consistent.

1.4 Circling the Earth

Learning objectives:

■ What is the centripetal force?

■ What is the relationship between linear and angular velocity?

■ What determines the period of a satellite?

Specification reference: 3.4.1A

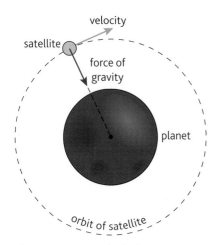

Figure 1 *Tangential velocity*

AQA Examiner's tip

Make sure that you label any force which is acting centripetally with its correct name. This is likely to be a gravitational force or weight in this module. You should never label a diagram with the term 'centripetal force'.

▦ Circular motion

In order for an object to move in a circle with a constant speed it must have a force acting on it which is always directed towards the centre of the circle. This is called the **centripetal force**. This is not a special category of force in its own right and must be provided by a force such as weight, tension, reaction or gravitation. For an object of mass m moving with a constant linear speed v in a circle of radius r the centripetal force required to keep the mass moving in that circle is given by the equation:

$$F = \frac{mv^2}{r}$$

Because the object is moving in a circle, its direction is continually changing; although its speed is constant its velocity is changing as a result of the change in direction (velocity being a vector). Consequently the object is continually being accelerated and therefore requires the centripetal force to do this. At any instant the direction of the object's velocity is tangential to the circle (Figure 1).

Angular velocity

A second form of the centripetal force equation can be written in terms of **angular velocity** (ω, the Greek letter omega). This is the rate of change of angle (in radians) with time.

When an object moves at a steady speed along the arc of a circle of radius r travelling a distance s in a time t its speed will be given by:

$$v = \frac{s}{t}$$

The angle θ moved through in this time is:

$$\theta = \frac{s}{r}$$

The steady angular speed is given by:

$$\omega = \frac{\theta}{t}$$

From these three equations it can be shown that the relationship between v and ω is:

$$v = \omega r$$

So the centripetal force equation becomes:

$$F = m\omega^2 r$$

Period and frequency

The time period (T) of an oscillation is related to the frequency (f) by the equation $T = \frac{1}{f}$. When an object moves around a complete circle it travels through an angle of 2π radians and the time that it takes will be T. This means that the object's steady angular speed (ω) can be found from:

$$T = \frac{2\pi}{\omega}$$

11

We now have all the tools that are needed to deal with the motion of satellites in circular orbits.

■ Satellites in orbit

Looking at Figure 1 it can be seen that gravity must provide the centripetal force for the satellite in orbit around the Earth. So if gravitational force = centripetal force:

$$G\frac{M_E m}{r^2} = \frac{mv^2}{r} \quad \text{so} \quad v^2 = G\frac{M_E}{r} \quad \text{or} \quad v = \sqrt{\frac{GM_E}{r}}$$

where m is the mass of the satellite, M_E the mass of the Earth, r the radius of the satellite's orbit and v the speed of the satellite.

We see that the velocity needed by a satellite to stay in orbit is independent of the mass of the satellite itself.

Geostationary orbits

At AS it was shown that communications satellites normally have orbits above the Equator and take up a west-to-east orbit with a period of 24 h; thus they remain above the same point on the Equator meaning that transmitters and receivers can point in the same direction without needing to track across the sky. We can easily calculate the angular velocity of the satellite since we know that its period of rotation (T) is 24 h or 86 400 seconds. Rearranging the equation $T = \frac{2\pi}{\omega}$ to give $\omega = \frac{2\pi}{T}$ we find that $\omega = 7.27 \times 10^{-5}\,\text{rad s}^{-1}$.

Gravity provides the centripetal force for the satellite so:

$$G\frac{M_E m}{r^2} = m\omega^2 r \quad \therefore \quad r^3 = \frac{GM_E}{\omega^2}; \quad \text{hence} \quad r = \sqrt[3]{\frac{GM_E}{\omega^2}}$$

substituting for ω, G ($= 6.67 \times 10^{-11}\,\text{N m}^2\,\text{kg}^{-2}$) and M_E ($= 5.97 \times 10^{24}\,\text{kg}$) we get a value for the radius of a geostationary orbit of $4.22 \times 10^7\,\text{m}$.

■ The effect of the rotation of the Earth on our apparent weight

When we are standing on the surface of the Earth the difference between our weight and the reaction of the Earth on us provides the centripetal force needed to keep us from flying off at a tangent to the Earth's surface, see Figure 2. The angular velocity of the Earth is the same as that of a geostationary satellite ($7.27 \times 10^{-5}\,\text{rad s}^{-1}$)

Since $mg - R = m\omega^2 r$ and remembering that it is the reaction that provides our sensation of weight, for a person of mass 65 kg and therefore actual weight 638 N, the reaction on the Earth's surface would be:

$$R = mg - m\omega^2 r$$

Taking the radius of the Earth to be $6.38 \times 10^6\,\text{m}$ the reaction on the person $R = 635\,\text{N}$. Thus the motion of the Earth reduces the perceived weight of a 65 kg person by a maximum of 3 N at the Equator – we think we weigh less than we really do! This effect is less than 0.5% and, as this is the maximum effect (it will be zero at the poles), it is sensible to equate the reaction to the weight under the vast majority of circumstances.

■ How science works

Geosynchronous orbits

A satellite with an orbital period of 24 h but not above the Equator is said to be in geosynchronous orbit. This means that it will pass over the same points on the Earth's surface at the same time each day.

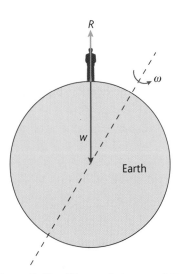

Figure 2 *The difference between weight and the reaction*

Finding the mass of the Sun

Exactly the same ideas used for satellite motion apply to the Earth's orbit around the Sun, see Figure 3. Equating the centripetal force equation to the gravitational attraction of the Sun we get:

$$G\frac{M_s M_E}{r^2} = M_E \omega^2 r$$

this shows that the mass of the Earth is not relevant to the calculation.

If $\frac{2\pi}{T}$ is substituted for ω the equation becomes $G\frac{M_s}{r^2} = \frac{4\pi^2 r}{T^2}$

or $M_s = \frac{4\pi^2 r^3}{GT^2}$

The Earth's period around the Sun is 365 days $(= 3.16 \times 10^7 \text{s})$ and the mean orbital radius is 1.5×10^{11} m. Taking the usual value for G gives a value for the mass of the Sun of 2.00×10^{30} kg.

Figure 3 *The Sun*

$\mathcal{AQA}$ **Examiner's tip**

The advantage of using the ω version of the centripetal force equation is that angular velocity does not vary with distance from the centre of the circle so the geostationary satellite and the Earth have the same angular velocity but the satellite is moving with a far greater linear velocity than the surface of the Earth.

Summary questions

1 A low polar orbiter Earth satellite has an orbital period of 90 min. Calculate the height above the Earth's surface corresponding to this orbit.

   $G = 6.67 \times 10^{-11}$ N m^2 kg^{-2}, mass of the Earth $= 5.97 \times 10^{24}$ kg, radius of the Earth $= 6.38 \times 10^6$ m

2 A planet has a moon with an orbital period of 6.2 days at an orbital radius of 4.5×10^7 m. Calculate the mass of the planet.

3 Explain the similarities and differences between geostationary and geosynchronous satellite orbits.

4 Two satellites, P and Q, orbit the Earth at radii of 8.5×10^6 m and 2.1×10^6 m, respectively. Calculate the ratio of the satellites' orbital periods.

1. Two planets P and Q with the same mass move in circular orbits about the same star. P is closer to the star than Q.
   (a) Explain, using a mathematical argument, whether P or Q has the greater
      (i) gravitational force acting on it due to the star, *(2 marks)*
      (ii) kinetic energy, *(2 marks)*
      (iii) orbital period around the star. *(2 marks)*
   (b) The data refer to the two planets.

planet	radius/km	density/kg m^{-3}
P	18000	6000
Q	36000	3000

   The gravitational field strength due to the mass of P at its surface is $30\,N\,kg^{-1}$.

   Calculate the gravitational field strength due to the mass of Q at its surface. *(7 marks)*

2. Stokes' law applies to small spheres moving through a viscous medium. It can be written in the form
   $$F = 6\pi a \eta v$$
   (a) For this equation, state the meaning and quote the SI unit of
      (i) F *(2 marks)*
      (ii) v *(2 marks)*
      (iii) η *(2 marks)*
   (b) Use Stokes' law to show that the time t taken for a small sphere of radius a to fall a distance s through a viscous fluid of density ρ is given by
   $$t = \frac{9s\eta}{2\rho a^2 g}$$
   (3 marks)
   (c) A student carries out an experiment in which she measures the times taken for small spheres of differing radii to fall a fixed distance of 1.5 m through water. The diagram shows the arrangement. She collects the following data having ensured that the spheres are travelling at terminal speed:

t/s	13	3.3	2.1	0.83	0.53
a/mm	1.0	2.0	2.5	4.0	5.0

   The density of water is $1.0 \times 10^3\,kg\,m^{-3}$
      (i) Plot a graph that will display the data as a straight line. *(3 marks)*
      (ii) Use your graph to find the viscosity of the fluid. *(3 marks)*
   (d) Explain why it is important for the sphere to have a much smaller radius than that of the tube that contains the oil. *(2 marks)*

3. Two hydrogen atoms are 3×10^{-10} m apart. Calculate the gravitational force between them. (Ignore the mass of the electrons.) *(2 marks)*

4. The giant Ferris wheel (the Riesenrad) in the Prater funfair in Vienna (**Figure 1**) has a diameter of 61 m and a journey time (one rotation) of 500 s.

Figure 1

Calculate

(a) the angular speed of the wheel, *(2 marks)*

(b) the tangential linear speed of a passenger 61 m from the centre of the ride, *(2 marks)*

(c) the centripetal acceleration of the passenger on the ride, *(2 marks)*

(d) the fractional change in total acceleration acting on a passenger between the highest and lowest positions on the ride. *(2 marks)*

5 Scientists wish to place a satellite in orbit around the Sun in order to study sunspots on the Sun's surface. The Sun rotates once every 27 days. The sunspot regions move with the surface.

Calculate the distance that the satellite needs to be placed from the centre of the Sun in order to remain stationary above a sunspot on the equator of the Sun.

mass of Sun = 2.0×10^{30} kg *(4 marks)*

6 Estimate the angular speed of

(a) a satellite in polar orbit around the Earth that takes 90 minutes to orbit once *(3 marks)*

(b) a satellite in geostationary orbit around the Earth (a geostationary satellite takes the same time to rotate about the Earth as the Earth takes to rotate on its axis) *(3 marks)*

(c) the Moon in its orbit around the Earth *(3 marks)*

(d) the Earth in its orbit around the Sun *(3 marks)*

7 At the end of the Apollo 15 mission to the Moon, Commander David Scott dropped a hammer and a feather simultaneously to repeat Galileo's experiment but this time in a vacuum.

A hammer was dropped from rest above the surface of the Moon and fell for 2.5 s.

The gravitational field strength of the Moon is one-sixth of that of the Earth.

Calculate the ratio

$$\frac{\text{momentum of the hammer after 2.5 s of free fall on the Moon}}{\text{momentum of the hammer after 2.5 s of free fall on the Earth}}$$ *(3 marks)*

8 A signal from a satellite orbiting the earth is received at the Earth's surface 79 ms after it was transmitted from the satellite.

(a) Show that the satellite is about 24 Mm above the surface of the Earth. *(2 marks)*

(b) Show that the gravitational field strength of the Earth at this orbital height is about $0.4 \, \text{N kg}^{-1}$. *(3 marks)*

(c) For the satellite in this orbit, calculate

(i) its linear speed, *(3 marks)*

(ii) its orbital period. *(2 marks)*

2 Leaving the Earth

2.1 Going up

Learning objectives:

■ How does the gravitational potential energy change as we move away from the Earth?

■ Should we consider the Earth's gravitational field to be uniform or radial?

■ What are equipotential surfaces?

■ How do equipotential surfaces relate to gravitational field lines?

Specification reference: 3.4.1B

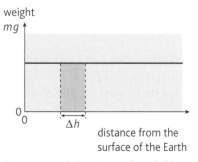

Figure 1 *Work done in a uniform field*

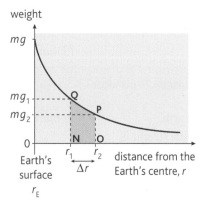

Figure 2 *Work done in a radial gravitational field*

Gravitational potential energy change in a uniform field

Close to the surface of the Earth the Earth's gravitational field is almost completely uniform and so g is a constant of value $9.81\,\mathrm{N\,kg^{-1}}$. This means that the work done in lifting an object through a distance Δh will be given by:

$$W = mg\Delta h$$

This is the amount of **gravitational potential energy** that the object gains (assuming no work is being done in moving the atmosphere out of the way). This potential energy can be calculated from the appropriate area under a graph of weight against distance from the surface of the Earth, as shown in Figure 1.

Gravitational potential energy change in a radial field

The gravitational field strength falls off with the square of distance as an object moves further from the surface of the Earth (the field is radial); this, of course, means that an object's weight will vary in this way too. The area under the relevant part of a curve of weight against distance from the centre of the Earth will give the change in gravitational potential energy. When a mass (m) is moved from r_2 to r_1, as shown in Figure 2, the decrease (in this case) of gravitational potential energy will be given by:

$$\Delta E_\mathrm{P} = GM_\mathrm{E}m\left(\frac{1}{r_2} - \frac{1}{r_1}\right)$$

The mathematics required to prove this relationship involves using calculus but the proof is not required for this course. For an object moving away from the Earth's surface there will be an increase in gravitational potential energy (it becomes less negative – see the How science works box). Radial gravitational fields are always produced by spherical or point masses.

Equipotential surfaces

The gravitational potential energy of an object at a particular height depends upon the mass of the object as well as that of the Earth. It is useful to be able to think of the space around the Earth as having a property which depends only on the mass of the Earth. This, of course, is the gravitational field strength.

There is a second way of thinking of the field. The **potential** at a point in a gravitational field is the potential energy experienced per unit mass at that point; it is therefore measured in $\mathrm{J\,kg^{-1}}$. The **gravitational potential** is **inversely proportional** to the distance from the centre of the Earth

$\left(V = \dfrac{GM_E}{r_E}\right)$, but you will not be examined on the derivation of this relationship in this course. Lines connecting points of the same potential are called lines of equipotential and, in three dimensions, the surfaces connecting these points are called **equipotential** surfaces. No work needs to be done in moving an object over an equipotential surface, which is why satellites in orbits outside the atmosphere will stay in a circular orbit indefinitely without the need for a source to power their motion.

Figure 3 shows how the gravitational potential varies with the distance from the Earth. If a space capsule moves towards the Earth, its gravitational potential energy is found by multiplying its mass by the value of the gravitational potential at that distance from the Earth. Since equipotential surfaces are really three dimensional, in three dimensions this graph resembles the horn of a trumpet and is called a 'potential well'. The Earth's gravitational field sucks the space capsule into its potential well.

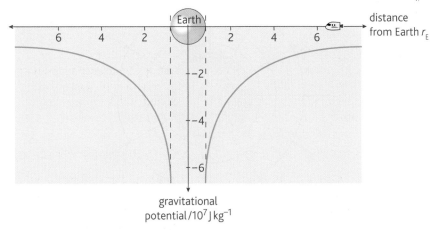

Figure 3 *The gravitational potential well around the Earth*

■ Application and How science works

Sign convention

As shown in Topic 1.3 Newton's law of gravitation should be written with a negative sign to indicate that it is always an attractive force. When considering changes in gravitational potential energy (gpe) the Earth's surface at sea level can be assigned as having zero gpe; moving upwards shows an increase in gpe and downwards a decrease in gpe. Absolute potential is measured from infinity where the potential is defined to be zero (the gravitational potential energy of an object is zero). As an object moves closer to the Earth the gravitational field of the Earth does work on it and so the object loses potential energy i.e., it gains bigger and bigger negative values. This means that the equipotentials around the Earth also take negative values.

AQA Examiner's tip

Although you will not be examined on the derivation of the equation $V = \dfrac{GM_E}{r_E}$ it is included here to help explain how equipotential surfaces come about and how they are labelled with their potential. You **do** need to be able to sketch the shape of the Earth's field lines and equipotential surfaces and to be able to interpret these.

Field lines and equipotentials

Figure 4 shows the equipotential surfaces and gravitational field lines around the Earth. The potential at the surface of the Earth is approximately $-62\,\mathrm{MJ\,kg^{-1}}$ $\left|\text{calculated from } V = \dfrac{GM_E}{r_E}\right|$. Note that the field lines are at right angles to the equipotentials and that as they become closer together the field strength increases. These equipotential surfaces are drawn at intervals of $10\,\mathrm{MJ\,kg^{-1}}$. r_E is the radius of the Earth which means by going to an altitude of r_E the potential will rise to $-31\,\mathrm{MJ\,kg^{-1}}$ (a negative number of smaller magnitude is increasing!), at an altitude of $2r_E$ the potential rises to $-20.7\,\mathrm{MJ\,kg^{-1}}$. The difference between the values of the equipotential divided by their distance apart gives the average gravitational field strength over that space.

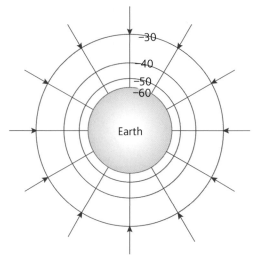

Figure 4 *Field lines and equipotential surfaces around the Earth*

Summary questions

1 Calculate the change in gravitational potential energy of a mass of 1.0 kg being raised to an altitude of 10 km

   a assuming the Earth's gravitational field to be uniform

   b assuming it to be radial. Explain which value is the more appropriate?

   $g = 9.81\,\mathrm{N\,kg^{-1}}$, $G = 6.67 \times 10^{-11}\,\mathrm{N\,m^2\,kg^{-2}}$, mass of the Earth $= 5.97 \times 10^{24}\,\mathrm{kg}$, radius of the Earth $= 6.38 \times 10^6\,\mathrm{m}$.

2 Using the graph of Figure 3 calculate the final speed of a space capsule of mass 2200 kg moving from $4r_E$ to $2r_E$ from the Earth. The capsule has a speed of $2.5\,\mathrm{km\,s^{-1}}$ at $4r_E$. State any assumption you have made.

3 Explain whether or not contour lines (lines of equal height above sea level) are lines of equipotential.

2.2 Energy changes

Learning objectives:

■ How much energy is needed to send an astronaut into space?

■ What is meant by escape velocity?

Specification reference: 3.4.1B

Escape from the Earth

When a ball is thrown up into the air it will usually come down again. The higher it is thrown, the longer it will stay in the air but eventually it will come back to the Earth. If we ignore the effect of air resistance, the energy change taking place is that the kinetic energy of the ball is converted into gravitational potential energy (gpe) on the way up and the gravitational potential energy is returned to kinetic energy (ke) on the way down. Throughout the motion the total energy is constant, being the sum of gravitational potential energy and the kinetic energy. The gravitation potential energy near the Earth is negative as shown in Topic 2.1 (being zero at infinity). The ball fails to escape from the Earth's gravitational field because it did not have enough kinetic energy initially (which when added to the negative potential energy would need to make the total energy at least zero).

Calculation of the escape velocity

In order to escape from the Earth's gravitational field the total energy of a body must be at least zero. Ignoring any energy transferred into the internal energy of the atmosphere or the body projected into the air

$$gpe + ke = 0$$

$$-G\frac{M_E m}{r_E} + \tfrac{1}{2}mv_e^2 = 0$$

where G is the gravitational constant, M_E the mass of the Earth, r_E the radius of the Earth, m the mass of the object being projected from the Earth and v_e its escape velocity.

Cancelling m gives

$$v_e^2 = \frac{2GM_E}{r_E}$$

$$\text{or} \quad v_e = \sqrt{\frac{2GM_E}{r_E}}$$

Using the values from the previous topic gives an escape velocity for the Earth of approximately $11.2\,\text{km s}^{-1}$.

Using the rotation of the Earth to help achieve the escape velocity

The Earth's rotational velocity is nearly $500\,\text{m s}^{-1}$ west to east at the Equator; an object projected tangentially from the Equator in an easterly direction requires an initial velocity of about $10.7\,\text{km s}^{-1}$ **relative to the surface of the Earth** in order to escape. If, however the object was projected tangentially from the Equator in a westerly direction it would require a velocity of about $11.7\,\text{km s}^{-1}$ **relative to the surface of the Earth**. The surface velocity of the Earth decreases with latitude, so space launch sites are usually located close to the equator in order to maximise the use of the Earth's rotation.

The Schwarzschild radius

The escape velocity equation $v_e = \sqrt{\dfrac{2GM}{r_E}}$ shows that if mass increases or there is a decrease in radius, the escape velocity needs to increase too.

Figure 1 *Hubble space telescope image of space surrounding a black hole*

How science works

Why the Earth retains its atmosphere

The Earth retains its atmosphere only because its escape velocity is appreciably larger than the mean speed of air molecules at temperatures found on the Earth. The Moon, which has a much weaker gravitational field strength than that of the Earth, has a much lower escape velocity – this means that even denser gas molecules have escaped, leaving it with no atmosphere.

Summary questions

1 What two factors does the escape velocity depend on?

2 Explain why Saturn, with a mass of over 95 times that of the Earth, has a smaller escape velocity than the Earth.

3 Show that the escape velocity from the Earth's surface can be given by $v_e = \sqrt{(2gr_E)}$, where g is the gravitational field strength at the surface of the Earth and r_E is the radius of the Earth.

4 Use the equation in question 3 to calculate the escape velocity of the Earth. ($g = 9.81\,\mathrm{m\,s^{-2}}$ and $r_E = 6.38 \times 10^6\,\mathrm{m}$.)

If a planet or star is sufficiently massive, the escape velocity equals the speed of light. Such an object would not emit or reflect electromagnetic radiation and would therefore appear 'black'. Einstein showed in the *Special Theory of Relativity* that it is not possible to exceed the speed of electromagnetic radiation in a vacuum. If the Earth was squashed so that its escape velocity were to become the speed of electromagnetic radiation in a vacuum (c), it would become a black hole, see Figure 1. The radius of a body under these circumstances is called the Schwarzschild radius (R_s). For the Earth:

$$R_s = \frac{2GM_E}{c^2} = \frac{2 \times 6.67 \times 10^{-11} \times 5.97 \times 10^{24}}{(3.0 \times 10^8)^2} = 8.85 \times 10^{-3}\,\mathrm{m}$$

This is approximately the radius of a large marble but with the mass of the Earth – very dense!

■ Application and How science works

Escape velocity, rockets and the air

Don't confuse escape velocity with launching rockets. The escape velocity should be thought of in terms of a cannon ball or bullet fired from the surface of the Earth (i.e. an unpowered object), it is not the velocity that a rocket or other powered object would need. Powered objects could leave the Earth at any speed if they had enough fuel; this is because the fuel is being used to increase the potential energy. Rockets leaving a space station in orbit around the Earth will need less fuel than from the Earth's surface because they have already gained considerable gravitational potential energy by virtue of having been taken to the space station in the first place.

Escape velocity and orbital velocity

As shown in Topic 1.4 the orbital velocity needed by a satellite is given by $v = \sqrt{\dfrac{GM_E}{r}}$. If this was a low polar orbit $r \approx r_E$ so the equation becomes $v = \sqrt{\dfrac{GM_E}{r_E}}$. Comparing this equation with the escape velocity equation $v_e = \sqrt{\dfrac{2GM_E}{r_E}}$ we see that $v_e = \sqrt{2}v$.

Energy of satellite in orbit

For a satellite in an orbit of radius r (above the atmosphere) about the centre of the Earth, its total energy (E_t) will be given by the sum of its kinetic energy (E_k) and its gravitational potential energy (E_p).

$$E_t = E_k + E_p$$

$$= \tfrac{1}{2}mv^2 + \left(-\frac{GM_E m}{r}\right) \text{ and since orbital velocity is given by } v = \sqrt{\frac{GM_E}{r}}$$

$$= \frac{GM_E m}{2r} + \left(-\frac{GM_E m}{r}\right)$$

$$= -\frac{GM_E m}{2r}$$

So the positive kinetic energy is half the magnitude of the negative gravitational potential energy giving a total energy that is still negative (i.e. it is less than it would be at infinity when the total energy would be zero).

2.3 Conservation rules

Learning objectives:

- What are the conservation rules of motion?

- How do the rules apply to collisions and explosions?

Specification reference: 3.4.1C

Conservation of energy

The concept of energy conservation has been used many times in this course already and you have undoubtedly come across this principle previously. The conservation of energy is arguably one of the most fundamental concepts in physics.

In any closed system the total energy remains constant although it may change form and internal work may also be done when one body interacts with another.

This law is very useful to physicists in problem solving since any apparent loss of energy suggests that we are not looking at the whole story of any situation.

Momentum and impulse

The importance of impulse and momentum was noted at AS when the safety features in cars were considered. To recap:

momentum is the product of mass and velocity ($p = mv$) and is a vector taking the direction of the velocity as its direction;

impulse is the product of force and the time for which the force acts (impulse $= Ft$), like momentum it is a vector taking the direction of the force as its direction.

Conservation of momentum

In any interaction between bodies the total momentum is constant providing no external force acts on the system. This relationship applies to any type of interaction and is useful in a range of situations from particle physics to rocket science. Later on it will be shown that if momentum is not conserved then there must be a resultant external force acting.

Consider the two objects shown in Figure 1.

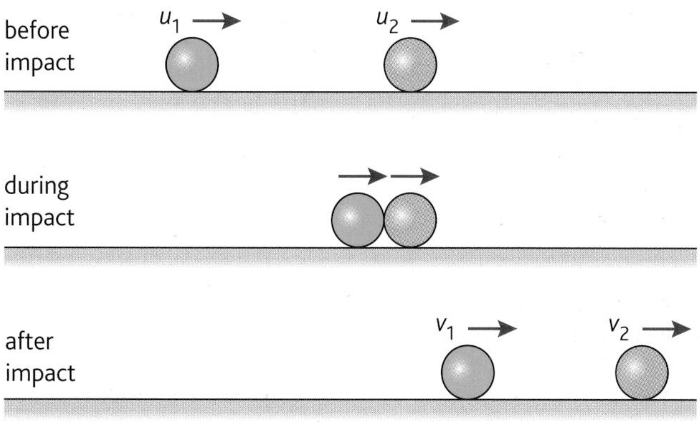

AQA Examiner's tip

Don't forget that the principles that you studied at AS may be assessed in your A2 examinations; the contexts, however, are unlikely to be revisited unless they are appropriate to the A2 context being tested.

Figure 1 *Conservation of momentum*

In this case the objects are moving separately, collide with each other, and then separate again. The momentum of each object changes but the total momentum of the 'combination of objects' remains constant at all times. In equation form:

$$m_1u_1 + m_2u_2 = m_1v_1 + m_2v_2$$

For each of the objects there will be a change in momentum from before the collision, during the collision and after the collision. This is perfectly acceptable physics since if we consider each object to be the 'system' then the interaction with the other object is an external force acting and this changes the momentum of the system. Newton's second law of motion tells us that the rate of change of momentum with time is directly proportional to the external force acting so during the collision we would expect there to be a change of momentum.

■ Newton's third law

The conservation of momentum is an alternative way of considering Newton's third law of motion. According to this law if two objects interact then the force exerted by the first object on the second must at any time be equal in magnitude and opposite in direction to the force exerted by the second object on the first.

In equation form: $\qquad F_1 = -F_2$

Newton's second law tells us that force is proportional to the rate of change of momentum with time, so in time Δt

$$\frac{m_1v_1 - m_1u_1}{\Delta t} = - \left| \frac{m_2v_2 - m_2u_2}{\Delta t} \right|$$

cancelling Δt and rearranging gives

$$m_1u_1 + m_2u_2 = m_1v_1 + m_2v_2$$

In other words this is the equation shown previously for the conservation of momentum.

Types of interaction

The conditions needed for momentum to be conserved have already been stated together with the fact that total energy is conserved in any closed system. Interactions (collisions) are labelled as a consequence of whether or not **kinetic** energy is conserved.

(Perfectly) elastic collisions

These are collisions in which kinetic energy (as well as momentum) is conserved. For macroscopic objects coming into contact there will always be some dissipation of kinetic energy; however collisions between snooker balls or the steel balls in a Newton cradle, see Figure 2, are nearly elastic. Interactions in which the objects do not come into contact, such as the 'gravity assist' of a space capsule around a planet or Rutherford alpha-scattering, are elastic collisions.

In a perfectly **elastic collision** between a moving object and a stationary object of equal mass, the moving object stops and transfers all of its momentum and kinetic energy to the initially stationary object, see Figure 3. However, in an elastic collision between two objects of equal mass travelling towards one another they swap both momentum and kinetic energy, see Figure 4.

Figure 2 *Newton's cradle*

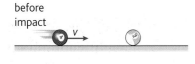

before impact

after impact

Figure 3 *Perfectly elastic collision between moving and stationary object of equal mass*

The equation for a perfectly elastic collision between two bodies of masses m_1 and m_2 is:

$$\tfrac{1}{2}m_1u_1^2 + \tfrac{1}{2}m_2u_2^2 = \tfrac{1}{2}m_1v_1^2 + \tfrac{1}{2}m_2v_2^2$$

(Partially) inelastic collisions

These are collisions in which some kinetic energy is converted into other forms of energy (often internal or elastic potential energy). All macroscopic interactions are inelastic to a degree in that some kinetic energy is dissipated. In a **perfectly inelastic collision** the colliding objects stick together after the collision. This does not mean that all the kinetic energy is dissipated just that the kinetic energy lost is a maximum. The two objects will move together as one and will still have some kinetic energy, see Figure 5.

Explosive collisions

These are collisions in which there is an increase in kinetic energy (with energy converted from elastic, chemical potential energy or nuclear energy). In many ways an explosion is a perfectly inelastic collision in reverse – an object initially at rest explodes and scatters with fragments going in all direction; the sum of all the momenta will add up vectorially to zero.

Momentum in space

Space is an ideal place in which to study the motion of objects; the external forces acting on astronauts are zero or negligibly small. How rockets make use of the conservation of momentum is shown in the next topic but firstly consider an astronaut undertaking a 'space walk'. Figure 6 shows the first American space walker, Edward White in June 1965. White carried a 'zip gun' which he used to control his motion by firing a blast of compressed gas. Using the zip gun was effectively an explosive collision; the astronaut and the zip gun behaved as the system. When the gas was released it produced momentum in one direction and in order to conserve momentum the astronaut moved with an equal and opposite momentum. White was tethered to the Gemini space capsule and pulling on the tether was another means of moving himself. The tension in the tether acted as an external force and therefore changed his momentum.

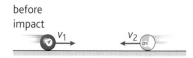

Figure 4 *Perfectly elastic collision between two objects of equal mass*

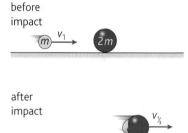

Figure 5 *Perfectly inelastic collisions*

Figure 6 *Space walk*

AQA Examiner's tip

Any collisions that you will be expected to analyse will be in a straight line but remember that momentum is a vector and so you can resolve momenta into components at right angles to each other. In each direction momentum must be conserved and therefore you can resolve momentum in perpendicular directions and it will be conserved in each of them.

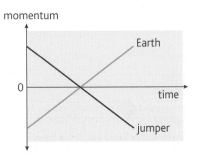

Figure 7 *Momentum of jumper and Earth during jump*

Momentum on Earth

How is it possible to jump up in the air and still conserve momentum? There are two ways of looking at this situation:

either we consider the person jumping to be the system. In this case the push up of the Earth on the jumper's feet (as a reaction to pushing down on the Earth's surface) acts as an external force and therefore momentum is gained by the jumper. There is an impulse acting which provides a change in momentum to the jumper:

$$Ft = mv - mu$$

or we consider the person **and** the Earth to be the system. In this case we have an explosive interaction when the person jumps i.e. the jumper and the Earth gain equal but opposite momenta. The mass of the Earth is so much greater than the mass of the person that the effect on the Earth is infinitesimally small.

Taking M_E to be the mass of the Earth and m_p that of the person, v_E to be the maximum velocity of the Earth and v_p that of the person due to the person jumping, the conservation of momentum gives:

$$0 = M_E v_E + m_p v_p \quad \text{or} \quad M_E v_E = -m_p v_p$$

Of course gravitation acts on the jumper and the Earth and the attractive forces slow them both down until they stop and move in the opposite directions. At every instant the total momentum adds up to zero, see Figure 7.

Summary questions

1 Explain what happens to each of two astronauts on a space walk when:

a one astronaut throws a tool which is caught by the second astronaut,

b the astronauts push against each other,

c one astronaut pulls on a tether attached to the space capsule, making it taut.

2 Using the internet, research how momentum is utilised in performing a gravitational assist (slingshot manoeuvre) to add momentum to a space capsule on long flights. Describe your findings.

3 A satellite has a mass of 250 kg. A broken panel of mass 15 kg is jettisoned with a velocity of 8.0 m s⁻¹. Calculate the recoil velocity of the satellite (neglect any initial velocity of the satellite).

4 An astronaut is outside her space capsule in a region where gravity can be neglected. She uses a gas gun to move herself relative to the capsule. The gas gun fires gas from a muzzle of area 160 mm² at a speed of 150 m s⁻¹. The density of the gas is 0.800 kg m⁻³ and the mass of the astronaut, including her space suit is 130 kg. Calculate:

a the mass of the gas leaving the gun per second and

b the acceleration of the astronaut due to the gun (assuming that the change in mass is negligible).

2.4 It is rocket science!

Learning objectives:

- How can rockets work in space?

- Why do spacecraft need to be so large when launched?

- What are the lift and drag forces and how do they arise?

Specification reference: 3.4.1C

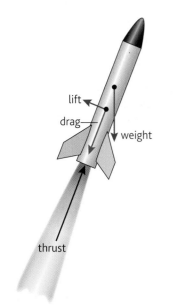

Figure 1 *Forces on a rocket*

Forces on a rocket

Figure 1 shows the forces acting on a rocket (they are similar to those acting on an aeroplane as described at AS). On an aeroplane, the **lift** overcomes the **weight** of the aeroplane; however it is the rocket's **thrust** that opposes its weight (when the rocket is close enough to the Earth for gravity to be significant). **Lift** is used to stabilise the rocket's flight path. Aeroplanes have a high lift to drag ratio but the **drag** of a rocket is usually much greater than the **lift**. The forces on a rocket vary throughout the flight, the **weight** reduces as the fuel is used up, the **thrust** changes when the rocket burns fuel at different rates and the **drag** increases with the square of the velocity. The density of the air changes with temperature and altitude and this affects the **drag**. Gravity becomes less as a rocket moves away from the Earth.

Rocket launch

The four major parts of a rocket are the payload, propellants, combustion chamber and nozzle (for a liquid-propellant rocket see Figure 2).

The payload is any cargo and equipment the rocket carries. Considering the space shuttle, its payload is the shuttle orbiter, its astronauts and any satellites or other scientific equipment that it may carry.

Rockets gain their thrust by the reaction to the ejection of fast moving exhaust gases. Most of a rocket's mass is made up of fuel and oxidiser (propellants). The fuel and oxidiser enter the combustion chamber where they react. As they burn, the propellants expand rapidly, creating intense pressure at a temperature high enough to melt the metal used for the construction of the rocket. The chamber thus needs insulation and a cooling system in order to cope with such high temperatures. The walls of the chamber must also be strong enough to withstand pressures of up to approximately 2×10^7 Pa (200 times atmospheric pressure at sea level). When the rocket is in flight the exhaust from the propellants is

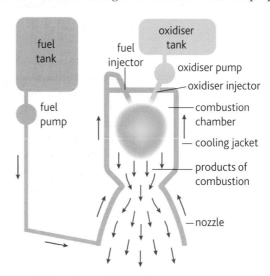

Figure 2 *Features of a liquid-propellant rocket*

ejected from the combustion chamber nozzle at the rear of the rocket. It converts the high pressure of the gases into thrust by forcing the exhaust through a narrow opening, which accelerates the exhaust to speeds of many $km\,s^{-1}$. This action produces a reaction force on the rocket itself which propels it forward; this is an example of Newton's third law of motion. An alternative way of explaining rocket motion is by using the conservation of momentum. Since the rocket has no momentum before it takes off, and since no external forces act on it, its total momentum must stay at zero. As the exhaust is ejected the exhaust gases have momentum in one direction and the rocket must have an equal momentum in the opposite direction (meaning that the rocket moves).

Loss of mass of a rocket

Assuming that a rocket can eject its mass at a constant rate and with a constant velocity relative to the rocket, then its thrust will remain constant. However the mass of the rocket will be decreasing as it uses up its fuel. Considering the equation $F = ma$ with a constant force and decreasing mass, it means that the acceleration of the rocket will increase. NASA design rockets to be as efficient as possible and this is done by having the mass of the payload (whatever the rocket is designed to carry, e.g. a satellite) as less than 5% of the total mass of the rocket. The rocket structure itself has about 5% of the mass and the fuel makes up over 90% of the total mass. To improve the payload to take-off mass ratio multistage rockets are often used. Each stage often carries a rocket motor, fuel, oxidant and reaction chamber. When the fuel is used up the stage is dumped or 'jettisoned'; this increases the payload-total mass ratio.

■ The rocket equation

This equation was first derived by Konstantin Tsiolkovsky in 1895 for straight-line rocket motion with constant exhaust velocity. The equation can be obtained from Newton's laws of motion (but involves calculus so you have no need to do this). If the effects of gravity or drag are ignored, the rocket equation can be written as:

$$v_f = v_e \ln\left(\frac{m_0}{m_f}\right)$$

where v_f is the maximum velocity of the rocket in gravity-free, drag-free flight, v_e is the effective exhaust velocity of the gas, ln is the natural logarithm, m_0 is the original or total rocket mass, and m_f is the final or empty rocket mass.

There are two things that affect the maximum velocity: the exhaust velocity and the ratio, m_0/m_f. In order for a rocket to go faster either the exhaust velocity can be increased by using more efficient propellants, or the m_0/m_f ratio can be increased by using lighter materials. This can be achieved by eliminating some of the rocket's structure or reducing the payload. Currently the most efficient propellants are liquid oxygen and liquid hydrogen so little can be done to increase the exhaust velocity meaning that the rocket's maximum velocity is heavily dependent on the m_0/m_f ratio. Making a rocket physically bigger means launching the same payload with a rocket with much larger fuel tanks. But this increases the mass of the empty rocket which means the rocket will need to carry an even greater quantity of fuel. Ultimately the rocket equation tells us that no rocket powered by conventional chemical propellants can ever achieve speeds approaching the speed of light simply because the mass ratio would need to be unimaginably large.

The rocket equation can be rearranged into the following form:

$$\frac{m_f}{m_0} = e^{-v_f/v_e}$$

A graph of $\frac{m_f}{m_0}$ against the final velocity v_f takes the shape of an exponential decay (like radioactive decay or capacitor discharge) as shown in Figure 3.

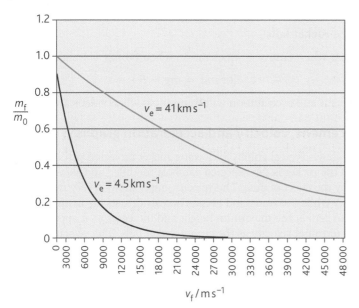

Figure 3 *Ratio of the final mass to the original mass for different final velocities*

Note the effect that altering the exhaust gas velocity has on the relationship between the final velocity and the mass ratio. For a higher v_e the same v_f can be achieved for a higher $\frac{m_f}{m_0}$ ratio, which means that a greater payload can be carried.

◼ Water rockets

Much interesting information about rockets can be found by investigating the motion of **water rockets**, see Figure 4. A water rocket is a model rocket in which water is ejected by means of a pressurised gas, usually air. The pressure vessel is usually a used plastic fizzy soft drink bottle. When the pressure vessel is partially filled with water, air is pumped into the bottle until the pressure is three or four times the atmospheric pressure. As the rocket is released from the pumping clamp the high air pressure drives the water out of a nozzle in the mouth of the tube. This action causes a reaction on the bottle which flies upwards, see Figure 5.

Forces on the water rocket

Typically it takes less than 0.1 s to eject all the water with another 0.05 s for the remaining pressurised air to be ejected. At the end of this time the rocket will be travelling with its maximum velocity and drag and gravity will be the only forces acting on it. Like any projectile the rocket will be brought to rest and then gravity will cause it to accelerate downwards with drag opposing its motion. The product of the thrust and the time for which it acts is the impulse and this will be equal to the change of momentum of the rocket. Since the thrust is derived from the periods when the water and then the air is expelled the impulse has two phases.

Figure 4 *An experimental water rocket*

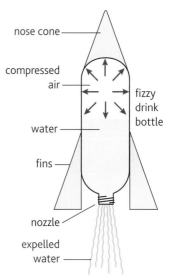

Figure 5 *How a water rocket is propelled*

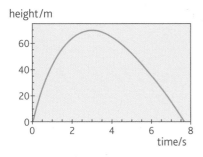

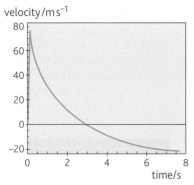

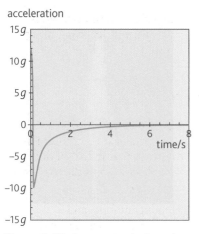

Figure 6 *Displacement, velocity and acceleration against time graphs*

If upwards is defined as being the positive direction, the force equation, at a particular instant, for a water **rocket when it rises vertically** is:

mass of rocket × acceleration when rising = thrust + weight + drag

$$(\text{or } ma_r = T + mg + F_d)$$

When values are substituted weight and drag will be negative. As time increases, the mass of the rocket and its weight will rapidly reduce until the rocket is empty, when its mass and weight will remain constant.

When the **rocket falls**:

mass when empty × acceleration when falling = weight + drag

$$(\text{or } ma_f = mg + F_d)$$

(both weight and acceleration will be negative when values are substituted).

Displacement, velocity and acceleration graphs

Figure 6 shows typical graphs for a water rocket projected vertically. The height of the rocket is the expected parabola modified and skewed (squashed a little) by the effect of drag. The velocity graph shows a very rapid increase in velocity while the water and pressurised air thrusts are acting; it then reduces to zero at the maximum height and increases as it approaches a negative terminal velocity as the empty rocket falls. The velocity at each instant is, of course, the gradient of the tangent to the displacement (height) against time graph at that instant. The acceleration is the gradient of the velocity–time graph. Notice the initial thrust reaches approximately $12g$, i.e. $12 × 9.8\,\text{ms}^{-2}$ but as the terminal velocity is reached it falls to almost zero.

■ **Application and How science works**

Safety with water rockets

Water rockets can be dangerous if misused or there is construction or material failure. Accepted good practice is to pressure test a fizzy drink bottle by completely filling the bottle with water before pressurising it to well above the normal pressure that is to be used. The low volume of air inside a full bottle should cause the bottle to split rather than explode. Other risks can be minimised by using the rocket in an open space, having a release mechanism that can be triggered from a distance and ensuring the rocket does not point at buildings, trees and especially people or animals.

Summary questions

1 Calculate the increase in velocity of a 150 g water rocket when a thrust of 20 N acts on it for 0.080 s; assume its mass is unchanged.

2 Explain why a rocket's acceleration will increase even though it experiences a constant thrust.

3 A rocket with final speed 9000 m s^{-1} could use chemical propellants ejected at a range of speeds from 2500–4500 m s^{-1}. Explain which ejection speed is preferable and calculate the mass ratio (m_f/m_o) for each propellant speed.

4 What safety considerations should be borne in mind when experimenting with water rockets?

2.5 Rocket propulsion

Learning objectives:

- How is the thrust produced by a rocket motor?

- How does the ideal gas equation apply to the gases produced in a rocket?

- How does the first law of thermodynamics apply to a rocket?

Specification reference: 3.4.1C

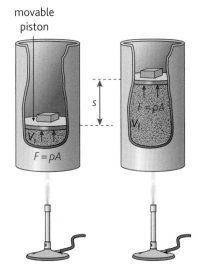

movable piston

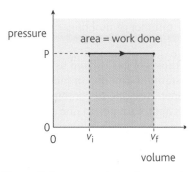

Figure 1 *Work done on the surroundings by an expanding gas*

Rockets and gases

The combustion of fuel in the combustion chamber of a chemical rocket produces a high pressure gas which is ejected through the rocket nozzle. The accelerated exhaust gas is called the **working fluid**. Turbine engines and propeller powered aircraft use air from the atmosphere as the working fluid. With no air, turbine and propeller powered aircraft cannot work. While in the combustion chamber the gas behaves as any other gas and exhibits the macroscopic properties of pressure, volume and temperature due to the microscopic properties of the gas molecules including the transfer of momentum and energy. The increase in gas pressure pushes on the rocket which causes the rocket to experience a thrust as discussed in the previous topic. The unbalanced force does work on the rocket at the expense of the chemical energy of the propellants.

The first law of thermodynamics

The first law of thermodynamics is a restatement of the conservation of energy and links the quantities of **work** (W), change in **internal energy** (ΔU) and **heat** (Q).

The equation for this law takes the form:

$$\Delta U = Q + W$$

The internal energy of a substance (working fluid) is the total kinetic and potential energy of all the molecules. Thus, for the change in internal energy of a substance (ΔU) to increase, heat must be supplied to the substance and/or work must be done on the substance; in other words the total of Q and W must be greater than zero.

At AS it was shown that work done is the product of force and displacement in the direction of the force ($W = Fs$). Remember that the definition of pressure is force per unit area:

$$p = \frac{F}{A} \longrightarrow F = pA$$

So the work done by a gas expanding at constant pressure (for example in a cylinder enclosed by a piston, as shown in Figure 1) will be given by $W = pAs$. As the piston area is constant $As = \Delta V$ (the increase in volume) giving $W = p\Delta V$.

This quantity is the area under a graph of pressure against volume, as shown in Figure 2. Here $\Delta V = V_f - V_i$.

For a gas the internal energy is proportional to the absolute temperature and so an increase in internal energy results in a temperature rise.

Figure 2 *Pressure against volume graph for gas*

■ Application and How science works

Sign convention

It is vital when using the equation for the first law of thermodynamics that you adhere to the sign convention. On this course we use the sign convention that quantities are positive when:

▨ there is an increase in internal energy of the working fluid,

▨ work is being done on the working fluid,

▨ heat is being transferred to the working fluid by conduction, convection and thermal radiation.

Quantities are negative when:

▨ there is a decrease in internal energy of the working fluid,

▨ work is being done by the working fluid,

▨ heat is being transferred away from the working fluid.

Thermodynamics of rocket propulsion

In a liquid fuel rocket the propellants react in the combustion chamber, converting their stored chemical energy into internal energy in the gases formed as products of the reaction. These high temperature and high pressure gases are then accelerated through the exhaust nozzle (exchanging internal energy for kinetic energy). As they pass through the exhaust nozzle they push on the walls of the nozzle doing work on the rocket. The kinetic and/or potential energy of the rocket increases as a result. Any energy left in the exhaust (internal and kinetic) is lost to the atmosphere which sees a very slight increase in its internal energy as a result of the whole process.

Now consider the rocket's exhaust gases as they exit the nozzle to be the system. The system loses internal energy (and cools) as a result of doing work on the rocket and the expansion happens in such a short time that no heat can transfer out of the rocket's nozzle (it is an **adiabatic** expansion). Thus ΔU and W are negative quantities and Q is zero.

The ideal gas equation

The high pressure produced in the nozzle of a rocket originates because of the combustion of the fuel. The mechanism for this increase in pressure can be simplified by considering the gas to be ideal. This is one which obeys the ideal gas equation: $pV = nRT$. Here p represents the pressure of the gas in Pa, V its volume in m^3, n the number of mol of gas, R the molar gas constant and T the temperature in K.

When gas is in the nozzle the number of moles of gas is fixed as is the volume of the nozzle and the gas constant. So the rise in pressure originates as a result of the increased temperature due to combustion. Having a fixed volume means that the gas approximates to one obeying the pressure law so that $p \propto T$. This gives a linear graph of pressure against temperature as shown in Figure 3.

Rocket propulsion systems

In this and the previous topics liquid fuel rocket propulsion has been discussed. However, liquid fuel is not the only type of propulsion system.

AQA **Examiner's tip**

R is the molar gas constant and has a value of $8.3\,J\,mol^{-1}\,K^{-1}$.

n is the number of moles (mol) of a substance. The mol being a quantity used to refer to the amount of substance present in a sample of material. It is defined as being the amount of a substance that contains as many atoms, molecules, ions, or other elementary units as the number of atoms in $0.012\,kg$ of carbon 12. The number is 6.0225×10^{23}, or Avogadro's number.

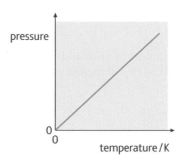

Figure 3 *p–T graph for the rocket gas*

Solid fuel system

Solid fuel propulsion systems provide large amounts of thrust but cannot be switched off once ignited. They are safe and stable until ignited and are used to power model rockets as well as to give the Space Shuttle its initial boost. The fuel and the oxidiser are combined to generate high temperatures and pressures. As with liquid systems, gaseous fuel then passes through a nozzle and is expelled. A solid fuel engine burns from the inside outwards and so the cavity inside the engine increases in volume. The temperature of the combustion is a constant and therefore (by the ideal gas equation: $pV = nRT$) when the volume increases the pressure must decrease. When the pressure falls the rocket motor works less efficiently.

Cold gas system

This is the simplest form of chemical propulsion, consisting of a single gas and a nozzle. When thrust is required the nozzle is opened and some of the gas is ejected. This is the safest of all of the chemical propulsion systems but less efficient than other chemical propellants. As gas is used the pressure goes down, reducing both the thrust and efficiency. This system operates in much the same way as when an inflated balloon is released; as the gas leaves the balloon the pressure drops and so does the thrust. In terms of the ideal gas equation p, V and n all fall.

Ion propulsion system

An ion propulsion system is a form of electric propulsion in which very small amounts of ionised gas are accelerated by an electrostatic field to produce a high-speed exhaust (typically $30\,\mathrm{km\,s^{-1}}$), unlike chemical systems which eject large amounts of gas at a slow speed. This means that an ion system uses far less fuel than a chemical system. It is, however, not effective in the atmosphere or as a launch vehicle, but extremely useful in space where a small amount of thrust acting over a long time period can result in a big difference in velocity. This makes an ion engine particularly useful either as a final thruster to position a satellite in a higher orbit or for deep-space exercises requiring thrust over a period of months to provide a high final velocity. The source of electrical energy for an ion engine can be either solar or nuclear.

Figure 4 *European Space Agency's SMART-1 ion thruster*
SMART-1 was launched in September 2003, and arrived at the Moon on 15 November 2004, during this time it tested new technologies, including solar-electric (ion) propulsion for future applications in interplanetary travels. The mission ended through lunar impact on 3 September 2006.

Summary questions

1 Apply the first law of thermodynamics to a rocket moving through the atmosphere into space. Consider the whole rocket to be the system.

2 Explain the advantages of an ion (electrical) propulsion system over chemical propulsion systems.

3 A water rocket of volume $1.0 \times 10^{-3}\,\mathrm{m^3}$ contains 0.250 mol of air at a pressure of $5.5 \times 10^5\,\mathrm{Pa}$ above atmospheric pressure.

   a Calculate the absolute temperature of the air.

   b Calculate the temperature of air remaining in the rocket when 0.044 mol of air remains at atmospheric pressure.

   c Using the first law of thermodynamics explain why the temperature of the air drops.

1 (a) Explain in terms of both its energy and its speed, what is meant by the *escape speed* of a space rocket. *(2 marks)*

   (b) Using the symbols M for the mass of the Earth and R for the radius of the Earth, show that the escape speed v for a rocket on the Earth is given by

$$v = \sqrt{\frac{2GM}{R}}$$

(2 marks)

   (c) The nominal escape speed from the Earth is $11.2\,\text{km s}^{-1}$. Calculate a value for the escape speed from a planet of mass six times that of the Earth and radius three times that of the Earth. *(2 marks)*

   (d) Explain why the actual escape speed from the Earth would be greater than $11.2\,\text{km s}^{-1}$. *(3 marks)*

2 A satellite is stranded on the Moon. NASA wishes to recover it and to place it in orbit around the Moon.

   The graph in **Figure 1** shows the variation of gravitational field strength against distance from the centre of the Moon.

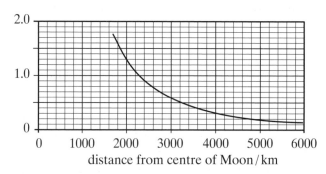

gravitational field strength / N kg^{-1}

distance from centre of Moon / km

Figure 1

   (a) (i) Explain why the line does not extend to the y-axis. *(1 mark)*

       (ii) Copy the graph and sketch on your copy the area that corresponds to the energy needed to move 1 kg from the surface of the Moon to a vertical height of 4000 km above the surface. *(2 marks)*

       (iii) The satellite has a mass of 450 kg. Estimate the change in gravitational potential energy of the satellite when it is moved from the surface of the Moon to a vertical height of 4000 km above its surface. *(5 marks)*

   (b) NASA now decides to bring the satellite back to Earth. Explain why the amount of fuel required to return the satellite to Earth will be **much** less than the amount required to send it to the Moon originally. *(5 marks)*

AQA, 2004

3 (a) Starting with the relationship between impulse and the change in momentum, show clearly that the unit, N, is equivalent to kg m s^{-2}. *(2 marks)*

   (b) A rocket uses a liquid propellant in order to move.

   Explain how the ejection of the waste gases in one direction makes the rocket move in the opposite direction. *(3 marks)*

   (c) A rocket ejects $1.5 \times 10^4\,\text{kg}$ of waste gas per second. The gas is ejected with a speed of $2.4\,\text{km s}^{-1}$ relative to the rocket. Calculate the average thrust on the rocket. *(3 marks)*

AQA, 2004

4 (a) (i) State the principle of conservation of momentum. *(2 marks)*

       (ii) Explain briefly how an elastic collision is different from an inelastic collision. *(2 marks)*

(iii) Describe and explain what happens when a moving particle collides elastically with a stationary particle of equal mass. *(4 marks)*

(b) **Figure 2** shows an astronaut undertaking a space-walk. The astronaut is tethered by a rope to a spacecraft of mass 4.0×10^4 kg. The spacecraft is moving at constant velocity.

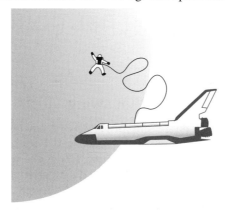

Figure 2

The astronaut and spacesuit have a total mass of 130 kg. The change in velocity of the astronaut after pushing off is 1.80 m s^{-1}.

(i) Determine the velocity change of the spacecraft. *(3 marks)*

(ii) The astronaut pushes for 0.60 s in achieving this speed. Calculate the average power developed by the astronaut. Neglect the change in motion of the spacecraft. *(3 marks)*

(iii) The rope eventually becomes taut. Suggest what would happen next. *(3 marks)*

AQA, 2000

5 (a) The first law of thermodynamics can be represented by $Q = \Delta U - W$.

State and explain, with reference to the equation, two ways in which the internal energy of a gas can be decreased. *(3 marks)*

A chemical rocket is launched. A volume of 20 m^3 of exhaust gas from a rocket leaves the rocket exhaust at a pressure of 1.0×10^5 Pa. The gas is cooled by the surrounding atmosphere, which is also at a pressure of 1.0×10^5 Pa, and, as a result, the gas contracts to half its volume.

(b) (i) Calculate the work done by the atmosphere on the gas during this contraction *(2 marks)*

(ii) 4.9 MJ of heat is transferred to the atmosphere during cooling. Using the first law of thermodynamics, calculate the change in internal energy of the gas. *(2 marks)*

(iii) Represent this process as a p–V diagram, showing the direction of the process. *(2 marks)*

AQA, 2004

6 This question is about the mechanics of establishing satellites above Mars to allow communication between possible human colonies on Mars and Earth. Use the data below to answer the questions.

mass of Mars = 6.4×10^{24} kg

radius of Mars = 3.4×10^6 m

period of rotation of Mars = 8.9×10^4 s

(a) Calculate the escape speed for Mars. *(3 marks)*

(b) For a 'geostationary' orbit above Mars, calculate the orbital height above the surface *(4 marks)*

(c) Discuss whether it is better to transport the satellite from Earth to its Mars orbit or to assemble it on Mars and insert it into orbit from the Mars surface. *(4 marks)*

What goes around comes around

3.1 Moving harmonically

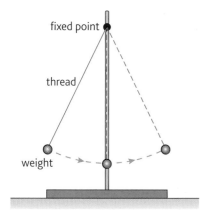

Figure 1 *Pirate ship*

Figure 2 *Simple pendulum*

▣ Rides that swing

The pirate ship of Figure 1 or any other swing boat ride found in an amusement park is essentially a large pendulum. As will be shown in more detail in Topic 3.2, at the top of each swing, the rider loses contact with the seat and experiences a sensation of weightlessness, having no reaction force. Although a more realistic model would be to consider the ride to be a compound pendulum (i.e., a rigid pendulum such as a metre ruler suspended from a pin), much information can be gained about the nature of the swing by considering the simple pendulum of Figure 2.

▣ Describing oscillatory motion

The pirate ship or pendulum moves repeatedly in one direction and then in the opposite direction, passing through its rest (or equilibrium) position. The displacement of the object from the equilibrium position continually changes with time during the motion following the shape of a sine or cosine graph, see Figure 3(a).

Three quantities help us to describe the motion:

▣ the amplitude (A) is the maximum displacement of the object from the equilibrium position,

▣ the time period (T) is the time taken for one complete cycle of the oscillation,

▣ the frequency (f) is the number of cycles per second made by the object.

At AS it was shown that the time period (T) of a wave or an oscillation is related to the frequency (f) by the equation $T = \dfrac{1}{f}$.

Displacement, velocity and acceleration

At AS it was shown that the gradient of a displacement-time graph gave the velocity and the gradient of a velocity-time graph gave the acceleration. This is true for the oscillation graph too. As Figure 3(a) is a cosine curve, a graph of the gradient of this gives a negative sine curve as the variation of velocity with time (Figure 3b). The gradient of the velocity–time graph gives the variation of acceleration with time and this is a negative cosine curve as shown in Figure 3c.

It should be noted that the shape of the acceleration graph is the negative of the displacement graph (although their amplitudes will be different, since they are different quantities). This is true for the many oscillations that are called **simple harmonic** and is how we define **simple harmonic motion**.

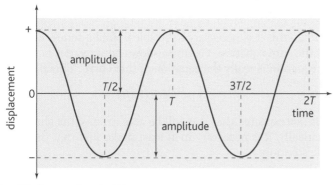

Figure 3 a *Displacement against time*

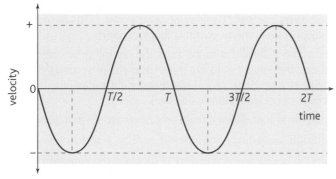

Figure 3 b *Velocity against time*

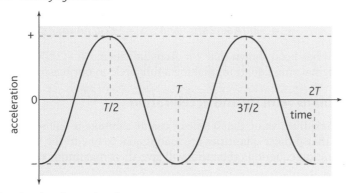

Figure 3 c *Acceleration against time*

■ Simple harmonic motion (shm)

This is defined as oscillatory motion in which the acceleration is always:

■ proportional to the displacement from the equilibrium point,

■ in the opposite direction to the displacement.

This can be written in equation form as:

$$a = -kx$$

where a is the acceleration, x is the displacement from the rest position and k is a constant which depends upon the time period of the oscillation. If the time period is shorter the oscillation changes direction more frequently and so you would expect the acceleration to be greater for the same displacement. It can be shown that k is, in fact, equal to the quantity $(2\pi f)^2$; although you do not have to be able to prove this for this course. This means that the shm equation can be rewritten as:

$$a = -(2\pi f)^2 x$$

Solving the shm equation

In order to do this it is necessary to be able to find a series of values of x which fit the shm equation. Figure 3a shows how x varies graphically and the shm equation is really the equation of that curve. This turns out to be:

$$x = A \cos(2\pi f t)$$

Since it is not expected that you will be able to solve the shm equation mathematically, it is necessary to at least make sure that the equation is a sensible solution:

■ The shape of the curve of Figure 3(a) is a cosine, so the shape and the equation match.

■ The maximum value that a sine or cosine can take is one so if the cosine term $(\cos 2\pi f t)$ equals one then $x = A$. This is sensible since the amplitude is the maximum displacement.

■ Since x and A have the same units the complete cosine term can have no units and since f is in Hz $(= s^{-1})$ and t is in seconds the units of ft inside the brackets cancel out leaving a dimensionless quantity, so that part of the equation fits as well.

■ If one period had elapsed from whenever we started measuring our oscillation and since $f = \dfrac{1}{T}$ then $ft = fT = 1$ and so $x = A\cos 2\pi$. The cosine of 2π radians is equal to 1; so again the equation makes sense.

In a similar vein it can be shown that the velocity and acceleration are given by the equations:

$$v = -2\pi f A \sin 2\pi f t \quad \text{and} \quad a = -(2\pi f)^2 A \cos 2\pi f t$$

Since it has been shown that $x = A\cos 2\pi f t$ then $a = -(2\pi f)^2 x$ which was the original shm equation, making a full circle in our reasoning.

Maximum velocity and acceleration

The maximum value that a sine or cosine can take is one so it is easy to see that if these quantities are made equal to one in the velocity and acceleration equations then this will give their maximum values.

$v = -2\pi f A \sin 2\pi f t$ leads to a maximum velocity of $v_{max} = -2\pi f A$

and

$a = -(2\pi f)^2 A \cos 2\pi f t$ leads to a maximum acceleration of $a_{max} = -(2\pi f)^2 A$

Back to the pendulum

It can be shown experimentally that the period of a simple pendulum is independent of the mass of the bob. You should investigate this statement by measuring the period of at least three pendulums of the same length but using bobs of different mass. The length of the pendulum is from the point from which the pendulum hangs (suspension point) to the centre of mass of the bob. The bobs must be made from dense materials if the air resistance is not to be significant and spoil the results.

The time period of a simple pendulum is given by the equation: $T = 2\pi \sqrt{\dfrac{l}{g}}$

Here l is the length of the pendulum from the centre of mass of the bob to the point of suspension and g is the gravitational field strength.

Rearranging this equation gives $T^2 = \dfrac{4\pi^2}{g} l$ and since $\dfrac{4\pi^2}{g}$ is a constant this means that $T^2 \propto l$. A graph of the period squared against l should give a straight-line graph that goes through the origin.

Application and How science works

Measuring the period

In the topics on practical work and ISAs or EMPAs the need to measure the time for several oscillations in order to improve the reliability of your measured period is discussed. In this case the time for at least twenty oscillations, three times for each length of pendulum should be recorded. The calculated period should be averaged before plotting the graph. In order to allow a reliable straight line to be drawn it is appropriate to measure the period for six different lengths over as large a range of values as possible. Shorter lengths will give less reliable results as the periods will be shorter.

How energy changes with time

When the pendulum is displaced the bob is slightly raised and so it gains gravitational potential energy. As the oscillation occurs this gravitational potential energy is converted into kinetic energy, which reaches a maximum as the pendulum passes through the rest position. The kinetic energy is then returned to gravitational potential energy as the pendulum swings past the rest position to a maximum displacement on the other side of the rest position from the original displacement. Assuming no energy is converted into internal energy of the air, the total energy of the pendulum remains constant.

Consider the variation in the kinetic energy. Velocity is given by the equation $v = 2\pi f A \sin 2\pi f t$ and kinetic energy by the equation $E_K = \frac{1}{2} m v^2$.

Substituting for velocity gives the equation:

$$E_K = \frac{1}{2} m (2\pi f A \sin 2\pi f t)^2 \quad \text{or} \quad E_K = 2\pi^2 f^2 A^2 m \sin^2 2\pi f t$$

Notice that square of sine (written $\sin^2$) is included in this equation. If this looks complicated, don't worry you won't have to use this equation in this form. One of the reasons for doing this manipulation is to see that the maximum kinetic energy (and therefore maximum gravitational potential energy or total energy) is proportional to the **square** of the amplitude of the oscillation. The $\sin^2$ is very similar to the sine in that its maximum value is 1. So the maximum kinetic energy is given by:

$$E_{Kmax} = 2\pi^2 f^2 A^2 m$$

The second reason is to see that the variation of the kinetic energy follows the shape of the $\sin^2$ curve; although the shape of $\sin^2$ is similar to that of a sine curve, it never goes negative. Figure 4 shows how the kinetic energy and gravitational potential energy vary with time and how the total energy remains constant.

These graphs show that:

- the kinetic (or potential) energy vary at twice the frequency of the pendulum oscillation (they reach a maximum twice each cycle),
- the potential energy at any instant can be found by subtracting the kinetic energy from the total energy,
- potential and kinetic energy are anti-phase (when one is at maximum the other is at a minimum).

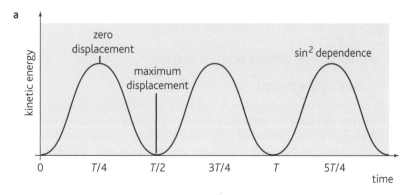

a

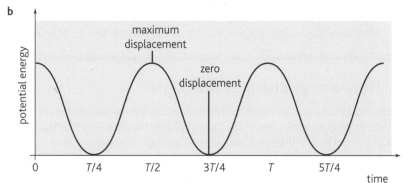

b

Figure 5 *Roller coaster*

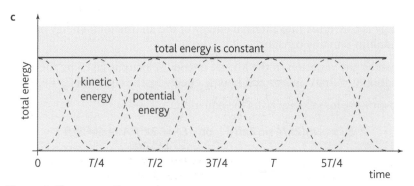

c

Figure 4 *Shm energy–time graphs*

The roller coaster

The profile of part of a simple roller coaster track can be sinusoidal. The motion when riding on one is simple harmonic. Figure 5 shows a rollercoaster with a sinusoidal profile. The riders experience different vertical reaction forces during the ride. As the carriage follows the shape of the track it moves up and down and this applies an up and down reaction to the riders. In a 'trough' the carriage starts to move upwards as the rider is moving downwards and it is here that the rider experiences the greatest 'g' force. At the top of a 'crest' the rider is moving upwards and the carriage starts to move downwards and so the rider gains the experience of weightlessness. In this way the vertical reaction force varies sinusoidally. Up and down motion will be studied in more detail in a later topic.

Summary questions

1. Draw graphs to show the variation of velocity and acceleration if the displacement varies as a sine function.

2. Explain the meaning of the quantities in the equation $a = -(2\pi f)^2 x$; what is the significance of the minus sign?

3. Calculate the time period of a pirate ship of 'rope' length 20.0 m, assuming it to swing as a simple pendulum ($g = 9.81\,\text{N kg}^{-1}$).

4. Calculate the displacement of a toy swing boat when it has an acceleration of $8.0\,\text{m s}^{-2}$ and a frequency of 4.0 Hz.

5. A pirate ship of total mass of 5570 kg swings with an amplitude of 15.0 m and a frequency of 0.16 Hz. Calculate its maximum speed and kinetic energy.

3.2 Back and forth

Learning objectives:

- What gives the thrill of an amusement park ride?

- How does the motion affect the rider?

- What are the energy changes that occur when swings are in different positions?

Specification reference: 3.4.2A

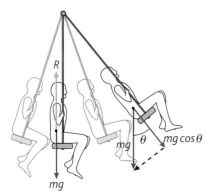

Figure 1 *Variation of reaction of someone riding on a swing*

Application and How science works

Thrill seeking

When we enjoy an amusement park ride it is noticeable that the straight sections at constant speed are boring. It is the changes in motion that give us the thrills! Newton's laws tell us that a force is needed to change motion (either when we are at rest or moving with a constant velocity). Acceleration is a direct result of the resultant forces acting. Amusement park ride designers are very skilled at making sure there is a significant variation of force and acceleration.

Why do riders experience high *g*-forces on pendulum rides?

As riders pass through the bottom of the circular arc, they experience high *g*-forces. These *g*-forces are the result of increases in the reaction force applied by the seat upon their bodies. The arc that the bob of a simple pendulum moves in is circular. An object moving in a circle requires centripetal force. This means that at the bottom of the circular swing there must be an upward force. Gravitational forces are always directed downward upon a rider's body; thus, gravitational forces cannot meet this centripetal force requirement. The seat must supply the centripetal force, pushing upwards on the rider with a force greater than the rider's weight. The size of the centripetal force is determined by the mass of the rider and the speed of the circular motion. If the reaction was insufficient to provide the centripetal force requirement the rider would move off at a tangent and so faster rides produce greater reactions and thrills!

Figure 1 shows the forces acting on a rider at the bottom of a swing.

At the bottom of the swing's arc the centripetal force is provided by the difference between the seat reaction (R) and the rider's weight (mg) thus:

$$R - mg = \frac{mv^2}{r}$$

where v is the rider's velocity and r the length of the swing rope (= radius of the circle that the swing moves in). This means that the reaction of the seat on the rider is given by:

$$R = \frac{mv^2}{r} + mg$$

At a later time the rider makes an angle θ with the vertical so the reaction is reduced. Here the centripetal force is given by:

$$R - mg\cos\theta = \frac{mv^2}{r} \quad \text{meaning that} \quad R = \frac{mv^2}{r} + mg\cos\theta$$

As $\cos\theta$ is less than one (as long as $\theta \neq 0°$) this means that the reaction decreases, giving a change in force, acceleration and thrill!

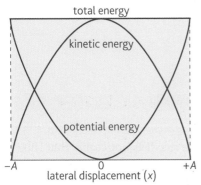

Figure 2 *Variation of kinetic and potential energy with distance*

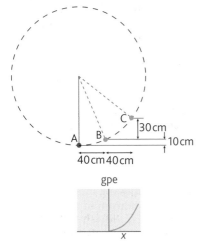

Figure 3 *Variation of gpe with lateral displacement*

Summary questions

1 For a swinging ride state and explain where the g-force is greatest and where it is least.

2 A swing of length 3.0 m supports a child of mass 35 kg. What is the maximum reaction that she will experience if her maximum speed is 4.5 m s^{-1}? ($g = 9.81$ N kg^{-1})

3 Explain why the two factors in the equation

$$R = \frac{mv^2}{r} + mg\cos\theta$$

mean that a rider on a swing boat needs securing in the boat if the boat is to reach the horizontal position.

4 What assumptions must be made when we say that the total energy involved in simple harmonic motion is constant?

■ Energy and position

In the last topic it was shown how the kinetic (and potential) energy of an object undergoing simple harmonic motion varies with time, in fact varying as a sin^2 curve. However, the kinetic energy varies with position in the shape of a parabola, see Figure 2.

Consider the energy changes of a pendulum. When the bob is displaced to the side of its equilibrium position it gains gravitational potential energy (gpe). This will be a maximum when the pendulum is displaced to its amplitude, when its speed is zero and it has no kinetic energy. As it passes through its equilibrium position, its speed and hence its kinetic energy are a maximum. Assuming that there is no friction or air drag, the total energy of the pendulum remains constant.

As the pendulum bob is raised, keeping the thread taut, the lateral (side-ways) displacement (x) can be quite a lot to start off with while the increase in height is not very much; however increasing the lateral displacement by the same amount again, increases the height and therefore the gpe by a greater amount. Thus the gpe increases parabolically with lateral displacement. Figure 3 shows how the gpe of a pendulum of length 1.0 m increases with two equal lateral displacements of 40 cm. For the first displacement the vertical height (h) increases by about 10 cm but for an additional 40 cm displacement h increases by a further 30 cm or so. Since gpe is related to h by the equation gpe = mgh, the gpe will be proportional to the height.

The kinetic energy will be zero at ± maximum amplitude (A) and a maximum when $x = 0$, so its graph is an inverted version of the gravitational energy graph. At any position kinetic + gravitational potential energy is a constant E.

Thus $E = \text{ke}_{max} = \text{gpe}_{max}$.

Remember that ke$_{max} \propto A^2$, so the total energy E of an object oscillating with shm is proportional to (amplitude)^2.

■ Application and How science works

Motion sickness

In humans, movement through the environment is inferred by our eyes (visual) and the inner ear (vestibular). This system includes the semicircular canals, which detect angular acceleration, and the otolith organs, which sense translational acceleration. It is now fairly widely accepted that motion sickness is caused by conflicting inputs to the brain between the visual and vestibular systems, or between the two vestibular systems, and comparison of those inputs with the individual's expectations derived from previous experience. Such sensory conflicts can typically happen in rough air turbulence, heavy waves at sea and when there is acceleration and sudden, unexpected motion in different directions. Motion sickness occurs most commonly with acceleration in a direction perpendicular to the longitudinal axis of the body. This means that head movements away from the direction of motion cause considerable motion sickness. Vertical oscillatory motion at a frequency of 0.2 Hz is most likely to cause motion sickness. However the likelihood of motion sickness decreases at higher frequencies.

3.3 Up and down

Learning objectives:

- What determines how far a bungee jumper falls?

- What is the period of a bungee jumper on one end of the tether?

Specification reference: 3.4.2A

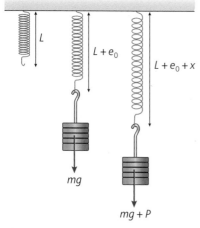

Figure 1 *Oscillations of a spring*

Modelling a bungee by using a loaded spring

The energy changes occurring when a bungee jumper is in flight were described at AS. The oscillations of a loaded spring will now be compared to the oscillations of the bungee jumper.

Figure 1 shows three diagrams of a spring: unloaded, loaded with a mass m and pulled down before releasing. By looking at the forces acting on the mass it is possible to derive an equation for the time period of the spring. **Although you will not be tested on this derivation** it is useful to be able to follow it through to see how a mathematical model holds together and matches the real world.

When a spring is stretched, there is a **restoring force** which (for small extensions) increases linearly with the extension of the spring; and conversely, if the spring is compressed, there is a restoring force, again proportional to compression. So if the length of a spring when it is neither stretched nor compressed is L, the tension T in the spring when it is stretched to a total length $L + e$ is given by:

$$T = ke$$

where k is the spring constant or stiffness of the spring.

If a mass m is added to the spring, the tension (acting upwards) increases in opposition to the weight. When the spring stretches by an amount e_0, the tension in the spring exactly balances the weight of the mass so

$$ke_0 = mg$$

If the mass is now displaced, by a downward pull P vertically from its new equilibrium position, by a displacement x (positive if downwards, negative if upwards) the length of the spring becomes

$$L + e_0 + x$$

The net downwards force on the mass is $P + mg$ and this will be equal to $k(e_0 + x)$ but will be in the opposite direction, so

$$P + mg = k(e_0 + x)$$

When P is removed the net upward force F acting on the mass will be given by

$$F = k(e_0 + x) - mg$$

and this means that the mass will accelerate upwards with a value $F = -ma$.

Equating these equations

$$-ma = k(e_0 + x) - mg$$

so

$$-ma = mg + kx - mg$$

cancelling mg gives

$$-ma = kx$$

or

$$a = -\frac{k}{m}x$$

Since k and m are constant this equation is actually the shm equation that was shown in Topic 3.1.

$$a = -(2\pi f)^2 x$$

meaning that

$$(2\pi f)^2 = \frac{k}{m} \quad \text{or} \quad f = \frac{1}{2\pi}\sqrt{\frac{k}{m}}$$

Using the fact that $T = \frac{1}{f}$ gives the final equation for the time period $T = 2\pi\sqrt{\frac{m}{k}}$.

Back to the bungee jumper

When the bungee jumper shown in Figure 2 jumps, their weight will be opposed by an air drag during the acceleration phase. This is identical to that of any jumper in free fall.

Once the bungee rope starts to tighten the jumper continues to fall but the motion is opposed by both the air drag and the tension in the rope. This means that the net downward force on the jumper is reduced but is still overall downwards until the jumper reaches the equilibrium position (the position at which the jumper will finally come to rest).

At this point there is zero net force on the jumper. The jumper will continue to move beyond the equilibrium position because of their momentum. Beyond the equilibrium position the tension in the rope plus the (varying) air resistance jointly act as a restoring force in the opposite direction to the jumper's velocity and therefore reduce the velocity to zero and the jumper is at the maximum amplitude.

The tension is now greater than the jumper's weight and the bungee rope begins to shorten and the jumper accelerates upwards (with weight and air drag opposing the motion). This continues until the tension falls to zero, at the equilibrium position once again, and then weight and air drag bring the jumper to rest.

The cycle then repeats.

The rope will transfer mechanical energy into internal energy as it stretches and slackens; this means that there is actually an extra factor that would need to be added to the equation derived above. This factor is known as a **damping** factor and reduces the amplitude of the oscillation. Figure 3a shows an undamped oscillation and Figure 3b includes the effect of damping.

Figure 2 *Bungee jumper*

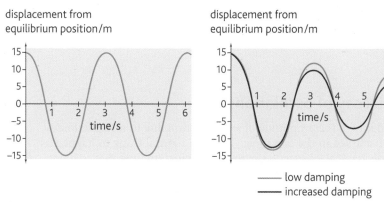

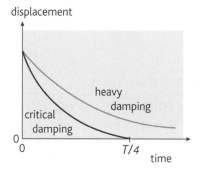

Figure 3 *Undamped and damped oscillations*

Figure 4 *Critical and heavy damping*

Damped oscillations

Damping originates because of frictional forces and always opposes the motion of an object. The presence of constant damping does not alter the time period or frequency of an oscillation but it reduces the amplitude. The degree of damping can be altered by increasing the friction. If a mass on a spring is oscillating in air there is very light damping on it and the mass will make many oscillations before coming to rest; if the spring is now placed in light oil the damping will be increased and the mass will make fewer oscillations before coming to rest, although the frequency will remain constant. Heavy damping reduces the amplitude more rapidly but also increases the period (or reduces the frequency). In the limit of critical damping the mass comes to rest as quickly as possible but without making a complete oscillation. Still heavier damping results in the displacement reducing to zero in a very long time, see Figure 4.

■ How science works

Damping can be a nuisance or lend a helping hand. When oscillations are intended to continue indefinitely such as a pendulum clock or signal travelling through a communications channel, damping is definitely a nuisance and needs to be compensated for by feeding energy into the system. On a car suspension system or door closure mechanism heavy damping is essential.

■ Summary questions

1. Explain how you might model the motion of a bungee jumper in the laboratory.

2. Calculate the time period and maximum acceleration of a mass of 200 g oscillating on a spring of stiffness 30 N m^{-1}. The amplitude of the oscillation is 12 cm.

3. Draw a graph showing five complete oscillations of a bungee jumper. Explain the features of your graph.

3.4 Gaining and losing height

Learning objectives:

- What energy changes occur during an oscillation?

- How does resonance occur?

- How do the resistive forces affect the resonance curve?

Specification reference: 3.4.2A

Figure 1 *Reverse bungee rider*

Decay of oscillations

The decay of the amplitude of an oscillation due to resistive forces was discussed in the last topic. This is a natural thing to happen as the mechanical energy dissipates to the surroundings due to damping forces. No system can be completely independent of damping forces. The amplitude of a bungee jumper's oscillations will naturally decay bringing the jumper to rest. In the **reverse bungee** or **ejector seat** ride, see Figure 1, two stretched elastic ropes are attached directly to the rider or to a spherical passenger car. The other ends of the ropes are attached to tall gantries. The ropes are stretched and the car is held to the base of the ride using an electromagnet. When the car is released, it is catapulted into the air to a height of over 50 m. The passenger car can rotate, giving the riders an exciting and chaotic ride. After several oscillations the amplitude of the oscillations has decayed so the tension in the ropes is reduced and the car lowered for the passengers to disembark.

The reverse bungee could be modelled using two expendable springs attached to a loaded mass hanger. The combination of the springs will have an effective spring constant (k). By measuring the time period of the combination the effective spring constant could be calculated using the equation $T = 2\pi\sqrt{\dfrac{m}{k}}$ derived in the last topic.

But really...

The motion experienced by the riders in a reverse bungee is far too chaotic to be truly considered to be shm. However, it is still possible to calculate the maximum speed of the oscillation from energy considerations.

When the bungee ropes are extended they store elastic potential energy ($\frac{1}{2}kx^2$) and this will transfer into kinetic energy as the car passes through the equilibrium position where the energy is $\frac{1}{2}mv^2$. Equating these two relationships shows that the maximum velocity v will be given by $v = \sqrt{\dfrac{kx^2}{m}}$.

Dealing with damping

To consider how amusement park rides deal with damping, think about pendulum rides or, more simply, consider a child's swing. Given a push the swing will oscillate several times but it will gradually come to rest as the amplitude decays. Air resistance and friction cause the swing to lose energy and its amplitude to decay. Of course in order to keep the swing swinging it needs either skilful movement of the rider's body or else someone pushing it. The person pushing the swing must supply energy to compensate for that lost. It is essential that the pushing does not occur randomly, but periodically. More energy will be fed to the swing if it is pushed in the same direction as the velocity. If the pushes are well synchronised the energy input is greater than the energy lost and the amplitude of swing will be increased. This phenomenon is called **resonance**. The effect of 'pushing' can also be provided by the rider in the swing by raising or lowering his or her centre of mass very slightly, achieved by changing the position of the legs or upper body. Again timing has to be very well synchronised to be of the same time period that the swing has when it is simply displaced and allowed to swing freely.

It would seem a natural consequence of resonance that the swing will go over the top of its mounting. However the equation of a pendulum $T = 2\pi\sqrt{\dfrac{l}{g}}$ only applies for small angles. When the swing goes beyond a certain height it is no longer possible for the rider to apply the necessary small force in synchronisation with the natural frequency of the swing because the natural frequency changes. In other words the motion of the system is naturally limited.

Resonance

The swing considered above can be generalised to any oscillating system. There are three conditions which must be applied for resonance:

- There must be an object with a natural frequency. This could be a mechanical or electrical system. The natural frequency of an object is the frequency that it will oscillate at when displaced. The oscillation could be a mechanical vibration such as a plucked guitar string. At AS it was shown that an object can have more than one natural frequency. These are called harmonics.
- For an undamped or very lightly damped system there must be a force applied at the same natural frequency as that of the object. Work is done on the object by the periodic force and this transfers energy to the object.
- Damping must dissipate less energy than the applied force provides the object with. For an object to resonate, mechanical or electrical energy has to build up in the object. Anything which removes energy restricts the resonance.

When the frequency of the applied force matches the natural frequency of an object, resonance occurs. The amplitude of oscillations could eventually become infinitely large; however, well before the oscillations reach infinite amplitude one of three things happens:

1 the object's dynamics change so that the resonant frequency and the frequency of the applied force no longer match, or

2 damping means that energy lost to the surroundings becomes equal to the energy input, or else

3 the object breaks!

Demonstration of resonance

Figure 2 shows Barton's pendulums; this is a demonstration which illustrates both resonance and the effect of damping. One of the pendulums, called the 'driver', has a heavy metallic bob. Paper cones are used as the bobs for light pendulums which are of a variety of lengths; the length of one light pendulum exactly matches that of the driver. The pendulums are suspended from a string loosely stretched between the two stands. The damping can be increased by adding masses (such as metal washers) to the paper cones.

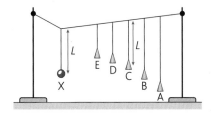

Figure 2 *Barton's pendulums*

From observations of this demonstration the following can be seen:

1 All of the pendulums vibrate at the same frequency as the natural frequency of the driver pendulum.

2 The light pendulum of the same length as the driver will vibrate with the largest amplitude because it is resonating.

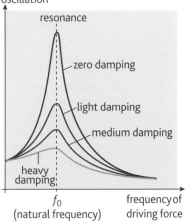

amplitude
of forced
oscillation

resonance

zero damping

light damping

medium damping

heavy
damping

f_0
(natural frequency)

frequency of
driving force

Figure 3 *Resonance curves*

3 The phase of the resonating pendulum is one-quarter of a period behind the driver pendulum. The shorter pendulums are all slightly out of phase with the driver whereas the longest one is almost half a period out of phase.

4 For a more heavily damped system the resonance occurs at a frequency less than that of the natural frequency of the driving pendulum.

Figure 3 shows how the amplitude of a driven pendulum changes with different applied frequencies.

From this graph a number of aspects relating to resonance are apparent:

■ The amplitude of the driven pendulum is a maximum when the driver frequency is equal to the natural frequency of the driven pendulum.

■ Lighter damping leads to sharper resonance with a larger amplitude.

■ Heavier damping leads the peak of the curve to move to a frequency slightly below the natural frequency of the driven pendulum.

Resonance on rides

There are two aspects of resonance that affect amusement park rides. Firstly resonances which could occur for the riders (see HSW below) and secondly resonance that affects the structure supporting the ride. Engineers designing structures must take care that the structures do not exhibit resonance frequencies. The most famous bad example is the Tacoma Narrows Bridge in 1940, when winds set up resonances in the bridge and the bridge began swaying and twisting uncontrollably, until it collapsed under the stress. The Millennium Bridge over the River Thames also initially suffered from resonances until dampers were installed. To prevent resonances from happening in structures designers dampen all of the **resonance** in the bridge; for example by adding plates that slide against one another as the structure bends so that sliding friction will dissipate energy and reduce the resonance. They also ensure that there are no mechanisms for resonant energy transfer. The wind blowing on the Tacoma Narrows Bridge excited the bridge by being at the right frequency. The bridge oscillated as the reed does in a musical instrument. Today bridges and ride structures are tested with computer modelling before they are built to make sure that they do not resonate in winds.

Summary questions

1 Calculate the effective spring constant of the combination of bungee ropes on a reverse bungee when the period of oscillation is 4.0 s and the total mass of the carriage and riders is 240 kg.

2 Calculate the maximum speed of the riders in the reverse bungee of question 1 when the amplitude of the oscillation is 27 m.

3 Describe the key features of Barton's pendulum experiment and explain how this experiment could be used to generate resonance curves similar to Figure 3.

4 Describe how you could investigate resonance using a signal generator and vibration generator attached to a loaded, stretched spring supported from a clamp.

Application and How science works

Avoid these frequencies

It is essential that continuous vibrations on rides are either eliminated by dampening or else the frequencies need to be outside the range 0.5–80 Hz; sustained vibrations in this range can have significant effects on the human body. The softer tissue in the human body is both flexible and deformable. Vibrations to the body can be severely damaging if they are at the resonance frequency of organs and connective tissues. The most effective resonant frequencies for vertical vibrations lie between 4 and 8 Hz. Vibrations between 2.5 and 5 Hz generate strong resonance in the vertebra of the neck and lower back region with amplification of up to 240%. Vibrations between 20 and 30 Hz set up the strongest resonance between the head and shoulders with an amplification of up to 350%. Whole body vibration may create chronic stresses and sometimes even permanent damage to the affected organs or body parts.

3.5 Round and round

Learning objectives:

- What centripetal force acts on a rider in circular motion?

- How is the centripetal force provided in the rotor?

- How do other rides involving circular motion at constant speed provide a centripetal force?

Specification reference: 3.4.2B

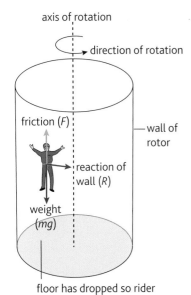

Figure 1 *Forces on a rider in the rotor*

How science works

Accidents on amusement rides

Although rides have a good safety record, accidents do happen. In 2000 two riders had their feet trapped in a rotor when the floor dropped at the wrong time, causing injuries to their feet. This accident resulted in a redesign of rotors in the US with the introduction of a guard to prevent feet from becoming wedged between the floor and wall of a rotor.

The centripetal force

In Topic 1.4 the necessity of a centripetal force is discussed in relation to satellites and other objects in circular motion due to gravity. The two versions of the centripetal force equation are:

$$F = \frac{mv^2}{r} \quad \text{and} \quad F = m\omega^2 r$$

where m is the mass of the object in circular motion, v its speed, ω its angular speed and r the radius of the circle. In order to maintain its motion in a circle an object must be subjected to a force which meets the requirements given by the equation. For example, for a child to stand on a roundabout which rotates at a steady angular speed the friction must be large enough to equal $m\omega^2 r$. Thus if the child were more massive ('heavier') or the angular speed of the roundabout were to increase or the child were to move outwards from the centre of the roundabout (increasing r) the friction would need to be larger or the child would shoot off at a tangent to the circle in which they were rotating. Many amusement park rides are based on this principle.

The rotor or gravitron

The rotor and the gravitron are two similar rides found in amusement parks. Riders are positioned around the inside of a cylinder which rotates. Once the speed of rotation is sufficient the floor drops and riders appear stuck to the wall. Figure 1 shows the forces which act on the rider. The frictional force must equal the weight of the rider, making the rider in vertical equilibrium ($F = mg$). The reaction of the wall on the rider's back provides the rider with the required centripetal force $\left(R = \frac{mv^2}{r}\right)$.

The rider's direction is continually changing and so, even though there is no change in linear speed, the rider is continually being accelerated. Thus the rider is not in horizontal equilibrium – there is a net inward force.

The big wheel

Figure 2 shows the London Eye; this is a very large version of a big wheel (sometimes called a 'Ferris wheel' after its designer). Although most big wheels rotate quite slowly the passengers still require a centripetal force to make sure they are moving in a circle. The motion of the riders is complicated somewhat by the fact that the seats are pivoted so that wherever they are on the wheel as it goes round in a vertical plane they remain upright. In fact this motion simply means that the riders move in a circle which is displaced to be a little lower than the circle that the wheel itself moves in. Let us consider the motion of a rider in a seat. The centripetal force will be the same value throughout the ride. However, the forces that combine to create the centripetal force change as the position on the circle changes. At all positions on the ride the forces add to give a total force towards the centre of the riders' circle. Figure 3 shows how the forces vary.

Position A – The reaction of the seat on the rider (R_A) and the weight (mg) are in opposite directions. The weight must be larger than the reaction of the seat on the rider to give a total downward force:

$$\frac{mv^2}{r} = mg - R_A$$

Figure 2 *The London Eye*

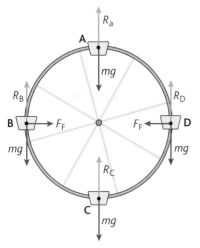

Figure 3 *Forces on a big wheel rider*

Position B – The reaction of the seat on the rider (R_B) and the weight are in opposite directions and are of equal magnitude but neither is directed towards the centre of the circle, so do not provide the centripetal force. The centripetal force acts on the rider through friction with the seat and through the back of the seat (F):

$$R_B = mg, \qquad \frac{mv^2}{r} = F$$

Position C – The reaction of the seat on the rider (R_C) and the weight are in opposite directions. R_C must be larger than the weight to give a centripetal force that is upward:

$$\frac{mv^2}{r} = R_C - mg$$

Position D – As for position B, the reaction of the seat on the rider (R_D) and the weight are in opposite directions and are of equal magnitude but neither is directed towards the centre of the circle, so do not provide the centripetal force. The centripetal force acts on the rider through friction with the seat or through the back of the seat (F).

$$R_D = mg, \qquad \frac{mv^2}{r} = F$$

The weight and the required centripetal force do not change and so this means that the reaction of the seat on the rider must change.

At positions in between those shown in Figure 3 the centripetal force will be provided by components of the weight, reaction of the seat on the rider and the friction with the seat and through the back of the seat.

Figure 4 shows the rider in between positions A and D. In this position it is the components of the forces along the line connecting the centre of mass of the rider to the centre of the circle which provide the centripetal force:

$$F \sin\theta + mg \cos\theta - R \cos\theta = \frac{mv^2}{r}$$

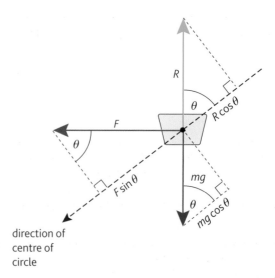

Figure 4 *Components of the forces providing the centripetal force*

Swing carousel

The ride is also known as the chair-o-planes and is illustrated in Figure 5. This ride is a modification of a carousel which has its seats supported by chains. As the carousel rotates the riders (having no centripetal force to keep them moving in the circle) will move along the tangent to the circle until the tension in the chains has a horizontal component which can provide the centripetal force required for that motion.

Figure 6 shows the forces acting on a rider on a swing carousel. Since the weight acts vertically, it cannot contribute to the centripetal force. Thus the centripetal force is entirely made up from the horizontal component of the tension in the chains. The vertical component of the tension will then also equal the weight. The rider (and chair) will be in equilibrium vertically but not horizontally; there is a net horizontal force acting which causes the usual centripetal acceleration:

$$\frac{mv^2}{r} = T\sin\theta \quad \text{and} \quad mg = T\cos\theta$$

Dividing the first equation by the second gives:

$$\frac{v^2}{gr} = \tan\theta$$

Thus the angle that the chair makes with the vertical is independent of the mass of rider or the chair but depends upon the speed and radius of the circle. The radius of the circle is that of the circle that the centre of mass of the rider and the chair sweep out.

Figure 5 *Swing carousel*

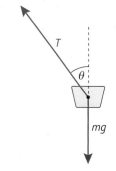

Figure 6 *Forces acting on a rider on a swing carousel*

Application and How science works

How else can centripetal forces be applied?

Cyclists in velodromes make use of the banking as they hurtle around the race track. The slope of the track (low nearest the centre and highest at the outside) means that the reaction of the track on the wheels of the cycle has a component towards the centre of the circle; this along with the friction is sufficient to provide the centripetal force unless the cyclist is going too quickly or the radius of the circle is too small.

Summary questions

1. A child of mass 30 kg is 1.50 m from the centre of a roundabout rotating with a period of 5.5 s. Calculate the centripetal force which would be necessary for the child to stay at that position.

2. A person of mass 62 kg is in a stable position on a rotor which rotates in a horizontal plane with an angular speed of 3.0 rad s⁻¹. Calculate

   a the frictional force acting on the rider

   b the radius of the circle in which the rider's centre of mass moves when the reaction of the wall is 900 N.

   ($g = 9.81$ N kg⁻¹)

3. Explain where riders feel lightest and where they feel heaviest when riding on a Ferris wheel (big wheel).

4. A swing carousel has a period of revolution of 6.7 s. Riders move in a circle of radius 4.7 m. Calculate the angle with the vertical that the riders make.

3.6 Spinning faster and faster

Learning objectives:

- What is the moment of inertia of an object?

- How does the moment of inertia affect the angular motion of a body?

- How can angular motion be compared with linear motion?

Specification reference: 3.4.2C

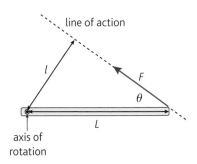

torque $= F \times l = F l \sin \theta$

Figure 1 *Calculation of torque*

Moment of inertia

When a spinning amusement park ride starts up the time that it takes to reach the working speed depends on how the ride's mass is distributed. In the same way if a disc and a hoop of identical masses and radii roll down the same incline the hoop will take longer to reach the bottom. The reason for this is that more of the hoop's mass is distributed further from the centre of its axis of rotation. The resistance to change in angular motion is measured by the moment of inertia (*I*) about a chosen axis for the object. The moment of inertia is measured in units of kg m².

Moment of inertia and torque

The moment of a force or **torque** about an axis is defined as the product of the force and the perpendicular distance between the line of action of the force and the axis. Figure 1 shows how this definition is applied.

Torque is a vector quantity and is measured in units of N m. Although this unit is dimensionally identical to the joule, you cannot use the joule as the unit of torque since the joule is derived from the force and displacement being in the same direction, not perpendicular directions.

When a net torque *T* is applied to an object of moment of inertia *I* the object will experience an angular acceleration α. The angular acceleration is the rate of change of angular speed (ω) with time and is measured in rad s⁻²:

$$\alpha = \frac{T}{I}$$

This equation is analogous to the linear equation $a = \frac{F}{m}$.

More analogies with linear motion

The analogies between linear and angular acceleration can be extended to all aspects of angular accelerated motion. The table below shows how the quantities can be compared with their symbols and respective units.

linear quantity and symbol	unit	angular quantity and symbol	unit
mass (*m*)	kg	moment of inertia (*I*)	kg m²
distance (*s*)	m	angle (θ)	rad
velocity or speed (*v*)	m s⁻¹	angular velocity or speed (ω)	rad s⁻¹
acceleration (*a*)	m s⁻²	angular acceleration (α)	rad s⁻²
momentum (*p*)	kg m s⁻¹	angular momentum (*L*)	kg m² rad s⁻¹
force (*F*)	N	torque (*T*)	N m

Using these quantities it is possible to easily write down equations for angular acceleration by replacing the linear quantities with angular quantities. So in addition to the analogy $F = ma$ leading to $T = I\alpha$ angular momentum can be linked to linear momentum meaning that:

$$p = mv \quad \text{leads to} \quad L = I\omega$$

In a similar way the work done by a force can be linked to the work done by a torque so:

$$W = Fs \quad \text{leads to} \quad W = T\theta$$

This idea can be extended to the equations of motion but symbols for initial angular velocity and final angular velocity are needed, these are ω_1 and ω_2, respectively.

This means that the equation $v = u + at$ leads to the equivalent angular equation $\omega_2 = \omega_1 + \alpha t$.

and $v^2 = u^2 + 2as$ leads to $\omega_2^2 = \omega_1^2 + 2\alpha\theta$, etc.

■ Rotational kinetic energy

As the hoop or disc, considered above, rolls down an inclined plane there are two aspects of kinetic energy that need to be considered: the normal translational kinetic energy ($= \frac{1}{2}mv^2$) and the rotational kinetic energy (which is $\frac{1}{2}I\omega^2$, by analogy with the linear kinetic energy).

Thus the total kinetic energy of a rolling object is given by

$$E_{k_{total}} = \tfrac{1}{2}mv^2 + \tfrac{1}{2}I\omega^2$$

When considering the conversion of gravitational potential energy into the linear kinetic energy of a rolling object the linear value will always be less than might be expected because of the portion of gravitational potential energy converted to rotational kinetic energy.

■ Conservation of angular momentum

The conservation of angular momentum is very appropriate to amusement park rides. In the same way that the conservation of linear momentum requires that the system is isolated from the surroundings so does the conservation of angular momentum. However, instead of the requirement that there be no external force acting on the linear system, here there must be no external torque. The total angular momentum of the system will remain constant. In practice, altering the moment of inertia is something that happens in many rides, this may be due to the distribution of the mass of the ride itself being deliberately changed during the course of the ride or because the passengers move into different positions.

When a child on a freely rotating roundabout moves closer to the centre of the roundabout, the radius of the circle that the child moves in is reduced. It would violate the conservation of angular momentum if the roundabout continued rotating at the same speed because the child would be closer to the axis of rotation meaning that the moment of inertia of the combination of the child and the roundabout is reduced. If the total angular momentum is to remain constant, reducing the moment of inertia about the axis around which the roundabout is spinning must be compensated for by an overall increase in its angular velocity. Since the child is already on the roundabout moving towards the centre produces no external torque. The same principle applies to ice skaters, trampolinist and divers as they perform twists or turns as part of a routine.

The waltzer

The 'waltzer' or 'tilt-a-whirl' is a ride in which rotating 'buckets' are mounted on a track attached to an oscillating segmented floor. The floor rides over a static but sinusoidally shaped track which means that as the ride goes round and round its floor surface follows the track up and down causing the floor to oscillate in a vertical plane. The peaks and troughs of the wave that the buckets follow cause them to roll around their individual tracks with angular speeds which depend on the total moment of inertia of the bucket and riders, see Figure 2. The motion of the bucket is quite complex since it is a combination of the vertical simple harmonic motion, horizontal circular motion and the oscillation of the bucket in its individual curved track.

The riders can alter the angular speed of the bucket in its curved track by changing the moment of inertia. When a number of riders move away from the centre the moment of inertia will increase and the angular speed will decrease. Moving in towards the centre of rotation of the bucket means that the moment of inertia decreases and the angular speed increases. Alternatively the ride operator may increase the angular speed by pushing on the edge of the bucket. This means that there is an external torque being applied and therefore that angular momentum will not be conserved.

Figure 2 *The waltzer*

Torques and rides

Figure 3 shows a swing ride in which the two 'cars' swing symmetrically in opposite directions. The design of this ride is sensible in that the cars will have equal and opposite angular momentum which will cancel out the torques placed on the supporting axle by either one of them. In a similar way pirate ships considered in Topic 3.1 often have a counterbalance which helps to reduce the net torque on the ride.

Figure 3 *Swinging ride*

The compound pendulum

In Topic 3.1 the pirate ship was mentioned as being a **compound pendulum** rather than a simple pendulum. When the dimensions of the suspended body are not negligible compared to the distance from the suspension axis to the centre of mass, the pendulum is called a **compound** pendulum. Any object mounted on a horizontal axis so that it oscillates in a gravitational field is a compound pendulum. The expression for the period of a compound pendulum is

$$T = 2\pi\sqrt{\frac{I}{mgh}}$$

where I is the moment of inertia of the pendulum about the axis of suspension, m is the pendulum's mass, and h is the distance from the suspension point to the centre of mass. For simple shapes such as cuboids, spheres and pyramids formulae can be derived for the moment of inertia but for complex shapes such as the pirate ship the moment of inertia is more likely to be determined experimentally. The equation can be rearranged into the form:

$$T^2 = 4\pi^2\frac{I}{mgh}$$

for the period of a compound pendulum.

Summary questions

1 Show that the units of angular acceleration are equivalent to the units of the ratio of torque to moment of inertia.

2 Write down the equivalent angular equations to

   a $s = ut + \frac{1}{2}at^2$;

   b $s = \left(\dfrac{v + u}{2}\right)t$;

   c $P = Fv$.

3 A playground roundabout has a radius of 2.0 m and moment of inertia 400 kg m^2 about the central vertical axis. The roundabout is initially at rest. A constant force of magnitude 120 N is applied tangentially at the edge of the roundabout for 4.0 s.

   a Calculate the angular momentum of the roundabout.

   b When a child climbs onto the moving roundabout the total moment of inertia increases to 450 kg m^2. Calculate the new angular velocity of the child on the roundabout.

4 A loaded pirate ship has a total mass of 1.6×10^4 kg and a period of oscillation of 12.4 s. The centre of mass is 4.5 m below the ship's point of suspension. Taking g to be 9.81 N kg^{-1}, calculate the moment of inertia of the pirate ship.

1. An 'orbiter' fairground ride consists of six vehicles each at the end of a horizontal support and initially 8 m from the axis of rotation (**Figure 1**).

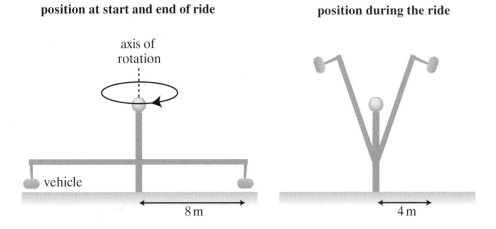

position at start and end of ride   **position during the ride**

diagram shows two of the six vehicles

Figure 1

The initial moment of inertia of the arrangement is $13\,000\,\text{kg}\,\text{m}^2$ and the angular speed of the ride is $2.2\,\text{rad}\,\text{s}^{-1}$.

(a) Calculate the angular momentum of the arrangement *(3 marks)*

(b) The ride mechanism is used to reduce the radius of the ride to 4 m by shortening the horizontal supports. This reduces the moment of inertia by a factor of 4. Calculate the new angular speed of the ride explaining the principles of your calculation. *(3 marks)*

(c) Calculate the change in rotational kinetic energy of the ride as a result of the change of radius. Make it clear whether the ride gains or loses this energy *(3 marks)*

2. In a 'rotor' ride a vertical cylinder rotates about a vertical axis and participants are held against wall of the rotating cylinder (**Figure 2**).

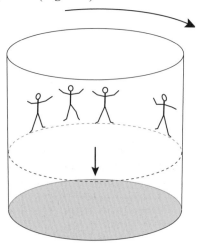

Figure 2

During the ride the floor of the cylinder moves downwards, leaving the participants pinned to the interior wall.

During testing the cylinder is spun to an angular speed of 15 rad s⁻¹. The emergency brakes are applied and the rotor makes three complete revolutions before stopping.

(a) Explain how the riders are held on the walls. *(2 marks)*

(b) Calculate the time taken for the system to come to rest assuming that the deceleration has a constant value. *(4 marks)*

(c) The total moment of inertia of the rotating system is 4500 kg m². Calculate the average frictional torque acting on the system due to the brakes. *(4 marks)*

(d) Without the emergency braking the rotor takes 30 complete revolutions to stop.

Calculate the power output developed by the ride motor to keep the ride turning at the test speed. *(5 marks)*

3   A bungee rope which obeys Hooke's law hangs vertically from a bridge and requires a force of 550 N to produce an extension of 27 m. A bungee jumper with a mass of 65 kg is attached to the rope and then jumps from the bridge.

(a) Show that the jumper will eventually oscillate with a frequency of about 90 mHz. *(3 marks)*

(b) On graph paper, sketch the variation of displacement of the jumper against time starting from the moment of release and continuing for two oscillations. Explain the shape of key regions of your graph. *(9 marks)*

4   A footbridge to celebrate the start of the new Millenium was designed and constructed across the River Thames in London between 1998 and 2000, shown in **Figure 3**. This bridge was subsequently closed for a period as it was discovered that large numbers of pedestrians crossing it could set it into oscillation with large amplitude.

Figure 3

(a) State the name of the physical phenomenon that gives rise to this effect. *(1 mark)*

(b) Explain the conditions under which this phenomenon could become hazardous. *(2 marks)*

(c) State and explain two ways in which engineers might reduce or eliminate the oscillations. *(4 marks)*

5   A bungee jumper oscillates with simple harmonic motion at the end of an elastic rope

(a) State two conditions for the acceleration of the jumper if the motion is to be simple harmonic. *(2 marks)*

(b) A jumper attached to a bungee rope jumps from a tower. After the initial jump the system oscillates , making 15 oscillations in 84 s. The distance from the bottom of the jump to the equilibrium position is 12 m. *(2 marks)*

(i) Calculate the frequency of the oscillations. *(2 marks)*

(ii) Calculate the maximum acceleration of the jumper due to the rope. *(2 marks)*

(c) Sketch a graph to show how the velocity of the mass varies with time over the first two cycles after release. Explain the main features of your graph. *(8 marks)*

6   A child on a swing oscillates with simple harmonic motion of period 3.2 s.

(a) Calculate the distance between the swing's point of support and the overall centre of mass of the child and the swing. *(2 marks)*

(b) The total energy of the oscillation is 20 J when the amplitude of the oscillations is 0.50 m. Sketch a graph showing how the total energy of the child varies with the amplitude of the oscillations for amplitudes between 0 and 1.0 m. Include suitable scales on your axes. *(4 marks)*

7   (a) Explain the significance of the minus sign in the simple harmonic equation

$$a = -(2\pi f)^2 x$$

(1 mark)

(b) A mass of 24 kg is attached to the end of a spring of spring constant 60 N m^{-1}. The mass is displaced 0.035 m vertically from its equilibrium position and released.

Show that the maximum kinetic energy of the mass is about 40 mJ. *(5 marks)*

(c) When the mass on the spring is quite heavily damped its amplitude halves by the end of each complete cycle. Sketch a graph to show how the gravitational potential energy of the mass on the spring varies with time over a single period. Start at time, $t = 0$, with your minimum gravitational potential energy. You should include suitable values on each of your scales. *(3 marks)*

AQA 2004

8   A girl sits at rest on a garden swing. The swing consists of a wooden seat of mass 1.2 kg supported by two ropes. The mass of the girl is 16.8 kg. The mass of the ropes should be ignored throughout this question. A boy grips the seat and gives a firm push with both hands so that the girl swings upwards as shown in the diagram.

Figure 4

(a)   The swing just reaches a vertical displacement of 0.50 m above its rest position.

   (i)   Show that the maximum gain in gravitational potential energy of the girl and the swing is about 90 J.

(2 marks)

   (ii)   The work done against resistive forces as the swing moves upwards is 20 J. Calculate the work done on the swing by the boy during the push.

(1 mark)

   (iii)   As he pushed, the boy's hands were in contact with the seat of the swing while it moved a distance of 0.40 m. Calculate the average force applied to the swing.

(2 marks)

(b)   Calculate the speed of the girl as she passes back through the lowest point of her ride for the first time. Assume that the work done against resistive forces is the same in both directions.

(4 marks)

(c)   The girl is not pushed again. Sketch a graph to show how the kinetic energy of the girl varies with time over two complete cycles of the motion. Start your graph from the time when she is 0.50 m above the rest position.

(3 marks)

AQA, 2005

4 Imaging the invisible

4.1 Beneath the Earth

Learning objectives:

▪ Why is non-intrusive exploration useful?

▪ How can buried ores and objects be found without digging?

▪ What techniques are available to geophysicists and archaeologists?

Specification reference: 3.4.3

Figure 2 *Petronas Towers*

How science works

Supply and demand

The increasing population of the world is placing an ever rising demand on the supply of raw materials which are becoming increasingly scarce and expensive. Recycling manufactured goods is one way of maintaining a supply of materials as geophysicists conduct the important task of discovering new sources of raw materials.

▪ Raw materials

The exploitation of the Earth's resources to provide necessities and luxuries has been a feature that sets human beings apart from other species. Wood, animal bones and stones that lay on or close to the surface of the Earth provided the first tools, weapons, utensils, ornaments and adornments. Gradually humans have developed skills and knowledge that have resulted in uses for an increasingly wide range of elements. Many of these are held in small concentrations in massive bodies of ore buried deep in the ground.

Figure 1 *Tara lead and zinc mine in Ireland*

Also, during the last century, human beings had an almost insatiable demand for gas and particularly oil for use both as a source of fuel and for its use in the manufacture of other materials. These mineral resources cannot be found simply by digging holes randomly and hoping that something will turn up. Random digging would be both environmentally damaging as well as being far too costly.

▪ Building for the future

Modern structures such as dams, bridges and buildings are built on a large scale and need well-constructed foundations. In order to evaluate the costs of building and to build safely it is important to understand what is beneath the Earth's surface to ensure that the structures are erected using appropriate building techniques and on suitable sites. The 452 m high Petronas Towers in Kuala Lumpur, shown in Figure 2 required foundations that were 120 m deep to ensure that the building was on suitable bedrock.

Rediscovering the past

The objective of an archaeologist is to explore the past through a study of the remains of past civilisations. Obviously this is a delicate task, so to avoid damaging the evidence they are looking for, it is useful to have a good idea where remains are buried. The remains may extend over areas that are large such as the remains of cities that have been built over or relatively small such as when investigating the remains of a Roman Villa, for example. To avoid damage to the remains it is useful to gain as much knowledge about the site as possible before starting excavations (Figure 3).

Techniques available

Sites that might possibly contain minerals and archaeological sites are often found from a study of aerial photographs taken from aircraft or satellites.

Figure 3 *Archaeologists at work*

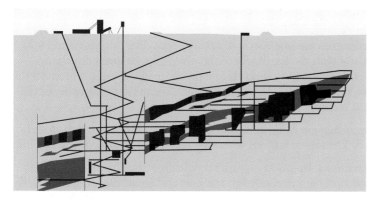

Figure 4 *Position of the Tara ore body*

Figure 4 shows a sketch of the position and extent of the ore body that is being exploited at the Tara mine in Ireland. The black lines are the mine shafts and tunnels. Before mining began geophysicists and other scientists and engineers had to find the location of the ore, determine whether it was worth exploiting and plan the best way of operating the mine.

Numerous measurements that depend on the physical properties of the Earth and its materials are available to investigate the substructure without the need for digging. Some of the following suitable properties will be discussed in more detail in the later topics:

■ electrical **resistivity**
■ velocity of sound waves transmitted through the ground
■ reflection of radio waves, allowing distance measurement
■ **gravitational field strength**
■ **magnetic field strength**
■ radioactivity.

Instruments which can be carried in aircraft can be made sensitive enough to measure natural and man-made radioactivity, the electrical **conductivity** of the surface material and variations in the magnetic field strength due to structural variations in the Earth's surface.

When searching for minerals, once the non-invasive physical evidence has been assessed boreholes can be drilled in suitable spots to gain evidence for the likely yield before deciding whether full extraction of the minerals is cost effective.

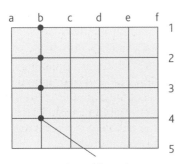

data collected at
each grid intersection

Figure 5 *Survey grid*

Application and How science works

Collaborative science

When the geophysicists have completed their work, boreholes can be drilled to produce an accurate pattern of the strata in the region under investigation. Metallurgists and chemists identify the useful minerals that could be extracted from a study of the material extracted from the borehole and the depth of the ore body at that point. By drilling many holes in a regular array, statisticians can work out the extent of the ore body and the likely yield of useful minerals.

General principles

If the Earth's crust was made of only one material, measurements of any physical quantity would not vary from place to place. However, even where the Earth's crust is reasonably homogeneous, slight differences occur and some properties such as gravity and magnetism vary around the Earth's surface. To investigate these variations geophysical survey measurements are made in a structured way. The purpose is to look for positions on the Earth where the physical measurement changes significantly enough to indicate the presence of something beneath the surface. This is called an **anomaly** which means a deviation from the expected reading.

Measurements are made at regular intervals using a grid system as shown in Figure 5. The area is laid out with each metre point marked on string lines.

Measurements are made along a straight line and the process is then repeated along a line parallel to the first and so on. Readings repeated along the lines at right angles give both fresh data and check repeatability at the crossing point. In this way a map similar to a contour map is built up. Some readings may be higher than usual and some lower.

The cause of the anomaly may be a denser body that contains useful ores or a less dense region which may contain lighter minerals or hydrocarbon deposits. Alternatively, it could indicate a cave or indicate where the Earth has been excavated in the past for some reason which may interest archaeologists. Figure 6 shows results of a typical **resistivity** survey in which the shape of a ditch beneath the surface can clearly be identified.

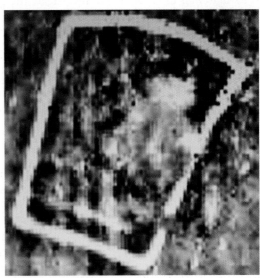

Figure 6 *Resistivity plot showing enclosure ditch*

Summary questions

1 Explain why geophysical surveys are employed in the search for new materials.

2 State two techniques that can be used to explore beneath the Earth that use waves.

3 Explain what is meant by an anomaly.

4.2 Gravity surveying

- How do local variations in the Earth's crust affect gravitational force?

- What is the magnitude of the changes that have to be measurable?

- What techniques are available to measure changes in gravitational field strength?

Specification reference: 3.4.3A

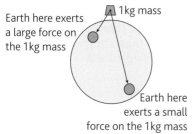

Earth here exerts a large force on the 1kg mass

1kg mass

Earth here exerts a small force on the 1kg mass

Figure 1 *Earth's gravity*

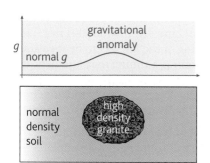

Figure 2 *Variation in g near an ore body*

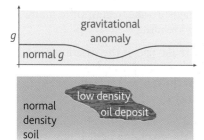

Figure 3 *Variation in g near an oil deposit*

Gravitational force

Newton's gravitational law states that the force between two objects of mass m and M separated by a distance r is given by $F = \dfrac{GMm}{r^2}$ where G is the universal gravitational constant ($6.7 \times 10^{-11}\,\mathrm{N\,m^2\,kg^{-2}}$).

The **gravitational field strength** at any point is the gravitational force on a mass of 1 kg at that point. This is found by adding (vectorially) all the forces exerted on the 1 kg mass by all the particles that make up the Earth. For particles of the same mass, those that are closest to the 1 kg test mass exert a larger force on it than those that are furthest away. For most purposes it is assumed that the Earth behaves as if the mass of all the particles that make it up is concentrated at the centre of the Earth.

Variations in the gravitational field strength (g) at the Earth's surface occur due to the Earth not being a perfect sphere and due to its rotation. This results in values for g that vary from $9.78\,\mathrm{N\,kg^{-1}}$ at the Equator to $9.81\,\mathrm{N\,kg^{-1}}$ in the UK and $9.83\,\mathrm{N\,kg^{-1}}$ at the North pole. Superimposed on this general variation of g are local variations that are caused by bodies in the Earth's crust that have a higher or lower density than usual. These bodies are close to the point of measurement so although the effect on the value of g is small it is detectable using suitable equipment.

The variations are significant enough to enable mapping of likely mineral bearing ores and hydrocarbon deposits and modern sensitive instruments can also detect variations due to buried structures that are of interest to archaeologists.

Magnitude of the change

When conducting gravitational surveys, the **changes** in the gravitational field that occur are more relevant than the actual value but many of the gravimeters used measure the absolute value of g. The magnitude of the change is caused by the difference in density of the body, its volume and its distance from the surface.

Suppose that there is a body of granite of density $2800\,\mathrm{kg\,m^{-3}}$ and a volume of $4.0 \times 10^7\,\mathrm{m^3}$ buried with its centre of mass 200 m below the surface, in a region where the density of the soil is about $1700\,\mathrm{kg\,m^{-3}}$.

The mass of soil displaced by the granite would normally produce a force of $\dfrac{6.7 \times 10^{-11} \times 4.0 \times 10^7 \times 1700}{200^2}\mathrm{N}$ on a 1 kg mass but the higher density increases the force to $\dfrac{6.7 \times 10^{-11} \times 4.0 \times 10^7 \times 2800}{200^2}\,\mathrm{N}$. The change in the gravitational field strength is the difference between these forces, $7.4 \times 10^{-5}\,\mathrm{N\,kg^{-1}}$. This is a change of only 0.00075% in g and such small changes require sensitive instruments to measure them.

The gal

This is the unit (named after Galileo) that geophysicists use for gravitational field strength. One **gal** is equal to $0.01\,\mathrm{N\,kg^{-1}}$ (equivalent to an acceleration of free fall of $1\,\mathrm{cm\,s^{-2}}$). This makes normal gravitational field strength 981 gal and the change referred to in the above example is 7.4 mgal.

Gravitational force changes with height

A height change of 1 m at the Earth's surface is an increase in radius of $1.6 \times 10^{-5}\%$. As the radius is a squared quantity in the calculation of g the value of g decreases by $3.2 \times 10^{-5}\%$. The gravitational field strength falls by about $3.1 \times 10^{-6}\,\mathrm{N\,kg^{-1}}$ (or $\mathrm{m\,s^{-2}}$). or 0.3 mgal. The gravitational force falls for distances further from the centre of the Earth and this has to be taken into account when undertaking gravitational surveys.

Gravimeters

A gravimeter is an instrument for investigating variations in g. Modern gravimeters are capable of measuring g or changes in g to 1 part in 1000 million. This is equivalent to a precision of about 0.001 mgal. The instruments are therefore capable of detecting small objects or large objects with smaller differences in density from the surrounding material.

Any measurement that depends on g can be used. Instruments that depend on timing freely falling objects measure the absolute value of the field strength to suitable accuracy. Those that depend on the stretching of weak springs or measurements of frequencies of simple pendulums and mass-spring systems are only suitable for registering changes.

Although they are sensitive instruments, surveys can be conducted with the instruments mounted in aircraft. Although the aircraft motion has accelerations many thousands of times greater than the changes in gravitational acceleration these can be removed from the instrument readings by electronic circuitry and computer calculations.

Free-fall gravimeter

Free-fall instruments are able to measure the absolute value of the gravitational field strength at a point whereas other methods can only detect changes.

To make a free-falling instrument of suitable size for field work a typical meter may measure the time for an object to fall a distance of about 20 cm. The time to fall is then about 0.2 s. A change of 0.001 mgal (equivalent to an acceleration of $0.000001\,\mathrm{cm\,s^{-2}}$ or $0.00000001\,\mathrm{m\,s^{-2}}$) is a change in g of about 1 in 10^9. The timing of the fall has to be measured to a similar degree of accuracy so this requires a timing measurement to better than 1 ns. The acceleration is found from the equation $s = \frac{1}{2}gt^2$ or, if two velocities are measured when the object is already moving, from $v = u + at$, where t is the time between the two velocity measurements.

There are many problems that have to be solved to make accurate measurements. These are similar to those encountered in a simple measurement of g in an A-level laboratory; reducing the effect of air resistance, starting and stopping the timing at well defined positions. In gravimeters the apparatus is evacuated to a low pressure and instruments can be designed to reset the object and measure the freefall time many times per minute and provide an averaged reading.

The most accurate free-fall instruments make use of the interference fringes formed by the superposition of laser light reflected from a reference mirror and a mirror attached to the falling body shown in Figure 4. The object falls inside a container that has been evacuated to a very low pressure.

As the object falls the detector monitors the changing light intensity. For a change of one wavelength of the laser light the falling object would have moved down half a wavelength. Laser light wavelengths and times

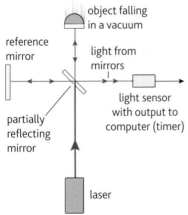

object falling in a vacuum

reference mirror

light from mirrors

light sensor with output to computer (timer)

partially reflecting mirror

laser

Figure 4 *Free fall gravimeter using interferometry*

can be determined to a high degree of accuracy. The system can measure the time for a set number of fringes to pass the detector and the distance and time measurements can then be used to determine a value for g. In a single fall this can be done many times and the results averaged to give g to a extremely high degree of accuracy.

Frequency measurements

The period T of a simple pendulum of length l is given by $T = 2\pi\sqrt{\dfrac{l}{g}}$.

Pendulums are never 'simple' however so the length, although constant for a given instrument, cannot be determined accurately enough to make absolute measurements to the accuracy required for gravitational surveying. However, the formula shows that for a given pendulum $g \propto \dfrac{1}{T^2}$ so as g increases the period decreases and vice versa so changes can be detected.

To see how difficult such measurements are, think about this. A change of 1 mgal is a change in g of 1 in 10^6 or 0.0001%. A change of this magnitude produces a change of 0.00005% in the period of the pendulum. If a pendulum has period of 20 s the change would be only 10 μs. Although very small, such a change is measurable by timing a large number of oscillations (maybe for an hour or more) and using a quartz clock. Because of the time required to make measurements of period other methods are generally preferred.

■ **Hint**

Uncertainty when squaring

Remember that when a quantity is squared in an equation the *percentage* uncertainty is doubled. So in this case if the uncertainty in T is 0.00005% the uncertainty in g is $2 \times 0.00005\%$

■ **Summary questions**

1 A 1 kg mass is 1 m above the Earth's surface. What is the ratio of the force on the 1 kg mass exerted by 1 kg of soil 1 m below the mass and 1 kg of soil on the opposite side of the Earth?

2 A free fall gravimeter records a time of 0.2023 s for the time taken for the mass to fall 0.2000 m from rest. Calculate the gravitational field strength in gal at that point.

3 A pendulum has a period of 20 s. What would be the change in g field strength that could be measured using a timer that can only record time intervals to the nearest 0.1 s? Give the answer in N kg^{-1}.

4 Why is gravitational surveying of little use when conducting archaeological surveys?

4.3 Magnetic field surveying

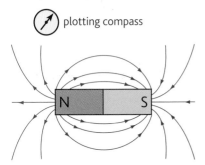

Figure 1 *Magnetic field near a bar magnet*

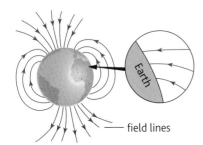

Figure 2 *The Earth's magnetic field*

Magnetic field surveying relies on differences in measurements of **magnetic field strength**. To understand why there are differences and how these can be detected it is necessary to understand what causes magnetism and what effects can be used to measure and detect it.

What is magnetism?

A magnetic field is a region in which a magnetic effect may be observed. The most familiar magnetic fields are the magnetic field of the Earth and that produced by a bar magnet. The most familiar effect is that on a compass needle. The direction of a magnetic field is the direction of the force on a magnetic north pole due to the field so the magnetic field of the Earth is toward the geographical north (although slightly deviated from it). This is the direction a compass needle points. For a bar magnet the direction of magnetic field (field line) is from the north pole to the south pole of the magnet. This is the direction of the force on the north pole of a compass needle or the direction in which a single north pole moves. It follows from this that the general shape of the Earth's field is produced by something that behaves as a giant magnet in the core of the Earth and which has its N pole toward the geographical S pole.

The field lines show the direction of the field. These are parallel to the Earth at the equator and dip down into the Earth in the northern hemisphere. The **angle of dip,** between the field direction and the horizontal, increases with latitude.

The field lines also give an idea of the relative strength of the field. Where they are closer the field is stronger.

Cause of magnetic fields

Magnetic fields are produced by the movement of charge, so in a laboratory magnetic fields are easy to produce by passing a current through a wire i.e. by the movement of electrons. The corkscrew rule can be used to predict the direction of the magnetic field around the wire.

Figure 3 shows the magnetic field for a straight wire. Notice that the field is in the form of closed circles. It is not a helix. The strength of the field is greatest close to the wire.

Most often, flat coils or solenoids produce the fields used in the laboratory. In these, the direction is still predictable using the corkscrew rule but there are other rules that may be used. The Earth's field may be caused by liquid iron and nickel spinning round in the Earth's core producing an electric current so that it behaves like a large coil carrying a current.

The magnetic field of a bar magnet is produced by the motion of electrons in atoms. Although there may be many electrons in motion in an atom the effects do not cancel and this leaves an atom with a net movement of charge. Each atom therefore behaves like a tiny magnet. In a bar magnet these atoms are arranged so that many of them are aligned in the same direction so producing a much stronger field.

Why magnetic field strength varies

The Earth's magnetic field is continually changing and every 300 000 years or so it even flips over. In most materials the magnetism of the atoms is very small and the random alignment of the atoms results in little or no overall magnetic field. In the past, however, the rocks in the Earth were molten and, in this state, the atoms aligned in the field as it existed at that time. As the rocks cooled and solidified they retained the magnetism. The variations in the magnetic field produced, due to this residual magnetism, can now be detected and geologists can use this to gain information about the Earth's past. Anomalies produced by different rocks also enable geophysicists to detect possible mineral bearing ores. Large variations in the field strength would be produced by ores that contain iron and smaller variations by other minerals.

On a smaller scale when building bricks are manufactured by heating in kilns some alignment of atoms in the Earth's field takes place. When the bricks cool they retain some of this magnetism. Although the magnetism is small, sensitive equipment enables the buried remains of buildings of ancient civilisations to be detected from magnetic anomalies on an archaeological site.

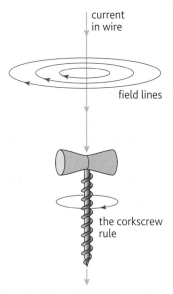

Figure 3 *Magnetic field near a wire*

Application and How science works

New evidence-new theories

Archaeologists investigating ancient aboriginal cooking sites have discovered that stones containing iron were magnetised the wrong way round. This suggests that the Earth's magnetic field can flip over changing the N pole to a S pole. Similar evidence from the study of volcanic ash suggests that this can happen four or five times every million years. Geophysicists try to find explanations of the effect.

Magnetic fields vary for other reasons too. Many of the devices that we use in our everyday lives produce their own magnetic fields. Electricity is conducted through overhead and underground cables to our homes producing magnetic fields. We communicate using electromagnetic waves and permanent magnets and electromagnets are used in motors that power machines. This restricts the places where magnetic surveying can usefully take place to those that are well away from modern buildings due to their magnetism and other electrical influences. Magnetic storms due to the effect of solar flares also affect the Earth's magnetic field so when conducting surveys over a period of time the daily fluctuations have to be accounted for.

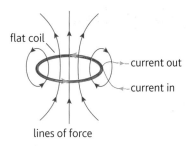

Figure 4 *Magnetic field in a flat coil*

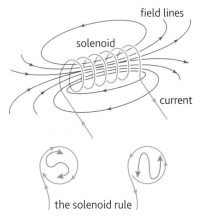

Figure 5 *Magnetic field in a solenoid*

■ Producing strong magnetic fields

In a laboratory the magnetic fields are produced by coils and solenoids.

The magnetic field strength at the centre of an air-cored coil depends on the number of turns, its radius and the current in it.

For a flat coil:

■ Each turn produces its own field and these add up to increase the overall field strength.

■ An increased current means a greater rate of flow of charge so a higher magnetic field.

■ A larger radius increases the distance of the current from the centre so decreasing the field strength.

Using a core of iron instead of air produces a field strength that is many hundreds of times greater than with the air core.

To produce a stronger field in a coil of a given radius requires more turns and larger currents. This presents design problems when using copper coils. To produce more turns without increasing the physical size of the coil requires the use of thinner wire. This increases the resistance of the coil. The wires necessarily have to be wound on top of one another. If the current is then increased to increase the magnetic field strength the energy dissipated in the wires increases (I^2R heating). This would result in the wire melting if the current is too great. So the size of the field obtainable from a coil of given dimensions is limited. Fortunately, these problems can now be overcome using coils of **superconducting** material.

Summary questions

1 Give reasons why you would not expect the magnetic field strength measured in different places in and around your home to be the same everywhere.

2 Explain briefly why a hydrogen atom may behave like a tiny magnet.

3 Draw a diagram showing the direction of motion of an electron and the magnetic field that the motion produces.

4.4 Measuring magnetic fields

Learning objectives:

- What are the units used to measure magnetic flux and magnetic flux density?

- How are magnetic flux densities measured in the laboratory?

- What is a protomagnetometer and how does it work?

Specification reference: 3.4.3B

Magnetic flux and flux density

When a current is passed through a coil, a certain amount of **magnetic flux** is set up inside the coil. This total magnetic flux is represented by the symbol Φ, the Greek letter phi. When more current passes through a coil or when there are more turns the total flux increases. The amount of flux also depends on the material that is in and around the coil. The atoms in a bar magnet also generate a magnetic field and so there is a magnetic flux in the space around and within the magnet.

The direction of the flux is the same as the lines of force that can be plotted using a compass. The strength of the magnetic field varies in the space around a magnet. When drawn carefully, the spacing of the lines can represent the strength of the magnetic field. Where the flux lines are close together there is a stronger field.

The magnetic field strength is defined by the **magnetic flux density B**. The SI unit for B is the **tesla** T.

The magnetic flux density is the *magnetic flux per unit area* so $B = \dfrac{\Phi}{A}$, where A is the area over which the flux is measured.

As the total flux, $\Phi = BA$, the unit of flux is $T\,m^2$.

An alternative unit for flux is the **weber**, Wb. One weber is the same as one tesla metre^2.

How big is a tesla?

We know a magnetic flux is present when there is a magnetic effect such as force exerted on a magnetic pole. To compare the strengths of magnetic fields that exist naturally and those produced in laboratories a standard of measurement is needed. Gravitational field strength is defined in terms of the force per kilogram when a gravitational field exists, and electric field as the force per coulomb when there is an electric field. Likewise, magnetic field strength was once defined in terms of the force on the unit pole. However this proves to be an unsatisfactory definition.

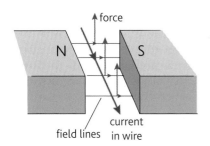

Figure 1 *Force on a current-carrying conductor*

Another important effect that occurs is the force exerted on a wire when it carries a current and there is a magnetic field perpendicular to the wire, as shown in Figure 1. This is easily reproducible so the strength of the field is defined by the magnitude of this effect. Fleming's left hand rule enables a prediction of the direction of the force to be made in relation to the current and magnetic field (Figure 2).

It is found that the magnitude of the force F increases when:

- the current increases,
- the length of the wire perpendicular to the field increases,
- the magnetic flux density increases.

The force on the wire is given by $F = BIL$ so the magnetic flux density is given by $B = \dfrac{F}{IL}$

The unit for B is the tesla, T, where $1\,T$ is $1\,N\,m^{-1}\,A^{-1}$.

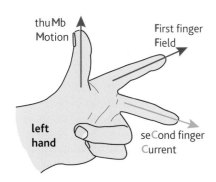

Figure 2 *Fleming's left hand rule*

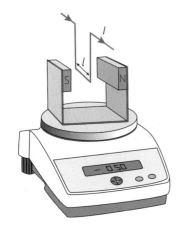

Figure 3 *Measuring **B** for a magnet*

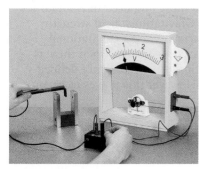

Figure 4 *Hall probe in use*

The magnetic flux density is 1 T when it causes a force of 1 N on a wire of length 1 m carrying a current of 1 A.

Because the changes that are detected in geophysics and archaeological surveys are often small the unit used is the '**gamma**'. This corresponds to a flux density of 10^{-9} T. Instruments that measure flux densities to $\pm 1 \times 10^{-10}$ T (0.1 gamma) are available. The changes in magnetic fields produced by a buried object depends on the material from which it is made, its size and how deeply it is buried. An old steel oil drum buried a few metres below the surface would produce an anomaly of about 50 gamma (50×10^{-9} T).

Measuring magnetic flux density

Measuring B for a magnet

Figure 3 shows a simple way of measuring the flux density between opposite poles of two magnadur magnets.

In this arrangement the length of wire in the field is 7.0 cm. A current of about 5 A is the typical current available from a laboratory power supply. When there is no current, the balance records the mass of the magnets and the yoke. When the current is switched on the reading on the balance will increase or decrease. This depends on the direction of the force on the wire which in turn depends on the direction of the current relative to the magnetic field.

Suppose the precision of the balance is ± 0.1 g. The smallest detectable change in the force on the wire would be 9.8×10^{-4} N. This corresponds to a magnetic flux density of 2.8 mT. A change of 1.5 g when the current is turned on or off would correspond to a magnetic flux density of 42 mT.

More sensitive arrangements can measure the force on the wire more accurately. Thus B can be found more accurately and smaller changes in B can be detected. If the force is measured in a field of known B, the current can be found. The arrangements are usually referred to as 'current-balances'. In the laboratory you may use instruments that use **Hall effect** sensors to investigate magnetic fields near magnets or coils. These are often calibrated to give the magnetic field strength in tesla.

When conducting surveys using aircraft the probe that measures magnetic field strength has to be kept well away from the aircraft structure. This reduces the effects of the metal structure and any other electronic instruments carried by the aircraft. Otherwise these would produce either a **systematic error** in the readings or a **random error** if the probe moves relative to the aircraft. The detector can be towed or it can be mounted on a long probe in front or at the rear of the aircraft.

Resolving B

B is a vector quantity. When making measurements with a current balance or with a Hall probe only the component of the field that is perpendicular to the wire or face of the probe is measured. If B is the flux density which is at an angle θ to the wire or the face of the Hall slice the measured flux density perpendicular to the slice $B_{\perp r} = B \sin \theta$.

The strength and inclination to the horizontal of the Earth's magnetic field varies across the UK. The value of B is approximately 48 μT inclined at about 66° to the horizontal.

This gives a horizontal component of the field of 19.5 μT.

Hall probe

A Hall probe consists of a small slice of semiconductor material that carries a steady current. When a magnetic field exists perpendicular to the probe the charge carriers are deflected to one side of the slice. Figure 4 shows what happens when the charge carriers are electrons. The top edge of the slice becomes negatively charged and the bottom edge positive as electrons are deflected toward the top edge.

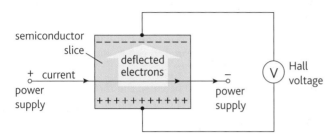

Figure 5 *A Hall probe (magnetic field direction into the page)*

A potential difference therefore exists that is **perpendicular** to the current due to the power supply. The magnitude of this potential difference is proportional to the magnetic flux density so the probe can by used to investigate variations in the flux density or, if calibrated using a known magnetic field, it can measure the actual value of B.

Instruments using the Hall Effect can be manufactured to measure fields to a precision of $\pm 1 \times 10^{-6}$ T.

Proton magnetometer

Archaeologists and geophysicists need instruments that can detect field changes much smaller than those detectable using a Hall probe. When surveying archaeological sites where small buried objects have to be detected, a change of 0.1 nT has to be detectable. A proton magnetometer is an instrument that is capable of detecting such a change and could even locate the magnetic field change due to a skier buried in snow. So how does this work?

The motion of a spinning top or gyroscope under the influence of a gravitational field is probably familiar to everyone. When the top is spun at a high speed, the gravitational force causes it to undergo **precession**. This means that the axis of rotation of the top rotates around the vertical axis through the point at which the gyroscope is in contact with the ground. The frequency of this precession depends on the mass of the top, the **gravitational field strength** and the rate at which the top is spinning. A proton magnetometer works in a similar way.

Figure 7 shows the structure of a proton magnetometer.

■ How science works

Locating hidden objects – a simulation

Ask a fellow student to bury a magnet or an iron bar in a box of sand and try to locate its position using a Hall probe.

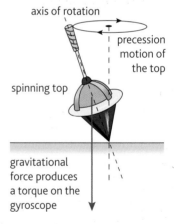

Figure 6 *Spinning gyroscope*

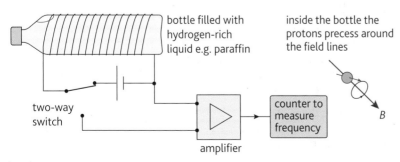

Figure 7 *Proton magnetometer*

■ Protons have charge and they also spin so they behave like tiny magnets. In hydrogen-rich liquids like paraffin these protons are normally aligned randomly producing no overall magnetism.

■ When a large current is passed through the coil the protons are in a strong magnetic field. The protons in the nuclei of the hydrogen atoms line up in the direction of the magnetic field just like the plotting compasses do in laboratory experiments.

■ When the power is switched off each proton behaves like the top. Each one precesses around the direction of the Earth's magnetic field.

■ The **frequency** of the precession (called the **Lamor frequency**) is extremely high and is proportional to the Earth's magnetic flux density at that point.

■ The precession can be detected because the motion of the protons induces an emf in the coil (see the next topic). The frequency is measured by timing the number of oscillations of this induced emf in a known time.

■ This frequency can either be used directly to compare the strengths of the field or the readings can be converted into values of flux density.

■ The frequency of the precession in Hz is $0.04258 \times$ the magnetic flux density in nT. So $B = 23.49f$.

In a place where the flux density of the Earth is $48\,\mu$T ($48\,000$ nT) the frequency would be about 2043 Hz.

A change in magnetic flux density of 0.1 nT is equivalent to a change in the precession frequency of 0.0043 Hz so the frequency has to be measured to a precision of at least 1 part in $500\,000$ and preferably better.

Clocks using the oscillations of quartz crystals are used to provide accurate timing and electronic circuits are used to define a precise time interval of about 0.5 s to 1 s over which the oscillations are counted.

Summary questions

1. A wire of length 0.75 m carries a current of 8.5 A. The wire is perpendicular to the Earth's field which has a strength of $50\,\mu$T. Calculate the force on the wire.

2. Explain the precautions you would take to eliminate the effects of other fields when investigating the field produced by the current in a coil.

3. A Hall probe produces a Hall voltage of 3.5 mV when in a field of flux density 0.030 T. What is the flux density of the field when the instrument reads 5.4 mV

4. Explain why archaeologists use a proton magnetometer rather than a Hall probe when conducting their surveys.

4.5 Using electromagnetic induction

Learning objectives:

- What is an induced emf?

- What factors determine the size of an induced emf?

- How are induced emfs used to detect movement?

Specification reference: 3.4.3B,C

Producing induced emfs

The emf produced by a battery is caused by the contact potential that exists when an electrode is in contact with a solution of ions. Emfs are also produced by solar cells and thermocouples which also depend on there being contact between two dissimilar materials.

An induced emf is different from these in that it requires only one material, the conductor itself. Faraday discovered two laws for electromagnetic induction.

Faraday's laws

Each of Faraday's laws can be expressed in two ways. The first law states:

> **When a conductor cuts magnetic flux an emf is induced in the conductor**

> or

> **When the magnetic flux linking a coil changes an emf is induced in the coil**

Faraday's second law governs the magnitude of the **induced emf which depends on**

> **the rate at which flux is cut**

> or

> **the rate of change of flux linkage**

Application and How science works

Faraday's contribution

Faraday's work on electromagnetism led to many applications which we often take for granted in our lives. It is instructive to reflect on how our lives would be different if this discovery had not been made and its applications recognised. The simple laboratory discovery led to the generation of electricity for our homes; the development of transformers, which play a crucial role in the transmission of electricity; and the design of early microphones, which led to the revolution in our ability to record information and to communicate over long distances with all its social and economic consequences.

Flux cutting

When an electrical conductor cuts magnetic flux as shown in the arrangement in Figure 1 a potential difference is produced between the ends of the conductor. The emf only exists if there is magnetic flux perpendicular to the conductor and only when the conducting wire is moving. This induced emf can produce a current in an electrical circuit.

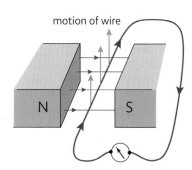

Figure 1 *Generating an induced emf*

The induced emf can be increased by:

■ using a stronger magnet; i.e. increasing the flux density
■ moving the wire faster.

When the wire in Figure 1 is moved in the opposite direction the induced emf is also reversed.

The emf arises because as the wire moves the electrons moving with the wire experience a force. The electrons are forced to one end making it negative and leaving the other end positive. The number of electrons that can move to that end is limited because the build up of electrons creates a force that balances the magnetic force on the electrons so preventing any further movement.

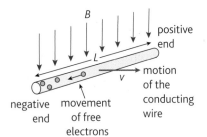

As the wire moves it cuts across the flux that exists in the area swept out by the wire.

The area swept out per second by a wire of length L moving at a velocity $v = Lv$.

The flux cut per second is therefore BLv. If B, L and v are in SI units (T, m and m s^{-1}, respectively) this gives the induced emf in V (Figure 2).

$$\varepsilon = BLv$$

Figure 2 *Emf produced by flux cutting*

Changing flux linkage

A simple laboratory demonstration is shown in **Figure 3**. When the magnet is moved into the coil a reading on the meter indicates that there is an emf produced. This emf only occurs while the magnet is moving. When the magnet is removed the emf is induced in the opposite direction. The size of the emf is greater if the magnet is moved more quickly into the coil.

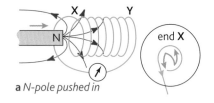

a *N-pole pushed in*

The flux linkage of a coil is the flux Φ through the coil multiplied by the number of turns N of the coil through which the flux passes.

$$\text{Flux linkage} = N\Phi = NAB$$

According to Faraday's law the magnitude of the induced emf is equal to the rate of change of flux linkage so:

$$\varepsilon = N\frac{\Delta\Phi}{\Delta t} = N\frac{\Delta(BA)}{\Delta t}$$

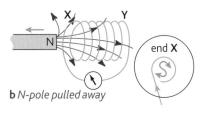

b *N-pole pulled away*

Figure 3 *Induced emf in a coil*

Remember that it is the value of the component of flux density that is perpendicular to the face of the coil that determines the flux linkage.

Direction of the induced emf: Lenz's law

Lenz was a scientist who amongst his other interests had studied geophysics. He discovered that induced currents are in a direction that produces a force to oppose the change that is producing the current.

So when the magnet in Figure 3 moves into the coil the charge in the coil always flows to produce a decelerating force on the magnet. The current direction makes the end X of the coil behave like an N pole so it repels the magnet. As the magnet is removed from the coil, the current is in the opposite direction making end X behave like an S pole. The induced S pole attracts the magnet's N pole and so opposes its motion out of the coil.

Lenz's law is a consequence of the law of conservation of energy. Energy has to be supplied to the magnet to move it into the coil because of the repulsive force experienced as the magnet moves. Thus work is done on the magnet and this work becomes the electrical energy dissipated in the circuit connected to the coil.

Geophone

A geophone is a device used by seismologists, geophysicists and archaeologists to measure Earth movements produced by earthquakes or those produced by even small explosions. The use is described in more detail in Topic 4.8 . Figure 4 shows the structure of a simple geophone.

The magnet has a large mass and is suspended between soft springs (low spring constant). The magnet–spring system is mounted inside a circular coil that is attached to the case of the geophone. If the magnet moves relative to the case there is a change in flux linkage through the coil. This is due to the coil moving into a region where there is a weaker magnetic field. The change produces an emf in the coil. The greater the movement of the coil relative to the magnet in a given time the greater the emf.

When in use, the spike of the geophone is inserted in the ground. If the ground moves upwards as a wave arrives the case of the geophone moves too. The magnet has a high inertia due to its large mass so it remains relatively still at first. It can only move upwards when there is an unbalanced force due to the stretching of the upper spring and compression of the lower one. As the coil moves, an induced emf is produced at the instant the wave arrives. Following the initial movement, the magnet then oscillates producing an alternating emf until it comes to rest due to damping by resistive forces, as described in Topic 3.3.

To produce a large voltage pulse the coil has a large number of turns and the rate of change of flux is further increased by using a strong magnet. The spring stiffness is a compromise between ensuring that the mass remains freely suspended and producing as small a force as possible during the initial movement of the case so that the magnet remains reasonably stationary.

The voltage pulse produced by the geophone can be used to start or stop a timing device.

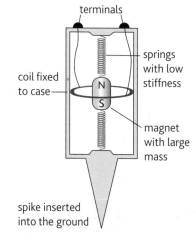

Figure 4 *Geophone*

Summary questions

1. State the SI units for magnetic flux and magnetic flux density.

2. A coil has an area of 8.0 cm² and consists of 150 turns. Calculate the induced emf in the coil when the magnetic flux density through the coil is changes at a rate of 0.25 T s⁻¹.

3. Explain how Lenz's law applies to the motion of a geophone when it has been set into oscillatory motion following the arrival of a disturbance

4.6 Eddy currents

■ What is an eddy current?

■ How is an emf induced using an alternating current?

■ How are eddy currents used to investigate soil conductivity and detect metallic objects?

Specification reference: 3.4.3B

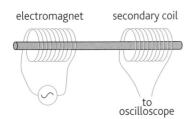

Figure 1 *Airport security scanner*

electromagnet   secondary coil

to oscilloscope

Figure 2 *Inducing emfs*

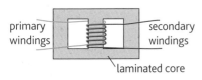

primary windings   secondary windings

laminated core

Figure 3 *Arrangement of coils in a transformer*

In the twenty-first century, eddy currents are increasingly used in security checks at airports and other public places. Those who have been through such a check will appreciate the high sensitivity of the detectors which respond to the presence of keys and coins (Figure 1). Metal detectors are useful tools for plumbers and electricians who are tracking pipes and cables and are well-established tools for amateur treasure hunters and professional archaeologists. They are also used in food processing plants to ensure that no metals have accidentally entered the food being prepared. There are a number of different designs for metal detectors but all depend on the production and detection of **eddy currents** that are set up by induced emfs in metallic conductors.

Flux change without movement

Using the arrangement shown in **Figure 2** induced emfs can be produced without moving the coils. When the switch is open there is no magnetic flux produced by the left-hand coil (the primary coil). When the switch is closed the current in the coil produces a magnetic field which passes through the right hand coil (the secondary coil). There is therefore a change in the flux linking the secondary coil and while the flux is increasing an emf is induced across it. As soon as the flux in the primary coil reaches its maximum value the induced emf ceases. The overall result is therefore a voltage pulse across the secondary coil.

The direction of the current in the secondary coil is in the opposite direction to the current in the primary coil because the secondary coil has to create a flux which opposes the increase in flux that is causing the induced current.

When the current is switched off the flux collapses and another emf is induced across the secondary coil, this time in the opposite direction.

For demonstration purposes in the laboratory the coils are usually linked with an iron core to increase the change in flux that is produced. If the flux is produced in a non-magnetic material like air then the flux change and the emf induced are smaller.

Transformer action

If the current in the primary coil is changed continually using an alternating supply then the **flux linkage** in the secondary will also change continually and generate an alternating emf. The size of this emf depends on the number of turns on the two coils and the emf that is applied to the primary. Increasing the ratio of the number of turns on the secondary coil to those on the primary coil increases the emf generated across it. This principle is used in transformers to increase voltages for transmission and then to decrease them again for use in mains-operated equipment (Figure 3).

In a practical transformer reducing energy loss within the transformer is important. This is achieved by:

■ using low-resistance coils,

■ maximising the amount of flux created by the primary coil that links with the secondary coil by winding the coils on top of one another,

■ laminating the core to reduce eddy currents which cause the temperature of the core to rise.

Investigating fields using induced emfs

In practical applications such as metal detectors, alternating fields are produced by coils and the designers need to know how the field strength varies with coil structure and with distance from the coil. Transformer action can be used to investigate alternating magnetic fields set up by coils in the laboratory using the arrangement shown in Figure 4.

So that the field in a small region can be investigated, the coil needs to have a small area. Therefore, in order to produce a measurable induced emf it has to have many turns. A typical search coil will have about 5000 turns. The induced voltages are larger if high frequencies from a signal generator are used as this leads to a larger maximum rate of change of current, a larger rate of change of flux and a larger maximum induced emf. In a laboratory, induced voltages are still small especially at large distances so an oscilloscope is used to measure them as shown in Figure 4.

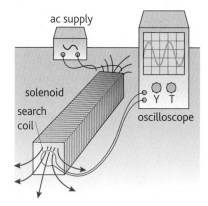

Figure 4 *Investigating fields using a search coil*

■ Eddy currents

Just as a changing magnetic flux can induce currents in a coil, a changing flux can also produce eddy currents in a solid metallic object. They are called eddy currents because they circulate within the conductor in complete loops (not spirals). The charged particles are made to go in circular paths first one way and then the other by the alternating magnetic field.

A metal object can be thought of as being built of many rings of conductor of different sizes as shown in Figure 5. The changing flux that links the dark blue loop causes the induced emf which drives the current around the loop. So in a field of given flux density, the emf in the larger loops is larger than in the smaller ones.

■ The change in flux linkage, and therefore the emf, is proportional to the area (πr^2).

■ The current in the loop depends on the resistance of the material in the loop, which is proportional to the length of the loop ($2\pi r$).

■ As the induced current is given by $\dfrac{\text{emf}}{\text{resistance}}$, the induced current in each loop is proportional to the radius.

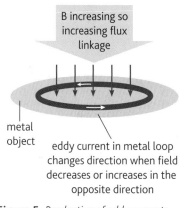

Figure 5 *Production of eddy currents*

Application and How science works

Uses of eddy currents

Eddy currents can cause I^2R heating. This principle is used in cooking where eddy currents are induced in the base of saucepans, induction welding and in many manufacturing processes such as the production of pure silicon crystals.

The direction of the induced currents opposes the change in the magnetic field that is producing them. These currents give rise to a repulsive force which provides the magnetic levitation that is used in maglev trains.

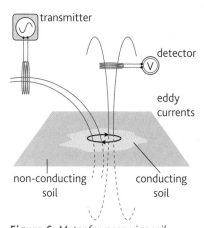

Measuring soil conductivity using magnetic fields

The electrical resistance of the ground varies according to the number of **ions** present in it. The ionic content can increase due to the presence of ions from ores that contain metals or from decomposing metallic

Figure 6 *Meter for measuring soil conductivity*

Figure 7 *Pulsed induction metal detector*

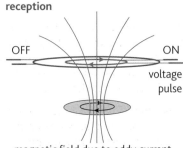

objects. The **conductivity** of the ground can be investigated by a direct measurement of **resistivity** (see Topic 4.7) or from variations in the magnetic field strength produced by eddy currents that are induced in the ground by a transmitter.

Figure 6 shows the components of a soil conductivity meter (SCM) schematically. The transmitter produces an alternating magnetic field. The detector coil about a metre away is orientated so that the field is along the face of the coil. There is no flux linkage in it due to this field. The transmitter produces eddy currents in the ground and these have a vertical component that produces an induced emf in the detecting coil. The magnitude of this emf depends on the conductivity of the soil.

Metal detectors

Small metal objects are also found by detecting the eddy currents generated in them by a transmitting coil. The design of the detectors depends on the size of the objects that have to be detected, what they are made of and how far away they are likely to be from the detector (Figure 7).

Pulsed induction metal detector

A pulsed metal detector is used in the walk-through security devices at airports and is the device preferred by gold prospectors (Figure 8). A current pulse in a transmitting coil produces a magnetic field lasting for a few microseconds. During this time the receiver is inactive so that it is not affected by this pulse. The magnetic field induces an eddy current in a metallic object. This current takes time to decay and, as it does so, it generates an induced emf across the receiver coil. The current in a good conductor (low resistance) takes a long time to decay as energy is dissipated slowly On the other hand, the eddy current dies away quickly in a poor conductor. So the length of the received pulse tells the user whether there is a metal present and may give an idea of the type of material being detected.

In use, the pulse is generated at a high frequency and when there is a metal object present the induced emf in the receiver also pulses at the same frequency. Electronic circuits analyse the signal and may give an audible sound or a digital readout interpreting the received signal.

Figure 8 *Operation of a pulsed induction detector*

Summary questions

1. Explain why it would be more difficult to locate a metal object submerged in sea water than it would if buried to the same depth on land.

2. An iron bar is placed inside a coil and an aluminium plate is placed on top of the iron bar. A switch and a supply capable of producing a large current through the coil are connected in series with the coil. Sketch a diagram of the arrangement and explain what would be observed when switching on a a dc supply b ac supply.

3. A pulsed induction metal detector is required to detect coins the size of a 5p piece buried a few cm below the surface. Discuss the factors that affect the ability of a pulsed induction metal detector to detect a coin the size of 5p piece that is buried a few cm below the Earths surface.

4.7 Resistivity surveying

- How do buried objects affect resistivity?

- How can changes in resistivity be detected?

Specification reference: 3.4.3C

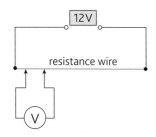

Figure 1 *Measuring the pd across a uniform wire*

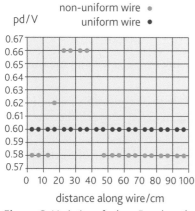

Figure 2 *Variation of pd per 5 cm length with distance from one end*

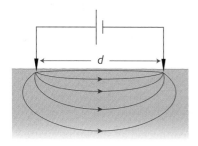

Figure 3 *Current paths in the ground*

Basic principles

When a potential difference of 12 V is applied across 100 cm of a uniform resistance wire as shown in Figure 1 the **potential difference** (pd) recorded by a voltmeter across each 5 cm length is constant at 0.6 V $\left(\frac{5}{100} \times 12\,\text{V}\right)$.

But suppose that the resistance wire is not uniform and has a narrower section somewhere along its length. The current in the wire is the same everywhere but lower than before owing to the higher resistance between the ends. Where the wire narrows the resistance per unit length increases so the potential difference across a 5 cm length increases. The graph in Figure 2 shows how the measured pd would vary for a uniform wire and some results for a non-uniform wire. The points are plotted at the centre point of the 5 cm intervals.

The wire becomes non uniform somewhere between the 12.5 and 17.5 cm readings and becomes uniform again at the 47.5 cm reading. To determine the non-uniform section more precisely the potential difference would need to be measured across shorter lengths of the wire.

The principles outlined above are those used in **resistivity** surveys. However, the three-dimensional electric field that produces conduction in the Earth produces more complex current patterns than the one-dimensional current in a wire.

When two metal probes are inserted into the ground and a potential difference is applied between them an electric field is established between the probes with field lines as shown in Figure 3. As the separation d of the probes increases the extra distance the charge has to flow tends to increase the resistance R between the electrodes. However, the area through which the charge flows also increases and, as area is a squared quantity, the overall effect is that the resistance decreases. The result is that $R \propto 1/d$.

Resistivities

If the soil contains ions then charge flows between the electrodes in the direction of the field lines. The electrical **resistance** between the probes depends on the mobility and concentration of ions in the Earth's crust as these factors affect the resistivity of the rocks and soil. If the resistivity of the soil decreases the resistance between the probes also decreases.

Typical resistivities of some materials are shown in Table 1. These show the range of resistivities but are subject to wide variations. For example the resistance of clay will depend on water content and temperature. Top soil that has 2% by weight of water might have a resistivity of about 250 Ω m whilst the same soil with 30% by weight of water would have a resistivity of 5 Ω m.

For the purposes of the geophysicist searching for minerals or the archaeologist looking for buried remains the actual values are not important. As with other techniques investigation only needs to identify any anomalies at a given site.

Investigation

You could design and carry out a laboratory experiment to investigate the way water content affects resistivity of sand or topsoil. This could be extended to study the variation when metal salts are added to reduce the resistivity.

Table 1 *Resistivity of material in Earth's crust*

Material	Typical resistivity/ Ω m
Rocks	1×10^6
Sand	300
Soil and Clay	5

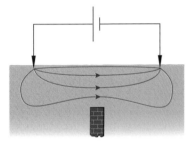

Figure 4 *Buried object restricting current*

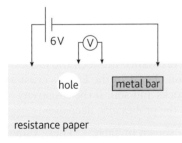

Figure 5 *Laboratory simulation*

Causes of anomalies

Where the ground has a constant resistivity the resistance measured between two probes inserted to the same depth is always the same. The resistance is given by $R = \frac{\rho}{2\pi d}$ (You do not need to remember this formula). If the resistivity of any of the material between the probes changes and is non-conducting material (or much higher resistivity) then the overall resistance will increase. This may be due to a buried rock or on an archaeological site due to the presence of a stone wall as shown in Figure 4.

On the other hand a buried object, such as an ore body, may decrease the resistance between the two probes. In this case the ore body may contain metallic salts that dissolve in the soil moisture thus reducing the resistivity in that region. On an archaeological site the presence of metallic objects buried in the soil have similar effects, either due to the metal's low resistivity or ions introduced into the soil as the metal corrodes. A buried pipe can be detected or even a ditch that has filled up as it can have a higher water content and hence a lower resistivity than the surrounding region.

Finding the anomalies

Based on the principles of resistivity the simplest approach to search for buried ores or objects is to:

- insert the probes a set distance apart, say 1 m,
- measure the potential difference and the current,
- calculate the resistance using $R = \frac{V}{I}$,
- calculate the soil resistivity using the simple formula $2\pi dR$, where d is the spacing of the electrodes,
- move the probes along the grid line being investigated and measure the resistance of the next 1 m length.

In the ground the resistivity is very unlikely to be constant so what is measured is the apparent resistivity of the material between the two probes.

Unfortunately, this simple approach is unreliable because of electrode contact resistances and polarisation due to the production of gases or other deposits on the electrodes. Furthermore, emfs may be generated at the electrodes as metals are in contact with salts. Contact resistances and polarisation can be reduced by the use of an interface made from a solution of ions (e.g. copper sulphate solution) and increasing the moisture content near the electrodes. Other problems can be avoided or minimised by using alternating power supplies or the potential divider techniques discussed below.

As shown in the simulation in Figures 5 and 6 a potential difference is established between the two outer electrodes. The potential difference between two electrodes a set distance apart is then measured along the line joining them. The potential difference will show small local variations due to different levels of moisture in the soil but wider variations will show the existence of buried objects.

Alternatively four equally spaced probes connected as shown in Figure 7, are all moved together at 1 m intervals along the grid line. These can be mounted on a base that makes it easy to move all four probes from one position to another. The potential difference between the inner electrodes

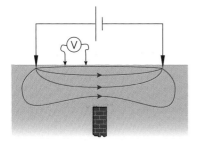

Figure 6 *Using pd measurements to find buried objects*

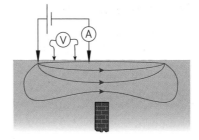

Figure 7 *Using four electrodes with fixed spacing*

divided by the current in the outer electrodes remains constant if the resistance of the soil remains the same. An increase or decrease is an anomaly that indicates the presence of buried material affecting the uniform conductivity of the soil.

Application and How science works

Modelling resistivity surveys in the laboratory

Resistance paper is impregnated with carbon to give it a uniform resistance per square. A hole can be cut in the paper producing a non-conducting region or high conductivity metallic objects (e.g. coins) may be placed on the paper. (These may be obscured and presented as problem situations) The arrangement can be investigated using the circuit shown in Figure 5.

Alternatively a 'tank' of copper sulphate can provide the homogeneous conducting medium which can be investigated using probes inserted at the surface. Conducting (lumps of metal) or non-conducting objects (stones) can be submerged in the copper sulphate and their location detected from anomalies found from the voltage readings as probes are moved along the surface.

Summary questions

1 Suggest why it would be difficult to use resistivity surveying in a desert region.

2 Give two reasons why the conductivity of the soil may vary.

3 A wire is made of two 50 cm lengths of two wires X and Y. X has a resistance per unit length which is twice that of Y. A pd is set up between the ends of the wires. Sketch a graph showing how the pd between a point P along the wire varies with the distance of P from the end of wire X.

4.8 Seismology

■ Background

Seismology is the field of study that monitors and investigates the propagation of waves through the Earth. From these studies scientists can gain information about the Earth's crust. Vibrations of the Earth's crust are caused by volcanic activity and the movement of tectonic plates over one another which produce earthquakes. These movements generate waves that travel through the Earth and the subsequent movement of the Earth's surface can be detected by sensitive sensors. These small tremors often occur before more violent activity and enable seismologists to warn the populations of vulnerable areas to take some action to reduce the risks when the more destructive earthquake occurs. As destructive tidal waves, known as tsunami, are often produced by earthquakes those people who live in coastal regions large distances from the epicentre of an earthquake also benefit from early warnings.

The waves generated during earthquakes allow geologists to build up a picture of the inside of the Earth. This is done by combining the signals received at the many seismic stations around Earth's surface following a tremor. Figure 1 shows some wave paths following such an earthquake.

Artificially generated waves can be used as an investigative tool for geophysicists and archaeologists to explore the substructure of the ground. These investigations may be on a large scale in which explosions are produced to discover the location of ore bodies buried deep in the ground. On a smaller scale, vibrations and waves generated by no more than a sledgehammer blow on to a metal block can be used to study a site containing structures of interest to an archaeologist.

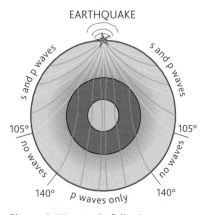

Figure 1 *Wave paths following an earthquake*

■ Detecting earthquakes

The geophone described in Topic 4.5 can detect any vertical oscillations of the Earth produced by an earthquake. To detect horizontal movement a **seismometer** (seismograph) is used.

The basic structure is shown in Figure 2. It consists of a pendulum with a large mass suspended inside a case. The case is firmly attached to the Earth or a building. When there is horizontal movement the case moves with the Earth or building but the large mass does not move initially because of its large inertia. The horizontal movement of the case produces a horizontal force on the suspended mass causing it to oscillate. The amplitude depends on how much the case has been moved by the earthquake which in turn depends on the magnitude of the earthquake. A pen fixed to the pendulum traces the displacement on a rotating drum producing a permanent record. Alternatively, the movement can be made to induce emfs like those in a geophone so that the movement can be recorded electronically.

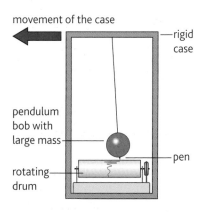

Figure 2 *Seismometer*

■ Wave speed

In the search for minerals it is not merely the detection of the waves that is of use. There are two types of wave: P waves and S waves. The P waves are **longitudinal** and these move more quickly than the **transverse** S waves, at about 1.8 times the speed in fact. The waves travel at different speeds in different types of material depending on both the **density** and **elasticity** of the material. Some typical values are given in Table 1.

Table 1 *Speed of P and S waves in different materials*

material	P wave velocity /m s^{-1}	S wave velocity /m s^{-1}
granite	5700	2900
sandstone	1500 to 4000	700 to 2400
clay	1000 to 2500	400 to 1000

The useful measurement is the time between the instant the disturbance is created by the explosion or sledge hammer blow and the time at which the wave energy reaches a detector. The timer can be started and stopped by the electrical pulse from two geophones placed a known distance apart (see Figure 3). Alternatively, the timer can be started by a short circuit to the 'start' input to a timer when the sledgehammer makes contact with the metal block as shown in Figure 4.

When carrying out surveys over small distances in an area such as an archaeological 'dig', the measured time is very short so high-precision timing is essential. For example if the timing is over a distance of 4 m then the energy takes about $\frac{4}{2500}$ seconds to travel from disturbance to receiver. For the investigation to make reliable observations of anomalous readings this time has to measured as precisely as possible. This requires the mechanism for starting and stopping the timing of the clock to be fast and consistent. The clock needs to record times to the nearest microsecond or better and, to achieve this clocks that use quartz crystals oscillating at frequencies of about 100 kHz are used.

Detecting buried objects

A geophysicist might be looking for the presence of granite rocks that might contain ore and an archaeologist might be trying to find an ancient wall. How might these affect the timings being made at the surface of the Earth?

If the Earth is a uniform structure then the speed of the waves would be constant and, since $s = vt$, as the geophones are moved apart the time should increase proportionally.

However, when waves travelling in surface soil meets a lump of granite some energy of the waves is **reflected** and some **refracted**. Because they can travel faster in granite the direction of travel bends away from the normal.

The **critical angle** c for a wave travelling from soil to granite is given by

$$\sin c = \frac{\text{speed of waves in soil}}{\text{speed of waves in granite}}$$

When the energy arrives at the critical angle some of the energy travels along the surface of the granite and, as it travels along, some is refracted back to the surface, again at the critical angle.

When measuring the time, the first wave to arrive at the geophone will trigger it. In Figure 5, the energy that arrives by the direct route is shown in red. For a certain separation between disturbance and geophone the energy that travels by the longer route shown in blue arrives at the same time as the direct route. This is because for some of the time it is

How science works

Earthquakes

The strength of an earthquake is measured on the Richter scale. The scale is a logarithmic one based on the amplitude of the movement of the Earth. A change of 1 on the Richter scale means that the amplitude of the vibration of a seismometer recording the event would change by a factor of 10. The table shows the sort of destructive effects of earthquakes of different magnitudes.

Magnitude 4	Strong enough to crack plaster on walls
Magnitude 5	Damage to chimneys; weak structures damaged
Magnitude 6	Ordinary homes damaged
Magnitude 7	Well-built strong buildings damaged
Magnitude 8	Damage even to buildings specially built to withstand earthquakes
Magnitude 9	Total damage caused, surface waves can be observed, objects thrown in the air

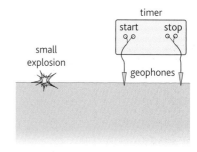

Figure 3 *Timing using two geophones*

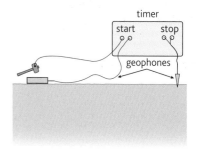

Figure 4 *Timing using one geophone*

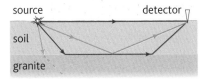

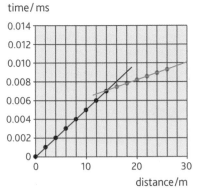

Figure 5 *Energy paths between source and detector*

time/ms

Figure 6 *Graph of time against distance showing discontinuity*

travelling at a higher velocity in the granite. For larger separations the wave taking the longer route arrives first.

Energy that is refracted into the granite (shown in orange) never reaches the geophone. The reflected wave (shown in green) clearly travels a longer distance and therefore takes longer to reach the geophone than that by the direct route.

The result is that, when times are measured for regular intervals of distance between the origin of the wave and the geophone, the graph shows a discontinuity as shown in Figure 6. From this graph the depth of the granite below the surface can be found.

Calculating the depth

Figure 7 shows data for one investigation in which the discontinuity in the gradient occurs after 7.5 ms and the direct distance between the origin of the wave and the geophone is 15 m. The speed of the wave in the soil is $2000 \, \text{m s}^{-1}$ and in granite $5700 \, \text{m s}^{-1}$. The critical angle at the interface between the soil and the granite is therefore 20.5°.

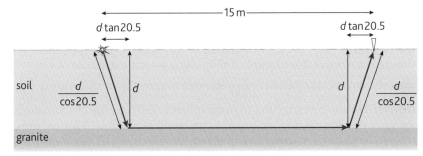

Figure 7 *Wave path corresponding to intercept of the graph*

The distance between the surface of the Earth and the granite $= d$

The distance travelled in the soil (down and up) $= 2 \times \dfrac{d}{\cos 20.5} = 2.14d$

The distance travelled in the granite $= 15 - 2 \times d \tan 20.5$

$= 15 - 0.75d.$

So the time to travel via the granite $= \dfrac{2.14d}{2000} + \dfrac{(15 - 0.75d)}{5700}$

This is the same as the time taken to travel directly via the soil $= 7.5 \, \text{ms}$

Solving for d shows that the depth of the surface of the granite mass below the surface $= 5.2 \, \text{m}$

Summary questions

1 State two ways in which the energy in a wave that is travelling toward the centre of the Earth may be returned to the Earth's surface.

2 The smallest time interval detectable using a clock is 1×10^{-4} s. A geophone is moved a distance of 0.10 m away from the point at which a wave is created by a small explosion. The wave travels in soil at a velocity of $2000 \, \text{m s}^{-1}$. Determine whether the clock is capable of detecting this change in position.

3 Calculate the critical angle for a wave travelling from clay into sandstone given that the velocity of waves in the clay is $1000 \, \text{m s}^{-1}$ and that in the sandstone is $1700 \, \text{m s}^{-1}$.

AQA Examination-style questions

1   Outline **three** methods by which geophysicists attempt to establish the presence of ore beneath the Earth's surface. Suggest advantages and disadvantages for each of the methods you suggest.

(9 marks)

2   **Figure 1** shows one type of free-fall gravimeter.

FG-5 principle of operation

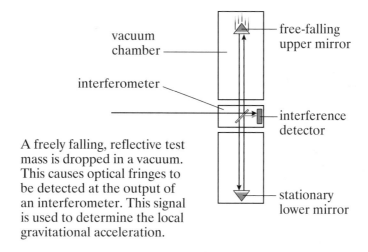

A freely falling, reflective test mass is dropped in a vacuum. This causes optical fringes to be detected at the output of an interferometer. This signal is used to determine the local gravitational acceleration.

Figure 1

Explain how the gravimeter is used to determine the local value of the gravitational field strength of the Earth.

3   **Figures 2 and 3** show two blocks of material: soil and a mineral bearing ore.

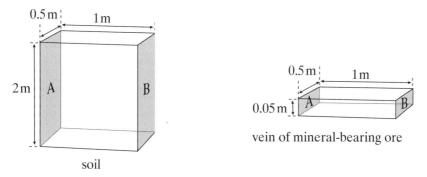

Figure 2   **Figure 3**

(a)   Calculate

    (i)   the resistance of the block of soil $2\,m \times 0.5\,m \times 1\,m$ between ends A and B (soil resistivity = $5\,\Omega\,m$)

(2 marks)

    (ii)   the resistance of the vein of mineral bearing ore $0.05 \times 0.5\,m \times 2\,m$ between ends A and B (ore resistivity = $4500\,\Omega\,m$)

(2 marks)

(b)   The soil in part (a)(i) overlays the ore in (a)(ii) as shown in the diagram.

Estimate the change in the total resistance between the ends A and B of the soil-ore block compared to the soil sample alone.

(3 marks)

(c)   Explain how the four-probe techniques can be used to detect the presence of a conducting object underground.

(4 marks)

4   The centre of an iron meteor density $7900\,\mathrm{kg\,m^{-3}}$ is buried $8.7\,\mathrm{m}$ below the surface of the ground after impact. The meteor is spherical and of radius $0.75\,\mathrm{m}$.

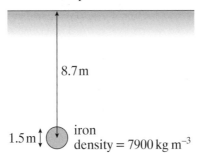

8.7 m

1.5 m   iron
density $= 7900\,\mathrm{kg\,m^{-3}}$

Figure 4

(a)   Show that the mass of the meteor is about $14\,\mathrm{Mg}$ *(2 marks)*

(b)   Calculate the gravitational field strength g due to the meteor at the surface of the Earth.

(c)   Calculate the change in g due to the presence of the meteor in the ground when it has replaced soil of density $1800\,\mathrm{kg\,m^{-3}}$.

(d)   A modern free-fall gravimeter can detect changes in g of 1 part in 10^9. Comment on whether the gravimeter could detect the presence of the meteor.

5   **Figure 5** shows a school bar magnet freely suspended for demonstration purposes on two pairs of jewelled bearings so that it can rotate freely in any direction.

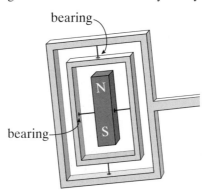

bearing

bearing

N

S

Figure 5

(a)   Explain, in terms of the Earth's field, why the magnet will not align itself to the horizontal in a school laboratory in the UK.   *(1 mark)*

(b)   Discuss the alignment of the magnet if it were to be placed:

at the Earth's magnetic north pole,   *(1 mark)*

at the equator.   *(1 mark)*

(c)   In the light of your answers to part (b), comment on the use of a magnetic compass for navigational purposes

at the magnetic poles   *(2 marks)*

in regions where there are significant deposits of iron ore under the ground.   *(1 mark)*

6 A Hall emf is produced when charge flows through a material as shown in **Figure 6**.

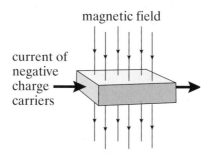

Figure 6

(a) Explain how the Hall emf arises. State the direction of the field produced by the Hall effect. *(7 marks)*

(b) A Hall probe is calibrated by placing it perpendicular to a magnetic field of flux density 1.5 mT. A Hall emf of 2.5 V appears across the device.

The probe is now held vertically in the Earth's magnetic field in a region where the resultant strength of the Earth's field is known to be 48 μT. The Hall probe registers an emf of 66 mV. Calculate the vertical component of the Earth's magnetic field. *(4 marks)*

(c) Calculate the angle of dip of the Earth's field at the point where the Hall probe is placed. *(3 marks)*

7 An archaeologist is using a metal detector to detect a horde of jewellery believed to have been buried underground (**Figure 7**).

Figure 7

He uses a device which can produce an alternating magnetic field of frequency 150 kHz.

(i) Calculate the time taken for the magnetic field to collapse from its maximum strength to zero.

(ii) The ring has a radius of 7.5 mm and is buried horizontally in the field some distance below the surface. The magnetic field at the gold ring due to the detecting device is directed vertically through the ring and has a strength of 2.3×10^{-4} T. Calculate the magnetic flux through the ring.

(iii) Estimate the maximum emf that can be developed in the gold ring.

8 (a) Seismic P waves travel through Earth faster than S waves. In terms of the damage they cause, Describe two differences between P and S waves. *(2 marks)*

(b) P and S waves are detected at a seismic station following an earthquake. The time interval between their arrival is 2.9 s. The speed of P waves is 7.0 km s^{-1} and that of S waves is 4.2 km s^{-1}. *(3 marks)*

Calculate the distance of the epicentre of the earthquake from the seismic station.

(c) Suggest what improvements in the positional data can be gained by the use of

(i) two seismic stations,

(ii) three seismic stations. *(2 marks)*

Inside the body

5.1 Using X-rays

Learning objectives:

- What techniques are available for unobtrusive clinical investigations?

- What properties of X-rays make them useful in diagnosis?

- What precautions are needed when using X-rays?

Specification reference: 3.4.3D

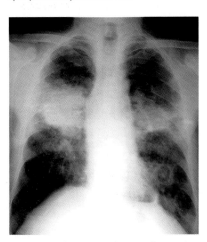

Figure 1 *Chest X ray showing diseased lung*

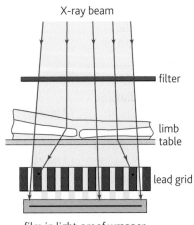

Figure 2 *Making an X-ray image*

■ Looking beneath the skin

Discovery of X-rays

Until Röntgen discovered **X-rays** in 1895, clinical investigations of disease in internal organs required, open surgery that was often unnecessary. Following Rontgen's first published X-ray of his wife's hand, X-rays soon became widely used by doctors. Although not without risk to the patient, the benefits of X-rays were soon seen to outweigh the possible side effects. For much of the twentieth century this remained the only tool available for unobtrusive investigations of broken bones and other internal problems.

The early techniques produced two-dimensional shadow images of the bones and organs inside the body. Images such as that shown in Figure 1 proved to be effective in diagnosing diseases that affect the lungs such as pneumonia, tuberculosis and cancers produced by the effects of asbestos and smoking. As well as the medical applications X-ray imaging is now used to monitor luggage at airports and other public places for security reasons.

Producing an X-ray image

Figure 2 shows the arrangement used to produce X-ray images. Lower energy X-rays are readily absorbed by the body and are harmful so a filter is used to remove them.

The X-rays that fall on the photographic plate form the image of the bones and organs. The **intensity** of the beam after passing through the body depends on the thickness and density of the tissue and bones through which the beam has passed. The intensity changes exponentially with thickness and is given by the formula $I = I_0 e^{-\mu x}$ where I_0 is the original intensity and μ is the **attenuation coefficient**.

The value of μ depends on the energy of the X-rays, the proton number (Z) of the absorbing material and its density. Elements with high Z have higher values of μ. For a given Z and photon energy, μ is proportional to the density.

As the change is **exponential**, the intensity always falls by the same factor when passing through a given thickness of the same material. Consequently the thickness of absorber that halves the intensity is constant and is called the **half-value thickness**, $x_{\frac{1}{2}}$. This is equal to $\dfrac{\ln 2}{\mu}$. The variation of transmitted intensity with absorber thickness is shown in Figure 3.

Most medical X-ray images are negatives. The dark parts of the image are formed where there has been little **absorption** of the radiation. Lighter images are formed by bones which have a high density, a high value of μ, and so absorb more radiation. Soft tissues, such as the liver or lungs, are seen as darker images on the exposed film. Diseased organs produce images of varying intensity that can be interpreted by doctors.

Improving the image

Because of their short wavelength, X-rays are not **diffracted** or **scattered** significantly by the atoms in the body so travel through the body in almost straight lines. The scattering of the beam that does occur would blur the image so the contrast of the image is improved by using a lead grid, as shown in Figure 2. The lead grid absorbs scattered X-rays so only radiation that travels directly through the grid channels reaches the photographic film.

The density of bone is much greater than that of the surrounding tissue so clear images are formed. However there is only a small difference in density between organs such as the stomach and the surrounding tissue so to improve the image a **contrast medium** is used. To produce good contrast a patient drinks a 'barium meal' which consists of barium sulphate. The barium absorbs X-rays improving the image. Similarly, blood vessels can be shown more clearly if a solution of iodine is introduced into the blood stream.

When using image intensifier tubes such as that in Figure 4 the image can be enhanced electronically and allows doctors to study real-time movement inside the body such as when a patient swallows. X-rays form the image on the fluorescent screen. This emits light photons that cause electron emission from the photocathode. These electrons are focused to produce an image on the fluorescent viewing screen. The image is enhanced by a factor of about 1000 so the radiation dose received by the patient is reduced significantly.

CT scanners

A flatbed office scanner can make copies of documents by detecting the intensity of the light reflected from the document as the light source and detector moves along it. In a similar way a CT (computerised tomography) scanner detects the intensity of X-rays transmitted through the body. The data is recorded as an X-ray source rotates around a patient. At the same time the patient travels slowly through the X-ray beam. The beam fans out from the X-ray source and sensors on the other side of the body record the intensity of the transmitted beam, see Figure 5. Each rotation of the beam provides data for a thin cross-section of the body. Analysis of all the data by powerful computer software produces a three-dimensional image of the body. This image can be manipulated so that the body can be viewed from different angles.

The British scientist Sir Godfrey Hounsfield was awarded the Nobel Prize for developing this technique. In early scanners it took many hours for him to produce an image but the times fell dramatically as X-ray production techniques improved and faster, more powerful computers were developed. By the mid 1970s an image of the cross-section of a brain could be produced in about 5 minutes. CT (or CAT, for computerised axial tomography) scanning is now commonly used for whole body investigations in hospitals all over the world using machines like that shown in Figure 6.

Some claim the CT scanner is the greatest legacy of the Beatles as it was the huge profits from their worldwide success that enabled EMI, to whom the band was signed, to fund scientific research (*Independent* 4 December 2007 http://news.independent.co.uk/health/article3196259.ece).

How science works

Use of data books

Data books quote a quantity called the mass absorption coefficient μ_m, which has the unit $m^2\,kg$. This is related to μ by the equation $\mu_m = \dfrac{\mu}{\rho}$.

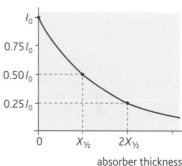

Figure 3 *Change of transmitted intensity with thickness*

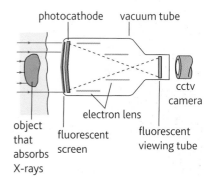

Figure 4 *Image intensifier*

Danger of X-rays

X-rays, like gamma radiations, are **ionising radiations** so high-energy X-rays can cause damage to cells. Because of this property they are used to kill malignant cells in the treatment of cancer. However, they damage healthy tissue too, so when conducting clinical investigations the benefits and risks have to be carefully assessed. The dose of radiation received by a patient when making an X-ray image is small and as any one individual has few X-rays taken during their lives there is little or no risk to the patient. X-rays are particularly dangerous to a foetus so X-rays are only used when absolutely necessary when a woman is pregnant.

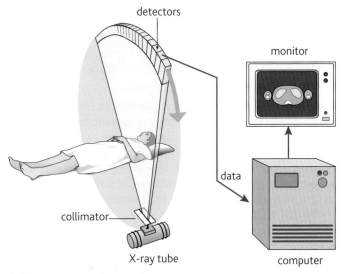

Figure 5 *CT scanner operation*

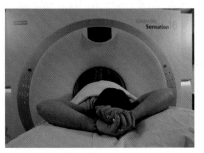

Figure 6 *CT scanner operation*

Radiologists have to take precautions to ensure that they are not affected by the radiation. A radiologist leaves the room when an X-ray is being taken and is protected by the screens that are designed to reduce radiation to negligible levels. Checks are made by using radiation badges to check the levels of radiation to which the operator has been exposed.

The received dose is reduced by up to 20 times using an intensifying screen on each side of the photographic plate but the spreading of the light radiated reduces the definition of the image. As in the image intensifier tube, the screens, made of a fluorescent material, absorb the energy from the X-ray photons and re-emit the energy as visible light.

Summary questions

1. State three ways in which X-ray images can be improved.

2. What is the advantage of the image produced by a CT scanner compared with an ordinary X-ray.

3. Describe the appearance of an X-ray image formed after passing through parts of a patient's body that contains regions where there is bone, air spaces and tissue.

4. A data book quotes the mass absorption coefficient as $0.014\,\text{m}^2\,\text{kg}^{-1}$ for 100 keV X-rays. Calculate the thickness of water that will halve the intensity of the X-ray beam. Density of water = $1000\,\text{kg}\,\text{m}^{-3}$.

5.2 Production and properties of X-rays

Learning objectives:

■ How is a continuous X-ray spectrum produced?

■ What are characteristic X-rays?

■ What are the principal components of an X-ray tube?

Specification reference: 3.4.3D

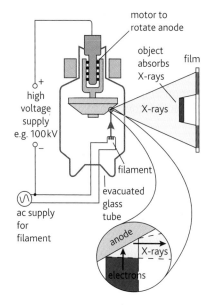

Figure 1 *Rotating anode X ray tube*

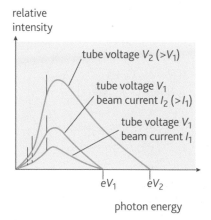

Figure 2 *X-ray spectrum*

What are X-rays?

X-rays are **electromagnetic radiation** with wavelengths from about 0.03 nm to 3 nm. Like all electromagnetic radiation (e-m) radiation they travel at $3 \times 10^8 \, \mathrm{m \, s^{-1}}$ in a vacuum and their frequency range can be found using $c = f\lambda$. Their short wavelengths means that the photon energies are very high, 6.6×10^{-15} J to 6.6×10^{-17} J $\left(\text{using } E = \dfrac{hc}{\lambda}\right)$.

Some X-rays have similar wavelengths to gamma radiation and where the wavelengths overlap they have indistinguishable properties. They are different only in the way that they are produced. Whereas gamma radiation comes from energy changes in the nucleus of an atom, X-rays are produced either by the rapid deceleration of electrons when they strike a metal target or by electron transitions between electron energy levels in atoms.

Producing an X-ray beam

Figure 1 shows the structure of a rotating anode X-ray tube. X-rays are emitted in all directions from the point at which the electrons strike the rotating anode. Those that pass through a window in the tube's lead shielding (not shown in Figure 1) are used to produce the X-ray image.

Electrons are produced at the heated filament by the process of **thermionic emission**. There is a high potential difference between the filament and the anode. This may be 30 kV to 100 kV in tubes used for diagnostic purposes and as high as 10 MV in tubes used for treatment. The potential difference produces an **electric field** in the region between the electrodes and the electrons are accelerated by this field.

A charge of 1 C accelerated through a potential difference of 1 V gains an energy of 1 J.

A charge Q accelerated through a pd V gains energy QV.

For an electron of charge e the energy gained is eV, where $e = -1.6 \times 10^{-19}$ C.

The energy of an electron accelerated through a pd of 1 V is therefore 1.6×10^{-19} J.

In nuclear and atomic physics the energy gained by an electron accelerated through 1 V is referred to as an **electron-volt** (eV). So 1 eV = 1.6×10^{-19} J. The electrons in a 100 kV X-ray tube have energies of 100 keV or 1.6×10^{-14} J.

When the electrons strike the atoms in the heavy metal target embedded in the anode they decelerate rapidly and the energy lost by each electron becomes a **photon** of X radiation. The radiation is call Bremsstrahlung (German for braking radiation). An electron may lose its energy in one collision or in many collisions in which different amounts of energy are lost by the electron. The resulting X-ray beam therefore has photons with a range of energies giving rise to a **continuous spectrum** of X-rays. The photon energies vary from 0 to the maximum, eV, which depends on the operating voltage of the tube, as shown in Figure 2. The three curves are for the same metal target.

The highest energy photons from an X-ray tube operating at 100 kV is 1.6×10^{-14} J corresponding to a wavelength of 1.2×10^{-11} m $\left(\text{given by } E = \dfrac{hc}{\lambda}\right)$.

Figure 2 shows the effect of increasing the beam current without changing the accelerating voltage and the effect of a higher accelerating pd on the X-ray spectrum.

Why does the anode rotate?

When the electron beam strikes the anode only about 1% of the energy becomes X radiation. The remainder becomes **internal energy** of the target, raising its temperature. The tube has to be designed to prevent the anode overheating and possibly melting.

A beam current of only 40 mA produces energy at a rate of 4 kW in a tube operating at 100 kV. About 3960 W of this would become thermal energy. In practice, a point source of X-rays is needed to give sharp images and enable fine detail in images, such as hairline fractures, to be seen. To produce the point source of X-rays the electrons must be focused on to a very small spot on the anode. Modern tubes use a rotating anode to overcome this problem because as the target rotates, the point at which the electrons strike the target changes continuously. Earlier tubes used fixed anodes which were cooled by passing oil through tubes embedded in the target. The oil removed the energy from the target and transferred it to the surroundings using fans and cooling fins in the same way that excess energy is removed from car engines.

■ Characteristic X-rays

Figure 2 shows 'spikes' on the continuous spectrum. The photon energies at which these sharp peaks occur depends on the target material. They would be different for a copper target and a tungsten target. The photons are produced in a similar way to that which produces photons of visible light that form a **line spectrum**.

The electrons striking the target ionise the atom. Some of the electrons that are removed from the target atom come from the inner electron **energy levels** (or shells) of an atom. When an electron falls from a higher level to fill the gap a high energy photon in the X-ray region is emitted. One such event is shown by the diagrams in Figure 3.

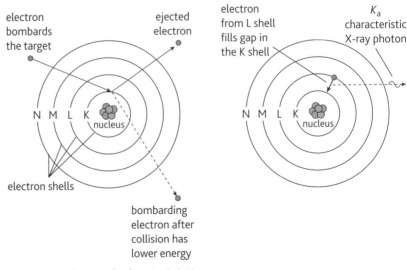

Figure 3 *Production of a characteristic X-ray*

Because the atoms have high proton numbers, the energy difference between energy levels of electrons close to the nucleus is large so that the photon energies are also large. The **characteristic X-ray** is named according to which level it falls to when it emits the X-ray photon. Those with the shortest wavelength fall into the K-level and give rise to K-lines in the spectrum. K_α and K_β lines are produced by electrons falling into the K-level from two different higher levels. The K-line in the tungsten spectrum corresponds to an energy of about 70 keV and a wavelength of 1.8×10^{-11} m.

Interaction of X-rays with matter

The intensity of an X-ray beam is reduced (**attenuated**) as it passes through matter, for a number of reasons:

- The energy may be **scattered** if the energy of the photon is too low to be absorbed. The photon retains all its energy in the process.

- The X-ray photons use all their energy to **ionise** an atom, knocking an electron out of one of the energy levels. This results in the emission of photons of different energies as electrons fill the gaps left by the electron that has been removed. These usually have lower energies and are easily absorbed.

- The X-ray photon may **excite** an electron inside an atom raising it into a higher energy level. As with ionisation this leads to the emission of photons of different energies.

- A high-energy photon can collide with an electron in a 'billiard ball' like collision giving the electron kinetic energy. This is called **Compton scattering**. The scattered photon has a lower energy due to the energy that it has given to the electron.

- At high enough energies the photon may collide with the nucleus of an atom leading to the production of an electron–positron pair. Using the mass–energy equivalence equation, $\Delta E = \Delta mc^2$, to produce two particles of mass 9.11×10^{-31} kg requires the X-ray photon to have an energy of $2 \times 9.11 \times 10^{-31} \times (3.0 \times 10^8)^2$. This is 1.64×10^{-13} J or 1.02 MeV. The electron and positron eventually lose their energy in the absorber, the positron finally annihilating with an electron to produce two 0.51 MeV photons.

Summary questions

1. State two ways in which X-rays are produced.
2. What do the wavelengths of characteristic X-rays depend on?
3. Calculate the minimum wavelength of the X-rays emitted when electrons of energy 50 keV strike a copper target.

5.3 Using ultrasound

Learning objectives:

- What is ultrasound?

- How is ultrasound used in clinical diagnosis?

- What are the advantages and disadvantages of using ultrasound compared with X-rays?

Specification reference: 3.4.3D

Ultrasound

Ultrasound consists of high-frequency **longitudinal waves** that are above the range of human hearing. A typical upper limit for the range of human hearing is 20 kHz so ultrasound frequencies are higher than this. In medicine ultrasound frequencies in the range 1 to 5 MHz are used in imaging for diagnostic purposes. Other uses include the cleaning of surgical instruments, cleaning teeth in dentistry and the generation of localised heating in the treatment of benign and malignant tumours. Ultrasound scanning equipment is very portable and this makes it very useful to veterinary surgeons for examining livestock on farms.

Production of ultrasound waves

Practical ultrasound transducers use a ceramic crystal called lead zirconate titanate. Like quartz this exhibits an effect called the piezoelectric effect. When the crystal is compressed a potential difference is produced across it and conversely when a potential difference is applied between opposite faces, it changes shape.

An alternating potential difference across the crystal forces it to oscillate so that its length increases and decreases at the same frequency as the applied voltage. The crystal size is chosen so that the **natural frequency** of oscillation of the crystal is the same as the frequency of the applied potential difference so that **resonance** occurs. This produces a large **amplitude** of vibration and waves are produced in the medium that is in contact with the crystal. The amplitude, and therefore the energy, of the ultrasound is controlled by the size of the voltage applied between the faces of the crystal.

In medical imaging the ultrasound is produced in pulses at a rate of 1000 pulses per second (1 kHz). If the crystal produces ultrasound of frequency 1.5 MHz there will be 1500 ultrasound waves generated in each pulse.

The wavelength of the waves depends on the speed of the waves in the medium. Table 1 shows some typical velocities. Notice the small variation in the speed between the different biological materials.

Table 1 *Variation of ultrasound velocity in different mediums*

medium	density ρ /kg m^{-3}	velocity v /m s^{-1}	acoustic impedance $Z(=\rho v)$ / kg m^{-2} s^{-1}
air	1.3	330	429
water	1000	1500	1.50×10^6
blood	1060	1570	1.66×10^6
fat	925	1450	1.34×10^6
muscle	1075	1590	1.71×10^6
bone	1400 to 1910	4080	5.71×10^6 to 7.78×10^6

Using $v = f\lambda$, it is easy to show that the wavelength for 1.5 MHz ultrasound varies from 0.22 mm in air to 0.96 mm in fat and 2.7 mm in bone.

■ Imaging using ultrasound

Ultrasound imaging depends on the ability of materials to transmit and **reflect** the waves.

The level of detail that can be observed depends on the wavelength of the waves and the diameter of the beam. These depend on the dimensions of the crystal that produces the ultrasound.

A shorter wavelength would provide better detail and this suggests that using a higher frequency would be best but higher frequencies are absorbed more readily so these are less useful for investigations deep inside the body. To obtain good images the energy needs to penetrate deep inside the body and to lose as little energy as possible due to **absorption** and **refraction**.

As much of the energy as possible from the transducer has to be transmitted into the body. At any interface energy is reflected and transmitted as shown in Figure 1. The energy reflected depends on the difference between a characteristic of the media called the acoustic impedance. Generally, the larger the difference between the acoustic impedances of the surfaces the more energy is reflected. The difference is very large for a skin interface. The use of a gel between the transducer and the skin ensures more efficient energy transfer into the body.

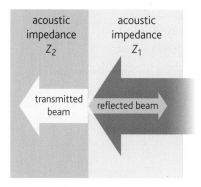

Figure 1 *Ultrasound energy at an interface*

Producing an image

The image is produced by waves reflected from parts of the body that are made of different tissue. The ultrasound image is built up by sending out pulses of ultrasound and changing the beam direction so that it scans the body. Some energy is reflected from any interface that the beam meets as it travels through the body. An image, such as that shown in Figure 2, consists of various shades of grey. The darker parts are where there is little or no reflection and the lightest parts where a higher proportion of the incident energy is reflected.

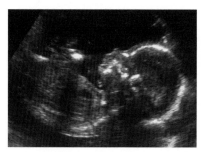

Figure 2 *Ultrasound image*

The depth of these surfaces is calculated from the time it takes the echo to return to the transducer after being emitted. The ultrasound pulses are sent out at 1 ms intervals and the depth of various reflecting surfaces are computed for that pulse direction. For computational purposes the speed is assumed to be constant at $1540 \, \text{m s}^{-1}$ so if a tissue interface is 15 cm below the skin the echo returns after $0.19 \, \text{ms} \left(\dfrac{2 \times 0.15}{1540} \, \text{s} \right)$.

Each pulse is sent out in a slightly different direction so that over a short period the ultrasound scans a cross-section through the body and this is displayed on a screen. As the transducer is moved over the skin images of different tissue can be investigated.

When ultrasound passes from one type of tissue into another $(1 \longrightarrow 2)$, the reflected intensity I_r depends on the acoustic impedances of the two tissue types and is given $I_r = I_i \left| \dfrac{Z_2 - Z_1}{Z_2 + Z_1} \right|^2$, where I_i is the incident intensity. As can be seen in Table 1, the difference between the acoustic impedances for some tissue types is quite small. So for some interfaces little energy is reflected and the image is not well defined.

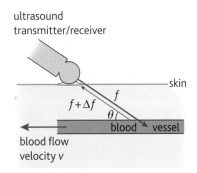

ultrasound
transmitter/receiver

skin

$f + \Delta f$

f

θ

blood   vessel

blood flow
velocity v

Figure 3 *Measuring blood flow*

■ Measuring blood flow

Using the **Doppler effect** the velocities of blood in a blood vessel can be found from the change in frequency of an ultrasound wave when it is reflected by a moving blood cell. The reflections from a scanning beam can be processed so that flows in different directions show up as different colours on the screen.

For blood flowing at an angle θ toward or away from the ultrasound transducer the velocity is given by: $\dfrac{2v\cos\theta}{c} \approx \dfrac{\Delta\lambda}{\lambda} \approx \dfrac{\Delta f}{f}$ where $v\cos\theta$ is the component of the blood's velocity toward the transducer and c is the speed of ultrasound in tissue (usually assumed to be $1540\,\mathrm{m\,s^{-1}}$). The factor of 2 occurs because the frequency shift is caused by the echo from a moving reflector and not simply from a moving source or moving receiver.

The volume flow rate of blood through an artery can be calculated from Av where A is the cross sectional area of the artery.

■ Comparison of ultrasound and X-rays imaging

X-rays	ultrasound
highly penetrating, produce images by transmission	images produced by reflection
ionising radiation so risk of damage to healthy cells	non-ionising so can be used for lengthy investigations
limitations on how often it can be used for examining a patient	can be used to provide real time images of organ functions
short wavelength produces more detail than ultrasound	can be readily moved to image different parts of the body
permanent images obtained using photographic plates	can monitor blood flow rates
careful precautions necessary to protect the operator	no danger to the operator
can be used for imaging in security screening.	readily absorbed so obtaining images may be difficult with obese patients

■ Application and How science works

Problem using ultrasound

The penetration of ultrasound falls exponentially with depth. For $1\,\mathrm{MHz}$ ultrasound the attenuation coefficient is about $0.6\,\mathrm{dB\,cm^{-1}}$. A fall of $3\,\mathrm{dB}$ is a halving of the intensity so the intensity halves when the wave travels through $5\,\mathrm{cm}$ of fat. Clearly if the ultrasound has to penetrate more fat then the reflected signal, which has to travel twice through the tissue, will be weaker and so more difficult or even impossible to interpret.

■ Summary questions

1 What is the purpose of the gel between the transducer and the skin of a patient?

2 Explain how a quartz crystal can be made to emit ultrasound waves.

3 What is the wavelength of $1.2\,\mathrm{MHz}$ ultrasound waves in water?

4 The $3.5\,\mathrm{MHz}$ ultrasound detected by a transducer/receiver after reflection from blood flowing in a blood vessel was found to increase in frequency by $0.85\,\mathrm{kHz}$. The incident and reflected wave travels at an angle of $30°$ to the blood vessel. Use the formula $\dfrac{2v\cos\theta}{1540} \approx \dfrac{\Delta f}{f}$ to calculate the velocity of the blood.

5.4 Magnetic resonance imaging

- What are the principles of magnetic resonance imaging?
- What are the advantages and disadvantages compared with other imaging techniques?

Specification reference: 3.4.3D

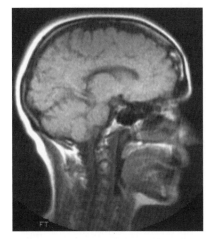

Figure 1 *An MRI scan of a head*

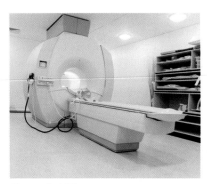

Figure 2 *MRI scanner*

Why is magnetic resonance imaging used?

As Figure 1 shows, the magnetic resonance imaging (MRI) method produces a detailed image of the inside of a body, better than any of the other available methods. The contrast between different tissue is much clearer than is possible using other techniques. This is because the image depends on the density of hydrogen nuclei in different parts of the body and not on **absorption** or the **reflective** properties of radiation or sound waves. It can therefore be used to look at regions that are obscured by bone, such as the bone marrow. Only radio waves are used so there is no **ionising** radiation to damage the patient. The technique can be used for extended investigations of sensitive parts of the body such as is required in the diagnosis of brain tumours. Furthermore, the doctor has fine control over which part of the body is investigated and of the orientation of the plane in which an image is produced, without the patient moving.

To make a scan, the patient is passed through a region where there is a strong uniform magnetic field produced by an electromagnet. The core of the magnet has a diameter of between 0.6 and 1 m. The larger diameter machines are much more expensive because it is more difficult to produce the required uniform magnetic field (Figure 2).

Basic principles

The idea of alignment and **precession** of protons in a magnetic field is similar to that in the proton magnetometer (see Topic 4.4). The actual operation is complex but is summarised in the following stages.

- Protons in the nuclei of hydrogen atoms are aligned in a strong magnetic field.
- A magnetic field of variable field strength (a **gradient field**) is produced across the body.
- Radio waves of suitable radio frequency (rf) are transmitted through the body. If there are protons that precess at this frequency (the Lamor frequency) they absorb energy from the radio waves, changing their spin state.
- The rf waves are switched off and the radiation from any excited protons is detected as the protons return to their original spin state.
- The data is stored and further data is collected for different radio frequencies and for different directions of the beam.
- The data is analysed by powerful computers to produce a final image.

More details

Spinning protons behave like tiny magnets due to their charge. The body contains many hydrogen nuclei contained in water and organic molecules. These are normally arranged at random but when a strong magnetic field (about 0.5–2 T) is applied a proportion of them line up in parallel to the field just like a compass needle does in field plotting experiments. Protons can spin in two directions so some line up one way and some the other but by chance there is always an excess in one direction and these are the ones that make MRI work.

When these protons lie in a magnetic field they precess around the field lines at the Lamor frequency. The Lamor frequency is $0.04258B$,

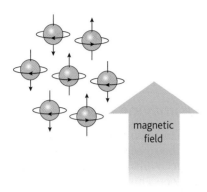

Figure 3 *Protons aligned in a magnetic field*

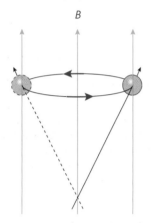

Figure 4 *Spinning proton precessing in a field*

where B is in nanotesla, so the precession frequency is proportional to the resultant field strength at the position of the hydrogen nucleus. Computer-controlled variable magnetic fields, called gradient fields, are applied to the body in three directions at right angles. These modify the magnetic field so that it is different in magnitude and direction in different places. The gradient fields define the 'slice' through the body that is imaged. The computer 'knows' the strength, and direction of the field at any point at any instant. Each point in space is therefore 'labelled' at any instant with a different magnetic field. As the Lamor frequency is proportional to B, protons in different places have different Lamor frequencies.

To obtain an image, a radio frequency at a particular frequency is directed though a slice of the body. Protons that have a Lamor frequency equal to the applied radio frequency undergo resonance and absorb energy from the rf beam. These protons move into a higher energy spin state. When the beam is switched off, any excited protons radiate energy and produce signals in the detector coil. The computer can identify the origin of the signal as it 'knows' the shape of the field and therefore 'knows' where the Lamor frequency is equal to the radio frequency. The amplitude of the signal depends on the density of protons that are radiating the energy and the type of tissue. This information is stored.

The gradient field changes direction so that protons in different 'slices' through the body resonate and the computer analyses the data to generate the final image.

Producing the magnetic field

The magnetic flux density inside a coil of radius r with N turns and carrying a current I is given by the formula $B = \dfrac{\mu_0 NI}{2r}$.

μ_0 is the **permeability of free space** and is equal to $4\pi \times 10^{-7}\,\mathrm{H\,m^{-1}}$. As B has to be about 1 T the product NI has to be about 480 000 A-turns. This means a 2000 turn coil would need to carry a current of 240 A.

Resistive coils producing the required fields would generate energies of more than 50 kW. They would therefore require cooling and be costly and wasteful of energy. The development of superconductors has overcome the problems and most MRI machines use superconducting magnets. Although they need to be cooled to very low temperatures in order for the conductors to become **superconducting**, the currents and therefore the fields can be larger without generating thermal energy. Larger fields lead to a greater proportion of the protons being aligned in the field and better quality images.

What are the disadvantages of MRI?

An MRI scanner is very expensive, about £750 000 at the time of writing. A hospital is only likely to have one machine and given that scans can take a long time (up to $1\frac{1}{2}$ h) patients may have to wait a long time for a scan.

When being scanned the patient has to remain still for a long period, and because the core of the magnet through which the patient passes is relatively small, some patients feel claustrophobic. Others can be unsettled by the noises made by the machine.

The limited size of the core means that the technique cannot be used for large patients.

Patients with pacemakers cannot be scanned and because the machine relies on the existence of a uniform magnetic field inside the core, metallic parts such as those used for knee and hip replacements also limit its use as these distort the field.

Summary questions

1. Explain why protons may line up in the direction of a magnetic field.

2. Explain why superconducting magnets are used in MRI scanners.

3. Use the expression for the Lamor frequency given in the above text to calculate the precession frequency when a proton is in a field of strength 0.25 T.

5.5 Endoscopy

Learning objectives:

- What is an endoscope?
- How does an endoscope produce images of the body?
- What are the advantages of endoscopy?

Specification reference: 3.4.3D

Figure 1 *An endoscope*

Advantages and use of endoscopy

Endoscopes are used for direct observations inside the body using light. Flexible versions are used to examine the gastrointestinal tract and the colon. Rigid versions are used in arthroscopy for examining and carrying out operations on damaged knee cartilage, for example.

The operation of an endoscope depends on the use of fibre optics to transmit light from an outside source into the patient and to carry the reflected light from the inside of the patient back to the outside to form an image. The image is then produced on a screen. The great advantage of the technique is that the image is high definition, true colour and is a real-time moving image which can be magnified. The image gives surgeons the ability to make a detailed study of the patient and allows them to carry out internal operations without the need for major surgery.

Figure 1 shows a typical flexible-tube endoscope and Figure 2 shows the components schematically.

All the components are contained in a tube which has a diameter of about 13 mm. The tube is designed to protect the optics and other parts, to prevent light entering the fibre from outside and to enable it to be easily inserted into the patient. The tube is inserted or swallowed by the patient who is usually sedated for comfort reasons.

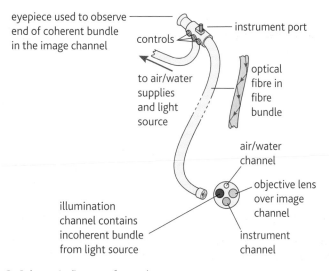

Figure 2 *Schematic diagram of an endoscope*

As well as the optical parts that are described in detail below, the tube contains a number of other channels. One enables air or water to be injected to keep the face of the endoscope clear. One carries controls for surgical tools fitted to the end of the endoscope, allowing surgeons to remove samples of tissue for testing or to carry out small repairs and another is a suction channel to remove material that is cut away.

The image formed by the endoscope can be viewed using a magnifying eyepiece or using a CCD camera (see Topic 5.6) attached to the end (Figure 3).

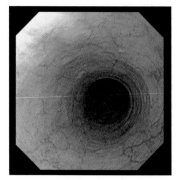

Figure 3 *Oesophagus image taken with an endoscope*

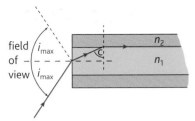

Figure 4 *Critical angle and field of view*

■ How science works

Other uses of endoscopes

Endoscopes can be used in any situation where direct observation is restricted and are commonly used to inspect inaccessible components that are part of complex machines, without having to undertake lengthy dismantling. They are commonly used to inspect jet engines.

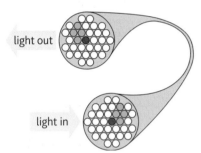

Figure 5 *A coherent bundle*

Summary questions

1 State the factors in an optical fibre that determines the critical angle for the total internal reflection of light.

2 State the purposes of four of the channels in an endoscope.

3 Describe the difference between a coherent and incoherent bundle of optical fibres.

4 Light enters an endoscope from a region that contains fluid of refractive index 1.3. The core has a refractive index of 1.50 and the cladding a refractive index of 1.42. Using the formula

$$n_0 \sin i = \sqrt{n_1 - n_2}$$

calculate the total angle subtended by the field of view.

■ Endoscope optics

Transmitting the light

The basic principles of the fibre optics in endoscopes is the same as that used in the communications fibre optics that were studied in AS. Bundles of cables transmit the light into and out of the body. The bundles consist of between 5000 and 40 000 single fibres that form a bundle with a diameter between 0.5 and 3 mm.

The core of each fibre, shown blue in Figure 4, has a circular cross-section of diameter about 30 μm of **refractive index** n_1. This is surrounded by a medium, shown green, that has a lower refractive index n_2. The **critical angle** at the interface is then given by $n_1 \sin c = n_2 \sin 90°$ so $\sin c = n_2/n_1$. To retain light in the core and allow the endoscope to be used when it has to bend around curves of a small radius the critical angle needs to be as small as possible. A fibre with a core of refractive index 1.55 with a cladding of refractive index 1.45 has a critical angle of 33°.

An important feature of the fibre is the **field of view**. This depends on the refractive index of the material from which the light enters the end of the fibre. It can be shown that for a fibre with a flat end, all light that is within a cone of half angle i_{max} given by $n_0 \sin i_{max} = \sqrt{n_1 - n_2}$ will be totally internally reflected and travel down the fibre.

If light enters the fibre from air, $n_0 = 1$, then the half-angle for the above fibre ($n_1 = 1.55$ and $n_2 = 1.45$) is 18° so all the light in a cone of angle 36° will be totally internally reflected and travel down the fibre.

Coherent and incoherent bundles

The purpose of one bundle of fibres is simply to provide illumination. The actual arrangement of the fibres in the bundle does not matter. This is called an **incoherent bundle**. However, for the bundle of fibres that is used to transmit the image it is important that each fibre retains the same spatial position relative to all the other fibres. This bundle of fibres is called a **coherent bundle** (Figure 5).

Provided this is done then light which arrives at, say, a fibre such as that shown black at the input end of the fibre emerges at the same position at the output end. Clearly, if the fibres were mixed up, the image would be useless.

Imaging problems

■ Light can take different paths down a fibre so that the received light may arrive at different times. This is called **multipath dispersion** and causes a blurred image. Use of thin fibres reduces the problem.

■ Fibres may become misaligned with use so that the bundle is no longer fully coherent.

■ Light may leak from one fibre to another. Coating each fibre with dark glass can reduce this effect.

■ Light intensity is reduced as it passes down the fibre. This may be as much as 50% for a 2 m length. Image intensity can be improved electronically.

5.6 Charge coupled device cameras

Learning objectives:

- What is a charge coupled device?

- How does a CCD produce an image?

- Why are CCDs useful in medical and astronomical applications?

- What is meant by the quantum efficiency of a CCD?

Specification reference: 3.4.3D

Figure 1 *Charge coupled device*

Uses of CCDs

Charge coupled devices were originally developed for use as computer memory devices. The potential of charge coupled devices (CCDs) for image production was first recognised for use in astronomy where light levels are often very low. Their advantages are that they are much more sensitive to light than photographic film and the image can be built up over a long time, which can be many hours or days. Because the image consists of electrical signals it can be enhanced electronically and can be used to produce moving images without any need for chemical processing.

The use of CCDs led to an escalation in the rate at which scientists gained an understanding of the Universe during the last decades of the twentieth century. Their use in medical applications too was soon recognised and CCDs were fitted to endoscopes in place of the magnifying lens. The digitised image could be converted to an image on a television screen making surgery easier. CCDs are now in common use in digital cameras.

Principles of CCD operation

Producing the image information

The CCD replaces the film of a conventional camera that uses photographic film. Figure 1 shows a CCD chip.

The image produced by the camera lens falls on the silicon integrated circuit (chip) which is an array of metal-oxide-semiconductor capacitors (MOS capacitors). These are called photosites, each photosite produces the image on one picture element (pixel) in the final image. In a 7.1 mega-pixel camera the image falls on an area that has 7.1×10^6 of these tiny semiconductor capacitors in an array 3072×2304. Figure 2 shows an array schematically.

Each photosite is a **photodiode** which has the ability to store the charge that is generated. When light falls on a photosite, photons liberate electrons from atoms. The photosites are insulated from one another and charge builds up on each site. Where the light is brighter more **photons** fall on the photosite during the exposure time liberating more electrons. The image is therefore represented by the variation in the electron distribution that builds up during the exposure time at the different photosites.

The detail (or resolution) obtained in the final image depends on the number of these photosites in the area where the image is formed. A clearer image is obtained if there are more photosites.

Quantum efficiency

Not all the photons that land on the sensitive area are used to generate the image. The percentage of the photons that are used is called the **quantum efficiency**. This must be constant for all the photosites so that the relative intensity of each part of the image is the same as in the scene being recorded. When an image is formed on the retina of an eye only about 1% of the photons are used. For a conventional photographic plate, this rises to 4%. For the photosites of a CCD the quantum efficiency is about 70%,

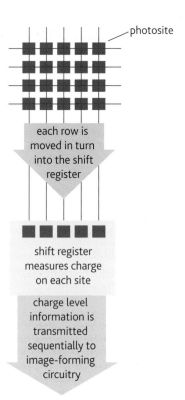

each row is moved in turn into the shift register

shift register measures charge on each site

charge level information is transmitted sequentially to image-forming circuitry

Figure 2 *Array of photocells linked by circuit connections*

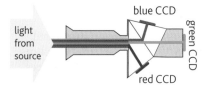

Figure 3 *Colour CCD camera*

which explains why it is so good at producing images of objects in low light conditions. In cameras it enables much shorter exposure times under normal lighting conditions so more images can be taken in a given time.

Transferring the image information to a screen

Following exposure the charge on each site has to be measured systematically and converted into the correct intensity light output of the corresponding pixel in a display screen. There are different ways of doing this, some faster than others. One way is illustrated in Figure 2.

- A clock pulse shifts the charge in each row downwards so that the charge on each photosite is transferred to the photosite below it.
- The bottom row is fed into a shift register where the charge is measured and another clock pulse empties the row by shifting each charge horizontally.
- The output of the shift register is a series of pulses that represent the charge level in each photosite.
- When it has been emptied, a clock pulse moves each row downwards again and the process is repeated until all the sites have been processed.
- The system can identify which charge level in the serial stream of information goes with which **pixel** on the screen and the image can be built up. For example, the first one in the complete stream goes with the bottom right-hand side of the image, and the last one with the top left-hand side.

Coloured images

Coloured images are produced by mixing the primary colours red, blue and green. The final colour depends on the relative intensity of each of the primary colours.

In cameras used for astronomy and in more expensive video cameras, three CCDs produce three different images that depend on the colour of the light. Mirrors and lenses direct the light to each CCD. Red, blue and green filters are placed in front of the CCDs so that each image depends on the intensity of these colours in the incident light. These three images are then processed to produce the final image.

Digital cameras use a simpler system that uses only one CCD array. In the simplest array a mask could be placed over the CCD array so that three adjacent pixels are covered by red, blue and green filters. So in a 6 mega-pixel array there would be 2 million photosites registering the intensities of each colour. The colours could then be processed to produce the final image.

In practice, the photosites are in pairs. One pair is red and green and the next pair blue and green and so on. The intensity of, for example, red and green in a particular region is measured directly. The intensity of blue is computed electronically from the averages of the signals from the adjacent green and blue covered photosites or by subtracting the red and green intensities from the intensity of white light.

AQA Examination-style questions

1 Metal oxides can be added to window glass to produce a material with a very high X-ray absorption coefficient of $3500\,m^{-1}$ at $30\,keV$.

  (a) Explain why glass of this specification is of use in the design of a hospital X-ray department. *(2 marks)*

  (b) Calculate the half-thickness of glass with an X-ray absorption coefficient of $3500\,m^{-1}$. *(2 marks)*

  (c) The X-ray absorption coefficient of dry air is $1.3\,m^{-1}$. Calculate the minimum distance in air required to replace a $2.0\,mm$ thickness of the glass. Assume that the beam is parallel. *(5 marks)*

  (d) Explain how the calculation would change if the beam were not a parallel one, but came from a point source of X-rays. *(2 marks)*

2 **Figure 1** shows an X-ray tube designed to produce X-rays for medical purposes.

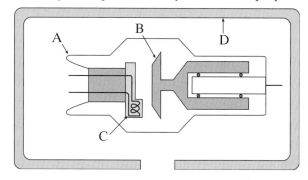

Figure 1

  (a) For each of the labelled parts A–D on the diagram, state what it is and explain its purpose. *(8 marks)*

  (b) State the direction in the diagram of

    (i) the electron beam *(1 mark)*

    (ii) the emerging X-ray beam *(1 mark)*

AQA, 1999

3 An X-ray beam energy of $30\,keV$ is commonly used in medical diagnosis. This is because at this energy, simple scattering is not an important attenuation mechanism and good contrast is produced in the image.

  (a) Outline the most important attenuation mechanism at this energy. *(6 marks)*

  (b) The attenuation coefficient μ at $30\,keV$ varies with atomic number Z as

$$\mu \propto Z^3$$

The table shows the typical values of Z for different tissues in the body

biological material	atomic number Z
bone	14
muscle	7
fat	6

Suggest, with a calculation, why a doctor finds $30\,keV$ X-rays useful in the diagnosis of a broken bone but will use a different technique for the examination of the boundary between fat and muscle. *(6 marks)*

4 (a) Suggest why a gel layer is used between an ultrasound transmitter/receiver and the skin of a patient undergoing an ultrasound scan. *(2 marks)*

(b) **Figure 2** shows the relative positions of the ultrasound transmitter and receiver, skin layer and an organ below the skin of a patient undergoing an ultrasound scan.

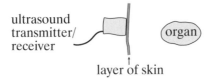

Figure 2

The graph in **Figure 3** shows the pulse strength of returned signals from the patient against time lapse between the pulse being transmitted and received.

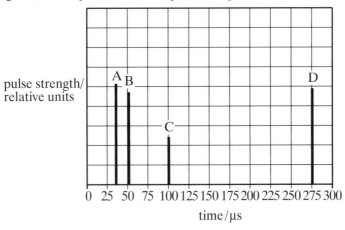

Figure 3

In terms of the diagram, suggest the origin of the reflected pulses A B C and D. *(4 marks)*

(c) The mean speed of the ultrasound used in the scan is $1600\,\text{m s}^{-1}$. Use the graph to estimate

   (i) the minimum distance between organ and skin

   (ii) the length of the organ *(5 marks)*

5 (a) By describing and explaining one situation in each case, explain how X-ray and ultrasound techniques are used in medical diagnosis. *(6 marks)*

(b) Many diagnostic techniques based on physics are now available to doctors, these include tracing of radioactivity in the body, scans, imaging techniques and so on. Apart from health hazards, explain why different diagnosis techniques are required in modern medicine. *(7 marks)*

6 Magnetic resonance imaging (MRI) techniques are now widely used in medicine.

(a) In the context of MRI, describe what is meant by proton alignment and precession and go on to explain how these effects are used to produce the image of the organs inside a patient. *(7 marks)*

(b) Explain the role in MRI scanners of:

   (i) the main magnets *(2 marks)*

   (ii) the gradient magnets *(3 marks)*

7 (a) An electron is accelerated through a potential difference of 78 kV. Calculate, in joules, the energy gained by this electron. *(2 marks)*

(b) Calculate the minimum possible wavelength of the X-rays that can be produced when a target is bombarded by electrons that have been accelerated through a potential difference of 78 kV. *(4 marks)*

(c) One of the K lines in the characteristic X-ray spectrum of copper has a wavelength of $1.54 \times 10^{-10}\,\text{m}$.

   (i) Explain what is meant by the characteristic X-ray spectrum of an element. *(3 marks)*

   (ii) Calculate the minimum accelerating voltage required to cause the K line to be emitted.

Unit 4 questions: Physics inside out

1   An engineer is designing a fairground ride in **Figure 1**. The ride consists of a capsule **A** which can carry two passengers. The capsule is attached to one end of a light inextensible rod **PA**. The total mass of the capsule plus passengers is 1500 kg; the mass of the rod is negligible compared to that of the capsule. The other end of the rod pivots about point **P**. The capsule is raised to point **A** and then released so that the centre of mass of the capsule moves freely along a circular arc of 7.5 m radius. The effect of air resistance can be neglected.

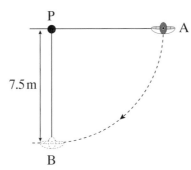

Figure 1

When the rod has moved through to the vertical position shown, the centre of mass of the capsule is at point **B**.

(a) For point **B**, calculate

    (i)   the kinetic energy of the capsule and passengers,   *(3 marks)*

    (ii) the velocity of the capsule and passengers,   *(3 marks)*

    (iii) the centripetal acceleration of the passengers,   *(2 marks)*

    (iv) the tension in the rod.   *(3 marks)*

(b) Comment, in the light of your answer to (a)(iv), on features of the design that an engineer would need to consider in attempting to make the design safe.   *(3 marks)*

2   (a) State, in words, Newton's law of gravitation.   *(2 marks)*

   (b) Some of the earliest attempts to determine the gravitational constant, G, were regarded as experiments to "weigh" the Earth. By considering the gravitational force acting on a mass at the surface of the Earth, regarded as a sphere of radius R, show that the mass of the Earth M is given by

$$M = \frac{gR^2}{G},$$

     where g is the value of the gravitational field strength at the Earth's surface.   *(2 marks)*

   (c) Use the data below to calculate the mass of the Moon and express its mass as a percentage of the mass of the Earth.

radius of the Moon	$= 1.74 \times 10^6$ m
gravitational field strength at Moon's surface	$= 1.62$ N kg^{-1}
mass of the Earth M	$= 6.00 \times 10^{24}$ kg
gravitational constant G	$= 6.67 \times 10^{-11}$ N m^2 kg^{-2}

     (3 marks)

3   The graph in **Figure 2** shows how the gravitational potential varies with distance in the region above the surface of the Earth. R is the radius of the Earth, which is 6400 km. At the surface of the Earth, the gravitational potential is -62.5 MJ kg^{-1}

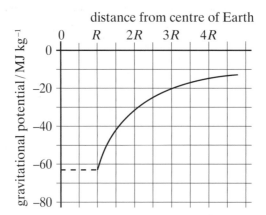

Figure 2

(a) A satellite is moved from the surface of the Earth to a circular orbit of radius $3R$.

Use the graph to calculate

   (i) The gravitational potential at a distance $3R$ from the centre of the Earth, *(1 mark)*

   (ii) The increase in the potential energy of a 1200 kg satellite when it is raised from the surface of the Earth into the circular orbit of radius $3R$. *(3 marks)*

(b) The satellite is now moved back towards the Earth's surface so that it is R above the surface $2R$ from the centre).

   (i) Write down an equation which relates gravitational field strength and gravitational potential. *(1 mark)*

   (ii) Using the graph in part (a), calculate the gravitational field strength at a distance $2R$ from the centre of the Earth. *(3 marks)*

   (iii) Show that your result for part (b)(ii) is consistent with the fact that the surface gravitational field strength is about $10\,N\,kg^{-1}$. *(3 marks)*

4 (a) A rocket uses a liquid propellant in order to move. The liquid is allowed to explode and the waste gases from this reaction leave the rocket at high speed.

Explain how the ejection of the waste gases makes the rocket move. *(6 marks)*

(b) The rocket ejects $1.5 \times 10^4\,kg$ of waste gas per second with a speed of $2.4\,km\,s^{-1}$ relative to the rocket. Calculate the average thrust on the rocket. *(2 marks)*

5 **Figure 3** shows a simple accelerometer designed to measure the centripetal acceleration of the car in a fairground gravitron ride that follows a horizontal circular path.

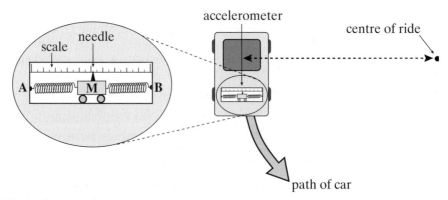

Figure 3

The two ends A and B are fixed to the car. The mass M is free to move between the two springs.

The needle attached to the mass moves along a scale to indicate the acceleration.

In one instant the car travels round a bend of radius 5.7 m in the direction shown in Figure 3. The speed of the car is $15\,m\,s^{-1}$.

(a) State and explain the direction in which the pointer moves from its equilibrium position. *(3 marks)*

(b) (i) Show that an acceleration of about $40 \, \text{m s}^{-2}$ would be recorded by the accelerometer.

   (ii) The mass M between the springs in the accelerometer is $0.35 \, \text{kg}$. A test shows that a force of $0.75 \, \text{N}$ moves the pointer $2.7 \, \text{mm}$. *(2 marks)*

   (iii) Calculate the displacement of the needle from the equilibrium position when the car is travelling with the acceleration in part (i). *(4 marks)*

(c) When the car leaves the bend the accelerometer eventually returns to its zero reading after a few cycles of damped simple harmonic motion.

   (i) Calculate the period of the oscillation of the mass M. *(2 marks)*

   (ii) Sketch a graph to show how the displacement of the mass varies with time from the instant the car leaves the bend. Include appropriate values on the axes of your graph. *(4 marks)*

6 (a) State what is meant by

   (i) a free vibration *(1 mark)*

   (ii) a forced vibration *(3 marks)*

(b) A roller coaster car and its suspension can be treated as a simple mass-spring system. When four people of total weight $3000 \, \text{N}$ get into a car of weight $6000 \, \text{N}$, the springs of the car are compressed by $150 \, \text{mm}$.

   (i) Calculate the spring constant of the system *(2 marks)*

   (ii) Show that, when the system, loaded with the four passengers, is displaced vertically and released, the time period of the oscillations is about $0.8 \, \text{s}$. *(2 marks)*

(c) The car and its passengers in part (b) travel at $25 \, \text{ms}^{-1}$ along the rollercoaster track one section of which has humps spaced $20 \, \text{m}$ apart.

   With an appropriate calculation, state and explain the effect the motion along the track will have on the oscillation of the car. *(5 marks)*

7 **Figure 4** shows a glass optical fibre used in an endoscope with a central core of refractive index 1.55 and a surrounding cladding of refractive index 1.40.

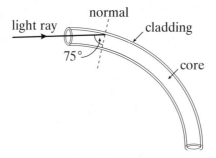

Figure 4

(a) Calculate the critical angle, C, for the boundary between these two types of glass. *(3 marks)*

(b) Copy Figure 4 and complete the path of the light ray shown in the diagram. *(2 marks)*

(c) State and explain whether the following changes in the optical fibre would increase or decrease the probability of light escaping from the fibre.

   (i) Increasing the refractive index of the cladding *(2 marks)*

   (ii) Bending the fibre into a tighter curve *(2 marks)*

8 A medical endoscope uses coherent and non-coherent optical fibre bundles.

(a) Describe the difference in structure between coherent and non-coherent bundles. *(1 mark)*

(b) State the use of

   (i) the coherent bundle *(1 mark)*

   (ii) the non-coherent bundle *(1 mark)*

(c) The fibres in the coherent bundle have very small diameters. State **two** advantages of using small diameter fibres. *(2 marks)*

9   The graph in **Figure 5** shows the X-ray spectrum, produced by an X-ray tube used to produce diagnostic images in medicine.

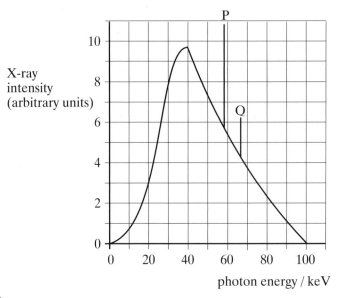

X-ray intensity (arbitrary units)

photon energy / keV

Figure 5

(a) Explain why the spectrum has

   (i)   a maximum photon energy and state the circumstances in which a photon of this energy is produced, *(4 marks)*

   (ii) two sharp peaks shown by the lines, P and Q. *(3 marks)*

(b) From the graph, estimate the accelerating voltage of the tube. *(1 mark)*

(c) Calculate the frequency of the radiation corresponding to line Q. *(2 marks)*

(d) Copy the X-ray spectrum and add an intensity curve which shows the output you would expect from the same tube when operated at 55 kV. *(2 marks)*

10   **Figure 6** shows an ultrasound transducer as used in medical diagnosis. The transducer produces short pulses of ultrasound.

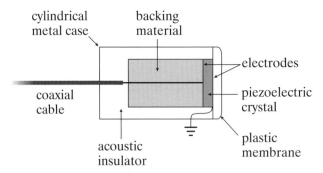

cylindrical metal case   backing material   electrodes

coaxial cable   piezoelectric crystal

acoustic insulator   plastic membrane

Figure 6

(a) Explain why it is necessary for the pulse to be short. *(2 marks)*

(b) State **one** advantage and **one** disadvantage of ultrasound compared with X-rays in medical imaging. *(2 marks)*

11   (a) State the factors that affect the gravitational field strength at the surface of a planet. *(1 mark)*

(b) **Figure 7** shows the variation, called an anomaly, of gravitational field strength at the Earth's surface in a region where there is a large spherical granite rock buried in the Earth's crust

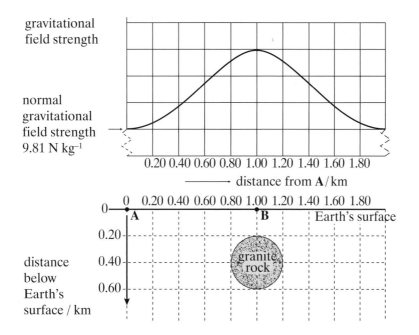

Figure 7

The density of the granite rock is $3700\,\text{kg m}^{-3}$ and the mean density of the surrounding material is $2200\,\text{kg m}^{-3}$. *(1 mark)*

   (i) Show that the difference between the mass of the granite rock and the mass of an equivalent volume of the surrounding material is $5.0 \times 10^{10}\,\text{kg}$. *(4 marks)*

   (ii) Calculate the difference between the gravitational field strength at **B** and that at point **A** on the Earth's surface that is a long way from the granite rock. *(4 marks)*

(c) Sketch a copy of the graph and add a further line to show how the variation in gravitational field strength would change if the granite rock were buried deeper in the Earth's crust. *(2 marks)*

12   A circular coil is part of a metal detector in **Figure 8**. The coil has 850 turns each with a diameter of $140\,\text{mm}$. In a series of tests of its correct operation, the coil is placed so that its plane is perpendicular to a horizontal magnetic field of uniform flux density $45\,\text{mT}$.

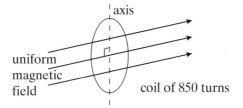

Figure 8

(a) Show that the magnetic flux passing through the coil when in this position is about $0.7\,\text{mWb}$. *(3 marks)*

(b) The coil is rotated through 90° about a vertical axis in a time of $120\,\text{ms}$.

    Calculate

   (i) the change of magnetic flux linkage produced by this rotation, *(4 marks)*

   (ii) the average emf induced in the coil when it is rotated. *(2 marks)*

(c) (i) Describe how a metal detector detects the presence of conductors underground. *(5 marks)*

   (ii) Explain how the properties of the underground conductor can enable the metal detector to indicate the type of metal that is buried. *(3 marks)*

Energy under the microscope

Chapters in this unit

6 Matter under the microscope

7 Breaking matter down

8 Nuclear radiation and its uses

9 Energy from the nucleus

In this unit the contexts bring together and develop further many aspects of physics that have been studied in earlier units so reinforcing understanding of the concepts that have been met earlier in the course.

Matter under the microscope

The motor car continues to be the internationally preferred mode of transport with an internal combustion engine providing the motive power. This section looks at the way the **gas laws** that relate pressure, volume and temperature of the gas, apply to the operation of the engine and how the laws can be explained using a **microscopic model.** The relationship between temperature and **internal energy** is also established using **the kinetic theory** of matter. The concept of **specific heat capacity** is studied in order to understand how the continuous flow cooling system for the engine works and this section goes on to look at how the **first** and **second laws of thermodynamics** apply to the engine and limit its efficiency.

Breaking matter down

The context in this section is the structure and operation of **particle accelerators**. Small accelerators are now commonplace in universities for research purposes and in many hospitals for producing the radioactive isotopes on site. The huge accelerators like those at CERN continue to explore the frontiers of scientific knowledge that relate to the nature of matter. This section looks at how the forces on charged particles, produced by electric and magnetic fields, accelerate and control the movement of protons, electrons and other charged particles. It goes on to consider how principles of mechanics are applied in the operation of these amazing devices and how relativistic mass increase at high speeds has influenced the design.

Energy from the nucleus

There are two contexts in this section. The first builds on earlier work on the nature and properties of radiation from **radioactive isotopes.** It leads on to a study of the properties of different types of radiation and how these properties and the **half-life** of an isotope affects the usefulness of the isotope for use in medical diagnostic or therapy. The second concentrates on the use of the energy liberated during **fission** and **fusion** reactions in the generation of electrical energy. The origin of the energy and how much is available from different fission and fusion reactions is described. It looks at the design features of a nuclear fission power station and issues related to the safe operation. The benefits that would result from the development of a practicable **fusion reactor** and the obstacles that have to be overcome to make this a possibility are also considered.

What you should already know:

From your studies at AS level on mechanics you should know that

- a scalar quantity has magnitude only whereas a vector quantity has magnitude and direction
- pressure = force ÷ area
- a force is necessary to produce an acceleration
- the magnitude of the force is proportional to the acceleration: $F = ma$
- change in momentum = impulse
- motion with constant acceleration is described by the equations of motion
- momentum is the product of mass and velocity
- kinetic energy $E_k = \frac{1}{2}mv^2$
- total energy is conserved
- work done = force × distance moved in the direction of the force
- power is the rate of doing work

From your studies at AS level on electricity you should know that

- resistance = potential difference ÷ current
- current = rate of flow of charge
- pd between two points is the work done per unit charge in moving a charged object from one point to the other; 1 volt = 1 joule per coulomb
- electrical power = potential difference × current
- for series components the total pd = sum of the pd across each component
- total current into a junction = total current out of the junction
- for parallel components, the pd across each component is the same
- area under a current–time graph gives the total charge that has flowed
- gradient of a charge–time graph at a given time gives the electric current at that time

From your studies of atoms and nuclei you should know that

- Rutherford scattering experiments suggest the existence of an atomic nucleus
- the nucleus consists of protons and neutrons
- the diameter of an atom is about 10^{-10} m and that of a nucleus about 10^{-15} m
- a nucleus may emit alpha, beta or gamma radiation
- when beta and alpha radiation is emitted the atom changes into a different element
- a neutrino is emitted in beta$^+$ decay and an antineutrino in beta$^-$ decay

6.1 Molecules in motion

Learning objectives:

- What is pressure?
- How does the kinetic theory of gases explain the existence of pressure?
- How does the gas volume or the number of molecules affect the pressure?

Specification reference: 3.5.1A

Figure 1 *Equal forces but different pressures*

Link

Diffusion and Brownian motion is covered in Topic 3.1 in the AS book.

Hint

There is no requirement for any derivation of the equations arising from the kinetic theory of gases in this course; however the assumptions that underpin the kinetic theory are required.

Pressure

Pressure is the force acting per unit area $\left(p = \dfrac{F}{A}\right)$. The concept of pressure adds to the understanding of matter since a particular force will have a significantly different effect on an object depending upon how large an area it acts on. Figure 1 shows a drawing pin being pushed downwards. The pressure on the pin point is high enough to penetrate the surface while the thumb, experiencing an equal and opposite force, is likely to be unharmed.

The SI unit of pressure is the pascal (Pa). 1 Pa is equivalent to $1\,\mathrm{N\,m^{-2}}$.

In a fluid pressure acts equally in all directions.

Kinetic theory of gases and pressure

Evidence for the belief in molecules was considered at AS to be based on the observations of Brownian motion and diffusion. The **kinetic theory of gases** is a statistical treatment of the movement of gas molecules in which macroscopic properties such as pressure can be interpreted by considering molecular movement.

Assumptions of the kinetic theory

- A gas consists of such a large number of molecules that statistical rules can be used with certainty.
- Each molecule has negligible volume when compared with the volume of the gas as a whole.
- Molecules are in constant rapid motion.
- At any instant as many molecules are moving in one direction as in any other.
- The molecules undergo perfectly elastic collisions with the walls of their containing vessel thus reversing momentum.
- There are no intermolecular forces between the molecules except during collisions (energy is entirely kinetic).
- The duration of a collision is negligible compared with the time between collisions.
- Each molecule produces a force on the wall of the container.
- The huge number of molecules (in even a small quantity of gas) will average out to produce a uniform pressure throughout the gas.
- Gravitational effects on the molecules are negligible.

It can be shown that the pressure within the gas is given by:

$$pV = \tfrac{1}{3}Nm\langle c^2 \rangle$$

Here p is the gas pressure, V is the gas volume, N is the number of molecules in the gas, m is the mass of each molecule and $\langle c^2 \rangle$ is the mean square velocity of the molecules.

■ Application and How science works

Note that the quantities on the left of the equation are macroscopic while those on the right are microscopic. The quantity $\langle c^2 \rangle$ is included because of the statistical nature of the derivation of this equation; it is the average of the square of the speeds of the molecules and has units of $m^2 s^{-2}$. The constant $\frac{1}{3}$ is included in the equation because on average one-third of the molecules are moving in each of the x, y and z directions of three-dimensional space.

Changing the pressure

If the number of molecules of a gas were to be increased in a container, collisions would also happen more frequently everywhere in the container and the pressure would increase as can be seen from the equation $pV = \frac{1}{3}Nm\langle c^2 \rangle$. Twice as many molecules would double the rate of collision with the walls and therefore double the pressure. Internal collisions have no effect on the rate of collision with the walls or pressure since all collisions are elastic and internal collisions would simply mean momentum is reversed. Each molecule therefore simply performs the role of the molecule with which it collided. It can also be seen from this equation that halving the volume of the gas (without changing the number of molecules) will also have the effect of doubling the pressure.

A slight re-arrangement of this equation gives $p = \frac{1}{3}\frac{Nm}{V}\langle c^2 \rangle$. The factor $\frac{Nm}{V}$ is the total mass of the gas divided by the volume of the gas; this is the gas density ρ. Unsurprisingly, the higher the gas density the higher the gas pressure. For a fixed mass of gas in a sealed container the pressure is proportional to the mean square speed of the molecules as shown in the graph of Figure 2.

Demonstration of gas pressure

Figure 3 shows a demonstration that can be used to model the effect of the number of molecules or the volume on gas pressure. Small steel balls, representing molecules, are caused to move randomly due to collisions with the motor-driven piston. The cylinder is sealed with a cardboard disc positioned above the steel balls. Adding further discs above the first one increases the pressure on the 'gas' and the volume occupied by the balls decreases, causing the balls to make more collisions with the bottom cardboard disc. The initial position of the single disc can be marked on the cylinder and discs added until they reduce the volume occupied by the balls to half its initial value. The motor is briefly stopped and twice the number of balls put into the cylinder. When the motor is started again (at the same setting as originally), the volume occupied returns to its original value. This demonstrates that a constant pressure can be achieved by doubling the gas volume and doubling the number of gas molecules.

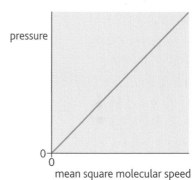

Figure 2 *Relationship between pressure and mean square molecular speed*

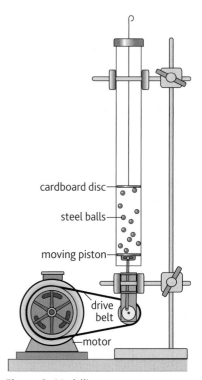

Figure 3 *Modelling gas pressure*

How science works

The bicycle pump

When a bicycle pump is used to inflate a tyre inner tube, the pump adds extra air molecules to the tube and this increases the pressure. The volume remains almost constant (it will expand a little against the surrounding air pressure). The rise in temperature of the pump itself is a good application of the first law of thermodynamics; this will be considered later in this chapter.

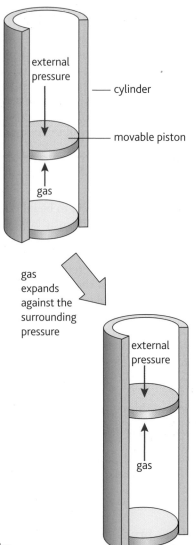

gas expands against the surrounding pressure

Figure 4 *Gas in cylinder*

Hint

It is useful to consider a gas contained in a cylinder enclosed by a movable piston. Figure 4 shows such a gas expanding against the pressure of the surroundings. This mirrors the cylinder of an internal combustion engine and also provides a useful representation of how the gas pressure or volume can easily be changed. This model will be used several times in this chapter.

Summary questions

1. Calculate the pressure, in pascal, at either end of a drawing pin when a force of 8.0 N is applied in each direction. Take the area of the ends of the drawing pin to be **a** 0.50 mm^2 and **b** 25 mm^2.

2. Explain how the ideal gas equation $pV = nRT$ is related to the equation derived using the kinetic theory of gases $pV = \frac{1}{3}Nm\langle c^2 \rangle$.

3. Calculate the mean square speed of the molecules in 1 mol of nitrogen occupying a volume of 1.5×10^{-3} m^3. The gas pressure is 2.5×10^5 Pa and the mass of each nitrogen molecule is 4.68×10^{-26} kg.

4. The density of nitrogen at a pressure 1.01×10^5 Pa is 1.25 kg m^{-3}. Calculate the mean square speed of the nitrogen molecules.

6.2 Energy in gases

Learning objectives:

- How can the behaviour of a gas be explained in terms of the molecular motion of the gas?

- How is the temperature linked to the kinetic energy of the molecules?

- What is absolute zero?

Specification reference: 3.5.1A

Kinetic theory and molecular energy

In Topic 6.1 the equation $pV = \frac{1}{3}Nm\langle c^2 \rangle$ was considered. This equation has a factor that may look familiar: $\frac{1}{3}m\langle c^2 \rangle$ is not far from the kinetic energy equation $\frac{1}{2}mv^2$ apart from the velocity being represented by c and the averaging of the squares of the velocities. Thus the original equation can be manipulated to give the total kinetic energy of all the molecules by multiplying each side of the equation by $\frac{3}{2}$:

$$\tfrac{3}{2}pV = \tfrac{1}{2}Nm\langle c^2 \rangle$$

In Topic 2.5 the ideal gas equation $pV = nRT$ was introduced for n mol of gas. In one mol of gas there is always the same number of molecules. This number is 6.02×10^{23} and is known as the **Avogadro constant**, N_A.

This means that N molecules must give $\dfrac{N}{N_A} = n$ mol.

Rewriting the ideal gas equation as $\qquad pV = \dfrac{N}{N_A}RT$

leads to $\qquad\qquad \dfrac{3}{2}pV = \dfrac{3}{2}\dfrac{N}{N_A}RT$

so that $\qquad\qquad \dfrac{3}{2}\dfrac{N}{N_A}RT = \dfrac{1}{2}Nm\langle c^2 \rangle$

Cancelling N and writing R/N_A as k gives us the equation

$$\tfrac{3}{2}kT = \tfrac{1}{2}m\langle c^2 \rangle$$

This equation gives the average kinetic energy per molecule of the gas. k is the **Boltzmann constant** and T is the absolute temperature (in K). So the mean kinetic energy of the gas molecules is directly proportional to the absolute temperature.

The Boltzmann constant has a value of $1.38 \times 10^{-23}\,\mathrm{J\,K^{-1}}$.

Temperature and internal energy

The kinetic theory has been linked with the temperature of a gas. Temperature, like pressure and volume, is a macroscopic property of a gas. In an ideal gas, the energy of the molecules is entirely kinetic (since there are no long-range intermolecular forces acting). This means that the **internal energy** of a gas (U) is made up of the total kinetic energy of the gas molecules. Thus

$$U = N \times \text{average kinetic energy per molecule.}$$

The average kinetic energy per molecule $= \frac{3}{2}kT$ so this leads to

$$U = \tfrac{3}{2}NkT$$

and shows that the internal energy of an ideal gas depends entirely on the absolute temperature of the gas.

When a gas is expanded or compressed isothermally (i.e., at constant temperature) there can be no change in the internal energy. This is an

Hint

If you are put off by algebra you can jump the next section and focus on the final equation; however it is vital that you do understand the differences between N, N_A and n and between R and k.

How science works

The kinetic theory of gases is one of the great success stories of physics. It links the microscopic with the macroscopic and produces equations for molecules which are in very close agreement with bulk properties of gases. Ideal gases are in good agreement with real gases at low pressure and fairly high temperatures. Outside these parameters factors must be introduced into theory to account for differences such as when gases liquefy. Such modifications are not considered on this course.

important aspect of the **first law of thermodynamics** which is considered in Topic 2.5 and will also be considered later in this chapter.

■ Application and How science works

The same temperature

For objects other than ideal monatomic (molecules made of only one atom) gases the internal energy is not simply the translational kinetic energy; it is the total kinetic and potential energy of the molecules of the object. For polyatomic gases there is rotational and vibrational kinetic energy in addition to translational kinetic energy. In liquids and solids, where there is very little translational kinetic energy, the internal energy is largely the potential energy associated with the intermolecular attractive forces. However, for all systems (whether solid. liquid or gas) at the same temperature, even though they may have different internal energies, the average kinetic energy of the molecules will be the same.

Absolute zero

It can be seen from the equation $U = \frac{3}{2}NkT$ that when T is zero U must also be zero. Thus at absolute zero the total kinetic energy per molecule would be zero and so they would be stationary. Quantum mechanics shows that this situation could never occur as there would always be fluctuations in kinetic energy. Thus it is better to say that a substance has a minimum kinetic energy per molecule at absolute zero. In polyatomic molecular gases, liquids and solids the idea of **entropy** must be used to define temperature. This is a statistical relationship of the number of ways in which molecules and their energies can be arranged within the system. Entropy will be considered in more detail later in the chapter.

■ Application and How science works

The quest for absolute zero

The COsmic Background Explorer (COBE) satellite has measured the temperature of the atoms, molecules and dust particles in space to be 2.73 K (the vacuum of space could not by definition have a temperature). This temperature is believed to be due to the cosmic background radiation: a remnant of the Big Bang. In the laboratory the lowest temperature achieved was in 2003 when Wolfgang Ketterle and colleagues at the Massachusetts Institute of Technology succeeded in cooling sodium atoms down to below 500 pK.

Figure 1 *Wolfgang Ketterle*

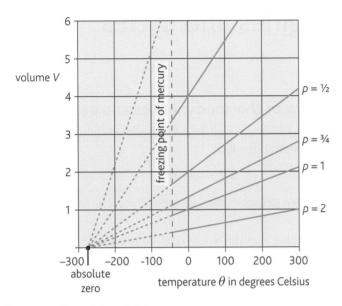

Figure 2 *V–θ graph for an ideal gas*

Summary questions

1
  a Calculate the mean translational kinetic energy per molecule of nitrogen gas at a temperature of 300 K. The Boltzmann constant has a value of 1.38×10^{-23} J K^{-1}.

  b Calculate the mean square speed of each nitrogen molecule. The mass of each nitrogen molecule is 4.68×10^{-26} kg.

  c Calculate the square root of the mean square speed (called the root mean square speed) and comment on the relevance to the atmosphere that this is very much less than the escape velocity on the Earth.

2 Calculate the mean square speed per molecule of hydrogen gas at 300 K. The mass of a mole of hydrogen = 0.002 kg; The Avogadro constant = 6.02×10^{23} mol^{-1}.

3 Sketch a $p–T$ graph for an ideal gas from absolute zero to 350 K.

Learning objectives:

- How is the first law of thermodynamics applied to a heat engine?

- What is the Carnot cycle?

- How does thermodynamics explain the workings of an internal combustion engine?

Specification reference: 3.5.1B

The first law of thermodynamics and gases

The quantities in the first law of thermodynamics are defined in Topic 2.5. This law is written in the form:

$$\Delta U = Q + W$$

Different changes in a gas are defined by controlling the three quantities in turn.

It is useful to remember that the work done (W) is given by the product $p\Delta V$ and that this quantity can be obtained by finding the area under a p–V curve.

When no heat enters or leaves a thermodynamic system the quantity Q is zero. Such a change is said to be **adiabatic**. There are two possibilities with an adiabatic change, either $\Delta U = W$ **or** $-\Delta U = -W$. Thermodynamically these two equations are not the same. The first equation represents an **increase** in internal energy (and temperature) of the system when **work is done on** the system. The second equation represents a **decrease** in the internal energy (and temperature) of the system when **work is done by** the system (and on the surroundings).

Isothermal changes occur when there is no change in the internal energy or temperature of a system and the quantity ΔU is zero. This means that $Q = -W$ or $-Q = W$. Again these are different thermodynamically. The first version means that heat is transferred to the system causing it to do work on the surroundings. The second version means that work is done on the system and that heat is transferred from the system to the surroundings.

When $W = 0$; $\Delta U = Q$ or $-\Delta U = -Q$. The first of these options means that the increase in internal energy occurs because heat is supplied to the system and the second means the internal energy falls because heat is taken from the system. For no work being done on or by a gas the volume cannot change.

Heat engines

A **heat engine** uses heat to do work and then rejects to the surroundings any heat which cannot be used to do work. The ratio of the useful heat (= the work done by the engine) to the total heat input gives a measure of the efficiency of the engine. Thus the thermal efficiency (η) of a heat engine is given by the relationship:

$$\eta = \frac{W}{Q_i}$$

where W is the useful work done by the engine and Q_i is the energy input to the engine. Assuming that there is no extra wasted work due to frictional forces, then when quantity of heat Q_0 is rejected to the surroundings this equation can be rewritten as:

$$\eta = \frac{Q_i - Q_0}{Q_i}$$

The Carnot cycle

A graph of pressure against volume for a gas can be very informative. This is because the area enclosed by a cycle of changes will give the total amount of work done by a gas (as a result of potential energy being changed by altering the gas's bonding).

Heat engines such as the internal combustion engine operate in a cycle, adding heat in one part of the cycle and using some of the heat to do useful work in another part of the cycle. The thermal efficiency is limited by the second law of thermodynamics which will be considered later in this chapter. The Carnot cycle represents the most thermally efficient sequence of changes that can convert a certain amount of heat into useful work.

Carnot chose an ideal gas to be the working substance in his ideal heat engine. The engine would operate between a hot reservoir at temperature T_H and a cold reservoir at temperature T_C. The cycle is shown in Figure 1. The paths are **reversible** which means that a small amount of heat supplied or extracted or work done on or by the system at any time will cause a change to reverse. The **Carnot cycle** is composed of two **isothermal** paths in which the temperature is constant and two **adiabatic** paths when no heat enters or leaves the system.

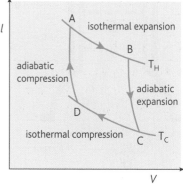

Figure 1 *The Carnot cycle*

If we think of a gas being trapped within a cylinder by a piston the piston will move back and forth as the gas goes around the cycle

From A to B: the gas expands and does work on its surroundings while the engine absorbs heat from a source (the hot reservoir). Along this isothermal, the internal energy and temperature of the gas does not change.

$$-W = Q$$

From B to C: the heat source is removed but the internal energy of the gas falls to allow the gas to continue expanding while cooling (lowering in temperature). This stage is called an adiabatic expansion since no heat enters or leaves the gas.

$$-\Delta U = -W$$

From C to D: the gas is recompressed as heat is extracted and the gas volume decreases. The pressure increases. The gas loses heat to the surroundings. This is an isothermal compression.

$$W = -Q$$

From D to A: the internal energy of the gas increases as the gas continues to be compressed. Its temperature rises to its original state whilst its volume decreases because work is done on the gas. This is an adiabatic compression.

$$\Delta U = W$$

It can be shown for an ideal gas undergoing a Carnot cycle that the thermal efficiency is given by

$$\eta = \frac{T_H - T_C}{T_H}$$

Here T_H is the absolute temperature of the hot reservoir and T_C is the temperature of the cold reservoir.

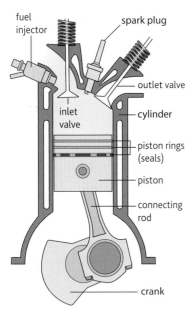

Figure 2 *Main features of an internal combustion engine*

■ The internal combustion engine

When a small quantity of high-energy fuel (such as petrol) is ignited in a small enclosed space, a large amount of energy is released as the fuel vaporises and expands. Petrol engines usually use what is called a **four-stroke combustion cycle** or 'Otto cycle' which converts the chemical potential energy in the fuel into kinetic energy. The four strokes of the Otto cycle are:

■ Induction stroke

■ Compression stroke

■ Combustion (power)stroke

■ Exhaust stroke

Figure 2 shows the main parts of one cylinder in a four stroke engine. In actual engines there are usually between four and twelve cylinders which help to ensure the smooth rotation of the engine. The four strokes of the internal combustion engine are always in the order: induction, compression, combustion and exhaust. This means that the piston moves down in the cylinder twice and up twice in any one cycle. These four strokes produce two revolutions of the crankshaft. The process continuously repeats itself during the operation of the engine.

On the induction stroke, the inlet valve opens. The piston moves downwards and the mixture of air and vaporised fuel is injected or pushed by atmospheric pressure into the cylinder through the inlet valve port.

After the piston reaches the bottom of the cylinder it starts to move upwards. As this happens, the inlet valve closes. The exhaust valve is also closed ensuring that the cylinder is sealed. As the piston moves upwards, the air/fuel mixture is compressed thereby increasing the pressure in the cylinder. The compression process causes the temperature of the air/fuel mixture to increase.

As the piston reaches the top of the cylinder an electric discharge is produced by the spark plug. The spark ignites the air/fuel mixture. The mixture combusts rapidly and cylinder pressure increases to a high level.

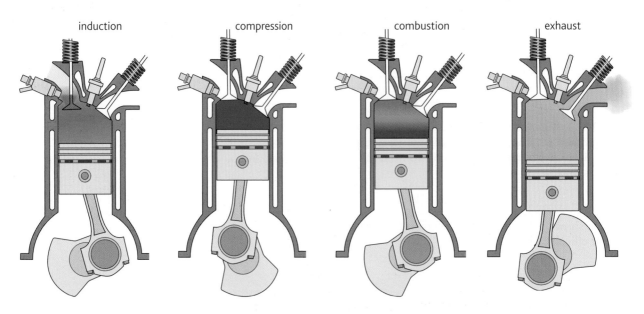

Figure 3 *Induction stroke*   **Figure 4** *Compression stroke*   **Figure 5** *Combustion stroke*   **Figure 6** *Exhaust stroke*

This high pressure now forces the piston back down in the cylinder. The force on the piston is now transmitted down through the connecting rod to the crankshaft. The crankshaft is rotated due to this force.

As the piston reaches the bottom of the cylinder for the second time the exhaust valve opens. As the piston moves up on the exhaust stroke it forces the molecules of the combusted gases through the exhaust port. As the piston reaches the top of the cylinder for the second time the exhaust valve closes and the inlet valve opens.

The p–V cycle for an internal combustion engine

The gas or 'system' in the case of an internal combustion engine is the air/fuel mixture in the internal combustion engine. The Otto cycle is shown in Figure 7.

Between points 1 and 2 the piston is pulled down the cylinder (by the crankshaft) with the inlet valve open. The pressure remains constant and the gas volume increases as the fuel/air mixture is drawn into the cylinder through the intake valve. At point 2 the inlet valve closes and the compression stroke starts. Between points 2 and 3 the piston moves upwards as an approximately adiabatic compression causes work to be done on the gas by the piston. At point 3 the spark is produced which starts the combustion of the fuel/air mixture. This combustion occurs very quickly and the volume remains constant. During this phase heat is released from the chemicals and this raises the internal energy (and temperature) of the gas and its pressure. Between points 4 and 5, the piston is driven downwards increasing the volume and decreasing the pressure as work is done by the gas on the piston; this is an adiabatic expansion of the gas. At point 5 the exhaust valve opens and the still hot gas transfers heat to the surroundings through the engine's cooling system. The volume remains constant and the pressure adjusts back to atmospheric conditions. Between points 5 and 6 the piston moves back up the cylinder decreasing the volume and expelling the combusted gases into the atmosphere at a constant pressure.

During the cycle, work has been done on the gas during the adiabatic compression and work is done by the gas during the adiabatic expansion. This means that the area enclosed by the curve is the net work done by the gas. The power of the engine is found by multiplying this work by the number of cylinders and the number of complete cycles per second.

How science works

In a diesel engine, fuel (with no air) is injected into the cylinder during the induction stroke. The fuel combusts because the diesel vapour reaches a high temperature as it is compressed.

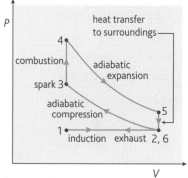

Figure 7 *The Otto cycle*

How science works

Real engines

The p–V diagram considered here is an ideal Otto cycle in which the compression and expansion are assumed to be adiabatic. In a real engine heat losses do occur and work will be done by friction causing a rise in the internal energy of the engine. This means that the enclosed area for a real engine will be less than the ideal one shown in Figure 7.

Summary questions

1. a Explain the difference between heat and internal energy.

   b What is meant by i an isothermal change ii an adiabatic change.

2. a Draw a p–V diagram for a Carnot cycle; label the isothermal compression, isothermal expansion, adiabatic compression and adiabatic expansion.

   b Calculate the thermal efficiency of a Carnot engine working between 20 °C and 120 °C.

3. a Explain the meaning of the term *four stroke petrol engine*.

   b A four stroke petrol engine has four cylinders and produces a power of 90 kW as its crankshaft makes 5800 revolutions per minute. Calculate the area that would be enclosed by cycle on the p–V diagram for this engine.

6.4 Cooling the engine

Learning objectives:

■ What factors determine the rise in temperature when an object is heated?

■ What is specific heat capacity?

■ How can liquids be used to cool hot objects?

Specification reference: 3.5.1B

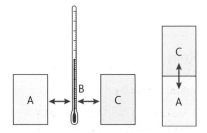

Figure 1 *Zeroth law of thermodynamics*

Heating objects

Heat may be defined as energy in transit from an object at a high temperature to one at a lower temperature. This can happen by conduction, convection, thermal radiation or a combination of these three processes. The idea that transferring heat from one object to another increases the internal energy of the receiving object has been considered earlier in this chapter. An increase in internal energy is detected by an increase in temperature of the object.

The zeroth law of thermodynamics

This law states that when two systems are separately in **thermal equilibrium** with a third system, they must be in thermal equilibrium with each other. In Figure 1 objects **A** and **C** are in thermal equilibrium with object **B**; this means that, although there is no direct thermal contact between **A** and **C**, they are still in thermal equilibrium with each other. Consequently the objects must be at the same temperature and object **B** can be thought of as behaving like a thermometer. Thermal equilibrium means that when there is exchange of heat between two objects the quantity of heat moving in one direction is identical to that moving in the opposite direction in the same time. Thermometers therefore are devices that are used to assess the internal energy of an object.

Raising the temperature

When heat is supplied to an object its temperature will rise or it will change state (from a solid into a liquid or from a liquid into a vapour). Assuming that the object is not near its melting or boiling point, the temperature rise of the object will depend upon:

■ the mass of the object,
■ the heat supplied to it (and/or the work done on it),
■ the material from which the object is made.

Car engine blocks made out of steel or aluminium will heat up (undergo a rise in internal energy) by different amounts depending upon the mass of the block and the energy supplied to them.

The **specific heat capacity** (c) of a material is defined as the energy needed to raise the temperature of 1 kg of the material by 1 K without any change of state. This can be written in equation form:

$$c = \frac{Q}{m\Delta T}$$

where Q is the total energy supplied to a sample of the material, m its mass and ΔT its temperature increase.

The unit of c is $J\,kg^{-1}\,K^{-1}$.

A material with a high specific heat capacity will require a lot of energy to raise its temperature but it will tend to retain that energy for a long time. Water has the specific heat capacity of $4200\,J\,kg^{-1}\,K^{-1}$ whereas steel has a specific heat capacity of $420\,J\,kg^{-1}\,K^{-1}$ and aluminium a value of $900\,J\,kg^{-1}\,K^{-1}$. Thus the temperature of water rises by only one tenth of that of steel given equal masses and equal quantities of heat supplied.

Equivalence of work done and heat supplied

Figure 2 shows a standard piece of equipment used to demonstrate the equivalence of work and heat. The handle is steadily turned at a rate which keeps the newtonmeter reading zero (this means that the hanging tensioning weight is balanced by the frictional force between the belt and the rotating drum). The number of turns of the handle and the change in temperature of the metal drum are recorded. Thus

the work done on the drum = (force) × (distance)

$$= (mg) \times (n2\pi r) = cM\Delta T$$

m = mass of tensioning weight, n = number of turns of handle, r = external radius of drum, M = mass of drum, c = the specific heat capacity of drum material (usually brass) and ΔT is the temperature increase of drum.

From these values the specific heat capacity of the material of the drum can be calculated.

It can also be calculated by removing it from the apparatus and by immersing it in hot water. The drum will eventually reach thermal equilibrium with the water.

The fall in temperature of the hot water should equal the rise in temperature of the drum giving.

$$m_w c_w \Delta T_w = Mc\Delta T$$

The subscripts refer to the water and the non-subscripted symbols refer to the drum. The value obtained for c by either method should be the same (if heat lost to the surrounding is minimised); thus showing the equivalence of heating and working as a mechanism for raising the temperature of an object.

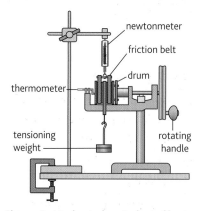

Figure 2 *Mechanical equivalent of heat apparatus*

▇ Internal energy in the internal combustion engine

The drawback as far as the efficiency of an internal combustion engine is concerned is that waste heat and the exhaust gas must somehow then be removed from the cylinder in preparation for the start of every consecutive cycle. The efficiency of these engines is very low (with typically only 20% of chemical energy in the fuel being converted into useful mechanical work). Around a third of the chemical energy is ejected as the internal energy of the exhaust gases with another third being transferred to the surroundings by the cooling fluid. Between 5% and 10% of energy is wasted as work being done by frictional forces. Without a cooling system the engine would become very hot and that would decrease the efficiency of the engine even more. Engines operate at their most efficient when the coolant is about 95°C. At this temperature the cylinders are hot enough to completely vaporise the fuel which gives more complete combustion and reduced emission of pollutant. This also means that the oil used to lubricate the engine has a reduced viscosity so that the friction is less on the engine's moving parts and that there is less wear.

Cooling systems

There are two systems used for cooling vehicle engines.

Some vehicles (especially motorcycles) are air-cooled. In these vehicles the engine block is covered by aluminium fins. These conduct the heat from

▇ How science works

Demonstration

The ability to raise the temperature of an object by doing work on it can easily be demonstrated by using a tube containing a quantity of lead shot as shown in Figure 3. The temperature of the shot should be measured and then the tube inverted 50 times and the temperature re-measured; there should be a measurable increase as a result of the mechanical work being done.

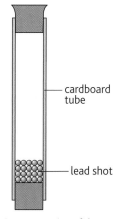

Figure 3 *Demonstration of the equivalence of work and heat*

the cylinder to the air which can also be forced over the fins by a fan.

The most common system in a car engine is the liquid cooling system (see Figure 4) in which a pump causes liquid coolant (a mixture of antifreeze and water) to circulate around the engine. As this liquid passes through the hot engine it absorbs heat, cooling the engine. After the liquid has passed through the engine it passes through the radiator (a heat exchanger). Air circulates around the radiator and picks up heat increasing its internal energy in the process. When the engine becomes particularly hot a fan cuts in to increase the rate of air flow. A thermostat is positioned between the engine and the radiator to make sure that temperature of the coolant remains above a certain preset temperature. If the coolant temperature falls below this temperature, the thermostat closes and blocks the coolant flow to the radiator, forcing the fluid instead through a bypass directly back to the engine. Once the temperature has reached the optimum value the thermostat opens and allows the coolant to pass through the radiator.

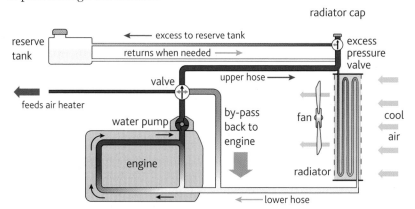

Figure 4 *Vehicle cooling system*

In order to prevent the coolant from boiling the cooling system is pressurised. This elevates the coolant's boiling point to up to 135°C (which means that it does not evaporate at temperatures below this). If the pressure becomes too great, the radiator cap releases pressurised coolant into an auxiliary system where it is stored in a reserve tank before automatically returning to the cooling system as the engine cools down.

Continuous flow systems

As a coolant flows around a system it absorbs heat from any hot objects that it makes thermal contact with. However the coolant will pass heat to the surroundings provided the surroundings are at a lower temperature. This is fine for a vehicle heating system because that is exactly what is required; the coolant can be considered to be a mechanism for taking heat from the engine and depositing it in the air more efficiently than by simply letting air circulate around the engine. In methods for measuring the specific heat capacity there is normally a systematic error in that heat is lost from the hot objects to the surroundings. By using a continuous flow method such that invented in 1902 by Callender and Barnes (see Figure 5) the heat lost can be eliminated (**this method will not be examined but is a valuable learning exercise**). Liquid passes through the apparatus at a constant rate past a thermometer registering temperature T_1. The heating coil passes heat to the liquid which then passes a second thermometer registering the temperature T_2 (which will be higher than T_1). When the thermometers give constant readings their values are noted and the mass (m) of liquid is collected in a measured time (t) to obtain the rate of flow. The heat generated in the coil ($= V_1I_1t_1$) will be equal to the heat transferred to the liquid + that lost to the surroundings by the apparatus Q

$$V_1 I_1 t_1 = m_1 c(T_2 - T_1) + Q$$

By altering the electrical power supplied and the rate of flow of liquid to keep the temperatures the same the experiment can be repeated and the heat loss will be constant. The new values will give:

$$V_2 I_2 t_{12} = m_2 c(T_2 - T_1) + Q$$

These equations can be re-arranged to make Q the subject of the equation and then they can be equated; from this the specific heat capacity of the liquid can be calculated.

Back to thermal efficiency

In Topic 6.3 the thermal efficiency of a Carnot engine was given by the equation:

$$\eta = \frac{T_H - T_C}{T_H}$$

This is the most efficient (and theoretical) type of engine. The only way to achieve 100% efficiency is for the cold reservoir to be at 0 K. Assuming the engine temperature to be around 400 K and that of the surrounding air to be 300 K the efficiency of the engine will be around 25%. The internal combustion engine is less efficient than the Carnot engine.

Application and How science works

Engine pollution and carbon offsetting

The flexibility and convenience of car travel makes it the most popular form of transport. However, increased car travel brings with it problems of congestion and pollution. All types of car emit pollutants into the atmosphere resulting in a detrimental effect on health and the environment. The UK Government website states: 'Climate change is a serious problem that affects us all. There is strong evidence that human emissions of greenhouse gases are changing the world's climate. The main greenhouse gas is carbon dioxide (CO_2), produced when we burn fossil fuels like coal, oil and gas for energy. Over 40% of CO_2 emissions in the UK come directly from what we do as individuals; for example, heating and using electricity in our homes – and driving vehicles.' As part of an individual's social conscience the UK population is encouraged to walk, cycle and use public transport. Individuals can become carbon neutral. Carbon offsetting is the act of an individual compensating their personal carbon footprint by 'offsetting' greenhouse gas emissions. Tree planting was the first common example of carbon offsetting. Recently, the use of renewable energy sources and methane capture offsets has become increasingly popular.

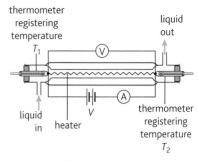

Figure 5 *Callender and Barnes' apparatus*

Summary questions

1 a Explain the meaning of thermal equilibrium.

b In order to measure the temperature of an object, why must a thermometer be in thermal equilibrium with the object?

2 Calculate the heat generated in a mass of 7.0 kg coolant in a cooling system. The specific heat capacity of the coolant is $3500\,J\,kg^{-1}\,K^{-1}$ and the coolant undergoes a temperature rise of 75 K.

3 A frictional force of 4.5 N is applied around the circumference of a copper cylinder of radius 5.5 cm. The cylinder is rotated 100 times. Calculate the increase in temperature of the cylinder if its mass is 120 g and the specific heat capacity of copper is $385\,J\,kg^{-1}\,K^{-1}$.

4 Explain why a liquid cooling system for a vehicle is similar to the Callender and Barnes' apparatus of Figure 5.

6.5 The arrow of time

Learning objectives:

- What is entropy?

- How does entropy change define events which happen spontaneously?

- How does the change in entropy explain the maximum efficiency achievable in an engine?

Specification reference: 3.5.1B and C

Figure 1 *House of cards*

The second law of thermodynamics

Although it is not necessary for you to learn it, this law is fundamental to an understanding of the concept of **entropy**. The second law of thermodynamics can be stated in a number of ways but one of them is that 'the entropy of a system can never decrease, the best it can do is stay constant but it usually increases'. Entropy (S) is a measure of the disorder of a system, as an alternative it can be said to be a measure of the number of ways in which a certain arrangement can exist, this is known as the multiplicity of the system. For example, ice has low entropy because the molecules are ordered and there only are few ways of arranging them. Liquid water has more entropy because groups of molecules are now free to move around so more arrangements possible. Steam has still more entropy because all the intermolecular bonds have been broken and the vapour can spread out in all directions and there are a very large number of distinct arrangements now possible.

The arrow of time

We have an intuitive understanding of entropy based on our common sense. If a house of cards is built as shown in Figure 1, we expect the order to very quickly turn into chaos as the house collapses. When a ball is taken to the top of a hill it easily rolls into the valley below. A small quantity of dye will soon spread throughout the water that it is dropped into. When a hot pan is placed in a sink of cold water, the pan cools down and the water warms up. Each of these instances demonstrates an increase in the entropy of the system as a whole and the reverse of each situation has a very low probability of happening: houses of cards do not build themselves when one card in a random pile of cards is moved slightly, balls do not run from a valley up to the top of a mountain to settle, a mixture of dye in water is very unlikely to clump together as a drop and the water never freezes as the hot pan placed in it starts to boil. Energy spreads out and becomes less localised as time goes on thus showing an increase in entropy.

Nature's heat tax

This second statement of the second law says that the entropy of the **universe** must increase with each process that occurs. However, this is **not** the same as saying the entropy of a **system** must increase with each process. A system is the thing that is of particular interest. The system can become more ordered, but the price paid is that the surroundings will become more disordered giving an overall increase in entropy of the universe. The human body can be considered to be a system, which develops from a fertilised egg. At this time the system is very ordered. As the body grows it becomes larger and more organised and so there is even more order, but this is at the expense of breaking down the food required for growth (which itself changes from an ordered system to a more disordered system). During growth heat is transferred to the surroundings and work is also done by the body. Transferring heat to the surroundings is therefore spreading out energy and increasing the entropy. The entropy of the 'universe' (that is, system and its surroundings) is increasing and the heat given out by the system is 'nature's tax' on the work that can be done; when a system takes heat from a hot reservoir and does work on the surroundings some heat must be deposited in the cold reservoir (to ensure that the entropy of the universe increases).

Heat engines and the second law

The Sankey diagram in Figure 2 illustrates a heat engine.

Yet another way of thinking of the second law of thermodynamics is by stating: no engine, that works in a cycle, can be devised that extracts heat from a hot reservoir and delivers mechanical work without also delivering heat to a cold reservoir. The **first law of thermodynamics** would not be violated by an engine that, say, powered a ship by extracting heat energy from cold sea water. It is the second law that says that this is not possible.

A further way of stating the second law of thermodynamics is in terms of the relationship:

$$\Delta S = \frac{Q}{T}$$

that is: the change in entropy of the system is equal to the heat transferred divided by temperature. This means that the units of change of entropy and therefore entropy are JK^{-1}.

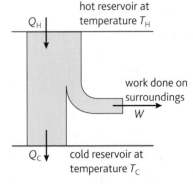

Figure 2 Sankey diagram for heat engine

Thermal efficiency of a heat engine

The gain in entropy by the cold reservoir must, at least, balance the loss of entropy in the hot reservoir

$$\Delta S_{tot} = \Delta S_H + \Delta S_C$$
$$= \frac{-Q_H}{T_H} + \frac{Q_C}{T_C} \geq 0$$

The inequality $Q_C \geq \left|\frac{T_C}{T_H}\right| Q_H$ means that the minimum value of Q_C occurs when it is equal to $\left|\frac{T_C}{T_H}\right| Q_H$.

As shown in Topic 6.3, $W = Q_H - Q_C$

so W could only be as large as the minimum value of Q_C can allow

$$W_{max} = Q_H - Q_{Cmin} = Q_H - \left(\frac{T_C}{T_H}\right) Q_H = Q_H\left(1 - \frac{T_C}{T_H}\right)$$

So the maximum efficiency of the engine is:

$$\text{maximum efficiency} = \frac{W_{max}}{Q_H} = \left(1 - \frac{T_C}{T_H}\right) = \frac{T_H - T_C}{T_H}$$

It can now be seen why in Topic 6.3 the Carnot cycle was considered as representing the most efficient heat engine possible and that the efficiency was given by:

$$\eta = \frac{T_H - T_C}{T_H}$$

So perfect efficiency is only possible if $T_C = 0\,K$.

Since the third law of thermodynamics says that it is not possible to reach absolute zero, it is not possible to have a perfectly efficient heat engine and as the temperature of the cold reservoir approaches that of the hot reservoir the efficiency drops to zero since no work can be extracted from the heat.

> **Hint**
> - This and similar equations must have the temperature in kelvin.
> - There is no need to learn this derivation.

In a reversible change such as with the Carnot engine, the change in entropy will be zero but in all other situations there will be an increase in entropy.

Suppose the hot reservoir is the water and the radiator of a car at a temperature of 350 K and the cold reservoir is the surrounding air at a temperature of 300 K. When 1050 J is transferred from the hot reservoir to the cold reservoir the changes in entropy will be:

for the hot body: $\Delta S_{\mathrm{H}} = \dfrac{Q_{\mathrm{H}}}{T_{\mathrm{H}}} = \dfrac{-1050}{350} = -3\,\mathrm{J\,K^{-1}}$ i.e., a loss of entropy

for the cold body: $\Delta S_{\mathrm{C}} = \dfrac{Q_{\mathrm{C}}}{T_{\mathrm{C}}} = \dfrac{-1050}{300} = +3.5\,\mathrm{J\,K^{-1}}$ i.e., a gain of entropy

From this it can be seen that the change of entropy of the 'universe' is an increase.

Application and How science works

What can be done with heat rejected to the cold reservoir?

Combined heat and power (CHP) or cogeneration is the simultaneous production of useful heat and electricity in the same power station. Conventional electricity generation in large power stations wastes considerable heat by releasing it into the atmosphere. Heat exchangers can be used to transfer some of this rejected heat to a hot water or air system for use in the surrounding locality. CHP plants can increase the overall efficiency of conventional power stations and provide heat to commercial, industrial or public sectors at the same time as producing electricity. In a motor vehicle in winter the same concept is used to provide the driver and passengers with space heating.

■ Hint

The idea of the 'universe' or 'total system' is very important: entropy can decrease locally but it must increase elsewhere by *a minimum of the same amount as the decrease*. No energy flows into or out of the universe: if it does, there's more to the system than there was initially believed to be.

■ Summary questions

1　Explain how the entropy of the gas molecules changes during the induction stroke in an internal combustion engine.

2　a Calculate the maximum efficiency of an engine working between a hot reservoir at 127°C and a cold reservoir at 27°C.

　　b 8.0 kJ of heat is transferred from the hot reservoir with 2.0 kJ of work being done. Calculate i the heat transferred to the cold reservoir ii the entropy change at the hot reservoir iii the entropy change at the cold reservoir iv the overall entropy change v comment on your answers.

3　Explain what is meant by the phrase 'nature's heat tax' with reference to entropy.

AQA⁄ Examination-style questions

1   **Figure 1** shows the relation between the product pressure × volume (pV) and temperature θ in degrees celsius for one mole of an ideal gas for which the molar gas constant is R.

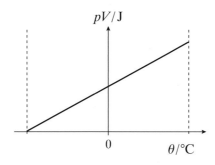

Figure 1

Which one of the following expressions gives the gradient of this graph?

A $\dfrac{1}{273}$ B $\dfrac{pV}{\theta}$ C $\dfrac{pV}{(\theta-273)}$ D R *(1 mark)*

2   **Figure 2** shows the pressure being increased in a bicycle inner tube.

When the piston is pushed in, all the air molecules from the pump are transferred into the inner tube.

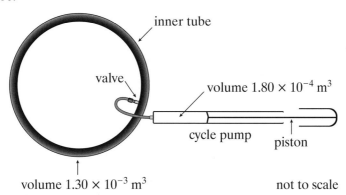

Figure 2

(a) (i)   The cycle inner-tube has a volume of $1.30 \times 10^{-3}\,\text{m}^3$ which remains constant as more air is pushed into it. Initially the air in the inner tube has a pressure of $1.50 \times 10^5\,\text{Pa}$ and a temperature of $300\,\text{K}$.

Calculate the initial number of moles of air in the inner tube.   *(2 marks)*

(ii) When full of air, the pump contains $1.80 \times 10^{-4}\,\text{m}^3$ of air at a pressure of $1.00 \times 10^5\,\text{Pa}$ and a temperature of $300\,\text{K}$.

Calculate the number of moles of gas transferred into the inner tube each time air is pushed into the tube.   *(1 mark)*

(iii) Calculate the new pressure in the inner tube after one stroke of the pump.   *(3 marks)*

(iv) State the assumptions you needed to make to answer part (a)(iii)   *(2 marks)*

(b) Explain how the kinetic theory model of an ideal gas predicts the existence of gas pressure and an increase in pressure when more molecules are transferred to the inner tube.   *(6 marks)*

3 The graph in **Figure 3** shows the variation of pressure with volume of the air in the pump system in Question 2 up to the time when it starts to enter the inner tube.

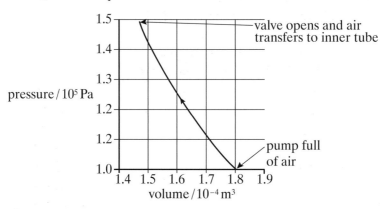

pressure / 10^5 Pa

volume / 10^{-4} m³

valve opens and air transfers to inner tube

pump full of air

Figure 3

(a) Use data from the graph to show that the change is not isothermal. *(3 marks)*

(b) Use the graph to estimate the work done on the gas whilst the gas is being compressed to the point at which the air enters the inner tube. *(4 marks)*

4 The first law of thermodynamics can be written $\Delta U = Q + W$

(a) State the meaning of each term in this equation. *(3 marks)*

(b) Explain why, for an isothermal expansion, the first law can be written $W = Q$. *(3 marks)*

5 **Figure 4** shows the energy transfers in an ideal heat engine operating between a source of heat at a temperature of 640 °C and a cold heat-sink at a temperature of 20 °C.

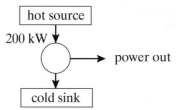

hot source

200 kW

power out

cold sink

Figure 4

(a) Calculate

   (i) the maximum possible efficiency, *(3 marks)*

   (ii) the maximum power output corresponding to this efficiency if the rate of energy supply from the hot source is 200 kW. *(1 mark)*

(b) A designer states that the two-stage ideal heat engine shown below would operate at a greater maximum overall efficiency, and hence provide a greater total power output, than the ideal heat engine in part (a).

The same heat source and sink are to be used, but the energy rejected from the first stage enters a reservoir which acts as a source of energy for the second stage.

The temperature of the reservoir is such that the maximum possible efficiency of the first stage is 34% and that of the second stage is 52%.

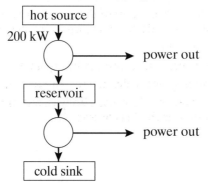

hot source

200 kW

power out

reservoir

power out

cold sink

Figure 5

For the two-stage engine, operating at its maximum theoretical efficiency, calculate:

(i)   the power output of the first stage,   *(1 mark)*

(ii) the power delivered to the reservoir from the first stage,   *(1 mark)*

(iii) the power output of the second stage,   *(1 mark)*

(iv) the overall efficiency of the two-stage engine.   *(1 mark)*

(c)   Comment on the validity of the designer's statement.   *(3 marks)*

6   Measurements made on a single-cylinder 4-stroke petrol engine produced the following data:

mean temperature of gases in cylinder during combustion stroke 820°C

mean temperature of exhaust gases   77°C

area enclosed by p–V diagram   380 J

number of power strokes every second   15 Hz

actual power developed by engine at output   4.7 kW

calorific value of fuel   45 MJ kg^{-1}

flow rate of fuel 2.1×10^{-2} kg min^{-1}

(a)   Estimate the maximum theoretical efficiency of this engine.   *(4 marks)*

(b)   (i)   Calculate the power of the engine as indicated by the p–V diagram. *(1 mark)*

(ii) Calculate the power dissipated in overcoming the frictional losses in the engine.   *(1 mark)*

(iii) Calculate the rate at which energy is supplied to the engine through the fuel.

(2 marks)

(c)   Calculate the overall efficiency of the engine.   *(3 marks)*

7   **Figure 6** shows a number of smoke particles suspended in air. The arrowheads indicate the directions and the length of the arrow the speeds in which the particles are moving at a particular time.

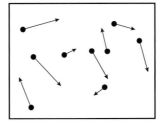

Figure 6

(a)   (i)   Explain why the smoke particles are observed to move.   *(1 mark)*

(ii) The smoke particles are observed to move randomly. State **two** conclusions about air molecules and their motion that arise from this observation.   *(3 marks)*

(b)   A sample of air has a density of 1.24 kg m^{-3} at a pressure of 1.01×10^5 Pa and a temperature of 300 K.

(i)   Calculate the mean kinetic energy of an air molecule under these conditions. *(2 marks)*

(ii) Calculate the root-mean-square speed for the air molecules.   *(3 marks)*

(iii) Explain why, when the temperature of the air is increased to 320 K, some of the molecules will have speeds much less than that suggested by the value you calculated in part (b)(ii).   *(2 marks)*

8   (a)   State what is meant by the increase in entropy of a system.   *(1 mark)*

(b)   Stating the meaning of your symbols, define entropy change.   *(4 marks)*

(c)   When a human embryo grows in its mother's body its entropy decreases. Explain how this is consistent with ideas of disorder.   *(3 marks)*

Breaking matter down

7.1 Accelerating charged particles

Link

The unit of capacitance is the farad (F). One farad = 1 coulomb per volt ($1\,F = 1\,CV^{-1}$). See Topic 8.6

How science works

A particular direction is chosen as being positive. Now imagine one charge firmly fixed at the origin of our measurement system and a second charge being brought close to it. If the charges are of the same sign then they will tend to repel each other and the movable charge will move in the positive direction (indicating that repulsive forces have a positive direction). If the charges are of the opposite sign then the movable charge will be attracted towards the fixed charge and move in the negative direction (indicating that attractive forces have a negative direction).

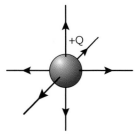

Figure 1 *Radial electric field*

Electric fields compared with gravitational fields

There are many analogies throughout physics. Models that are applicable in one area can often be modified to be used in other areas of physics. This is the case with gravitational and electric fields. Electric fields are regions in which charged objects will experience forces. This statement is comparable to that for gravitational fields as regions in which masses experience forces. Naturally the definition for electric field strength (E) becomes the force per unit (positive) charge and is measured in NC^{-1}.

Gravitational forces are always attractive as there is no evidence to support 'negative mass'. Electric forces may be either attractive or repulsive with like (same sign) charges repelling and unlike charges attracting. The law of forces also mirrors that of gravitation. It is an inverse square law force taking the form:

$$F \propto \frac{Qq}{r^2}$$

Here F is the force in newtons, Q and q are the charges in coulombs and r is the separation of the charges in metres (we imagine the charges to be point charges, taking up no physical size).

The constant of proportionality to convert this relationship into an equation is interesting. It would be nice to make this number a simple one like '1' but all units need to tie together in SI units and it ends up having a value of $9.0 \times 10^9\,N\,m^2\,C^{-2}$ for charges in a vacuum or air! If that wasn't complicated enough, the constant is written as $\frac{1}{4\pi\varepsilon_0}$ with ε_0 being called the 'permittivity of free space' where ε_0 is defined to have a value of about $8.85 \times 10^{-12}\,F\,m^{-1}$ and can be thought of as a measurement of how strongly charges interact in a vacuum. The 4π is included to simplify many equations which involve the idea that forces act in all directions around point charges (i.e. spherically).

The complete equation takes the form $F = \frac{1}{4\pi\varepsilon_0}\frac{Qq}{r^2_0}$ and is known as 'Coulomb's law'. Conventionally this is taken as being a positive force if it is repulsive and negative if it is attractive.

It follows from this equation that the electric field strength around a point charge (or a charged sphere – which behaves as if the charge were concentrated at its centre) will be given by:

$$E = \frac{F}{q} = \frac{1}{4\pi\varepsilon_0}\frac{Q}{r^2}$$

An electric field can be represented by drawing lines of force as shown in Figure 1. This is a radial field since the lines of force radiate from the charge in all directions. Radial fields are not uniform and charged objects will experience different forces and accelerations at different positions in the field.

Uniform fields

Uniform electric fields mean that a charged object will experience a constant force and acceleration at any position within the field. It is quite easy to produce a uniform electric field; a potential difference needs to be connected across a pair of parallel metal plates as shown in Figure 2. The field lines are parallel and perpendicular to the plates. The electric field strength (E) is easily calculated for a uniform field between a pair of parallel plates:

$$E = \frac{V}{d}$$

where V is the pd across the plates and d their separation.

We can see that the unit for uniform field strength can be written as being $V\,m^{-1}$ as an alternative to NC^{-1}; this is true for all electric fields.

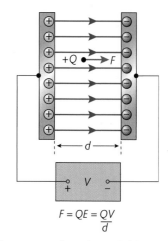

$$F = QE = \frac{QV}{d}$$

Figure 2 *Uniform electric field*

Application and How science works

Context is everything!

There are many situations where the units of quantities are commonly written differently depending on the context. At AS the idea of gravitational field strength was introduced as being equivalent to the acceleration due to gravity and having equivalent values of $9.81\,N\,kg^{-1}$ and $9.81\,m\,s^{-2}$, respectively. It was also shown that the unit of work was equivalent to that of energy ($N\,m \equiv J$). The unit of impulse is equivalent to the unit of momentum ($N\,s \equiv kg\,m\,s^{-1}$). Now we see that the unit of electric field strength can either be NC^{-1} or $V\,m^{-1}$! It is usual to use the former unit when comparing field strengths outside any particular context but the latter unit is usually used when a field is set up to accelerate charged particles. Whichever version of the unit you use it is correct and you will not be penalised for using it whatever the context.

Generating electrons – the thermionic effect

This is how the electrons are generated in cathode-ray oscilloscopes, X-ray tubes, older style cathode-ray tube televisions and visual display units, and 'valves' used in some high-quality sound system amplifiers. A heated metal filament or metal cathode in a vacuum will eject electrons from the surface if it can overcome the electrostatic forces holding the electrons to their parent atoms. Two heating methods are used: direct heating where the filament itself is heated by passing a current through it and indirect heating where a cathode is heated by a separate filament close to it. The emitted electrons produce an electric field. These electrons repel other electrons and disperse whilst forming a 'cloud' around the filament or cathode which has become positive due to the loss of electrons. (The term **thermionic emission** is also used to refer to any thermally excited charge emission process in which heating ejects charge carriers which subsequently are attracted by the field that their emission sets up). In all metals there are a small number of 'free' electrons per atom not tied to a parent atom. This is similar to atoms in a gas and there will be a distribution of electrons with different velocities. Occasionally an electron will have enough velocity to escape from the metal. The minimum amount of energy needed for an electron to leave the surface is called the **work function** of the metal. The work function is a characteristic of the actual metal being heated. The lower the work function, the more likely

Link

See Topic 5.2 for the thermionic effect used to generate electrons in X-ray tubes.

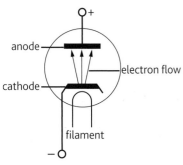

Figure 3 *Thermionic effect – the diode valve*

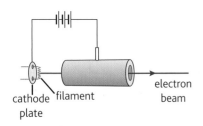

Figure 4 *Electron gun*

AQA **Examiner's tip**

You may be given energies in electron volts. This is a sensible unit for atomic and nuclear physics because many energies are a few eV or keV (kilo-electron volts) or MeV (mega-electron volts). 1 eV is the kinetic energy gained by an electron when it is accelerated by a pd of 1 volt. 1 eV = 1.60×10^{-19} J.

thermionic emission is to occur. By coating metals with different metallic oxides the work function can be reduced. In a diode valve (see Figure 3) a second electrode is included to set up an electric field which accelerates the emitted electrons through the vacuum in the tube.

The electron gun

The thermionic effect is used to generate electrons which can be accelerated through a vacuum towards a positively charged anode. When the anode takes the shape of a hollow cylinder, most of the electrons reaching it will pass through it into the region beyond. This combination of a filament or heater, a cathode and an anode is known as an electron gun, see Figure 4.

Equating the two equations for electric field strength $E = \dfrac{V}{d}$ and $E = \dfrac{F}{Q}$ the relationship $Fd = VQ$ is obtained. This equation may be familiar, since Fd is the work done and potential difference is the work done per unit charge. The work done on an object of charge Q being accelerated by an electric field in a vacuum will be equal to the gain in kinetic energy of the charge. This leads to the charged object losing electrical potential energy and gaining kinetic energy so that:

$$QV = \tfrac{1}{2}mv^2 \quad \text{or} \quad eV = \tfrac{1}{2}mv^2$$

when the charged object is an electron of charge e.

Here V is the pd between the anode and the cathode and m the mass of an electron. This leads to the velocity of the electron entering or leaving the anode of the electron gun being given by:

$$v = \sqrt{\frac{2eV}{m}}$$

The ratio $\dfrac{e}{m}$ included in this equation is called the **specific charge of an electron** and has a value of 1.76×10^{11} C kg^{-1} when the speed of the electron is small compared to the speed of light.

The electric field inside a hollow conductor is zero. This means that an electron inside a hollow cylindrical anode will not be accelerated – see the drift tube in the linear accelerator in Topic 7.4.

■ **Summary questions**

1 Make a table comparing electrical quantities with the gravitational quantities of: mass, Newton's law of gravitation, gravitational field strength, gravitational potential and gravitational potential energy. Include units and any relevant equations.

2 Calculate the force on an electron when it is 8.5×10^{-10} m from a second electron in a vacuum.

Electron charge = 1.60×10^{-19} C, $\dfrac{1}{4\pi\varepsilon_0} = 9.0 \times 10^9$ N m^2 C^{-2}

3 Calculate the field strength between two parallel metal plates separated by 1.50 cm. The pd across the plate = 4.52 kV.

4 Calculate the velocity of an electron accelerated through a pd of 10.0 kV.

Use $\dfrac{e}{m} = 1.76 \times 10^{11}$ C kg^{-1}.

7.2 Deflecting particles

Learning objectives:

■ How can the path of a charged particle be changed?

■ What factors affect the path followed by a charged particle?

Specification reference: 3.5.2D

■ Deflection by a uniform electric field

In Topic 7.1 the acceleration of charged particles by electric fields was considered. Electric fields can be used to deflect the path of a beam of charged particles when the field is applied at right angles to the path of the beam. This is the equivalent to projectile motion in a gravitational field; the presence of the field will not change the velocity of the beam which is perpendicular to the field. Consider a particle of charge Q and mass m initially moving with a speed u, moving into an electric field of strength E.

$$E = \frac{V}{d}$$

where V is the pd across the plates and d is their separation as shown in Figure 1. The plates are of length L and it takes time t to pass through them.

The motion of the particle should be considered both horizontally and vertically.

The horizontal speed will not be changed by the presence of the field and remains at the initial speed u_h.

Thus $u_h = \frac{L}{t}$.

The initial vertical speed of the particles is zero.

Their acceleration will be given by the force on each particle divided by its mass i.e., $a = \frac{F}{m} = \frac{EQ}{m}$.

Using the equation of motion $v = u_v + at$ gives $v = \frac{EQ}{m} \times \frac{L}{u_h}$ as the vertical velocity with which the particle leaves the plates. The overall velocity will need to be found by combining u_h and v using Pythagoras' theorem.

Using exactly the same reasoning as for projectile motion, a constant horizontal velocity combined with a uniform vertical acceleration leads to a parabolic trajectory for the charged particle.

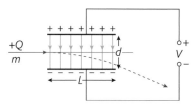

Figure 1 *Deflection of charged particle by a uniform electric field*

■ Deflection by a magnetic field

When a current-carrying conductor is positioned inside and at right angles to a magnetic field the conductor is found to experience a force. The magnitude of the force (F) in newtons is given by $F = BIl$ where B is the strength of the magnetic field in teslas (T), I the current in amps and l the length of the conductor in metres. The direction of the force is given by Fleming's left-hand rule as shown in Figure 2. This rule has nothing to do with the physics behind the force, it is simply a method of remembering the relative directions of the force, current and magnetic field (from north to south). The current used in this rule must be the conventional current: i.e. positive charge in motion. You need to take care when considering electrons because they travel in the opposite direction to the conventional current.

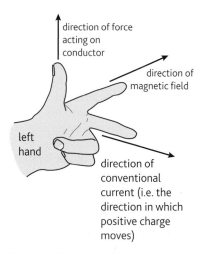

direction of force acting on conductor

direction of magnetic field

left hand

direction of conventional current (i.e. the direction in which positive charge moves)

Figure 2 *Fleming's left hand rule*

Equivalence of $F = BQv$ and $F = BIl$

Current is the rate of flow of charge with time and can be written as $I = \dfrac{Q}{t}$ if the current is constant. Substituting for I in the second equation above gives $F = \dfrac{BQl}{t}$ and if the speed is constant then $v = \dfrac{l}{t}$ giving $F = BQv$.

Charged particles moving through a vacuum represent a flow of charge just like electrons moving through a conductor. This means that when charged particles are moving at right angles to a magnetic field they will experience a magnetic force equivalent to that experienced by the current-carrying conductor. The magnitude of the force on a particle of charge Q, travelling with a velocity v in a magnetic field of strength B will be given by the equation:

$$F = BQv$$

Figure 3 shows a particle of positive charge Q and mass m moving in a uniform magnetic field of strength B at **X**. It experiences a force at **X** which alters its motion according to Fleming's left-hand rule deviating the particle to **Y** and then to **Z** etc. Thus the particle moves in a circle of radius r. The magnetic force is providing the centripetal force needed to move the particle in this circle so:

$$BQv = \frac{mv^2}{r}$$

Cancelling v gives a value for the radius of the circle of $r = \dfrac{mv}{BQ}$.

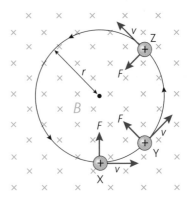

The speed of the charged particle doesn't change, but the direction does so continuously.
The force is always towards the centre of the circle – the magnetic force is providing a centripetal force.

Figure 3 *Force on a charged particle in a magnetic field*

Demonstrating the magnetic force on an electron

Figure 4 is an image of a fine-beam tube in operation. In this experiment thermionically emitted electrons are accelerated through a potential difference in an electron gun inside a glass tube. The tube contains a gas (often neon or nitrogen) at low pressure. The electron beam starts moving vertically but is then deflected in a circular path by the magnetic field produced by a pair of Helmholtz coils placed on either side of the bulb. By measuring the accelerating voltage, the radius of the circle in which the electrons travel and the magnetic field strength a value for the **specific charge** on an electron can be calculated (see below). The gas atoms in the tube are excited along the length of the circular path due to collisions with the beam of electrons; this means that the gas atoms emit light as they relax to lower energy levels thus making the circular path of the electrons visible.

Figure 4 *The fine-beam tube*

The kinetic energy of the electron beam is related to the pd between the filament and the anode by the equation:

$$\tfrac{1}{2}mv^2 = eV \text{ meaning that } v = \sqrt{\frac{2eV}{m}}$$

As shown above $BQv = \dfrac{mv^2}{r}$, this leads to $v = \dfrac{Ber}{m}$ when e is substituted for Q.

Equating the two equations for v gives $\dfrac{Ber}{m} = \sqrt{\dfrac{2eV}{m}}$

or squaring gives $\dfrac{B^2e^2r^2}{m^2} = \dfrac{2eV}{m}$

cancelling one $\dfrac{e}{m}$ produces $\dfrac{e}{m} = \dfrac{2V}{B^2r^2}$

How science works

Helmholtz coils

These are a pair of large coils which fit in a holder so that they are symmetrically positioned around electron tubes like the fine-beam or deflection tubes. The coils provide a uniform magnetic field the strength (B) of which can be calculated from the formula:

$$B = \left(\frac{8}{\sqrt{125}}\right)\frac{\mu_0 NI}{r}$$

where N = number of turns in each coil, I = current through the coils in amps, r = radius of coils in metres and μ_0 = permeability of free space $(4\pi \times 10^{-7}\,\mathrm{N A^{-2}})$.

Crossed fields

In 1897, J. J. Thompson measured the specific charge on an electron by using crossed electric and magnetic fields to deflect electrons with equal and opposite forces as shown in Figure 5. In the deflection tube a pair of parallel metal plates provide an electrical force F_E which is balanced by the magnetic force F_M provided by the Helmholtz coils,

$$F_E = F_M \quad \text{so} \quad Ee = BeV$$

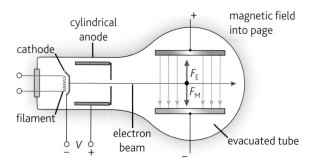

Figure 5 *Measuring $\dfrac{e}{m}$ with a deflection tube*

Cancelling the electron charge e gives $v = \frac{E}{B}$

As with the fine-beam tube the electron beam is accelerated by the pd between the anode and cathode and so the kinetic energy of the electrons is given by:

$$\tfrac{1}{2}mv^2 = eV$$

So again

$$v = \sqrt{\frac{2eV}{m}}$$

Equating this to $\frac{E}{B}$ and squaring gives

$$\frac{E^2}{B^2} = \frac{2eV}{m}$$

and so

$$\frac{e}{m} = \frac{E^2}{2VB^2}$$

This equation can be simplified by making the pd across the parallel plates equal to that between the anode and the cathode. This will mean that $E = \frac{V}{d}$ and modify the $\frac{e}{m}$ equation to:

$$\frac{e}{m} = \frac{V}{2d^2B^2}$$

How science works

Danger with high voltages

When handling EHT (extra high tension) power supplies there is potentially a great deal of danger. To reduce any risk shrouded leads (with a plastic sleeve over the metal contact) and a large protective resistor should be used in the circuit. The current will be limited to less than 5 mA if power supplies designed for educational use are used.

Summary questions

1 Explain why a beam of electrons would be expected to spread out as it moves along a straight path.

2 A uniform electric field of strength $150\,\text{N}\,\text{C}^{-1}$ is set up between a pair of parallel plates each 0.08 m long. The plates are separated by a distance of 0.05 m. An electron with a speed of $1.8 \times 10^6\,\text{m}\,\text{s}^{-1}$ enters the field perpendicular to the field lines.

   a Calculate the acceleration of the electron when it is between the plates.

   b Calculate the time for which the electron travels between the plates.

   c Calculate the vertical distance the electron moves in between the plates.

3 A beam of protons travels parallel to a magnetic field. Explain whether or not any force will act on the beam.

4 A beam of electrons moves with a speed of $1.4 \times 10^7\,\text{m}\,\text{s}^{-1}$ at right angles to a magnetic field of strength 5.0 mT. The beam moves in a circular orbit.

   a Explain why the beam moves in this path.

   b Calculate the radius of the orbit.

   Electron mass $= 9.11 \times 10^{-31}\,\text{kg}$; electron charge $= 1.60 \times 10^{-19}\,\text{C}$.

7.3 Mass spectrometers

Learning objectives:

- How are the masses of atoms measured?

- How are the ions produced and detected?

Specification reference: 3.5.2D

Measuring atomic masses

Originally atomic masses were found using chemical methods. Only the relative masses of elements could be determined in this way. They were usually close to whole number multiples of the mass of hydrogen but not always. The reason for this is that many elements have different isotopes (each having the same number of protons but different numbers of neutrons). Chemical properties depend on the number of orbital electrons, which (if the element is neutral) equals the number of protons (Z) in the nucleus. The neutron number (N) however, can vary without affecting the chemical properties of elements. To allow more accurate determinations of masses, physical methods have to be used. A very accurate method is to use a **mass spectrometer** (see Figure 1).

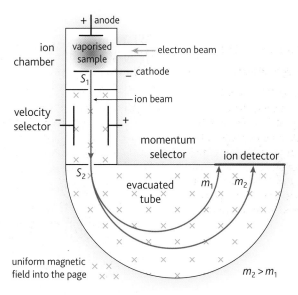

Figure 1 *Bainbridge mass spectrometer*

What is a mass spectrometer?

A mass spectrometer is a device which is used to measure the relative numbers of molecules and atoms of different masses. Modern mass spectrometers are commonly based on the mass spectrograph designed by Bainbridge in 1932 and have four parts: the ion chamber, the velocity selector, the momentum selector and the ion detector.

The ion chamber

Before the mass of these particles can be measured, samples of solids or liquids need to be converted into a gas (volatilised). In some forms of the apparatus, samples are volatilised by rapid heating of the sample using a laser, other types use a heating coil to heat the sample electrically. An inert gas carries the volatilised particles into the mass spectrometer itself. On entering the mass spectrometer the atoms are ionised by bombardment with high-energy electrons. A collision with a high-energy electron means that the target atoms each lose one electron converting them into positive ions (having a relative charge of +1). Ions with a net positive charge are called cations as they are attracted by a cathode (negative electrode). Mass spectrometers separate ions according to the ratio of their mass to their charge. Because most of the ions have a charge of +1, it can be considered that the mass spectrometer separates ions with different masses.

The velocity selector

From the ion chamber the ions are accelerated through a hole in the cathode into the velocity selector. The purpose of this chamber is to select only particles with a certain velocity (and charge). To do this both an electric and a magnetic field are applied to produce forces in opposite directions so that they exactly cancel out only for particles with a certain velocity. These ions then will move straight through the chamber through the slits S_1 and S_2, which ensure that the ion beam is moving in a straight line (collimated). Ions with velocities higher or lower than the required value do not pass through slit S_2.

As discussed in the previous topic, for an electric field E the force on an ion of charge Q is given by: $F_E = EQ$

and the magnetic force by: $F_M = BQv$ (where B is the magnetic field strength and v the velocity of the ion). In this case the magnetic field is shown going into the plane of the diagram meaning that the electric force (provided by the electric field between the parallel plates) and the magnetic force are in opposite directions. This means that the ions on which no net force is exerted are those for which: $EQ = BQv$ and

therefore those ions having a velocity which is given by $v = \dfrac{E}{B}$.

The momentum selector

Now the ions enter a momentum selector all with the same velocity. Here there is no electric field but a uniform magnetic field that bends the beam of ions into a circular path with radius r. As the centripetal force is provided by the magnetic force:

$$BQv = \frac{mv^2}{r}$$

hence the radius of the path of the ion beam is given by:

$$r = \frac{mv}{BQ}$$

The ion beam consists of singly ionised particles (each of constant charge, Q) of constant velocity (v) travelling in a uniform magnetic field (of constant magnetic field strength, B).

Thus $r \propto m$, i.e. the radius of the circular arc followed by each ion is proportional only to its mass.

This is an extremely effective way of distinguishing between different isotopes of an element – allowing the relative abundance of the isotopes to be found from the relative densities of the signals detected by the detector.

Ion detector

In the original form of Bainbridge's mass spectrograph, the ion detector was a photographic plate – this produced an image in which the degree of exposure was proportional to the intensity of the ions (i.e., a graph

– which is why this was called a mass spectrograph). Modern mass spectrometers have detectors which monitor and amplify the ion current transmitting it to a data system where it is recorded in the form of mass spectra ready for analysis.

Application and How science works

Carbon dating (See also Topic 9.1)

Neutrons produced in the upper atmosphere collide with nitrogen atoms converting them into the radioactive isotope carbon-14 (^{14}C). ^{14}C combines with oxygen and passes into living animals and plants through respiration. ^{14}C is produced at a constant rate and can only be absorbed by organisms which are alive. By comparing the activity of ^{14}C emitted by a living organism with that of similar matter that was once alive but is now dead the time elapsed can be measured. Mass spectrometers can be unreliable for ^{14}C dating because of the low concentration of ^{14}C and the presence in the samples of particles having almost identical masses to ^{14}C (particularly ^{14}N and ethene (CH_2)). Particle accelerators can be used with mass spectrometers to improve the reliability of the analysis by removing ions of similar mass to ^{14}C. A sensitivity of 10^{-15} in the $^{14}C : {}^{12}C$ ratio is reported to have been achieved with a sample of mass 1 mg.

Summary questions

1. Explain why it is essential that ions are produced for use in a mass spectrometer.

2. Describe the main features of a mass spectrometer; explain the role of the velocity selector and the momentum selector in separating a beam of singly charged ions.

3. The isotopes of iron ^{54}Fe, ^{56}Fe and ^{57}Fe are singly ionised in a mass spectrometer operating with a constant magnetic field of 45 mT and an electric field of 600 V m^{-1} in the velocity selector. Assuming the mass of a proton or neutron to be 1.66×10^{-27} kg and the charge on a proton to be $+1.60 \times 10^{-19}$ C, calculate the radius of the path for each isotope.

Link

See Topic 9.1 for more details of carbon dating.

7.4 Linear accelerators

Learning objectives:

■ How are charged particles accelerated in a linear accelerator?

■ What are the problems which exist with high energy particles?

■ How does travelling at speeds close to the speed of light modify mass, length and time?

Specification reference: 3.5.2D

Figure 1 *The Stanford linac*

■ Accelerating charged particles

Linear accelerators or 'linacs' are some of the simplest accelerators of charged particles. The total length of the accelerator depends on the use to which it will be put. When accelerating electrons for the production of X-rays for medical use they may be around a metre long. When used as the particle injector for a synchrotron, the linac is likely to be a few tens of metres long. However, primary accelerators in nuclear research will be much longer than this as is the case with the Stanford Linear Accelerator in California (SLAC), see Figure 1. This is 3.2 km long and accelerates electrons to energies of 50 GeV.

Electron, proton or ion beams may be accelerated by another accelerator such as one based on a Van de Graaff generator before entering the linear accelerator itself. The beam passes through several hollow metallic cylindrical electrodes called 'drift tubes' which are connected to a radio-frequency alternating supply. The ions are accelerated by the electric field that exists between each pair of drift tubes. In order to use a constant frequency supply each drift tube needs to be longer than the previous one. As they are moving faster charged particles will travel a greater distance in the time for which the alternating supply has the 'wrong polarity'; to accelerate them, therefore, they must be shielded from the effect of the field for a greater time. On leaving the linear accelerator the particles are made to collide with a target. Stanford's linac is an electron–positron collider designed to collide two beams of particles accelerated on different tracks of the accelerator.

Figure 2 shows part of a linear accelerator which accelerates protons or positive ions along the axis of a line of drift tubes (**A–F**). Alternate drift tubes are connected together and an alternating voltage is applied to **B**, **D** and **F** etc., whilst the other drift tubes remain at zero volts.

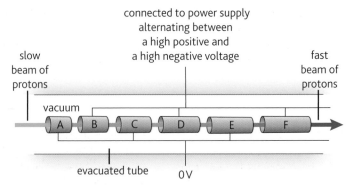

Figure 2 *A linear accelerator*

Protons are accelerated in the following sequence:

■ A bunch of slowly moving protons enters the tube **A** from a Van de Graaff generator.

■ Whilst inside **A** the protons move at a constant speed.

■ The proton beam accelerates across the gap between tubes **A** and **B** as drift tube **B** is negative with respect to drift tube **A**.

- The ions move with constant speed inside tube **B** for nearly half a period of the alternating voltage. The polarity of drift tubes **B**, **D** and **F** reverses whilst the ion is inside **B**.
- The proton beam emerges from **B** and accelerates across the gap between **B** and **C**. As **B** is now positive and **C** has remained at zero volts, this means drift tube **C** is now negative with respect to **B**.

This process continues as the proton beam passes through the tubes. At high energies the accelerated particles approach the speed of light. The energy they gain goes into their mass, which increases because of relativistic effects, rather than extra speed. This means that the length of the drift tubes has to be adjusted to allow for this.

Relativistic corrections

For everyday speeds (i.e., those very much less than the speed of light) Newton's laws of motion work very well as a model describing matter. However, accelerated particles may well travel close to the speed of light; this means that Einstein's Special Theory of Relativity must be used to describe the motion of these particles. Although some of the predictions of this theory do not seem to agree with our everyday experiences, over 50 years of experimentation with high-energy particles (which do travel close to the speed of light), has always produced results which agree with Einstein's theory.

The Special Theory of Relativity is developed from two fundamental ideas:

- The speed of light is the same for all observers irrespective of how they move relative to one another.
- The laws of physics are the same in any inertial (i.e., non-accelerated) frame of reference. This means that the laws of physics observed by an imaginary observer travelling with a very fast moving particle would be identical to those observed by someone who is not moving with the particle.

Einstein showed how quantities such as mass, length and time must change so that all observers obtain consistent results irrespective of the reference frame in which the observer may be moving.

Although you are not required to study the details of the Special Theory of Relativity on this course, you are expected to know the effect that travelling at relativistic speeds has on the mass, length and time measured. Einstein showed that each of these quantities is modified by a factor

$$\gamma = \frac{1}{\sqrt{\left(1 - \frac{v^2}{c^2}\right)}}$$

For non-relativistic objects, mass is constant. However relativity predicts that mass becomes larger and larger as the speed gets closer to the speed of light. A particle would have infinite mass if it could reach the speed of light. This means that mass should be defined by the equation

$$m = \gamma m_0 = \frac{m_0}{\sqrt{\left(1 - \frac{v^2}{c^2}\right)}}$$

where m_0 is the rest mass of the object (i.e. its measured mass when it is stationary relative to the observer making the measurement).

If the half-life of a large number of particles travelling close to the speed of light was to be measured from the Earth it would be found to be much longer than that of a similar sample of stationary particles. The time is 'dilated' or prolonged as a result of travelling at such a high speed. Time, like mass, needs to have a relativistic correction so that the measured time elapsed (t) for a relativistic object is given by

$$t = \gamma t_0 = \frac{t_0}{\sqrt{\left(1 - \frac{v^2}{c^2}\right)}}.$$

where t_0 is the time of the event measured when stationary relative to the observer.

Therefore, the half-life of moving particles appears, to the stationary observer, to be increased by the factor γ.

Accompanying time dilation is another relativistic effect which is length contraction. To a stationary observer the length of an object moving close to the speed of light appears to be shorter than if the object was stationary relative to the observer. This time, the 'rest length', must be corrected by the factor γ^{-1} so that the measured length will be given by:

$$l = l_0 \gamma^{-1} = l_0 \sqrt{\left(1 - \frac{v^2}{c^2}\right)}$$

Muons and relativity

Cosmic rays are mostly composed of long-lived protons from outer space. When high-energy protons reach the Earth's atmosphere there is a strong probability of a collision between a proton and a gas molecule in the atmosphere leading to the production of high-energy pions which subsequently decay into muons. Muons do not interact with matter easily and they are too massive to be significantly deflected by atomic electric fields that they encounter. The half-life of muons generated on Earth is found to be about 2.2 μs. It might be expected that at the top of a high mountain the measured muon flux would be much greater than that measured at the bottom of the mountain because many will have decayed on the way. However, because of relativistic time dilation, many more muons reach sea level than is predicted if relativity is ignored.

Assume the muons travel at a speed of $0.998c$ (where c is the speed of light $= 3.00 \times 10^8$ m s^{-1}). Using non-relativistic Newtonian equations (and thus $s = vt$) the muons would be expected to travel

$$0.998 \times 3.00 \times 10^8 \times 2.2 \times 10^{-6} \text{m} \approx 660 \text{m}$$

Using the time dilation factor the muons' half-life becomes

$$t = \gamma 2.2 \times 10^{-6} = \frac{2.2 \times 10^{-6}}{\sqrt{\left(1 - \frac{0.998^2 c^2}{c^2}\right)}} = \frac{2.2 \times 10^{-6}}{0.063} = 3.5 \times 10^{-5} \text{s}$$

This allows them to travel $0.998 \times 3.00 \times 10^8 \times 3.5 \times 10^{-5} = 10\,500$ m. Since this length is greater than the height of any mountain on Earth it confirms that the muons will have a very high probability of being detected at sea level.

Alternatively from the muons' 'perception' the distance they travel will be contracted so 10 500 m from the Earth reference frame becomes

$$l = 10\,500 \gamma^{-1} = 10\,500 \sqrt{\left(1 - \frac{0.998^2 c^2}{c^2}\right)} \approx 660 \text{m}$$

This value is identical to the distance expected without using relativistic ideas. In other words the two relativistic effects cancel telling us that the laws of physics will give the same result whatever reference frame is used.

■ **How science works**

Einstein versus Newton

The laws of motion based on the Special Theory of Relativity are correct for all objects. This doesn't, however, mean that Newton's laws are incorrect. In fact they are an excellent approximation to Einstein's relations when the speeds of the object are very much less than the speed of light. For everyday speeds it is appropriate to use Newtonian mechanics but for speeds close to the speed of light, Einsteinian mechanics must be used.

Advantages and disadvantages of linacs

One of the advantages of linacs is their simplicity; it is much cheaper to build a straight accelerator because no high power deflecting magnets need to be installed. However, for large energies, this also means that linacs need to be very long. The space taken up is a major drawback and many 'driver devices' and their associated power supplies are required. This increases the construction and maintenance expense. The SLAC is 3.2 km long and is very expensive to maintain (the budget for 2006 being in excess of US$10 000 000).

Linacs can accelerate ions to greater energies than other circular accelerators, which are limited by the strength of the magnetic fields needed to deflect the ions. These accelerators tend to lose energy by producing synchrotron radiation (see Topic 7.6). Linacs can operate continuously whereas other accelerators tend to work in bursts; however the large amount of internal energy generated in the accelerator cavity tends to mean that linacs too are not operated continuously.

Application and How science works

The UK and particle physics

In the delivery plan for 2008/9–2011/12 the UK Science and Technology Facilities Council stated that:

'Our highest priority will be to exploit the Large Hadron Collider (LHC) at CERN, which starts operation in 2008; this is because discoveries are guaranteed. This accelerator is the first with sufficient energy to access the regime where our existing knowledge breaks down: at the very least, we hope to find the Higgs Boson, which is postulated to give particles their mass; theoretical models suggest we will likely observe new symmetries of nature, new particles and forces beyond those known. With the commissioning of the LHC, CERN will be for at least the next decade the world's most advanced particle physics laboratory. Our membership of CERN gives us a strong and central role in this transformative project: one of the two major experiments at LHC is UK-led. ... The UK research community has been a major player in constructing the LHC and the highly advanced computing infrastructure to handle the data. The community is now prepared and ready to exploit the results from the machine and we will support the community to do so, within our financial constraints. We will cease investment in the International Linear Collider. We do not see a practicable path towards the realisation of this facility as currently conceived on a reasonable timescale.'

The International Linear Collider (ILC) is a proposed 35 km collider consisting of two linacs facing each other. The ILC is intended to collide 10^{10} electrons with positrons, using superconducting cavities operating at temperatures near absolute zero and making 14 000 collisions per second with energies of 5×10^{11} GeV. Each collision could create an array of new particles that could answer some of the most fundamental questions of matter and energy. The design of this accelerator would allow for an upgrade to a 50 km, 1 TeV collider at a later stage.

Watch this space.

Summary questions

1. Explain why the drift tubes in a linear accelerator must be of increasing length. How does the Special Theory of Relativity modify this situation?

2. Explain how an alternating field accelerates bunches of charged particles through the gaps between the drift tubes and why they are not accelerated inside the drift tubes.

3. Tau particles have half-lives of 3.05×10^{-13} s. How far would a tau travelling at $0.99c$ be expected to travel in this time using

   a Newtonian mechanics and

   b relativistic mechanics? ($c = 3.00 \times 10^8$ m s^{-1})

7.5 Cyclotrons

Learning objectives:

- How does a cyclotron accelerate charged particles?
- How can higher energy ions be achieved?

Specification reference: 3.5.2D

How the cyclotron works

The cyclotron (see Figure 1) is a particle accelerator designed by E O Lawrence in 1930 at the University of California, Berkeley. Despite being one of the earliest particle accelerators, cyclotrons are still used today, as the first stage in some hybrid accelerators and in some hospitals to accelerate particles used in the treatment of cancer.

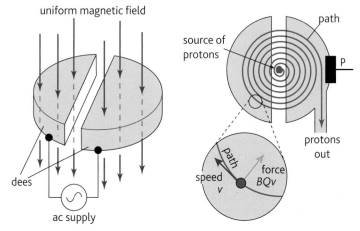

Figure 1 *The cyclotron*

Charged particles enter the accelerator with a small velocity at the centre of one of a pair of D-shaped electrodes called 'dees' because of their shape. The dees are enclosed in an evacuated chamber. A magnetic field is applied at right angles to the dees; this accelerates the charged particles in a semi-circular path until they reach the gap. An alternating voltage is applied to the dees; this produces an electric field which reverses every half cycle and always accelerates the charged particles across the gap between the dees. The frequency of the electric field must be precisely matched to the particle reaching the gap. The particles gain energy as they spiral around. As the particles travel faster they trace a larger arc meaning that they always take the same time to travel each semi-circle. This allows the voltage applied to the dees to be of a constant frequency.

Lawrence's first cyclotron was 12 cm in diameter and accelerated hydrogen ions to an energy of about 1 MeV. In the typical cyclotron, each particle may make up to 50 to 100 revolutions before reaching its final energy. By 1936 Lawrence had built a 1 m diameter cyclotron, which could accelerate deuterons (a particle consisting of a proton and a neutron), up to 8 MeV and alpha particles up to 16 MeV. This cyclotron was used to create radioisotopes including the first artificial element, technetium. In 1946 a 4.5 m cyclotron was completed at Berkeley. This was eventually converted into a **synchrotron.**

The cyclotron equation

As we have seen, charges inside a magnetic field obey the relationship $BQv = \dfrac{mv^2}{r}$, giving $r = \left|\dfrac{m}{QB}\right|v$ so the particles move in circles with radii proportional to their speed.

Ignoring the acceleration that takes place in the gap between the dees, the time taken for one orbit is:

$$T = \frac{2\pi r}{v} = \frac{2\pi}{v}\left(\frac{m}{QB}\right)v = \frac{2\pi m}{QB}$$

This means that the orbital frequency is $f_{cyclotron} = \frac{1}{T} = \frac{QB}{2\pi m}$ which does not depend upon the velocity of the particle. Similar particles (i.e. with equal charges to mass ratio) will all orbit with the same period regardless of their speed. High cyclotron frequencies require strong magnetic fields.

From the equation $BQv = \frac{mv^2}{r}$ we can see that the maximum speed as particles reach the outside of the dees is given by $v = \frac{QBr_{max}}{m}$ (where r_{max} is the radius of a dee) and therefore their maximum kinetic energy is:

$$\frac{1}{2}mv^2 = \frac{m}{2}\left(\frac{QBr_{max}}{m}\right)^2 = \frac{B^2 r_{max}^2 Q^2}{2m}$$

The problems with cyclotrons

We can see, from the kinetic-energy equation, that in order to obtain the maximum kinetic energy possible, the cyclotron should have as large a radius as possible and as large a magnetic field as possible. However, it is difficult to produce strong uniform magnetic fields acting over a large area. As explained above the cyclotron design means that all particles must orbit at the same frequency, whatever their speed. As particles approach the speed of light relativistic factors mean that their mass increases. Accelerating them becomes more difficult as a slower speed means that they lag behind the applied electric field.

Targets

Fast moving particles are used to probe the nuclei of atoms. Although electron beams can be used, protons have a much higher mass and are more common 'atom smashers'. The simplest target is liquid hydrogen which has the proton as its nucleus. Having a large number of essentially stationary protons gives a high probability of collision with a beam of protons and this can release an array of particles including other baryons, mesons and leptons. When two beams of protons are made to collide by travelling in opposite directions the total kinetic energy will be twice that of a single proton. Thus annihilation of a pair of colliding protons releases much more energy which results in the release of many particles. So in cyclotrons and synchrotrons, with modern focussing techniques, a multitude of particles can be produced to be studied by particle physicists.

How science works

Charged particles are detected by their ionisation of a gas or liquid through which they pass. A bubble chamber is filled with liquid hydrogen in which the particles leave a trail of ions as they pass through (see Figure 2). The array of tracks is produced by the particles originating from the collision of a single neutrino with a hydrogen atom in a bubble chamber – it is computer enhanced.

Figure 2 *Bubble chamber image of the effect of a single neutrino*

Summary questions

1 A 30 cm radius cyclotron has a magnetic field of about 0.5 T. Estimate the energy in MeV gained by accelerated protons.

2 Protons are accelerated in a cyclotron that has a magnetic field of 1.0 T. The maximum pd between the dees is 2.0 kV.

   a Explain why the protons move in a semi-circular path inside a single dee.

   b Calculate the time taken for a proton to make a semi circular path inside a dee.

   c Calculate the supply frequency.

   d Calculate the increase in kinetic energy gained by a proton in passing from one dee to the next.

   e Neglecting the input speed of the protons calculate the number of revolutions needed for the protons to gain a speed of 20 000 km s^{-1}

   Assume the proton mass $= 1.67 \times 10^{-27}$ kg and proton charge $= +1.60 \times 10^{-19}$ C.

7.6 From the first synchrotron to the LHC

Learning objectives:

- What is a synchrotron?
- Why develop the large hadron collider?

Specification reference: 3.5.2D

Synchrotrons

These accelerators use many of the concepts of the linac and cyclotron. The particles are accelerated through an evacuated chamber in a circular path of fixed radius using synchronised electric and magnetic fields that increase in strength as the particles get faster. As the particles move faster, in a magnetic field the radius would normally increase as this is given by

$r = \dfrac{mv}{BQ}$. Thus B must increase with v if r is to stay constant. Unlike in

the cyclotron the deflecting magnets in a synchrotron are situated along the beam path rather than over the whole area of the orbit. This means that the chamber can be much larger than is practicable with a cyclotron. The LEP (Large Electron Positron collider) at CERN (The European Organisation for Nuclear Research) was built in 1987 in a circular tunnel 27 km long and 100 m below ground and ultimately produced 105 GeV electron beams (see Figure 1). A high-frequency alternating voltage is applied between electrodes positioned round the ring; this accelerates the charged particles to high energies. The particles are initially injected into the ring with relatively high energy before having the energy boosted as they are accelerated by the electrodes (see Figure 2).

Figure 1 *The LEP/LHC tunnel under CERN*

Synchrotron radiation

One property of any accelerated charged particle is that it emits electromagnetic radiation; the charged particles in a synchrotron are accelerating when they are deflected in a circular path and therefore emit radiation. Synchrotron radiation is the electromagnetic radiation emitted when charged particles, moving at velocities close to the speed of light, are forced to change direction under the action of a magnetic field. The electromagnetic radiation is emitted in a narrow cone in the forward direction, at a tangent to the charged particle's orbit. This radiation

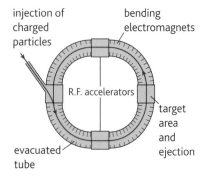

Figure 2 *The synchrotron*

(labels: injection of charged particles; bending electromagnets; R.F. accelerators; target area and ejection; evacuated tube)

is of very high intensity and it can be generated across the range of the electromagnetic spectrum, from infrared to X-rays. For electron synchrotrons, the maximum energy attained by the accelerated electrons is limited by the losses to synchrotron radiation which increases with the fourth power of the particle energy. The intense beams of synchrotron radiation have many uses, enabling scientists and engineers to investigate the structure of matter. This has led to scientific breakthroughs in the fields of biotechnology, medicine, environmental studies and material science. Such is the usefulness of synchrotron radiation that the UK Government (through the Science and Technology Facilities Council) and the Wellcome Trust jointly fund the synchrotron operated by Diamond Light Source Ltd. At the heart of the Diamond synchrotron is a 'storage ring'. Electrons are accelerated first by a linac and then a booster synchrotron before being transferred to the storage ring (see Figure 3). There are 22 straight sections coming off the accelerator; these are available for the insertion of experimental devices and are called 'beamlines'. The Diamond synchrotron produces X-rays a million times more intense than a hospital X-ray machine.

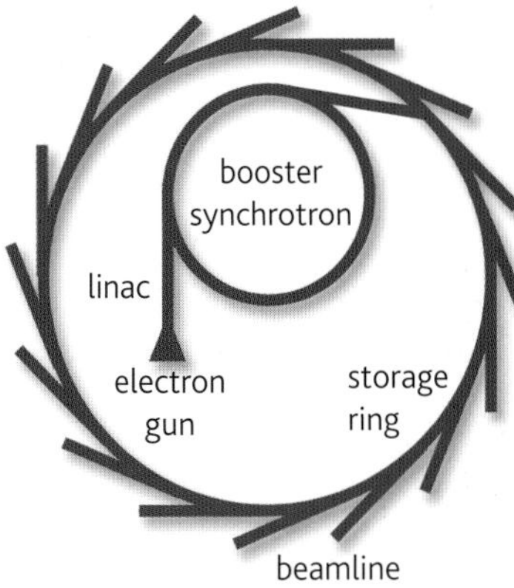

Figure 3 *The Diamond synchrotron*

■ The large hadron collider (LHC)

The LHC is a synchrotron and the world's largest particle accelerator. It operates by accelerating two beams of protons in opposite directions and then causing them to collide. By analysing the collisions, physicists are hoping to discover new particles and to answer some of the fundamental questions about matter. The LHC has been built in the underground tunnel previously occupied by LEP at CERN. Figure 4 shows the layout of the LHC and its feeder accelerators. Protons are initially accelerated along a linac followed by two smaller synchrotrons before they are fed into the LHC. Each beam of protons consists of 'bunches' or groups of protons. The reason for having bunches rather than a continuous beam is that it is not possible to accelerate a continuous beam using accelerating electrodes. The LHC is not quite circular. There are straight sections where radiofrequency (rf) cavities provide an electric field to accelerate the protons and where the four particle detectors (for the ATLAS, CMS, ALICE and LHC experiments) are located (see Figure 4). Protons are accelerated to a speed very close to the speed of light. This is done by the electric field in an rf cavity. The strength of the field in each cavity is $6\,MV\,m^{-1}$. The protons are held in place by the magnetic fields provided by superconducting magnets cooled to $-271°C$ (i.e., just $2\,K$ above absolute zero). 1232 'dipole' magnets, each $15\,m$ long, bend the proton beam while 392 'quadrupole' magnets, each $5–7\,m$ long, focus the beams.

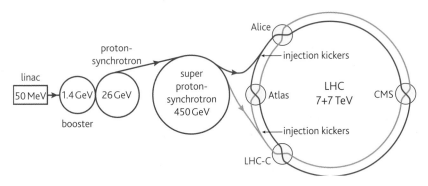

Figure 4 *LHC experiments*

Why has LEP been superseded by the LHC?

Data already gained from LEP's electron–positron collisions will be used to test aspects of the standard model (describing three of the four known fundamental interactions between the elementary particles that make up all matter). However, the small rest mass of the electron and subsequent energy losses due to synchrotron radiation means that the energy achievable from electron–positron collisions is too low to allow the production of some 'exotic' particles thought to exist. The LHC will allow scientists to penetrate still further into the structure of matter and recreate the conditions prevailing in the early universe, just after the Big Bang. By using more massive particles it is hoped that rare interactions can be achieved. It is hoped that the LHC could reveal the super-symmetric partners of ordinary matter particles and the Higgs particle – the link that may explain why particles have mass. In less than 100 years, the energy available to particle physicists has increased from 10 MeV in Rutherford's alpha scattering experiments to around 7 TeV with the LHC proton beams (a factor of nearly 10^6). This has meant that the known particles have increased from protons, electrons and implied neutrons to a huge number of already discovered particles.

■ The way forward

The production of synchrotron radiation is a limiting factor when accelerating electrons in a circular accelerator such as the cyclotron or synchrotron. However the low rest mass and availability of the electron makes it an ideal particle to accelerate in a linear accelerator. CERN has proposed a Compact Linear Collider (CLIC) which would use superconducting magnets and produce electron–positron collisions in the 3 TeV range. There has been consideration of the feasibility of a neutrino/muon factory by scientists at the Fermilab in the US. Under discussion is the feasibility and potential of high-energy, high-luminosity muon colliders operating in the range 100 GeV–4 TeV. The problem with muons is that, although they have a rest mass of some 200 times that of an electron, their half-life is around 2 μs. Although this would increase due to relativistic time dilation it means that storage of the beam, as in a synchrotron, would be very problematic. The muons decay into neutrinos but the intensity of the neutrino beam may prove to be too low to be viable for neutrino research. A working party at the Fermilab in 2001 produced a feasibility study of a VLHC (very large hadron collider) with a 233 km ring of circumference and beam energy 175 TeV! In January 2008 the host country for the international linear collider (ILC) (referred to in Topic 7.4) had not been determined. The ILC is considered as being of much lower energy than the LHC but will allow measurements to be made more accurately since a collision between an electron and a positron is much simpler than a collision between many quarks, anti-quarks and gluons that occur with proton-proton collisions. Hence the LHC and ILC are seen as being complementary accelerators.

Safety and energy in the LHC beam

Published in the journal *Proceedings of EPAC 2004, Lucerne, Switzerland* a document called the 'Interaction of the CERN Large Hadron Collider (LHC) Beam with Solid Metallic Targets' concludes that 'This paper presents two-dimensional numerical simulations of thermodynamic and hydrodynamic response of a solid copper target irradiated by one of the two LHC beams. It has been found that after about 2.5 µs when only 100 out of 2808 bunches [of protons] have delivered their energy to the target, the density at the centre of the beam heated region is substantially reduced due to the hydrodynamic expansion (about a factor 10 compared to the initial solid density). This implies that the bulk of the protons that will be delivered in the subsequent bunches will penetrate deeper into the target which means that the effective length of the material needed to stop the beam will be significantly longer than predicted by using static conditions. Preliminary estimations based on the simulations indicated that this length may be 10–40 m of solid copper.'

It is clearly much more cost effective to sacrifice huge blocks of copper than multi-million Euro technology!

Summary questions

1. Describe how a synchrotron differs from a cyclotron.

2. Explain the advantage of the LHC over its predecessor the LEP.

3. Perform an internet research to find uses of synchrotron radiation. Explain why this should be viewed as an additional benefit to particle acceleration and particle research.

1   The emission of electrons from a filament wire and their subsequent attraction towards a metal plate can produce a narrow beam of electrons (**Figure 1**).

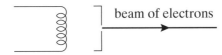

Figure 1

(a) Explain how an electric current through the filament wire can cause the wire to emit electrons. *(2 marks)*

(b) Explain why the filament wire and the metal plate must be in an evacuated tube *(3 marks)*

(c) The voltage between the filament wire and the plate is 3600 V.
    For each electron emerging through the hole in the plate, calculate

    (i) its kinetic energy in joules *(2 marks)*

    (ii) its speed *(2 marks)*

2   **Figure 2** shows a narrow beam of electrons entering a uniform electric field between two plates. The electrons travel initially parallel to the plates.

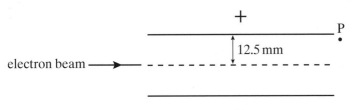

Figure 2

(a) Copy Figure 2 and sketch the path of the electrons whilst they are in the electric field and also when they have left it. *(4 marks)*

(b) The speed of the electrons is $3.6 \times 10^7 \, \text{m s}^{-1}$. The electric field is due to two oppositely charged parallel plates of length 60 mm.
    Calculate the time for which each electron is between the plates. *(2 marks)*

(c) The potential difference between the plates is adjusted to 1250 V so that the beam just emerges from the field at P without touching the positive plate. The plates are separated by a distance of 25 mm.
    Calculate the specific charge of the electron e/m_e. *(5 marks)*

3   π mesons, travelling in a straight line at a speed of $0.95c$, pass two detectors 34 m apart, as shown in **Figure 3**.

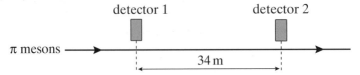

Figure 3

(a) Calculate the time taken, in the frame of reference of the detectors, for a π meson to travel between the two detectors. *(2 marks)*

(b) π mesons are unstable and decay with a half-life of 18 ns when at rest in the frame of the detectors. Show that approximately 75% of the π mesons passing the first detector decay before they reach the second detector. *(5 marks)*

4   An electron beam enters a uniform magnetic field and leaves after having been deflected through 90°, as shown in **Figure 4**.

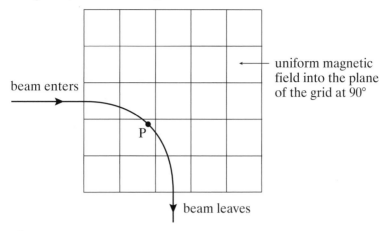

Figure 4

(a) State the direction of the force on an electron in the beam.   *(5 marks)*

(b) Explain why the kinetic energy of an electron in the beam is constant.   *(4 marks)*

(c) The squares on the diagram have sides of length 1 centimetre.

The electron beam was produced by means of an electron gun in which each electron was accelerated through a potential difference of 3.2 kV The magnetic flux density was 7.6 mT. Use these data and measurements from the diagram to determine the charge of the electron.   *(4 marks)*

5   **Figure 5** shows a narrow beam of electrons directed at right angles into a uniform electric field between two oppositely-charged parallel metal plates having a fixed potential difference across them.

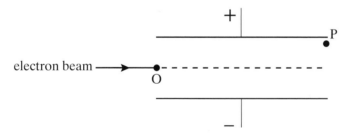

Figure 5

The electrons enter the field at O and leave it at P. A uniform magnetic field is applied into the plane of the diagram, perpendicular to the electric field and to the direction of the beam. The magnetic field reduces the deflection of the beam from its initial direction.

(a) Explain why the magnetic field has this effect on the beam.   *(2 marks)*

(b) The magnetic flux density is adjusted until the beam passes through the two fields without deflection.

Show that the speed v of the electrons when this occurs is given by

$$v = \frac{E}{B}$$

where E is the electric field strength and B is the magnetic flux density.   *(3 marks)*

6   **Figure 6** shows a diagram of parts of a mass spectrometer.

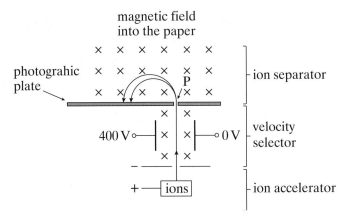

Figure 6

(a) Define the unit for magnetic flux density, the tesla. *(2 marks)*

(b) The magnetic field strength in the velocity selector is 0.14 T and the electric field strength is 20 000 V m^{-1}. Show that the velocity selected is about 140 km s^{-1}. *(4 marks)*

(c) A sample of nickel is analysed in the spectrometer. The two most abundant isotopes of nickel are $^{58}_{28}$Ni and $^{60}_{28}$Ni. Each ion carries a single charge of $+1.6 \times 10^{-19}$ C. The $^{58}_{28}$Ni ion strikes the photographic plate 0.28 m from the point **P** at which the ion beam enters the ion separator.

   (i) Calculate the magnetic flux density of the ion-separator field. *(4 marks)*

   (ii) Calculate the separation of the positions where the two isotopes hit the photographic plate. *(3 marks)*

7   **Figure 7** shows the plan view of a cyclotron in which protons are emitted in between the dees. The protons are deflected into a circular path by the application of a magnetic field. **Figure 7** shows a view from in front of the cyclotron.

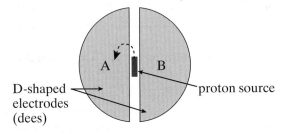

Figure 7

(a) State the direction of the magnetic field in the region of the dees such that it will deflect the proton beam in the direction shown. *(1 mark)*

(b) (i) Show that the velocity of the proton, v, at some instant is given by:
$$v = \frac{Ber}{m}$$
where m is the proton mass, r the radius of its circular path, B the magnetic flux density acting on the proton and $+e$ the proton charge. *(2 marks)*

   (ii) Write down an equation for the time T for a proton to make a complete circular path in this magnetic field. *(2 marks)*

   (iii) Explain how your equation leads to the conclusion that T is independent of the speed with which the proton is moving. *(2 marks)*

(c) In addition to this magnetic field there is an electric field provided between the dees. This accelerates the proton towards whichever dee is negatively charged. An alternating potential difference causes each dee to become alternately negative and then positive. This causes the proton to accelerate each time it crosses the gap between the dees.

(i)   Describe and explain the effect the acceleration has on the path in which the proton moves. *(3 marks)*

(ii) In terms of T, write down the frequency with which the p.d. must alternate to match the period of motion of the proton. *(1 mark)*

8   **Figure 8** shows a proton synchrotron in which protons are accelerated to high speeds in a horizontal circular path.

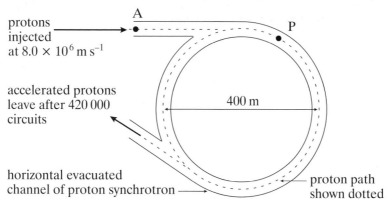

protons injected at $8.0 \times 10^6 \, \text{m s}^{-1}$

A

P

accelerated protons leave after 420 000 circuits

400 m

horizontal evacuated channel of proton synchrotron

proton path shown dotted

Figure 8

Protons of mass $1.7 \times 10^{-27} \, \text{kg}$ are injected at point **A** with a speed of $8.0 \times 10^6 \, \text{m s}^{-1}$. The diameter of the path taken by the protons is 400 m.

(a)   Calculate the force that has to be provided to produce the circular path when the speed of a proton is $8.0 \times 10^6 \, \text{m s}^{-1}$. *(3 marks)*

(b)   Sketch a graph to show how this force will have to change as the speed of the proton increases over the range 0 to $2 \times 10^7 \, \text{m s}^{-1}$. Give appropriate scales on both axes. *(3 marks)*

(c)   (i)   Before reaching their final energy the protons in the synchrotron in part (b) travel around the accelerator 420 000 times in 2.0 s.

            Calculate the total distance travelled by a proton in the 2.0 s time interval. *(3 marks)*

      (ii) Unless a vertical force is applied the protons would fall as they move through the horizontal channel.

            Calculate the vertical distance through which a proton falls in the 2.0 s time interval. *(2 marks)*

      (iii) Determine the force necessary to prevent the vertical movement. *(2 marks)*

9   A narrow beam of protons and positrons travelling at the same speed enters a uniform magnetic field. The path of the positrons through the field in the plane of the paper is shown in **Figure 9**.

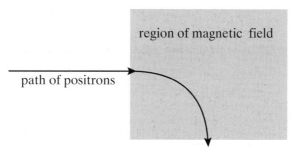

region of magnetic field

path of positrons

Figure 9

(a)   State the direction of the uniform magnetic field. *(2 marks)*

(b)   Copy Figure 9 and sketch on it the path that you would expect the protons to take *(2 marks)*

(c)   Explain why the protons take a different path. *(3 marks)*

Nuclear radiation and its uses

8.1 Radiated energy

Learning objectives:

■ What types of radiation come from the nucleus?

■ What is the effect on the nucleus when the radiation is emitted?

■ What are the important characteristics of nuclear radiation?

Specification reference: 3.5.3A

Figure 1 *Marie Curie*
Marie Curie established the nature of radioactive materials. She showed how radioactive compounds could be separated and identified. She and her husband Pierre won the 1903 Nobel Prize for their discovery of two new elements, polonium and radium. After Pierre's death in 1906 she continued her painstaking research and was awarded a second Nobel Prize in 1911 – an unprecedented honour.

■ Nuclear radiation?

The discovery of radiation from the atom by Becquerel and the work of Marie Curie and other scientists was initially of academic interest in understanding the nature of the world we live in but, as with many other discoveries, the properties of the radiation soon led to applications in engineering and medicine. The dangers as well as the uses became apparent in early research. Medical physicists now deal not only with the use of radiation for diagnostic and therapeutic purposes but also in monitoring the radiation in the environment and monitoring food to confirm that it is safe to consume.

Radiation medicine

In the treatment of cancer, malignant cells are severely damaged by radiation so that they cannot reproduce themselves and eventually they die. Normal tissue that is irradiated during treatment is also damaged but these cells are able to repair the damage when treatment ceases.

In order to understand how and why radiation is used together with its associated dangers, it is necessary to know both where the radiation comes from and what its properties are. To select the appropriate **nuclide** for a particular purpose it is necessary to know:

■ the types of radiation the nuclide emits

■ the ability of the different types of radiation to penetrate matter

■ the effect of the different types of radiation on the material it passes through

■ the rate of decay of the source (referred to as the **activity** of the source).

■ Radiations and their effect on the nucleus

Types of nuclear radiation

Alpha-particle scattering experiments showed the structure of the atom to be a small, positively-charged nucleus surrounded by negatively-charged electrons. Further experiments showed that the nucleus of an atom consists of protons and neutrons. A neutral atom has the same number of electrons surrounding the nucleus as there are protons in the nucleus.

When considering the use of radioactive sources for medical applications remember that the body uses the atoms in chemical processes. Nuclides with the same proton number (**isotopes**) may be stable or radioactive depending on the number of neutrons that the nucleus contains. However, the chemical behaviour of the atoms is identical for the stable and unstable isotopes of the element. The body will therefore use the radioactive isotopes in the same way as the stable ones. Some radio-nuclides are inserted in sealed capsules while others are selected so that when injected they will go to the appropriate part of the body for treatment to be effective.

For example, iodine-131, in the form of iodine chloride, is used in the treatment of thyroid carcinoma (cancer). This can be taken orally and the natural bodily function takes the iodine to the thyroid where the radiation can treat the disease.

In radioactive decay the unstable nucleus (called the parent) decays spontaneously, that is without any outside influence, into a more stable nucleus (called the daughter). Energy is released in the process. When particles are emitted the number of protons or neutrons in an unstable nucleus is changed producing a more stable structure.

A naturally occurring radionuclide may decay by emitting an alpha (α) or a negative beta (β^-) particle and gamma (γ) radiation.

- An α particle is a stable helium nucleus $^4_2\alpha$ or ^4_2He so its charge is $+2e$ ($3.2 \times 10^{-19}\text{C}$)
- A β^- particle is a fast moving electron ($^0_{-1}\text{e}$ or $^0_{-1}\beta$) with charge $-1.6 \times 10^{-19}\text{C}$. This emission is accompanied by the emission of an antineutrino $^0_0\overline{\nu}_\text{e}$.
- Gamma radiation is a photon (hf) of electromagnetic radiation. This usually occurs following the emission of an α or β^- particle.

Some artificially produced radio-nuclides may also decay by the emission of a positron ($^0_{+1}\text{e}$ or $^0_{+1}\beta$) and a neutrino $^0_0\nu$.

The energy released by the nucleus appears as kinetic energy of the particles formed as a result of the decay or as the energy of an emitted gamma-ray photon. Some of the energy becomes kinetic energy of the daughter nucleus as it recoils to conserve momentum.

Figure 2 *Recoil of nucleus in alpha and beta decay*

The charge on the radiation can be identified by applying a magnetic field perpendicular to its direction of travel. As shown in Figure 3, for a given field direction the α and β^- radiations deflect in opposite directions and this is consistent with the signs of their charges. Gamma-ray photons are unaffected by a magnetic field. However, note that Figure 3 is simply a diagrammatic representation. In a field with the same magnetic flux density a β^- particle might bend into a path with very small radius and an alpha particle with a mass almost 8000 times larger would hardly deflect at all.

Alpha decay

When an alpha particle is emitted by a nucleus the Z number decreases by 2 and the A number decreases by 4:

$$^A_Z\text{X} \longrightarrow \; ^{A-4}_{Z-2}\text{Y} + ^4_2\alpha$$

Alpha particles are particularly damaging so they are rarely used for therapy. Americium-241 emits 5.5 MeV alpha particles and this is used in smoke detectors that are now commonplace in homes and public places.

Link

The basic ideas of atomic and nuclear structure were studied in Topic 3.3 of the AS book. Recall that:

- a nuclide of an element X is represented as ^A_ZX where X is the symbol for the element; H, He, Li,...C, U, etc.
- Z is the proton number; the nucleus contains Z protons.
- A is the nucleon number (sometimes called the mass number); the nucleus contains A nucleons.
- a neutral atom contains Z electrons (number of protons = number of electrons).
- there are (A – Z) neutrons in the nucleus.

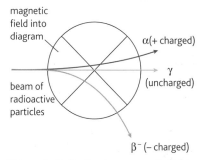

Figure 3 *Deflection by a magnetic field*

AQA Examiner's tip

The electron volt, eV, is a unit of energy.

1 eV is 1.6×10^{-19} J

1 MeV is 1.6×10^{-13} J

To ionise a hydrogen atom requires 13.6 eV.

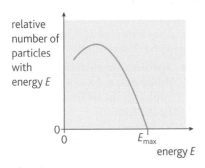

Figure 4 *Beta particle spectrum*

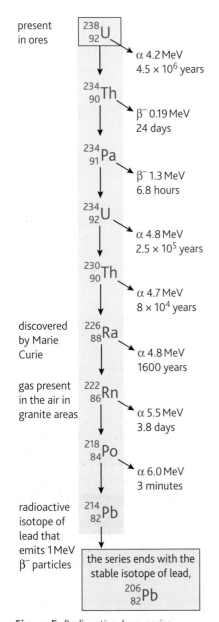

Figure 5 *Radioactive decay series*

Beta decay

The β⁻ particle is a fast moving electron $_{-1}^{0}$e or $_{-1}^{0}$β.

When a β⁻ particle is emitted a neutron effectively becomes a proton so the Z number increases by 1 and the A number remains the same. An anti-neutrino is emitted at the same time as the β⁻ particle:

$$_{Z}^{A}X \longrightarrow \ _{Z+1}^{A}Y + \ _{-1}^{0}\beta + \bar{\nu}_{e}$$

Strontium-89 $(_{38}^{89}Sr)$ emits 1.5 MeV β⁻ particles and is injected to relieve pain in patients suffering from bone cancer. In this decay the result of the decay is stable nuclide yttrium-89$(_{39}^{89}Y)$ The energy emitted is the same in each decay but the β⁻ particles have a range of energies (see Figure 4) from almost zero to the maximum available. The remaining energy is taken up by the antineutrino.

Gamma decay

Gamma radiation is short-wavelength electromagnetic radiation $(\approx 1 \times 10^{-11}\,\text{m})$. The photons have a high energy given by $\frac{hc}{\lambda}(\approx 2 \times 10^{-14}\,\text{J})$. A gamma-ray photon is emitted when the nucleus is in an **excited state** following the emission of an α or β⁻ particle.

The intense gamma rays that follow the β⁻ emission from cobalt-60 are used in the treatment of cancer. Gamma radiation is also used to kill bacteria in food and to sterilise equipment in hospitals.

Radioactive decay series

Radioactive nuclides that occur naturally occur in one of four radioactive decay series. Each one starts with a different nuclide at the head of the series and this defines the whole series. The names given to the series are the 'thorium' series $(_{90}^{232}Th)$; the 'neptunium' series $_{93}^{237}Np$; the 'uranium' series $_{92}^{238}U$ and the 'actinium' series $(_{92}^{235}U)$.

Figure 5 shows most of the nuclides in a series decay starting with U-238 together with the **half-lives** of the nuclide and the radiation energies.

Summary questions

1. How many protons and neutrons are there in a nucleus of $_{93}^{237}Np$?

2. $_{11}^{21}Na$ is produced artificially and decays by positron emission. What are the proton number and nucleon numbers of the resulting nucleus? State the name of the other particle emitted in the decay.

3. How many α and β⁻ particles would be emitted by $_{82}^{214}Pb$ before reaching the stable form $_{82}^{206}Pb$?

4. An α particle has a mass of 6.8×10^{-27} kg. Calculate the energy in J and the speed of a 5 MeV α particle.

8.2 Radiation through matter

Learning objectives:

■ What is meant by ionising radiation?

■ What are the typical ranges of α, β and γ radiation?

■ What is meant by the inverse-square law for gamma radiation?

■ How do the penetrative properties affect safety precautions?

Specification reference: 3.5.3A

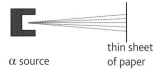

α source   thin sheet of paper

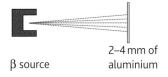

β source   2–4 mm of aluminium

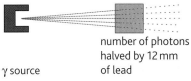

number of photons halved by 12 mm of lead

γ source

Figure 1 *Penetration of α, β and γ radiation*

■ Ionising and penetrating properties

Ionising radiation travels between atoms in solids, liquids and gases but when it interacts with an atom it removes an electron from the atom and loses some or all of its original energy. This process is called **ionisation**. How far the radiation travels through matter depends on how quickly it loses its energy. In a vacuum all the radiations have unlimited range. As they travel through matter collisions occur with the atoms and these are more likely in denser materials. This means that the range is greater in gases than in liquids or solids where atoms are more densely packed.

Alpha particles are stopped completely by a thin sheet of paper and travel only about 4–5 cm in air at normal atmospheric pressure. This is because alpha particles interact easily with matter. Beta particles are stopped by a sheet of aluminium a few millimetres thick. The most energetic travel about 0.5 m in air. Gamma radiation interacts poorly with atoms and the intensity is never completely reduced to zero as it travels through matter. The intensity is, however, halved by a centimetre or so of lead.

Alpha particles

To remove an electron from a typical air molecule (usually nitrogen or oxygen but sometimes traces of other gases) requires about 28 eV. A 5 MeV alpha particle can produce about 180 000 ions as it passes through air. At normal atmospheric pressures these ions are produced in a distance of about 5 cm. This is therefore the range of the alpha particle as it has no more kinetic energy and stops moving. The alpha particle finally combines with stray electrons in the air to form helium.

In denser material the alpha particle collides more often with atoms so its range is less. Even a thin sheet of paper stops the alpha particles and alpha particles cannot therefore penetrate the skin. Alpha particles are particularly dangerous though as they cause considerable localised damage if ingested into the body. Swallowing an alpha emitter or breathing in an alpha emitter in the form of a gas is likely to be fatal.

Beta particles

Beta particles are smaller and collide less often with atoms so in a given material a negative beta (β⁻) particle with similar energy travels much further than an alpha particle. In air, a β⁻ particle can have a range of up to 0.5 m but can be stopped by a thin sheet of aluminium. When beta particles interact with atoms some of the energy becomes gamma radiation. As a result the intensity of the radiation from a beta source does not drop to zero when the beta particles have been stopped (see Figure 3 below).

Figure 2 shows an arrangement for investigating the absorption properties of radiation. The Geiger–Müller (G–M) tube and scaler counter records a count rate that is proportional to the intensity of

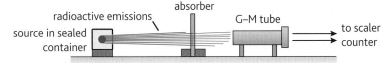

Figure 2 *Investigating absorption*

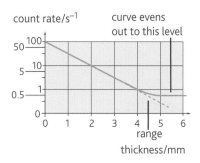

count rate/s^{-1}

curve evens out to this level

range

thickness/mm

Figure 3 *Absorption curve for β particles*

the radiation. Figure 3 shows typical results for the variation of count rate with thickness for aluminium for 2.5 MeV beta radiation (note the logarithmic count rate scale). The higher the energy of the beta particle the greater the range.

The intensity due to a source of positrons (β$^+$) falls more rapidly than that of a source emitting β$^-$ particles with similar energy. As well as causing ionisation the positrons can be annihilated when they interact with electrons that orbit the nuclei of the absorbing material.

Gamma radiation

Gamma rays are highly penetrating and the energy they possess is high so when they interact their effect is very damaging to cells in the body. Gamma rays may lose energy by ionising atoms or by other processes. The absorption processes results in the intensity falling exponentially with distance (x) travelled through an absorbing medium.

$$I = I_0 e^{-\mu x}$$

In exponential changes, the dependent variable falls by a constant fraction when the independent variable changes by a given amount. In this case, the intensity falls by the same fraction for a given change in distance. So the **intensity** will always halve when it passes through a particular thickness of absorber (not surprisingly called the **half-thickness**). The value of μ and hence the half-thickness depends on the absorber and the photon energy. Dense metals like lead result in low values of half-thickness and higher photon energies give rise to greater half thicknesses.

Background radiation

Background radiation comes from many sources. Figure 4 shows the relative amounts of radiation from different sources that forms the

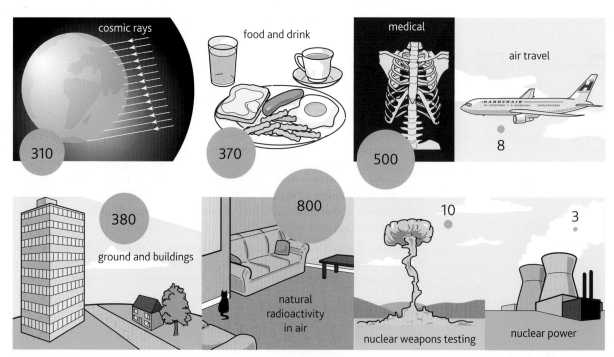

Figure 4 *Sources of background radiation in the UK. The numbers in the circles show the relative number of units emitted per year by the source.*

background radiation in the UK. Some may come from ores that contain elements such as uranium and some from radon gas formed by the decay of radioactive elements in the ores. Radioactive carbon (carbon-14) is formed in the atmosphere by cosmic radiation so all things that contain carbon, including ourselves, are radioactive. Some radiation may arise due to fall-out from testing of atomic weapons and from nuclear disasters. For safety reasons the background radiation should be continually monitored especially in a working environment so that the cause of any sudden increase can be investigated. A typical count rate using a G–M tube in the laboratory may be about 20 counts per minute but this depends on the location. In experimental work, the background count rate has to be deducted from the count rate caused by radiation sources used in the experiment. This is particularly important when low count rates are involved.

▮ Inverse-square law for gamma radiation

Over short distances in air the total number of gamma-ray photons in the radiation from a source does not change significantly. This means that, as with a point light source, the intensity varies approximately according to an inverse-square law.

A radioactive source is a small 'point' source and will emit N gamma ray photons per second uniformly in all directions. The gamma ray intensity is the number of gamma ray photons per second per square metre. At a distance r from the source the N photons will be spread over an area $4\pi r^2$ so the intensity is $\dfrac{N}{4\pi r^2}$.

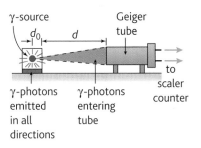

The count rate C recorded by a radiation detector is proportional to the number of photons passing through the detector. This means that the count rate also varies with r and is given by $C = \dfrac{C_0}{4\pi r^2}$ where C_0 is a constant for the source.

Practically the distance r cannot be determined directly. It is not possible to identify exactly where the source is due to its protective container nor where the actual detection point of the radiation is as this can be anywhere in the Geiger tube. i.e. there is a systematic error d_0, which has to be added to the measurement made, shown as d in Figure 5. The equation for the variation of count rate will be

$C = \dfrac{k}{(d + d_0)^2}$ (where k is a constant)

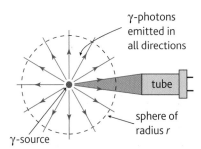

Figure 5 *Investigating the inverse-square law*

Rearranging this leads to $d = \dfrac{\sqrt{k}}{\sqrt{C}} - d_0$. A graph of d against $\dfrac{1}{\sqrt{C}}$ should therefore be a straight line if the inverse square law is obeyed. The gradient of the graph will be $\sqrt{k}$ and the intercept on the d axis will be d_0.

▮ **Summary questions**

1 How many ions could a 1.5 MeV alpha particle produce when passing through hydrogen which has an ionisation energy of 13.6 eV?

2 Explain why the variation of count rate with distance for alpha and beta particles do not obey an inverse square law.

3 A detector which is 5.0 cm from a gamma ray source records a count rate of 80 s⁻¹. What would the count rate change to at a distance of 12 cm from the source?

8.3 Radioactive decay rate

Learning objectives:

▪ What is meant by activity?

▪ What is the relationship between decay constant and half-life?

▪ How does activity change with time?

Specification reference: 3.5.3A

▪ Radiation dose

A patient undergoing radiation treatment has to receive an appropriate dose of radiation. Too little and the treatment will be ineffective, too much and the radiation will do more harm than good. The dose of radiation depends on the effect of the radiation on tissue. This depends on the ionising effect of the radiation which is different for alpha, beta and gamma radiation and the rate at which the source is emitting the radiation. The dose received therefore depends on the nuclide used and the number of radioactive nuclei that decay each second.

Activity and decay constant

The **activity** (A) of a radioactive nuclide is the number of nuclear disintegrations of the nuclei that take place each second. The unit of activity is the **becquerel** (Bq). One becquerel is one nuclear disintegration per second.

The activity of a particular nuclide depends on:

▪ the number of radioactive nuclei, N

▪ the probability of decay of a nucleus in a 1 s time interval.

When a die (a single dice) is thrown the probability of it showing a '6' is 1 in 6 so if one die is thrown 60 times it is likely to show a '6' on 10 throws, a 1 on 10 throws, etc.

If a large number (N) of six-sided dice is thrown it is impossible to tell which will show a '6'. However, $\frac{1}{6}N$ should show a 6. With a small number of dice the number will vary from this theoretical value but the more dice that are thrown, the more likely this will happen.

The same thing occurs with radioactive nuclei. The nuclei decay randomly. For a given nuclide, each nucleus has the same chance of decaying in a 1 s time interval. The likelihood of an atom decaying is not influenced by changes in physical conditions, such as temperature and pressure, or when it is combined with other atoms in a chemical compound.

For a nuclide, the probability of it changing by radioactive decay is the **decay constant** λ (unit s^{-1}). The decay constants vary widely. A very short-lived isotope might have a decay constant of perhaps $0.5\,\text{s}^{-1}$. The commonly used nuclide, iodine-131, has a decay constant of $9.9 \times 10^{-7}\,\text{s}^{-1}$ compared with $3.1 \times 10^{-14}\,\text{s}^{-1}$ for a long-lived source such as uranium-235.

In a similar way to the dice, if the probability of decay is λ then λN should decay each second.

The **activity** is the number of particles emitted per second and is therefore given by:

$$A = \lambda N$$

Although there are a very large number of nuclei present in even a small sample of a radioactive nuclide, the randomness of the decay means that the activity will most likely differ from this theoretical value. In any given second, either more or fewer of the radioactive atoms will disintegrate than expected so the actual count rate recorded may be higher or lower than the theoretical value.

▪ How science works

Total activity

Because a nuclide is usually part of a decay series the total activity of a radioactive source is not due to one nuclide alone. The activity is the sum of the activities of all the nuclides present in the source which may be emitting all three types of radiation.

This random variation is superimposed on the general trend of changes that are taking place. The statistical variation means that the uncertainty in a measurement in which the recorded count is C is $\pm\sqrt{C}$. If the count is 100 the uncertainty is ±10 (i.e. 10%). If the count is 1000 the uncertainty is ±32 (i.e. 3.2%). This illustrates how data can be improved by making a measurement taken over a longer period of time when possible. When count rates are being recorded the higher count rates will be more reliable than the lower ones.

Calculating mass from number of nuclei

The **mole** (symbol mol) is the measure of the amount of a substance.

1 mol of a nuclide contains 6.02×10^{23} atoms. This number is the **Avogadro constant N_A**.

Just as one can talk of 5 dozen eggs meaning 60 eggs, so one can talk of 5 mol of carbon-12 to meaning 30.1×10^{23} atoms of carbon-14. It is a convenient unit to use when referring to the very large numbers of atoms involved.

So what mass of carbon-12 contains 6.02×10^{23} atoms? The answer is 12 g as this is how the mole was defined. For other nuclei it is the mass that has an equivalent number of atoms to 12 g of carbon. To a reasonable accuracy this is the nucleon number expressed in g.

For iodine-131, 6.02×10^{23} atoms have a mass of 131 g (strictly 130.9)

So 2.0×10^{14} atoms of iodine-131 have a mass of $\dfrac{2 \times 10^{14}}{6.02 \times 10^{23}} \times 131$ $= 43 \times 10^{-9}$ g.

The total activity of a source depends on the activity of all the radioactive nuclei in it. There may be more than one nuclide present.

Given the particular dangers involved in radiation, correct handling of powers of 10 in such calculations of dose is vitally important.

▪ Application and How science works

Exponential changes

The mathematical equation for the effect of the decay on the source is $\dfrac{dN}{dt} = -\lambda N$.

This equation shows the rate of decrease of the radioactive atoms is proportional to the number of radioactive atoms present. Equations in which the rate of change of a quantity is proportional to how much of that quantity there is result in an exponential change. The minus sign signifies that the number of radioactive nuclei is decreasing with time and this leads to an exponential decay. (See also capacitors in Topic 8.6 where the rate of change of charge is proportional to the charge present.)

Changes in radioactive decay rate

The decay of a radioactive material is exponential. How does this arise?

Suppose a source starts with 10 000 radioactive atoms and has a decay constant of $0.1\,\text{s}^{-1}$.

▪ Hint

When designing a radioactivity experiment, try to vary the time for the count as the count rate changes so that there are roughly the same number of counts recorded each time. In this way, the uncertainty in each count rate will be approximately the same.

AQA Examiner's tip

Take care not to confuse count rate with activity. Activity is a property of the source and is measured in Bq. Count rate depends on the source and the detecting equipment and is measured in counts per second, written as s^{-1}.

Count rate is the number of particles or photons of radiation that are detected by a counter such as a solid state detector or Geiger–Müller tube each second. This value depends on the size of the detector and its efficiency at detecting the particles. Some particles emitted by the source are never counted because they miss the detector. Others are absorbed by the source or the medium between the source and the detector. Some gamma-ray photons pass through without causing ionisation in the detector and some that cause ionisation in the detector are not recorded because the detector is inactive for a short period after it has detected a particle (called the 'dead time').

In the first second 1000 atoms will decay leaving 9000 radioactive atoms. In the next second 900 will decay leaving 8100 radioactive atoms. The table shows how the decay progresses. The table shows that the number of radioactive atoms remaining will halve sometime between 5 and 6 s.

time t/s	number of radioactive atoms after time t/N	number decaying per second/A	number left
0	10000	1000	9000
1	9000	900	8100
2	8100	810	7290
3	7290	729	6561
4	6561	656	5905
5	5905	591	5314
6	5314	531	4783
7	4783	478	4305
etc	etc	etc	etc

The graph in Figure 1 shows the variation of N with t. The gradient of the graph is the rate of decay and can be seen to decrease as the number of radioactive nuclei decreases.

An important feature of any exponential change is that the time-dependent variable always takes the same time to undergo the same fractional change. In Figure 1 the change from 10000 to 8000 is a fall of 20%. A 20% change from 8000–6400 always takes the same time. In particular, the time-dependent variable always halves in the same time.

The **half-life** of a radioactive nuclide is the time taken for the number of radioactive nuclei of that nuclide to halve.

The half-life is related to the decay constant by the equation

$$T_{\frac{1}{2}} = \frac{\ln 2}{\lambda} = \frac{0.69}{\lambda}$$

In the above example the half-life is $0.69/0.1 = 6.9$ s. The value of 5–6 s suggested by the data in the table is too low because in each second the activity is falling so the actual number decaying is lower that that given in the third column. Try producing a similar table using time intervals of 0.5 s and plotting the data. The half-life should be closer to 6.9 s.

Tables usually give the half-lives of radionuclides rather that the decay constant. The half-life of iodine-131 is 8.1 days $\left(= \frac{0.69}{9.9 \times 10^{-7}} \text{s}\right)$

Since the number of radioactive atoms remaining is proportional to the activity and also to the mass, these also take the same time to halve. The A–t graph and the m–t graphs have the same shape as the N–t graph.

Decay equation

The number (N) of radioactive nuclei of a given nuclide at a given time t is found from:

$$N = N_0 e^{-\lambda t}$$

where N_0 is the number of radioactive nuclei at time $t = 0$ and λ is the decay constant.

Since A is proportional to N, the activity due to that nuclide is $A = A_0 e^{-\lambda t}$.

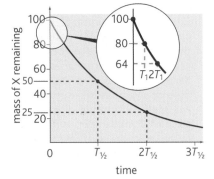

Figure 1 *Radioactive decay curve*

This equation can be used to find how long it will take for activity to fall to a given value, or to find the activity after a given time.

Suppose a source of iodine has an initial activity of 300 MBq. When will the iodine activity be 200 MBq?

$$200 = 300e^{-9.9 \times 10^{-7}t} \longrightarrow \frac{200}{300} = e^{-9.9 \times 10^{-7}t}$$

$$\longrightarrow \ln 0.667 = -9.9 \times 10^{-7}t \longrightarrow t = 4.09 \times 10^5 \text{ s}$$

So the 200 MBq activity is reached after 4.09×10^5 s (4.7 days).

Measuring half-life

Figure 2 shows apparatus that can be used to measure the half-life of protactinium-234 ($^{234}_{91}$Pa).

The thin polythene bottle contains a solution of a uranium salt in the lower layer. The upper layer is an organic solvent. Thorium-234 is one of the isotopes formed in the decay series of the uranium and this decays to protactinium-234. The bottle is shaken to mix up the chemicals and, when the layers separate again, the Pa-234 remains in the solvent layer. The G–M tube placed close to the solvent layer in the bottle detects the beta radiation from the decay of protactinium. The count rate is measured at regular intervals and the half-life (about 72 s) calculated.

Figure 3 shows a typical curve of count rate C (corrected for background count) against time from which the half-life can be found.

The scatter of the points around the line of best fit occurs because of the random nature of radioactive decay. Although there is an expected count rate based on the probability of decay, the count rate may be higher or lower. Statistically there is a greater uncertainty when the count rate is low, which is usually the case in this experiment.

An alternative way of treating the data is to plot a graph of ln(count rate) against time, as shown in Figure 4.

The equation for count rate, $C = C_0 e^{-\lambda t}$, can be written in the form $\ln C = \ln C_0 - \lambda t$. Therefore a graph of $\ln C$ against t gives a straight line of gradient $-\lambda$. Using this approach it is easier to account for the random nature of the decay because it is easier to draw a line of best fit for a linear graph than for a curve.

Effect of background radiation

Because of the low count rates involved it is essential to account for this by determining the mean background count rate and subtracting this from the measured count rates made during the experiment. If the background count is not taken into account all the values will be too high and the half-life obtained would be higher than the correct value.

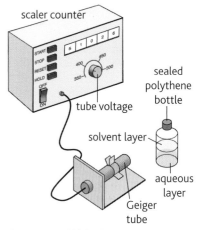

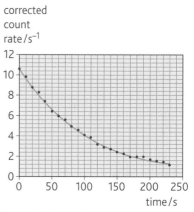

Figure 2 *Half-life of protactinium*

Figure 3 *Decay of protactinium*

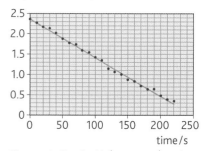

Figure 4 *Graph of ln(count rate) against time*

Summary questions

1 The half-life of plutonium-239 is 2.4×10^4 years. Calculate its decay constant.

2 The decay constant of phosphorus-32 is 3.9×10^{-7} s^{-1}.

   i How many atoms of phosphorus-32 will produce an activity of 1.5×10^7 Bq?

   ii What will be the mass of the phosphorus-32 with this activity?

3 In the experiment to determine the half-life of protactinium, explain why the bottle is made of thin polythene rather than glass and why the G–M tube is placed close to the bottle.

4 Strontium-90 has a half-life of 28 years. How long would it take for the activity of strontium-90 produced in a nuclear reactor to fall to 1% of its initial activity?

8.4 Radiation in medicine

Learning objectives:

- What uses are made of radioisotopes in medicine?

- How are radioisotopes for medical use produced?

- What is meant by biological half-life?

Specification reference: 3.5.3A

The isotopes used in medicine have relatively short half-lives which affects where and how they are produced. Some are made in nuclear reactors and some by using particle accelerators. They are then transported to hospitals as required. If the transport distance is large they may lose a significant amount of their activity before they are delivered and this has to be accounted for when determining the patient dose. Alternatively, some isotopes are produced in 'generators' on site. In this case the radioactive nuclide is extracted from the generator as it is needed. Larger hospitals may have their own small cyclotrons.

The type of radiation emitted and the decay constant are both properties of the nucleus and these are unchanged when the atom is attached to other atoms or molecules. The radioactive nuclide is attached to molecules that are used by the body in known ways. For example, iodine is used almost exclusively in the thyroid gland and radioactive iodine-131 has been used for many years to investigate whether the thyroid gland is functioning correctly.

PET scanners

PET stands for positron emission tomography. The positron emitter commonly used is fluorine-18 with a half-life of 110 minutes. Carbon-11 and nitrogen-13 are also used but as they have half-lives of only about 10 minutes these have to be manufactured on site. The fluorine atoms are attached to glucose which the body uses to continually replenish cells in the body.

PET imaging depends on the annihilation of the positrons with their antiparticle, the electron. By analysing the gamma rays that are emitted the detectors can identify the points of origin of the gamma ray pairs and build up a three-dimensional image of the body.

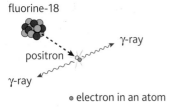

Figure 1 *Electron–positron annihilation*

The fluorine-18 is produced in cyclotrons that accelerate particles to between 10 and 20 MeV. Because of the short half-life of the nuclide the cyclotrons have to be on sites close to the hospitals where the isotopes are needed.

The change in activity of the source has to be accounted for. The activity is measured in activity per unit volume. Suppose a volume V of a particular sample labelled with fluorine-18 is needed at a particular time. If the scan were delayed by 110 min then twice the volume would have to be administered to give the same initial activity. Such calculations are important to ensure that the dose given is suitable to form the images and to ensure that the patient is not given more radiation than necessary.

Technetium-99m

This is the most commonly used radioactive isotope in medical applications. Tc-99m is the daughter of the decay of molybdenum-99 which has a half-life of about 67 hours. The molybdenum-99 is produced in the fission of uranium-235 in nuclear reactors. After processing it is transported to hospitals where it is stored and the Tc-99m is extracted from the 'Tc-99m generators' when it is needed. As the half-life is almost 3 days the activity of the molybdenum falls to about 25% of its original activity in a week, after which it has to be renewed.

In the generators the radioactive molybdenum is in the form of MoO_4 ions and as the molybdenum nuclei decay $^{99m}TcO_4$ ions are formed. The technetium-99m oxide is removed from the generator by passing salt solution through it.

Tc-99m emits $140\,keV$ gamma radiation which is a relatively low energy for gamma radiation. The radiation is less likely to produce damaging ionisation in a patient than gamma radiation of higher energies but it can still be easily monitored by detectors outside the body. The 'm' signifies that the isotope is **metastable.** This means that the nucleus remains in an excited state for a longer period than is usual for gamma emitters, 6 hours rather than a few seconds, which is fairly common. After it has emitted the gamma radiation it becomes Tc-99 which emits low energy beta radiation with a very long half-life $(2 \times 10^5\,\text{years})$. This again means that a patient receives only a low dose during investigations.

The Tc-99m is used for gamma ray scanning, producing images of the body, and also as a tracer for investigating the function of different organs in the body including the brain, bone marrow and heart.

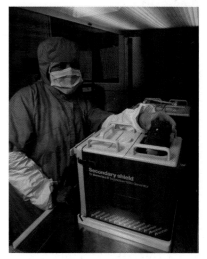

Figure 2 *A technetium generator*

Biological half-life

The activity of a source injected into a patient does not remain the same. In order to determine the correct dose it is necessary to know:

- How long the radioactive nuclide will remain in the patient,
- The way the activity of the source varies with time.

Radioactive substances like other elements will gradually be excreted from the body in urine and by perspiration. The time taken for half of the atoms of an element to be lost by the body is the **biological half-life**.

The activity measured after a time t will therefore be lower than if no radioactive material is lost. Consider a simple (unlikely) case where the biological and physical half-life of the source are the same. After one half-life half the original number of atoms would have left the body. Of those that did not leave half would have decayed inside the body so the activity remaining would be $\frac{1}{4}$ the original activity.

The calculation for unequal half-lives is quite straightforward.

The biological decay constant $\lambda_b \left(\dfrac{0.69}{\text{biological half-life}} \right)$ and the physical decay constant for the nuclide λ_p are added to give the effective decay constant for the element in the body.

This decay constant is then used in the equation $A = A_0 e^{-\lambda t}$.

If the expected activity for a healthy patient after a given time following a dose of a radioactive element is known then if the count rate is high it means that more of the element is being retained than is normal and vice versa.

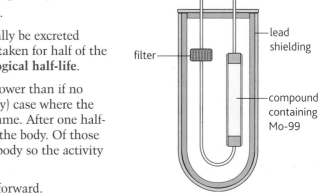

Figure 3 *Principal parts of a technetium-99m generator*

Summary questions

1 What radiation is detected in a PET scanner?

2 Why are positron emitters so useful in medicine?

3 A nuclide has a biological half-life and a physical half-life that are both 4 days. A sample injected into a patient has an activity of 640 kBq when it is injected.

   a What will be the activity 8 days later.

   b What would be the activity after 14 days?

8.5 Atomic batteries

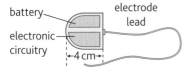

Figure 1 *Pacemaker system*

The need for long-life batteries

The need for long-life batteries arose with the beginnings of space travel and the development of heart pacemakers. In space exploration solar panels are often used but are not appropriate for all situations so atomic sources were developed and new methods are still being investigated. Pacemakers are devices used to control the heartbeat of patients who have an irregular heartbeat by sending short pulses of electric current to the heart. To avoid the patient having to have frequent operations to replace the battery long-life batteries are essential (Figure 1).

Pacemaker batteries

A pacemaker has two parts. A sealed battery supplies the energy and an electronic circuit produces pulses. Early devices simply produced pulses at a set rate. Modern devices can alter the pulse rate cleverly so that the heart beats at a rate that depends on the activity of the patient.

Some pacemakers have only one electrode that provides a pulse of current that stimulates a single chamber of the heart. Others have two electrodes that send pulses at suitable times to both chambers. Circuits that control the size and frequency of the pulses depend on the use of capacitors. This is covered in the next topic.

When pacemakers were initially developed, the batteries that power the pacemaker were large and lasted only about 2 years so the pacemaker was, inconveniently, fixed outside the patient's body. Modern batteries, with a mass of only 20–50 g last anything from 5 to 15 years, depending on the rate at which energy is used. Their size is about 40 mm × 40 mm × 8 mm so they can now be inserted inside the body giving patients much greater freedom of movement.

At present, the preferred type of battery derives its power from the chemical energy released when lithium combines with iodine to form lithium iodide. This cell can supply an emf of about 1.5 to 3 V. It has a high internal resistance so is only suitable for low current applications. The capacity of a typical battery is about is about 10 Wh. It can only deliver currents of 10–200 μA but this is all that is necessary for a pacemaker.

There are no gases formed in the cell so there is no risk of explosion. The terminal potential difference eventually falls due to contamination by the lithium iodide but the fall can be monitored externally so that the cell is replaced before placing the patient at risk

Atomic batteries

These convert the energy emitted in radioactive decay into electricity. Their main use at present is in powering the equipment used in spacecraft but research into the use of these for medical purposes is ongoing.

To be useful for space travel the source of radiation must:

■ be long enough to generate sufficient energy over the duration of any project,

- be short enough to produce thermal energy at a suitable rate,
- have a high ratio of energy per unit mass and per unit volume,
- produce high energy radiation that is readily absorbed,
- require little shielding to minimise the mass carried (Shielding is needed to prevent damage to equipment or radiation exposure of astronauts.)

There are a number of nuclides that could be used in atomic power supplies. Some are shown in the table.

Table 1 *Nuclides for power supplies*

nuclide	emission	half life /y	Energy /MeV	comment
curium-244	α	18	5.8	half-life too short for long projects
plutonium-238	α	88	5.5	commonly used
polonium-210	α	0.38	5.3	high power for small mass. Short half-life makes it suitable for very short projects. Used for power supplies in early space flights
strontium-90	β	28	0.54	β emission increases shielding requirements and half-life too short for long projects. Useable for terrestrial projects
caesium-137	β	28	1.2	

Some have relatively short half-lives and some require more shielding than others because of the beta radiation and the gamma radiation produced when beta particles are decelerated. The nuclide most commonly used is plutonium-238 which emits alpha particles of energy $5.5\,\text{MeV}$ $(8.8 \times 10^{-13}\,\text{J})$.

Calculating the energy available

The energy available from one gram of a nuclide is the number of radioactive atoms in one gram multiplied by the energy per decay.

One gram of Pu-238 contains $\frac{1}{238} \times 6.02 \times 10^{23} = 2.52 \times 10^{21}$ atoms.

The total energy available from $1\,\text{g}$ of Pu-238 is $2.2 \times 10^{9}\,\text{J}$ $(= 2.52 \times 10^{21} \times 8.8 \times 10^{-13}\,\text{J})$

Calculating the power available

This is the activity of one gram multiplied by the energy available per emission.

The half-life of Pu-238 is 88 years so its decay constant is $2.52 \times 10^{-10}\,\text{s}^{-1}$

One gram of Pu-238 has an activity of about $6.3 \times 10^{11}\,\text{Bq}$ $(= \lambda N = 2.5 \times 10^{-10} \times 2.52 \times 10^{21})$.

Power available = activity × energy per decay.

Therefore the power from $1\,\text{g}$ of Pu-238 is $0.55\,\text{W}$, $(= 6.3 \times 10^{11} \times 8.8 \times 10^{-13})$.

This initial power falls with time. The power is about 85% of its initial activity after 20 years and is halved after 88 years.

The density of Pu-238 is $20\,\text{g}\,\text{cm}^{-3}$ so this initial power of $0.55\,\text{W}$ is available from a volume of only $0.05\,\text{cm}^{3}$ of material.

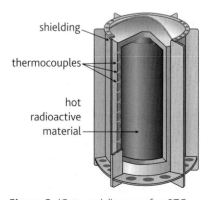

Figure 2 *'Cutaway' diagram of an RTG*

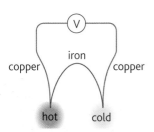

Figure 3 *Thermocouple*

Link

In a solar (photovoltaic) cell, photons of light release electrons at the junction of P-type and N-type semiconductor material and this process generates a useable emf. More detail can be found in Topic 13.1 of the AS book.

Summary questions

1. What is the origin of the energy used to power a pacemaker?

2. An alpha source has an activity of 4.0×10^6 Bq. The energy released in each decay is 3.5 MeV. Calculate the power, in W, generated by the source.

3. Using data from Table 1, calculate the activity of 1 μg of curium? (Avogadro constant = 6.0×10^{23} mol^{-1})

4. Use the answer to 3 to find the mass of curium that would generate a power of 10 mW?

5. What methods are used to convert the thermal energy generated by a radioactive source into electricity?

Application and How science works

Energy density

One important feature of battery selection is the **energy density**. This may be expressed as the energy available per kilogram or per cubic metre of the battery. Both are important. For motive power carrying a higher mass leads to a demand for even more energy for propulsion. Increased volume leaves less space for other things and small batteries carrying as much energy as possible are needed for medical applications. Typical batteries for everyday use have electrodes of lithium and manganese dioxide with a lithium salt as electrolyte. Some approximate energy densities of batteries is shown in the table

battery type	energy density /kJ kg^{-1}
lead–acid	140
nickel–cadmium	240
lithium ion	1000

Practical power sources

A power source using a radioactive nuclide is called a radioisotope thermoelectric generator (RTG). A cutaway diagram is shown in Figure 2 on page 167. An RTG for deep-space exploration produces an output of about 500 W with an efficiency of about 5% so about 18 kg of Pu-238 is needed.

The source itself absorbs most of the alpha particles that it emits and this raises the temperature of the source. The conversion of the **thermal energy** to electrical energy is by means of thermocouples usually made from two different metals or metal alloys. The low efficiency of the power supply is due to the low efficiency of the thermocouples.

A thermocouple generates a thermoelectric emf when the two junctions are at different temperatures. The emf produced by a **thermocouple** can be investigated using metals such as copper and iron (Figure 3). This generates an emf of a few millivolts. Because the emf from a thermocouple is low, many are needed to generate the emf necessary to operate the electrical equipment and electronic systems of a spacecraft. This is called a thermopile. Practical thermopiles use different combinations, for example, germanium and silver. Such combinations convert the energy more efficiently. In an RTG one terminal of each thermocouple is in contact with the hot radioactive source and the other is well away from it so that the terminals are at a different temperature.

The power output falls with time due to the reduced activity of the radioactive nuclide and deterioration of the thermocouple.

Alternative power source

The use of a beta-voltaic is another way of generating a useable emf and the technique is in the early stages of development. A beta-voltaic cell works in a similar way to that in which a solar cell generates electrical energy from solar energy. In beta-voltaics the energy comes from beta particles that are emitted by a radioactive source. As beta particles are used, more screening is necessary because of the penetrating gamma radiation produced when the beta particles decelerate.

8.6 Keeping a regular heartbeat

Learning objectives:

- How is the physics of capacitors involved in the design of pacemakers?

- How much energy can a capacitor store?

- How does the charge on a capacitor vary with time?

- What is meant by the time constant?

Specification reference: 3.5.3B

▇ Controlling heartbeat

A pacemaker has to deliver electrical pulses to the heart so that it beats regularly at a suitable rate. The pacemaker has to deliver energy in short electrical pulses that are sufficient to stimulate the muscles in the heart to contract and force blood round the body. The heart has to ensure that there is a suitable blood flow-rate to enable the body to function properly in doing whatever tasks it is doing. If the activity is energy consuming such as running or digging the garden then a higher rate of flow of blood is necessary than when the body is in a more relaxed mode such as watching TV. Modern pacemakers are intelligent devices that can sense the level of activity and respond accordingly.

The electronics in a pacemaker are quite complex but the basis for timing is based on the physics of the capacitor. The timing depends on the charging and discharging of a capacitor through a resistor. The amount of energy in the pulse depends on the energy stored in a capacitor and the **pulse length** on the characteristics of the discharge circuit through the heart.

▇ Charging a capacitor

Capacitors and capacitance

Capacitors consist of two conducting plates separated by a non-conducting gap. The gap may be air-filled or filled with an insulating material such as polythene. For investigations in the laboratory the plates are usually two square or circular sheets of metal. When a power supply is connected to the plates it causes charge (in the form of electrons) to move from one plate to the other (see Figure 1). This causes a potential difference, equal to the emf of the supply, to build up between one plate and the other.

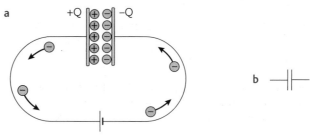

Figure 1 *(a) Charged capacitor* *(b) Capacitor symbol*

The quantity of charge Q necessary to produce a potential difference V between the plates depends on the structure of the capacitor (see below).

The **capacitance** C of the capacitor is defined as the charge necessary to change the potential difference between the plates of the capacitor by $1\,V$ (the charge per volt) so

$$C = \frac{Q}{V} \text{ (This is usually remembered as } Q = CV)$$

The unit of capacitance is the **farad** F. One farad = 1 coulomb per volt $(1\,F = 1\,C\,V^{-1})$.

$E\sim F = V$

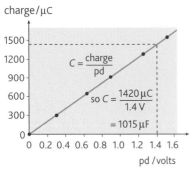

Figure 2 *Graph of charge against pd for a capacitor*

Notice that the charge Q in the equation is the charge on **one** of the plates. When a capacitor is charged there is $+Q$ on one plate and $-Q$ on the other.

A farad is a relatively large capacitance and although capacitors of this value are available, for many practical applications the capacitors have values of the order of mF, μF, nF or pF.

Figure 2 shows a graph of charge against potential difference for a capacitor showing that the charge is proportional to the pd. The gradient of this graph is C.

Energy stored

When a battery charges the capacitor, energy is transferred from the battery to the capacitor. So how much energy is stored?

When a charge flows between two points which have an electrical potential difference between them, the energy transferred is equal to the voltage multiplied by the charge transferred.

When a charge ΔQ moves from one plate of a capacitor to the other at a time when the pd between them is v, the energy transferred is $v\Delta Q$. The addition of the charge increases the pd between the plates so more energy is transferred when the next ΔQ of charge is transferred between the plates.

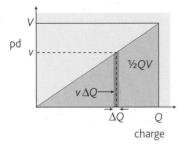

Figure 3 *Energy stored by a capacitor*

In Figure 3 the shaded area represents $v\Delta Q$ and this is the area beneath the graph line (if ΔQ is very small). When the potential difference is V and the charge is Q the total energy stored is the sum of all similar shaded areas under the graph line. The total energy stored is therefore the area of the triangle beneath the graph line.

The energy stored $E = \frac{1}{2}QV$.

Using $Q = CV$, other useful forms of this equation are $E = \frac{1}{2}CV^2$ and $E = \frac{1}{2}\frac{Q^2}{C}$.

The energy is in joule (J) when C is in farad, V in volt and Q in coulomb.

In the laboratory, experiments are usually conducted with capacitors up to about 1000 μF and with voltages of about 6 V. In this case the energy stored is about 0.018 J.

Defibrillators

When a patient suffers a cardiac arrest, in which the heart actually stops beating, a much larger energy pulse may be used to resuscitate the patient. In its simplest form a capacitor is charged to a high pd and is designed to deliver a short pulse of energy. Typically, the energy comes from a bank of capacitors of capacitance about 0.3 mF charged to around 1000 V. The energy stored is therefore about 150 J ($\frac{1}{2}(0.3 \times 10^{-3})1000^2$). This energy may be delivered in a single direction over a controlled period of about 5 ms.

To deliver the pulse the electrodes are placed on the patient using a gel to ensure good electrical contact. Because high voltages and energies are used precautions have to be taken to ensure the safety of the operator.

Some defibrillators stimulate the heart using pulses, which go first in one direction and then the other over a 10 ms time interval.

Pacemakers

In a pacemaker, the regular pulses may have a maximum voltage of 3 V and each pulse may deliver a total energy of 20 μJ in 1 ms.

$A\overline{Q}A$ **Examiner's tip**

Notice that the total energy is the energy between the graph line and the Q axis. The area between the graph line and the V axis gives the same result but is physically the incorrect area. This is because energy is calculated by summing the areas $V\Delta Q$ and not $Q\Delta V$. If the V–Q graph were non-linear this would be an important distinction.

Assuming that this energy comes from the discharge of a capacitor, the capacitor has a value of $4.4\,\mu F$. The charge delivered in each pulse is $13\,\mu C$ (from $Q = CV = 4.4 \times 10^{-6} \times 3\,C$) and the mean current about $13\,mA$ $\left(\text{from } I = \dfrac{Q}{t} = \dfrac{13 \times 10^{-6}}{1 \times 10^{-3}}\right)$.

These pulses are delivered at a rate of about 60 per minute so each day the energy delivered is $1.73\,J$. A battery that is to last 10 years therefore needs to store $6300\,J$.

Practical capacitors

Experiments show that the capacitance of a capacitor depends on:

- the overlapping area of the plates (greater overlap leads to more capacitance $C \propto A$),
- the separation of the plates (smaller separation leads to more capacitance $C \propto 1/d$),
- the insulating material (called the dielectric) between the plates.

The use of materials like polythene increases the capacitance by about 2.2 times compared with an air space. The factor is equal to the relative permittivity ε_r of the material between the plates.

Practical capacitors need to be more convenient shapes than the two parallel plates used in laboratory experiments.

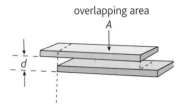

Figure 4 *Parallel plate capacitor*

Figure 5 shows an electrolytic capacitor. The capacitor is labelled with its value and the maximum potential difference that can be connected across it. If a higher pd is used then the insulation breaks down and charge leaks through the insulator from one plate to the other. Particular care has to be taken with electrolytic capacitors as these have to be connected with the correct polarity. The terminal marked '−'must be connected to the negative terminal of the supply. If connected the wrong way round, gases may be released inside the capacitor which increase the internal pressure and can lead to a dangerous explosion.

Capacitors in microcircuits consist of conducting layers of doped semiconductor separated by non-conducting pure silicon. The area of the capacitor storing the charge is necessarily small so thin insulating layers are needed to produce useful capacitors.

Figure 5 *Electrolytic capacitor*

Application and How science works

Capacitance of isolated conductors

Any isolated object made of an electrical conductor can store charge and has a capacitance. For an isolated object, charge would be brought from 'infinity' to charge the capacitor. The potential V of a sphere of radius r with a charge Q is given by $V = \dfrac{Q}{4\pi\varepsilon_0 r}$. This means that a spherical conducting sphere has a capacitance $\left(\dfrac{Q}{V}\right)$ equal to $4\pi\varepsilon_0 r = 1.1 \times 10^{-10}r$ farad. Assuming the Earth to be a conductor its capacitance is $1.1 \times 10^{-10} \times 6\,400\,000 = 700\,\mu F$.

Capacitors as timing devices

Because the voltage across a capacitor varies with time in a predictable way when being charged or discharged through a resistor, it can be used for measuring time intervals.

In Figure 6 the capacitor charges when the switch connects the capacitor to the cell and discharges through the resistor when the switch is moved to the right.

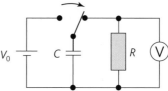

Figure 6 *Capacitor discharge circuit*

The potential difference across the capacitor is monitored by a voltmeter or a data logger.

The capacitor charge at any instant can be calculated using $Q = VC$.

Figure 7 shows how the capacitor charge varies with time. The graph of pd against time has the same shape.

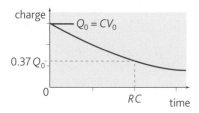

Figure 7 *Capacitor discharge*

The magnitude of the discharge current, $I = \dfrac{\Delta Q}{\Delta t}$ which is the rate of change of charge on the capacitor.

The discharge current $= \dfrac{V}{R}$, where V is the instantaneous value of the potential difference across the capacitor.

As $V = \dfrac{Q}{C}$ it follows that $\dfrac{\Delta Q}{\Delta t} = -\dfrac{Q}{RC}$.

The minus sign indicates that the charge is decreasing.

This equation shows that the rate of change of charge $\propto$ the charge present.

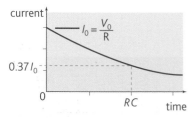

Figure 8 *Current–time graph for capacitor discharge*

This is analogous to the radioactivity situation in which $\dfrac{\Delta N}{\Delta t} = -\lambda N$.

So just as the number of radioactive atoms decreases exponentially with time so does the charge on a capacitor.

For a capacitor that initially has charge Q_0 the equation that models the change of charge with time is $Q = Q_0 e^{-t/RC}$.

Similarly since the charge on the capacitor, the pd and the discharge current are all directly proportional to each other the equations relating V and I with time are $V = V_0 e^{-t/RC}$ and $I = I_0 e^{-t/RC}$ (see Figure 8)

Time constant

The shape of the discharge curve depends on the value of RC. This is the **time constant** of the circuit.

If R is in Ω and C is in F then the time constant is in s.

The time constant is the time for the charge to fall to $\dfrac{1}{e}$ (0.37) of its original value.

The time to halve is $0.69 RC$. This is often loosely referred to as 'the half-life of the capacitor' because of the analogy with radioactive decay but the term should be avoided.

Capacitor charging

The variation of charge with time during charging depends on the **internal resistance** of the supply and any resistances that are in series with the capacitor. The charging rate falls as the pd across the capacitor increases.

This is because the charging pd at any instant = $\varepsilon - V_C$ (emf of the supply – pd across the capacitor)

So as V_C increases the charging current, $\dfrac{\varepsilon - V_C}{R}$, falls.

Producing regular pulses

The time for the potential difference across a capacitor to fall to a given value when discharging (or to rise to a given value when charging) is predictable and, unlike radioactive decay, is not subject to random fluctuations.

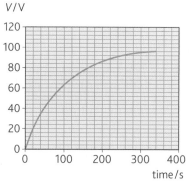

*Figure 9 **V–t** graph for capacitor charging*

Circuits can therefore make use of this fact to produce pulses. In such circuits, the electronics is designed to produce a pulse when the voltage falls, or rises, to a predetermined value.

Suppose a pulse is required at 1 s time intervals so that 60 pulses are produced in a minute such as might be required in a pacemaker.

If a 1.0 μF capacitor is discharged through a 1.0 MΩ resistor the time constant is 1.0 s.

If the initial charge is 3.0 V then after 1.0 s it will be 0.37 × 3.0 V which is 1.11 V. The electronics would therefore be designed to produce a pulse when the pd reaches this value.

In pacemakers, the timing of the pulses may be fixed or it may be varied automatically in response to the patient's activity.

To illustrate the timing effect a simple neon lamp can be made to flash regularly using the circuit in Figure 10.

A small neon discharge lamp will not conduct until the voltage reaches the 'striking voltage' (about 110 V). It then conducts with a very low resistance until the pd reaches a lower voltage.

In the circuit, the capacitor charges through the resistor. When the striking voltage is reached the resistance of the neon lamp is low and the capacitor discharges very rapidly through the lamp until the extinguishing voltage is reached. The process then repeats itself. The repetition rate depends on the value of the resistor.

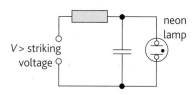

Figure 10 *Flashing neon lamp circuit*

Summary questions

1 A 470 nF capacitor is charged to a potential difference of 3.5 V. Calculate the charge on the capacitor and the energy stored.

2 Calculate the potential difference across a 2200 μF capacitor that stores an energy of 150 J.

3 A 100 μF capacitor is charged to a potential difference of 25 V. It discharges through a 270 kΩ resistor. How long would it take for the potential difference to reach **a** 22.5 V; **b** 5 V.

4 Describe two ways in which capacitors might be used in pacemakers.

1 In an experiment to verify the inverse-square law for gamma radiation, a student used the arrangement shown in the diagram.

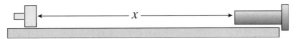

Figure 1

The distance from the front of the radioactive source to the window of the Geiger–Müller tube is x and the observed count rate is C. The data are given in the table.

x/cm	10	20	30	40	50	60	70
C/s^{-1}	29.1	10.5	4.7	2.8	1.8	1.3	1.0

(a) Plot a suitable graph that will display the data as a straight-line. *(6 marks)*

(b) Use the graph to determine the distance between the unknown position of the radioactive source in its holder and the effective point inside the Geiger–Müller tube at which the radiation is detected. *(2 marks)*

2 The chart in **Figure 2** shows how the nucleon number A changes with proton number Z for part of the decay series that starts with uranium-238. The half-lives of each decay are also shown.

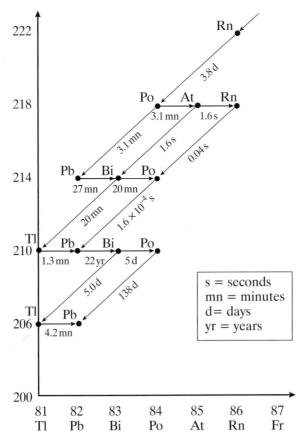

Figure 2

A sample containing only bismuth-214 has an initial mass of 0.60 g.

(a) After what period of time will the mass of bismuth-214 (Bi) present in the sample be 0.15 g? *(2 marks)*

(b) (i) Calculate the number of bismuth-214 atoms present in the sample after the time you determined in part (a). *(3 marks)*

   (ii) Calculate the activity of the bismuth-214 in the sample after the time you determined in part (a). *(4 marks)*

   (iii) State and explain how the total activity of the sample will be different from the value calculated in (ii). *(2 marks)*

(c) The bismuth-214 decays into polonium-214. Explain why there is very little polonium–214 in the sample. *(2 marks)*

3 The table shows the count rate from a radioactive isotope. The background count rate is 0.4 counts s^{-1}.

time, t / s	0	30	60	90	120
count rate /C s^{-1}	14.0	9.6	6.6	4.6	3.2

Plot a graph of the **corrected count rate** against time and use it to determine the half-life of the isotope. *(9 marks)*

4 (a) The isotope iodine-131 is a beta emitter used in medical diagnosis. It can help to locate sites inside the body where bleeding occurs. The table gives some of the properties of this isotope when used with adult patients.

isotope	physical half life/ day	biological half life/day	type of isotope
Iodine-131	8	75	Beta- emitter

   (i) Calculate the effective half-life of the isotope. *(2 marks)*

   (ii) Explain why the properties outlined in the table make it suitable for the identification of sites inside the body *(4 marks)*

(b) Technetium-99m in the *metastable* form is a daughter product of the isotope molybdenum-99. $^{99}_{43}$Tc decays by beta emission to give rubidium.

   (i) Explain what is meant by a metastable state. *(3 marks)*

   (ii) The technetium emits electromagnetic radiation of energy 140 keV.

   Calculate the wavelength of this radiation and state the region of the electromagnetic spectrum to which it belongs. *(4 marks)*

   (iii) Write down the equation that represents the decay of the technetium-99 to rubidium (Ru) *(1 mark)*

   (iv) The emitted beta particle has an energy of about 300 keV. The decay constant of the technetium-99 is about 1×10^{-13} s^{-1}.

   Comment, with an estimate, on the maximum energy that can be delivered as a result of the injection of 1.0 mg of technetium-99 into a patient. *(5 marks)*

5   The graph in **Figure 3** shows the variation of potential difference V with time across a $470\,\mu\text{F}$ capacitor discharging through a resistor in a pacemaker circuit.

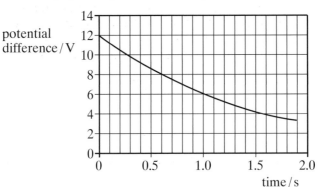

Figure 3

(a) The resistance of the resistor is approximately

A $900\,\Omega$

B $1300\,\Omega$

C $3000\,\Omega$

D $4700\,\Omega$ *(1 mark)*

(b) The potential difference across the capacitor falls from $12\,\text{V}$ to $4\,\text{V}$. The best estimate of the change in the energy stored by the capacitor is

A $7.5\,\text{mJ}$

B $15\,\text{mJ}$

C $30\,\text{mJ}$

D $60\,\text{mJ}$ *(1 mark)*

6   The back-up power system in a satellite is provided by the radioactive decay of plutonium-239 enclosed in a sealed container. The container absorbs all the energy released by the isotope. Energy from the radiation is converted to electrical energy by means of a thermopile.

(a) Outline how the thermopile carries out the energy conversion.   *(4 marks)*

(b) The isotope has an initial activity of $1.3 \times 10^{14}\,\text{Bq}$ and produces α particles of energy $5.1\,\text{MeV}$. Calculate the initial rate at which the container absorbs energy from the α particles .   *(3 marks)*

(c) (i)   The isotope has a half-life of 90 years. Calculate the decay constant λ of this isotope.   *(2 marks)*

     (ii)   The overall thermopile efficiency is 17%. Calculate the mass of plutonium-239 that will be required to give an initial power of $100\,\text{W}$.   *(4 marks)*

7   Iodine is found naturally in the world as the isotope I-127; it is not radioactive and it is essential to life.

Other isotopes of iodine are formed in nuclear reactors. In the Chernobyl nuclear power station disaster in the Ukraine, an explosion caused a large quantity of the radioactive isotope iodine-131 to be released into the atmosphere. Iodine-131 is radioactive.

The table shows the proton and mass numbers of these two iodine isotopes.

	proton number	mass number
iodine-127	53	127
iodine-131	53	131

(a)   Explain, in terms of particles found in the nucleus, how an iodine-131 nucleus is different from an iodine-127 nucleus.   *(2 marks)*

(b)   Explain why iodine-131 could be dangerous to animals.   *(4 marks)*

(c)   Iodine-131 and iodine-127 have the same chemical properties. Explain why this would be a problem if iodine-131 was taken into our bodies.   *(1 mark)*

(d)   The Chernobyl disaster took place in 1986.

State and explain whether you think that iodine-131 from the disaster is still a threat to us today.   *(2 marks)*

9 Energy from the nucleus

9.1 Nuclear reactions and mass–energy equivalence

Learning objectives:

■ What is meant by mass–energy equivalence?

■ What units are used to measure nuclear masses and energies?

■ How does mass affect whether a nucleus can decay?

■ How can new heavy nuclei and particles be made?

Specification reference: 3.5.3C

Energy conservation

A statement of the law of conservation of energy is that 'energy cannot be created nor destroyed but may be changed from one form into another'.

When a stationary nucleus emits alpha or beta radiation, the particle and the recoil nucleus possess kinetic energy so the question arises 'Where does the energy come from?' The same question may be asked of the energy produced when hydrogen and other hydrocarbons are burned in oxygen. The resulting gases are hot. So the kinetic energy of the molecules (water in the case of hydrogen; carbon dioxide and monoxide in the case of coal) has increased. At first sight, it appears that the principle of conservation of energy has been violated.

Einstein resolved the problem by stating that energy and mass are equivalent. He went on to formulate what is probably the most well-known law in physics, $E = mc^2$, c being the velocity of light $(3.00 \times 10^8\,\mathrm{m\,s^{-1}})$. Mass is just another form in which energy can appear.

As many observations explained using this equation involve **changes in mass** and the consequential **change in energy**, the law is often stated in terms of changes and this is how it appears on the examination formula sheet.

When mass changes by an amount Δm the change in other forms of energy is ΔE. The equation on the formula sheet is therefore $\Delta E = \Delta mc^2$

Having said this, the masses of nuclei are often quoted in terms of their energy equivalence.

For example:

The mass of a proton is $1.673 \times 10^{-27}\,\mathrm{kg}$.

The mass could also be quoted as $1.51 \times 10^{-10}\,\mathrm{J}$ $(= 1.673 \times 10^{-27} \times (3.00 \times 10^8)^2)$.

Recall, however, that the MeV is used by physicists for small energies where $1\,\mathrm{MeV} = 1.60 \times 10^{-13}\,\mathrm{J}$. This gives yet another alternative of $941\,\mathrm{MeV}$ for the mass of a proton.

To complicate matters further the atomic mass unit (u) is also used for nuclear masses.

One u = 1.661×10^{-27} kg

This give a proton mass of $1.00728\,\mathrm{u}$.

Chemical reactions

The energy released when hydrogen burns is relatively small. When $1\,\mathrm{kg}$ of hydrogen reacts with oxygen to form water the energy released is about $140\,\mathrm{MJ}$. Using Einstein's equation, the change in mass is only $1.6 \times 10^{-9}\,\mathrm{kg}$ $(1.6\,\mu\mathrm{g})$ so the change in mass is negligible and hard to measure. It is not surprising therefore that the earlier scientists did not make the connection between mass and energy.

Stretching springs, heating and running around

The equation always works in the same way when a spring is stretched. If a spring with a spring constant of $25\,\text{N}\,\text{m}^{-1}$ is stretched by $0.1\,\text{m}$ the energy stored is $0.125\,\text{J}$. The spring increases in mass by $1.4 \times 10^{-18}\,\text{kg}$!

When the temperature of an object is increased using an electric heater there is an energy input. If a $20\,\text{W}$ heater is used for $5\,\text{min}$, the energy supplied is $6000\,\text{J}$. This means that the mass of the heated object increases by $6.7 \times 10^{-14}\,\text{kg}$.

The equivalent mass increase of a $60\,\text{kg}$ athlete running at $10\,\text{m}\,\text{s}^{-1}$ is $3.3 \times 10^{-14}\,\text{kg}$, equivalent to the $3000\,\text{J}$ of kinetic energy.

In each case, the theoretical increase in mass is small and negligible compared with the mass of the object. However, when a proton is accelerated to a speed of, say, $5 \times 10^7\,\text{m}\,\text{s}^{-1}$ the kinetic energy of $2.13 \times 10^{-12}\,\text{J}$ equates to a mass change of $2.4 \times 10^{-29}\,\text{kg}$, an increase of 1.4% which cannot be ignored.

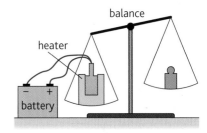

Figure 1 *Gaining mass by electrical heating*

Nuclear decay

When a uranium-235 nucleus emits an alpha particle, the alpha particle has an energy of $4.56\,\text{MeV}$. The total change in the energy of the nucleus is $2.86 \times 10^{-10}\,\text{J}$. The energy change when $1\,\text{kg}$ of uranium-235 disintegrates is $7.3 \times 10^{14}\,\text{J}$ which is equivalent to $81 \times 10^{-3}\,\text{kg}$ ($81\,\text{g}$), which is easily measurable.

One guiding feature of alpha decay is that it can only be spontaneous if the total mass of the alpha particle and the daughter nucleus is less than the mass of the parent nucleus.

So for example

$^{241}_{95}\text{Am} \longrightarrow {}^{237}_{93}\text{Np} + {}^{4}_{2}\alpha$ decay occurs spontaneously because there is a decrease in mass $241.0566\,\text{u} \longrightarrow 237.0480\,\text{u} + 4.0026\,\text{u}$ (total $241.0506\,\text{u}$)

The energy released in the americium reaction is $0.0060\,\text{u}$ which is equivalent to about $1.0 \times 10^{-30}\,\text{kg}$ or $9.0 \times 10^{-13}\,\text{J}$ or $5.5\,\text{MeV}$.

This energy is shared between the alpha particle and the recoil nucleus in such a way that momentum is conserved. In the decay of Americium-241 the alpha particle takes about 99.5% of the energy available.

recoil of
neptunium
nucleus

alpha
particle

Figure 2 *Alpha decay*

Nuclear stability and instability

Whether or not a nucleus is stable depends on the balance between the protons and neutrons in the nucleus. Protons being positively charged repel each other and a nucleus of protons without neutrons would just fly apart.

Hydrogen-1 is the only nucleus that does not contain any neutrons. For other light stable nuclei the number of protons Z and neutrons $N\,(= A - Z)$ are the same. After about $Z = 20$, the stable nuclei contain more neutrons than protons and the difference becomes greater for higher Z. For the stable nucleus of gold (Au-197) there are 79 protons and 118 neutrons.

Figure 3 shows how N varies with Z for some nuclides. The orange shading shows the stable nuclei and these lie close to a line of stability. The nuclei represented by the purple shading decay by β^- emission because they contain too many neutrons. Those shaded green lie below the stability line and decay by β^+ emission so increasing the number of neutrons. Alpha emitters (shown shaded red) all have Z greater than 84. Uranium is the naturally occurring nuclide with the highest Z (92 protons in its nucleus). In each case, the decay of a nucleus by alpha or beta emission results in a **daughter nucleus** that lies closer to the line of stability.

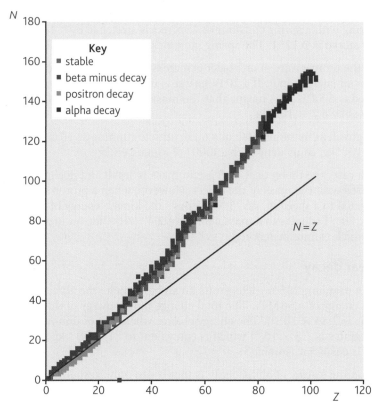

Figure 3 *Plot of N against Z*

Making new particles

The equivalence formula works both ways. It is possible to produce new heavier particles from less massive particles. One or both particles can be given kinetic energy in an accelerator and the particles that result from the collision will have a total mass that is equal to the sum of the mass of the colliding particles plus their kinetic energy.

To produce new nuclei the interacting particles have to get close enough together so that the strong nuclear force comes into play. The neutron flux produced in reactors can achieve this easily because, being uncharged, the neutrons are not repelled by the nucleus. When protons, deuterons or alpha particles are used they have to be accelerated to a high kinetic energy so that they can overcome the coulomb repulsion due to the like positive charges on the particles. (See Topic 9.4.)

Radioactive iodine-124 for medical use can be made by bombarding antimony-121 with alpha particles accelerated in a cyclotron.

The equation for the reaction is $^{121}_{51}\mathrm{Sb} + {}^{4}_{2}\alpha \longrightarrow {}^{1}_{0}\mathrm{n} + {}^{124}_{53}\mathrm{I}$

The mass equation in terms of u is

$$120.90382\,\mathrm{u} + 4.00260\,\mathrm{u} \longrightarrow 1.00867\,\mathrm{u} + 123.90621\,\mathrm{u}$$

There is a mass increase of $0.00846\,\mathrm{u}$ or $1.405 \times 10^{-29}\,\mathrm{kg}$.

The alpha particle therefore needs at least $1.26 \times 10^{-12}\,\mathrm{J}$ or $7.9\,\mathrm{MeV}$ of kinetic energy to induce this reaction.

Production of radioactive carbon and carbon dating

When neutrons in cosmic rays enter the atmosphere, they can interact with nitrogen nuclei and form radioactive carbon-14 and a proton. The equation for this reaction is: $^{14}_{7}N + ^{1}_{0}n \longrightarrow ^{1}_{1}p + ^{14}_{6}C$

In terms of the masses in atomic mass units the equation is

$$14.00307\,u + 1.00867\,u \longrightarrow 1.00728\,u + 14.00324\,u$$

$$15.01174\,u \longrightarrow 15.01052\,u$$

The loss of mass in the process means that the carbon nucleus and proton have more kinetic energy than the original particles. The mass decrease is $0.00122\,u$ or $2.03 \times 10^{-30}\,kg$. This converts to an increase of $1.82 \times 10^{-13}\,J$ in the kinetic energy of the particles.

$$^{14}_{6}C \longrightarrow ^{14}_{7}N + ^{0}_{-1}\beta + ^{0}_{0}\overline{v}$$

The basis for radiocarbon dating is the assumption that the proportion of radioactive carbon-14 in carbon in the atmosphere has been the same for thousands of years.

Carbon-14 behaves chemically like other isotopes of carbon and exists in the atmosphere as radioactive carbon dioxide. This enters plants and animals when they are alive and ceases when the plant or animal dies. The radioactive carbon decays to $^{14}_{7}N$ by β^- emission with a half-life of about 5800 years.

The age of an old wooden boat, for example, can therefore be found by comparing the activity A of a given mass of wood from the boat with the activity A_0 of the same mass taken from new wood.

The boat's age t in years is given by $A = A_0 e^{-(0.69/5800)t}$.

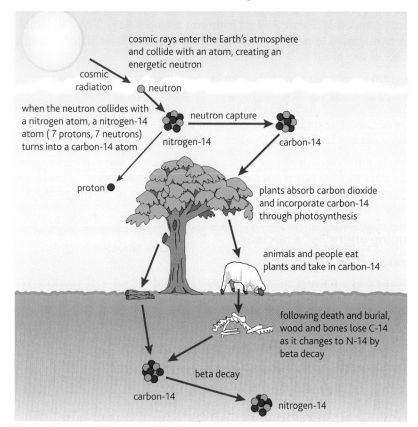

cosmic rays enter the Earth's atmosphere and collide with an atom, creating an energetic neutron

cosmic radiation

neutron

when the neutron collides with a nitrogen atom, a nitrogen-14 atom (7 protons, 7 neutrons) turns into a carbon-14 atom

neutron capture

nitrogen-14

carbon-14

proton

plants absorb carbon dioxide and incorporate carbon-14 through photosynthesis

animals and people eat plants and take in carbon-14

following death and burial, wood and bones lose C-14 as it changes to N-14 by beta decay

beta decay

carbon-14

nitrogen-14

Figure 4 *Radiocarbon enters living things*

How science works

Carbon-14 content in the atmosphere

Variations in the neutron flux in the atmosphere changes the rate of production so the take-up of carbon-14 by wood and animals from different periods will have been different. This has to be accounted for when estimating the age of ancient artifacts.

Summary questions

1. The temperature of 1 kg of copper is raised by 100 K when 38 kJ of energy is supplied. What is the change in mass of the copper produced by the heating.

2. The calorific value of petrol is about $45\,MJ\,kg^{-1}$. The density of petrol is $730\,kg\,m^{-3}$. What is the change in mass when 1 litre of petrol is used?

3. Explain how it is possible for the total mass of the particles produced in a nuclear interaction to be greater than the rest mass of the colliding particles.

4. The activity of a sample of carbon from new wood is 9000 Bq. What would be the expected count rate of wood taken from a boat that is thought to be 3000 years old?

9.2 Nuclear binding energy

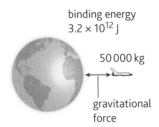

binding energy
3.2×10^{12} J

50 000 kg

gravitational
force

Figure 1 *Binding energy due to gravity*

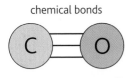

chemical bonds

C ═ O

binding energy 1.8×10^{-19} J

Figure 2 *Chemical binding energy*

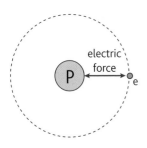

electric
force
P ← e

binding energy 2.2×10^{-18} J

Figure 3 *Binding energy due to attraction of charges*

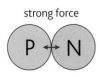

strong force

P ↔ N

binding energy 2.2×10^{6} eV

Figure 4 *Nuclear binding energy*

Binding energy

The term relates to the energy needed to separate one particle from another. Although this section is primarily concerned with nuclear **binding energy**, the term binding energy applies in other situations.

A man of mass 70 kg is bound to the Earth by the gravitational force between him and the Earth. The energy required to separate him from the Earth can be calculated from his gravitational potential energy at the Earth's surface, as shown in Topic 2.1. The gravitational potential energy is equal to -4.4×10^{9} J. $\left(\text{using } E_{\mathrm{p}} = \dfrac{GMm}{R}\right)$. So to remove the man to a point a long way away from the Earth where his potential energy is zero requires an input of 4.4×10^{9} J. We are bound to the Earth by about 63 MJ per kg of our mass. To separate us from the Earth this amount of energy has to be supplied (Figure 1).

In chemical combinations, molecules consist of two or more atoms that are bound together. When carbon and oxygen combine to form carbon monoxide (CO) 110 kJ of energy is released for every mole of carbon monoxide that is formed. To separate the CO molecule back into carbon and oxygen this energy would have to be supplied in some way. The binding energy of one CO molecule is therefore 1.8×10^{-19} J (about 1.1 eV) (Figure 2).

Ionisation energy is the energy needed to remove an electron from an atom or molecule (Figure 3). In a hydrogen atom 13.6 eV (2.2×10^{-18} J) of energy is needed to remove an electron in the ground state. The binding energy of this electron is therefore 13.6 eV.

The same applies in a nucleus. The binding energy of a nucleon is the energy needed to remove that nucleon from the nucleus (Figure 4). However, a single nucleon is not usually a concern in discussing nuclear interactions. The total binding energy of a nucleus and the **binding energy per nucleon** are much more useful concepts.

In each of the cases discussed above the total mass of the particles after the separation has taken place is greater than the mass before. This is because energy has to be put into the system to separate all the particles from each other.

Binding energy of a nucleus

Total binding energy

The mass of a nucleus containing Z protons and N ($=A - Z$) neutrons is less than the sum of the masses of the individual protons and neutrons that make up the nucleus.

Mass of a nucleus $^{A}_{Z}X$, $M_{\mathrm{nucleus}} < Zm_{\mathrm{p}} + (A - Z)m_{\mathrm{n}}$.

For example the mass of an iron-56 $\left(^{56}_{26}\mathrm{Fe}\right)$ nucleus is 55.921 u.

The mass of 26 protons and 30 neutrons is $26 \times 1.00728 + 30 \times 1.008$ $67 = 56.449$.

The difference is 0.528 u. This is equivalent to 8.765×10^{-28} kg.

This difference in mass between the masses of the individual protons and neutrons and the mass of the resulting nucleus is called the **mass defect.**

Using $\Delta E = \Delta mc^2$. This mass defect equates to 493 MeV.

This binding energy is the energy that would be necessary to split the nucleus up into its constituent protons and neutrons.

Alternatively, it is the energy that would be released when a nucleus is formed from individual protons and neutrons.

Examiner's tip

Defining binding energy

Take care to make clear that the formation is from the individual protons and neutrons. As shown in Topic 9.4 a nucleus may be formed by fusing two larger nuclei. The energy release in this case is different from the binding energy.

Binding energy per nucleon (BEPN)

The binding energy per nucleon for the iron-56 in the above example is

$8.8 \, \text{MeV} \left(= \frac{493}{56} \, \text{MeV} \right)$.

This is a simpler and more useful form for recording the binding energy of a nucleus.

The binding energies of different nuclei vary as shown in the graph in Figure 5.

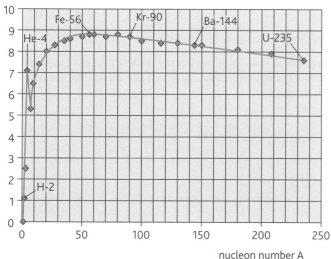

Figure 5 *Binding energy per nucleon against A*

The total binding energy = the binding energy per nucleon × the nucleon number A.

The binding energy of hydrogen-1 is 0, as it only has one nucleon.

Deuterium, which is hydrogen 2, has a total binding energy of 2.2 MeV or 1.1 MeV per nucleon.

A helium-4 nucleus (an alpha particle) is a stable nucleus requiring about 28 MeV to split it up completely, about 7 MeV per nucleon.

Using BEPN in decay calculations

A nucleus can only decay spontaneously if there is an increase in the total binding energy when the decay occurs. The energy released when a nuclide decays can be calculated directly using values for binding energy per nucleon.

For example uranium-238 decays by alpha emission to thorium-234. The equation is:

$$^{238}_{92}\text{U} \longrightarrow {}^{234}_{90}\text{Th} + {}^{4}_{2}\alpha$$

The binding energies per nucleon for the nuclei involved are given in the following table.

nucleus	BEPN/MeV
uranium-238	7.57
thorium-234	7.60
alpha particle; helium-4	7.08

The total binding energy of uranium-238 $= 238 \times 7.57\,\text{MeV}$
$= 1801.7\,\text{MeV}.$

The binding energy of thorium-234 $= 234 \times 7.60\,\text{MeV}$
$= 1778.4\,\text{MeV}.$

The binding energy of an alpha particle $= 4 \times 7.08\,\text{MeV} = 28.3\,\text{MeV}.$

The total binding energy before the event $= 1801.7\,\text{MeV}.$

The total binding energy after the event $= 1778.4 + 28.3\,\text{MeV}$
$= 1806.7\,\text{MeV}.$

There is an increase in total binding energy $= 5.0\,\text{MeV}.$

The **increase** in total binding energy means that **energy was released** in the decay. This is the kinetic energy of the alpha particle and the recoiling thorium nucleus.

Summary questions

1 The binding energy of $^{8}_{4}\text{Be}$ is 56.5 MeV. Calculate the binding energy per nucleon.

2 The binding energy per nucleon of helium-3 is 2.573 MeV and that of helium-4 is 7.074 MeV. How much energy would be needed to remove a neutron from a helium-4 nucleus.

3 How much energy in joule would be needed to create a plasma of free protons and electrons from 1.0 mol of hydrogen?

4 Explain what is meant by: a binding energy of a nucleus, b mass defect.

5 Explain how mass defect and binding energy are related.

9.3 Energy from nuclear fission

Learning objectives:

- Where does energy come from during fission reactions?
- How much energy is produced for each fission?
- What are the principal parts of a pressurised water reactor?
- How is the energy converted into electricity?

Specification reference: 3.5.3D

Figure 1 *The first nuclear reactor*

Figure 2 *Sizewell B nuclear power station*

What is nuclear fission?

Fission means 'splitting up' and nuclear fission is a process in which a nucleus is split into two smaller nuclei. Spontaneous nuclear fission occurs when a nucleus decays by alpha emission without outside help. In the process commonly referred to as 'splitting the atom' certain nuclei split up into smaller nuclei when an extra neutron is introduced into the nucleus. Energy is released when **neutron-induced fission** occurs and this forms the basis of nuclear reactors and nuclear weapons.

Application and How science works

Discovery of nuclear fission

Following the discovery of the neutron in 1932 many scientists were experimenting with neutron bombardment. Results of experiments suggested that other elements were being produced but scientists were, at first, sceptical. Hahn and Strassmann proved conclusively that fission of the nucleus was taking place. Research accelerated during the Second World War when the potential of fission for nuclear weapons was identified. Fermi first demonstrated in 1942 how the power output from the nuclear reaction could be controlled. After the war, as well as continuing with weapon development, scientists also focused on the development of power producing reactors which paved the way for today's nuclear industry.

Neutron-induced fission

The nuclides most commonly used in fission reactors are uranium-235 and plutonium-239.

When a uranium-235 nucleus absorbs a slow-moving neutron, it forms a new intermediate nucleus, uranium-236, which is very unstable. This nucleus splits up immediately into smaller fragments. Two smaller nuclei are produced and two or three neutrons are formed too. Figure 3 shows a diagram of one typical fission reaction.

The nuclear equation for the reaction is:

$$^{235}_{92}U + n \longrightarrow {}^{236}_{92}U \longrightarrow {}^{144}_{56}U + {}^{90}_{36}Kr + 2\,{}^{1}_{0}n + energy$$

Notice that, as in all nuclear equations, the sum of the proton numbers Z and nucleon numbers A are the same before and after the reaction.

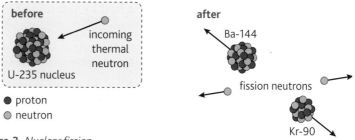

Figure 3 *Nuclear fission*

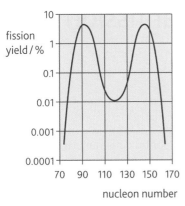

Figure 4 *Yield of fission products from U-235*

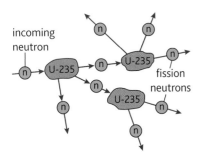

Figure 5 *Chain reaction*

The nucleus rarely splits into two equal parts. Figure 4 shows the yield of fission products from a large number of fissions of U-235. Note that the *y*-axis scale is logarithmic so that only about 1% of the fissions produce two similar nuclides with nucleon number around 118. The most likely outcome is a heavy and a light nucleus such as that in Figure 3. The Ba and Kr nuclei are formed in about 7–8% of fissions.

The number of neutrons increases as a result of the reaction and these neutrons can go on to produce further fissions resulting in a chain reaction shown in Figure 5.

■ Energy release

The graph in Figure 5 in Topic 9.2 shows that the binding energies per nucleon for nuclides such as Kr-90 and Ba-144 are higher than that for U-235. This increase in binding energy per nucleon results in the release of energy when a U-235 nucleus splits. The change in binding energy per nucleon means that there is also a decrease in mass.

The table shows the binding energies per nucleon and the nuclear masses of a neutron and the nuclei involved for the fission described above.

nucleus /particle	BEPN /MeV	mass /u
uranium-235	7.59	234.993
barium-144	8.26	143.892
krypton-90	8.59	89.901
neutron	0	1.009

Energy release calculated using binding energies

Total binding energy of uranium-235 $= 235 \times 7.59 = 1784$ MeV.

Total binding energy of barium-144 $= 144 \times 8.26 = 1189$ MeV.

Total binding energy of krypton-90 $= 90 \times 8.59 = 773$ MeV.

Total B.E. before the reaction $= 1784$ MeV.

Total B.E. after the reaction $= 1962$ MeV.

Increase in binding energy $= 178$ MeV.

The energy released as a result of this increase in binding energy appears as kinetic energy of the fission products; the two lighter nuclei and the neutrons.

Energy release calculated using masses

From the nuclear equation $^{235}_{92}\text{U} + ^{1}_{0}\text{n} \longrightarrow ^{144}_{56}\text{Ba} + ^{90}_{36}\text{Kr} + 2\,^{1}_{0}\text{n}$

mass of U-235 + mass of 1 neutron $= 234.993\,\text{u} + 1.009\,\text{u} = 236.002\,\text{u}$.

mass of Ba-144 + mass of Kr-90 + mass of 2 neutrons
$$= 143.892 + 89.901 + 2 \times 1.009 = 235.811\,\text{u}.$$

Decrease in mass $= 0.191\,\text{u}$, which is equivalent to
$$3.17 \times 10^{-}\text{kg}\ (0.191 \times 1.661 \times 10^{-27}\,\text{kg}\,)$$

Using $\Delta E = \Delta mc^2$ this is equivalent to 2.85×10^{-11} J or 178 MeV.

Compare this with the energy released when an atom of carbon combines with an atom of oxygen to release energy when burning. This is of the order of 1 eV.

Energy from a kilogram of U-235

235 g of uranium-235 contains 6.02×10^{23} atoms so 1 g contains
2.56×10^{21} atoms $\left(= \dfrac{1}{235} \times 6.2 \times 10^{23} \text{ atoms}\right)$.

The number of fissions possible from 1 kg is therefore 2.56×10^{24}.

The total energy available $= 2.85 \times 10^{-11} \times 2.56 \times 10^{24} = 7.3 \times 10^{13}$ J.

Compare this with the energy available from burning 1 kg of coal which is about 2.4×10^7 J.

The energy available per kilogram is some 3 million times greater.

■ Fuelling reactors

The supply of uranium ores is not unlimited and of this only about 0.72% of the uranium is U-235. Most is U-238 ($\approx 99.27\%$) and the rest is U-234. Plutonium-239, the other useful fissile nuclide, has a long half-life (2.4×10^4 year) but does not occur naturally. However, it is formed in reactors following the capture of neutrons by U-238 nuclei. The resulting U-239 nucleus decays first to neptunium-239 and then to Pu-239.

$$^{238}_{92}\text{U} + {}^{1}_{0}\text{n} \longrightarrow {}^{239}_{92}\text{Pu} + \gamma \text{ then } {}^{239}_{92}\text{Pu} \longrightarrow {}^{239}_{93}\text{Np} + {}^{0}_{-1}\beta^- + \bar{\nu}$$

then $\quad {}^{239}_{93}\text{Np} \longrightarrow {}^{239}_{94}\text{Pu} + {}^{0}_{-1}\beta^- + \bar{\nu}$

The plutonium produced in fuel elements captures neutrons and undergoes fission to produce useful energy. In commercial reactors about a third of the energy is produced by the fission of the plutonium. The reactors are called breeder reactors because they produce fuel as well as using it to produce energy.

■ The pressurised water reactor

A schematic diagram of a pressurised water reactor (PWR) is shown in Figure 6.

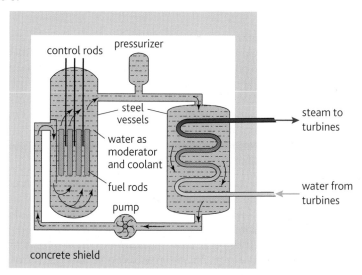

Figure 6 *A pressurised water reactor*

The key features of the reactor are:

■ a strong containing vessel, made of steel about 20 cm thick, surrounded by a reinforced concrete shield

■ the **fuel rods** which are regularly spaced in an array inside the reactor vessel

■ water which acts as a **moderator** to slow the neutrons down and as the coolant which takes the energy away from the fuel rods

■ the pressuriser which maintains a high pressure in the reactor ensuring that the water does not boil

■ **control rods** which can be raised or lowered to increase or decrease the power output of the reactor or to shut it down altogether

■ the heat exchanger which transfers the energy in the **coolant** to water in a secondary circuit causing water to boil and produce steam to drive the turbines.

Critical mass

This is the minimum mass of fuel which will produce a self-sustaining chain reaction. To start the chain reaction a source of neutrons is needed. For example, this could be neutrons produced when alpha particles collide with a beryllium nucleus. When the mass is 'critical' the number of neutrons that produce fission is constant. If the mass is too small then too many neutrons escape and the reaction rate cannot keep going. The number of fissions depends on the volume of the fissile material and the number lost depends on the surface area of the shape the mass takes. A sphere has the smallest surface area for a given volume of material so the critical mass is smallest for a sphere than any other shape.

The moderator

The moderator slows down the neutrons that are emitted when the uranium undergoes fission. At high energies too many neutrons would be absorbed by U-238. Slowing them down is necessary to make them more likely to be captured by the U-235 and cause fission.

The slow neutrons are called thermal neutrons because their kinetic energy is such that they are in thermal equilibrium with the moderator. On average they neither gain energy from the moderator nor give energy to it.

Slowing down occurs when the neutrons collide with the nuclei of the moderating material. Carbon was used in early moderators but the PWR uses water. A neutron colliding head-on with a stationary proton in a hydrogen nucleus would transfer all its energy to the proton. In other collisions, neutrons are scattered in different directions (in billiard-ball-type collisions), losing some of their energy to the protons. They subsequently reach thermal equilibrium with the moderator.

Absorption cross-section

The chance of a neutron being absorbed depends on the **absorption cross-section**. Two solid objects such as billiard balls will collide provided that the centre of each ball falls within a circle of radius equal to twice the radius of one of the balls, see Figure 7. That is within an area of πd^2, where d is the diameter of one of the balls. For billiard balls this area depends only on the physical size of the balls. For nuclei the cross-sectional area determines the probability of a particle being scattered or a reaction occurring.

In the case of nuclear interactions such as neutron absorption, the cross-section is not simply related to the diameter of the nucleus. It depends on the type of the nucleus **and** the speed of the neutron. For U-235 the absorption cross-section for slow neutrons is greater than that for fast neutrons.

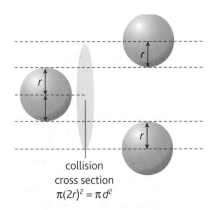

collision
cross section
$\pi(2r)^2 = \pi d^2$

Figure 7 *Scattering and absorption cross-section*

Absorption cross-sections are very small so they have their own unit, the barn:

$1\,\text{barn} = 10^{-28}\,\text{m}^2$.

For 10MeV neutrons, the fission cross-sections of U-238 and U-235 are about the same (1–2 barn). For neutrons below 1 MeV, the cross-section for U-238 is negligibly small (<0.01 barn) whilst that for U-235 increases to about 10 barn for 100 eV neutrons.

The coolant

The coolant is the fluid that absorbs the thermal energy from the fissile material and then transfers this in a heat exchanger to produce steam. The coolant has to flow past the fuel rods so it is important that it does not cause a reaction with the materials in the reactor core. Carbon dioxide gas is used in a Magnox and an Advanced Gas-Cooled Reactor (AGR) but in a PWR the water that acts as the moderator is also the coolant.

The control rods

The control rods are made from a material that absorbs neutrons such as boron. Neutrons are readily absorbed by the stable isotope boron-10 ($^{10}_{5}\text{B}$) to form another stable isotope of boron, boron-11 ($^{11}_{5}\text{B}$). The number of neutrons removed from the neutron flux depends on how far the boron rods are inserted into the reactor, in this way the power output can be controlled. The reactor can be shut down quickly in an emergency by inserting more rods into the core.

Producing electricity

Remember that the reactor simply generates thermal energy. A nuclear power station therefore contains many of the same generating features of conventional power stations that use coal or gas as can be seen in Figure 8.

The thermal energy in the reactor raises the temperature of water to produce steam. The steam drives the turbines. The turbines turn the generators producing the electricity for the national grid. The steam condenses as it drives the turbines and further cooling takes place in a heat exchanger using water from the sea or from a river. The cold water returns to the reactor to be re-heated and the warm water returns to the sea or river.

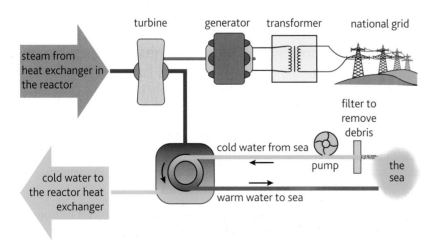

Figure 8 *Electricity generating system*

Link

Temperature change of the coolant

The rate of fluid flow $\dfrac{\Delta m}{\Delta t}$ determines the temperature change $\Delta\theta$ of the fluid as it passes through the reactor.

This is calculated from $\dfrac{\Delta Q}{\Delta t} = \dfrac{\Delta m}{\Delta t} c \Delta\theta$

where $\dfrac{\Delta Q}{\Delta t}$ is the rate of production of energy in the fuel rods and c is the specific heat capacity of water. (See Topic 6.4)

Summary questions

1 Explain the difference between the effect of the moderator and the control rods on the neutron flux in a nuclear reactor.

2 Nuclei may split up by spontaneous or induced fission. Describe the difference between these processes.

3 When a uranium-235 nucleus undergoes induced fission by absorbing a neutron, about 6% of the reactions produce molybdenum-99 ($^{99}_{42}\text{Mo}$) that is used in hospitals to generate technetium-99. If the process produces 2 neutrons what other nucleus is produced in the reaction.

4 When a neutron (mass 1.009 u) is absorbed by a uranium-235 nucleus (mass 234.993 u) the two nuclei $^{143}_{55}\text{Cs}$ and $^{90}_{37}\text{Rb}$ may be formed together with 3 neutrons. The nuclear mass of Cs-143 is 142.900 u and the mass of Rb-90 is 89.894 u. Calculate the mass change in u and the energy, in J and in MeV, for this fission reaction.

9.4 Energy from nuclear fusion

Learning objectives:

- How much energy is produced by nuclear fusion?

- How is energy produced by fusion in the Sun?

- What are the problems involved in fusion reactor design?

Specification reference: 3.5.3E

particle	binding energy /MeV	mass /u
proton	0	1.00728
deuteron ($_1^2$H)	2.2246	2.01355
helium-3	7.7181	3.01493
helium-4	28.2957	4.00160

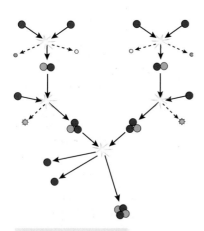

● proton
◌ neutron
✦ gamma ray photon

Figure 1 *Hydrogen cycle*

Nuclear fusion is considered to be the 'holy grail' of energy production. The 'fuels' that could be used are plentiful but at present a workable technology still has to be developed. In this topic, the principles and problems are discussed.

The energy that we receive on Earth from the Sun and stars comes from nuclear fusion processes. The development of nuclear weapons, notably the hydrogen bomb, demonstrates in a dramatic fashion that the fusion process can be replicated on Earth but only, as yet, in an uncontrolled way.

Fusion in the Sun

Fuel cycles

The principal process by which energy is generated in the Sun is a cycle called the hydrogen cycle. It is called a hydrogen cycle because the process involves fusion of protons, the nuclei of hydrogen. At the temperature of the Sun's core the hydrogen atoms that were originally present in the stellar gases are stripped of their electrons and so the Sun's core is a **plasma** of positively charged nuclei of atoms and free electrons. The cycle within the plasma takes place in the following way.

1 Two protons fuse to form a **deuteron** in the reaction
   $_1^1\text{p} + _1^1\text{p} \longrightarrow _1^2\text{H} + _{+1}^0\text{e} + \nu$.

2 The deuterium fuses with another proton to form helium-3 in the reaction $_1^2\text{H} + _1^1\text{p} \longrightarrow _2^3\text{H} + \gamma$.

3 Two helium-3 nuclei, formed in reaction 2 fuse to form helium-4 and 2 protons in the reaction $_2^3\text{H} + _2^3\text{H} \longrightarrow _2^4\text{He} + _1^1\text{p} + _1^1\text{p}$.

4 The two protons go on to fuse in further type 1 reactions.

The positron produced in stage 1 annihilates with an electron in the Sun's plasma to produce more gamma radiation.

In stage 1 the energy released = 2.2246 MeV.

In stage 2 the energy released = 7.7181 – 2.2246 = 5.4935 MeV.

In the cycle, **two** stage 1 and **two** stage 2 reactions occur to produce the two helium-3 nuclei that react in stage 3 so the energy released is 15.4362 MeV

In stage 3 the energy release = 28.2957 – (2 × 7.7181) = 12.8595 MeV.

So overall the energy release = 15.4362 + 12.8595 = 28.2957 MeV.

Figure 1 illustrates the hydrogen cycle. Notice that there are 6 protons going into the cycle and 2 are released in the final stage so that the net effect is the combination of 4 protons to produce helium-4. The energy calculated above is therefore equal to the binding energy of helium-4 given in the table.

The same overall effect of four protons combining to form helium-4 takes place in the 'carbon cycle' in which the protons in the plasma fuse with carbon and nitrogen nuclei in the cycle of changes shown in Figure 2.

How much energy?

One kilogram of hydrogen contains 6.0×10^{26} atoms. As four protons are used in each cycle, 1.5×10^{26} helium nuclei are formed per kilogram of hydrogen. So 1 kg of hydrogen produces 4.2×10^{27} MeV ($1.5 \times 10^{26} \times 28.2957$ MeV) of kinetic energy. This is 6.8×10^{14} J.

The Sun radiates energy at rate of about 3.9×10^{26} W so, assuming that all the energy is produced by the **fusion** of protons the mass fused per second is 5.8×10^{11} kg. Estimates for the mass of hydrogen in the Sun vary but assume that about 75% of its mass (2×10^{30} kg) is hydrogen and that only the hydrogen cycle is producing energy. On this basis the Sun can produce energy for about 2.6×10^{18} s or about 8×10^{10} years.

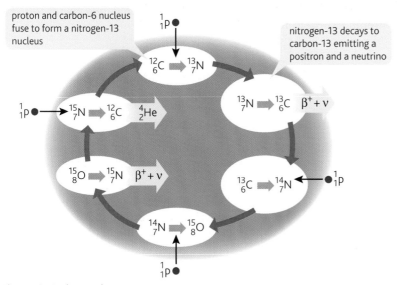

proton and carbon-6 nucleus fuse to form a nitrogen-13 nucleus

nitrogen-13 decays to carbon-13 emitting a positron and a neutrino

Figure 2 *Carbon cycle*

Why is nuclear fusion so difficult to achieve?

For reactors on Earth one of the promising fusion reactions appears to be that of fusing deuterons. Deuterons are the nuclei of hydrogen-2 which occurs naturally in water. About 0.015% of the hydrogen nuclei in water contain a proton and a neutron so there is no shortage of fuel for this type of reaction.

The energy using deuterons can be produced in stages (Figure 3):

1 Two deuterons fuse to produce a nucleus of tritium (hydrogen-3) and a proton.

2 A second deuteron fuses with the tritium nucleus to produce helium-5, a beta particle and an anti-neutrino

3 The helium-5 decays and the overall effect is the fusion of three deuterons to produce helium-4 and a proton and neutron.

Before the reaction, the binding energy is 6.674 MeV (3×2.2246 MeV) and after the reaction it is 28.296 MeV.

The binding energy has increased by 21.6 MeV so this is the energy released in the fusion processes.

So what's the problem? Because the nuclei carry a positive charge, in order to fuse they have to get close enough for the nuclear strong force to come into play. This means that the separation has to be equal to the sum of their radii. For two deuterons this separation is equal to the nuclear diameter 1.5×10^{-15} m (see Figure 4). In this position there is a strong electrostatic repulsive force.

The **electrical potential energy**, calculated from $E_P = \dfrac{Q_1 Q_2}{4\pi\varepsilon_0 r}$

is 1.5×10^{-13} J $= \left[\dfrac{(1.6 \times 10^{-19})^2}{4 \times 3.14 \times 8.9 \times 10^{-12} \times 1.5 \times 10^{-15}} \right]$.

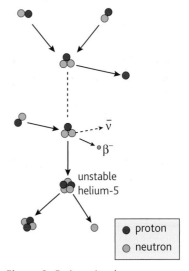

Figure 3 *Fusion using deuterons*

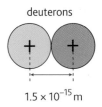

deuterons

1.5×10^{-15} m

Figure 4 *Nuclear separation necessary for fusion*

Figure 5 *Culham Science Centre*

The deuterons would have to have at least this kinetic energy if they are to come close enough to fuse.

This kinetic energy. has to be given to the deuterons by increasing the temperature of the plasma containing them. Using the gas laws, the mean kinetic energy of molecules of an ideal gas is $\frac{3}{2}kT$, where k is the Boltzmann constant and T is the temperature, in kelvin, see Topic 6.2.

Assuming that each of the deuterons has half the required energy the minimum temperature required is given by

$$\frac{1.5 \times 10^{-13}}{2} = \frac{3}{2} \times 1.38 \times 10^{-23}\,T$$

This gives a temperature of $3.7 \times 10^9\,\text{K}$. Containing the plasma at these temperatures poses significant problems for the designers.

The Joint European Torus (JET) reactor

The reactors that have been operated using fusion up to the present time are experimental reactors and have not been designed to produce electricity.

The JET reactor at the Culham Science Centre (see Figure 5) is the largest of its type in the world and has been an important first step in gaining information as to how a practical reactor might operate.

The maximum output of the JET was 16 MW but this lasted for less than a second. The JET is a 'tokomak' fusion reactor and is shown schematically in the diagram in Figure 6.

Figure 7 and Figure 8 show views of the whole reactor and the inside of the torus where the fusion takes place. The physical size of the JET can be judged from the people in Figure 7.

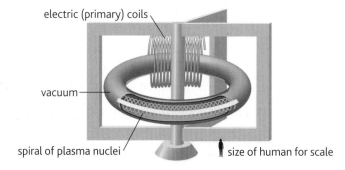

Figure 6 *Schematic diagram of the JET reactor*

Figure 7 *The JET machine*

The conditions required to produce a sustained fusion reaction depends on the confinement time and the density of the plasma. For, example, a plasma with a density of about $1 \times 10^{-6}\,\text{kg}\,\text{m}^{-3}$ would need to be confined for about 5 s.

Containing the plasma

The plasma is contained in the cavity of a torus which is shaped like the inner tube of a tyre. This is shown schematically in Figure 6, The inside of the torus used in the JET is shown in Figure 8.

The high temperature plasma must not touch the wall of the torus as this would cool it down so that fusion would not be possible. The technique used copies nature. Charged particles from space are sometimes trapped by the Earth's magnetic field. They move toward the North pole in a spiral path in the direction of the magnetic field. Near the pole they become more concentrated so they collide and produce the Aurora Borealis (northern lights). In the reactor a circular magnetic field is produced using large coils around the torus. The charged particles travel in spiral paths around the torus and are kept away from the walls. The path is however unstable and this has been a significant problem as the particles drift out of the region where they should be confined.

Heating the plasma

The plasma can be heated to a high temperature by a number of methods and these may be used at the same time. One method is to pass an electric current of about 5×10^6 A through the plasma. The temperature increases by I^2R heating and uses a few megawatts of power to do this. Another method is to inject energy in the form of electromagnetic waves rather like when using a microwave. The particles in the torus move in spiral paths with a frequency corresponding to radio frequencies. By injecting energy from a radio-frequency transmitter, the charged particles, that resonate with the frequency transmitted, gain energy.

Removing the energy

In the reactors, tritium is also produced using a lithium blanket that surrounds the plasma. The neutrons from the plasma undergo a fission reaction with the lithium-6 producing helium-4 and tritium. The tritium can be removed from the lithium blanket and then be injected into the plasma.

$$^6_3\text{He} + \,^1_0\text{n} \longrightarrow \,^4_2\text{He} + \,^3_1\text{H} + 4.8\,\text{MeV}$$

The energy of the helium nuclei (alpha particles) produced in the reactions and the energy released in the lithium neutron reaction raises the temperature of the plasma and the lithium blanket. The reaction therefore is theoretically self-sustaining. In a commercial reactor, energy could be extracted by pumping a coolant through the lithium blanket and then producing the electricity as discussed in the previous section.

Conclusion

There are many problems still to be overcome. However, the benefits of producing a commercial reactor are significant. Unlike fission reactors, fusion reactors do not have the problem of dealing with nuclear waste. The deuterium from water is plentiful and estimates of the availability of lithium suggest that there is enough to last for a thousand years. The challenge is to produce such a reactor by joint international effort over the next half century. Could it be that some of the students working for this examination will be involved in making the breakthrough?

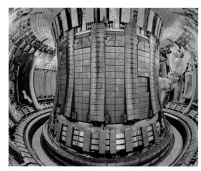

Figure 8 *Interior of the JET vacuum vessel (2005)*

Summary questions

1 The binding energy for helium-4 is 28.296 MeV. The binding energy of beryllium-8 is of 56.499 MeV. Deduce whether or not energy is released when two helium nuclei fuse to produce beryllium-8.

2 How much energy in joule could be produced from the fusion of 1 mole of hydrogen nuclei to form helium-4?

3 Give two advantages of producing energy using fusion reactors compared with fission reactors.

4 Describe and explain one major problem that has to be overcome in the design of a practical nuclear reactor.

9.5 What's the risk?

Learning objectives:

■ What is meant by risk?

■ What risks are associated with the generation of nuclear power?

■ What are the risks in diagnosis and treatment using applications of physics?

■ How is risk minimised?

Specification reference: 3.5.3F

What is meant by risk?

Risk is the probability of harm being caused by an activity. Everyday life is full of risks. What we eat and drink, how we travel to work and how we play poses possibilities of harm to ourselves. Even staying in bed to avoid these risks poses a health hazard so we have to accept the everyday risks and do whatever is sensible and practical to ensure that serious harm does not come to us.

When an activity is undertaken it will have positive effects. This may be simply entertainment for the individual as when participating in, say bungee jumping, or for spectators, as when watching a motor race. It may be the type of activity that progresses human knowledge, such as that gained from space travel, or the diagnosis and treatment of an illness.

The activity could be harmful to:

■ the health of the person undertaking the activity

■ the health of others not directly involved in the activity

■ the equipment that is used

■ the natural environment including plant and animal life.

On a larger scale, we now live in a world where science has enabled technological developments that enhance our lives. During this course many examples of these developments have been discussed such as different methods of producing electrical energy, methods of communication, thrilling fairground rides and medical diagnosis and treatment using new methods. Scientists have to advise decision makers on the benefits of developments using new discoveries and the possible negative impact the developments may have.

The risks associated with the activity have to be assessed. This includes the probability of a particularly harmful occurrence and the subsequent consequences. Once the particular risks have been identified steps have to be taken either to eliminate the risks altogether or to reduce them to an acceptable level.

Assessing risk

In carrying out risk assessment of an activity the following steps are needed:

■ Identification of the hazards.

■ Consideration of who or what might be harmed and how this harm occurs.

■ Evaluation of the level of risk involved and how this can be reduced to an acceptable level or eliminated.

■ Implementation of the decisions.

■ Continual review of risks as the activity progresses.

The level of risk is measured by the probability of something going wrong during an activity and the level of harm that occurs when it does go wrong. For example, the chance of being run over when crossing a road, the probability of a driver in any given age group having an accident, or the probability of a house being flooded during any one year. Risks like these are analysed by government to produce laws such as imposing speed limits and by insurance companies to fix the size of insurance premiums.

Assessment activity

In an A level science laboratory, there are hazards that need to be considered carefully. For example, the use of high voltage supplies, heavy masses, hot objects, toxic liquids, and radioactive materials could harm the experimenter or others in a laboratory. Equipment is costly and care is needed to prevent damage to apparatus such as by dropping thermometers or by overloading resistors, ammeters or voltmeters. Every experiment has to be assessed for the risks involved. Criteria in the practical assessment refer to your ability to carry out risk assessment.

At this stage in the course it is instructive to think about some of the risks associated with topics that have been studied and discuss them with others. Some questions worthy of discussion are listed in the 'Worth the risk?' feature.

 Application and How science works

Worth the risk?

1 Is listening to loud music risky?
2 Does the radiation from mobile phones and telecommunication masts affect health?
3 How risky is a roller-coaster fairground ride?
4 What are the risks of building particular types of power stations?
5 What are the risks of not building them?
6 What are the risks involved in space travel? Are the risk levels acceptable?

The internet provides a wealth of information on such matters, some biased and some objective.

Public perception of risk

The public gain their appreciation of risk mostly from the media. Their perception may be influenced by the scale of disastrous events. For example, some members of the public may feel that rail travel is particularly dangerous because when disasters happen there are often many deaths that occur at once. However, when the data for each mode of travel are expressed in terms of deaths per miles travelled, rail deaths may carry a much lower risk. Data are often difficult to compare. Statistics may be provided in a way that makes comparison difficult. For example, in one publication, the annual number of fatalities when travelling by rail is quoted in terms of number of fatalities per **billion passenger-kilometres** whereas fatalities by road travel is quoted in terms of the number of fatalities per **100 000 vehicle-kilometres**.

Pressure groups tend to select and promote the risks associated with carrying out a particular proposal and the risks that could result from **not** carrying out the particular proposal often receives less publicity.

Here are some questions that may be asked regarding the public perception of the risks:

■ Are the risks associated with going ahead with a proposal and not going ahead with it presented in a balanced way?

■ Do the public have sufficient information to form a sensible judgement?

 How science works

Putting it in perspective

At present the estimate of cancer risk at low doses recommended by NRPB (National Radiological Protection Board) for use in the UK predicts that a lifetime of exposure of the population to all sources of ionising radiation (natural plus man-made) could be responsible for an additional risk of fatal cancer of about 1% – this can be compared with a life-time risk of cancer of about 20–25% from all causes. The very small doses from non-medical, man-made radiation would be responsible for only a tiny fraction (about one-hundredth) of this 1% radiation risk. Therefore, compared with other known cancer risk factors in the population such as cigarette smoking, excessive exposure to sunlight and poor diet, the risk to the population from non-medical man-made radiation is generally agreed to be very small indeed.

Health Protection Agency

Figure 1 *Radiation sign*

Figure 2 *Radiation film badge*

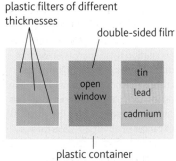

Figure 3 *Structure of a film badge*

■ What is the role of scientists in informing the public and decision makers on risks?

Risk in medicine

Doctors often have to make a decision based on a comparison of the risks of different alternative treatments or the risks of doing something compared with the risk of doing nothing. For example, for a patient with a cancer the risk of providing no treatment must be compared with the risks associated with an operation or the side effects of radiation treatment.

The risks of X-ray examinations can be quantified by gathering data over a period of time. A typical X-ray of an arm or leg is equivalent to about 1.5 days worth of background radiation. The lifetime additional risk of this causing a fatal cancer is reckoned to be 1 in a few million. In more sensitive parts such as the abdomen, the X-ray dose is larger and equivalent to about 4 months worth of background radiation so the risk is far greater, an increase of 1 in about 30 000.

Radiation protection

The rules governing the handling of radioactive materials are very strict. The sign in Figure 1 indicates the presence of a radiation hazard. Students, research workers and radiologists need to take great care to protect themselves from ionising radiation. The following is a list of some rules that govern workers in a typical laboratory. Consider why these rules were devised and how someone disobeying each rule would put their health at risk from radiation.

■ Eating or drinking are prohibited and no food should be taken into the work area.

■ Self-adhesive labels should be used; **do not use** labels that have to be moistened to become adhesive.

■ A laboratory coat should be worn and fully buttoned.

■ Gloves must be worn when handling radioactive substances.

■ Any cuts or abrasions of the hands should be covered.

■ Unsealed radioactive substances should be moved, carried or used only within secondary containment.

■ Handle sources with tongs.

■ Working surfaces should be covered with absorbent, disposable material.

■ Appropriate shielding should be used.

■ The working area should be monitored before and after an experiment.

■ People should stay away from areas where radioactive materials are being used unless necessary.

■ Before leaving the laboratory, gloves should be removed without hands touching the outside. Hands should be washed. Protective clothing should be monitored before removal.

In an A-level laboratory most sources are sealed and have a low activity so some of the rules relating to open sources are less significant. However, the source in the protactinium experiment is a liquid source so particular care has to be taken.

The main protection for workers is focussed on how to handle sources and reduce the dose of radiation received. Swallowing of any radioactive material is extremely hazardous so many of the rules are designed to eliminate this risk. The protection required depends on the radiation used. Alpha particles cannot penetrate the skin so the harm these do is limited to the outer layer of the body. An operator will receive no dose from beta radiation that is more than about 0.5 m away but because gamma radiation is emitted when the beta particles are stopped, this has to be taken into account too.

When working with gamma sources it is important to use suitable screening such as a few centimetres of lead between the source and the body. Remember too that the intensity of radiation from gamma radiation obeys an inverse-square law so by moving twice as far away the dose is reduced to a quarter.

Monitoring radiation dose

Although care in the working environment minimises the dose received, monitoring still takes place. The dose a worker receives may be monitored weekly, monthly or quarterly depending on the nature of the work and particularly vulnerable people, such as pregnant women, are monitored more often. Radiation badges (or dosimeters) are used for monitoring.

The dosimeters may be in the form of a ring or badge, depending on the type of work an employee undertakes. In one type, the radiation falling on aluminium oxide puts electrons into an excited state where they remain until radiation from a laser causes them to relax emitting visible light. The intensity of this light is a measure of the dose. Alternatively, radiation falling on photographic film causes a change in colour and the depth of colour can be measured to find the dose.

Absorbers made of different materials and thicknesses can be placed in front of different parts of the film so that the dose of each type of radiation is known. This information is necessary to account for the different ionising abilities of different types of radiation which also affects the damage that the radiation can do.

Nuclear power

The hazards associated with nuclear power are probably discussed with more emotion than most other activities. The devastating effects of the events at Chernobyl were felt around the globe and the consequences are still being dealt with in the health of the people most affected. Because the consequences of reactor failure are so great the rules governing the design of reactors are very strict and research to further improve the safe operation of reactors continues.

Apart from the release of radiation into the atmosphere from reactor meltdown the other issue of concern is the transport and disposal of nuclear waste. The transport of nuclear waste through urban areas and sites for burial of the waste are contentious issues. At present the waste from UK nuclear power stations is processed at Sellafield in Cumbria.

To minimise risks, the spent fuel is transported in strong steel flasks that are designed to withstand any likely collision. The spent fuel rods are stored in cooling ponds such as that shown in Figure 4. After removal of any useful isotopes the remaining waste is buried in deep caverns where it will have to remain for many hundreds of years.

Low-level waste such as that from hospitals can be stored in metal drums and buried in large trenches on selected sites.

Figure 4 Spent fuel rods in a cooling pond

Summary questions

1. Give two reasons why the use of tongs is advised for safe handling of radioactive materials.

2. Explain why eating and drinking is not permitted where radioactive materials are being used?

3. What do the data in the quotation from the health agency suggest is the approximate additional risk of cancer that is caused by non-medical man-made radiation?

4. Imagine you are opposed to the building of a nuclear power station. Write a short letter to a newspaper supported by scientific argument explaining your opposition.

5. Someone has written to a newspaper expressing opposition to the building of a nuclear power station expressing views about the risks involved. Write a letter explaining how developers minimise the risks involved so that they are reduced to acceptable levels.

1 (a) In the reactor at a nuclear power station, uranium nuclei undergo *induced fission* with *thermal neutrons*. Explain what is meant by each of the terms in italics.   *(4 marks)*

A typical fission reaction in the reactor is represented by

$$^{235}_{92}\text{U} + {}^{1}_{0}\text{n} \longrightarrow {}^{92}_{36}\text{Kr} + {}^{141}_{56}\text{Ba} + N$$

where N is the number of neutrons emitted in the reaction

   (b) Calculate N.   *(1 mark)*

   (c) Explain how the neutrons produced in this reaction differ from the initial neutron that begins the reaction   *(1 mark)*

   (d) Calculate the energy released in MeV when one uranium nucleus undergoes fission in this reaction.

mass of neutron   = 1.00867 u

mass of ^{235}U nucleus   = 234.99333 u

mass of ^{92}Kr nucleus   = 91.90645 u

mass of ^{141}Ba nucleus   = 140.88354 u   *(4 marks)*

2 (a) Sketch a graph to show how the neutron number, N, varies with the proton number, Z, for naturally occurring stable nuclei over the range $Z = 0$ to $Z = 90$. Show values of N and Z on the axes of your graph and draw the $N = Z$ line.   *(4 marks)*

   (b) On your graph mark points, one for each, to indicate the position of an unstable nuclide which would be likely to be

an α emitter, labelling it A,

a β$^-$ emitter, labelling it B.   *(2 marks)*

   (c) State the changes in N and Z which are produced in the emission of

   (i) an α particle,   *(2 marks)*

   (ii) a β$^-$ particle.   *(2 marks)*

3 A proton and a deuterium (^2_1H) nucleus can fuse together to form a helium nucleus (He).

$$^{1}_{1}\text{p} + {}^{2}_{1}\text{H} \longrightarrow {}^{3}_{2}\text{He} + Q$$

Calculate, in joules, the energy Q released in this reaction.

mass of a proton   = 1.00728 u

mass of a $^3_2$He nucleus   = 3.01493 u

mass of a $^2_1$H nucleus   = 2.01355 u   *(4 marks)*

4 (a) The mass of a nucleus ^4_ZX is M.

Determine an expression for the binding energy per nucleon of this nucleus, taking the speed of light to be c and the masses of the proton and neutron to be m_p and m_n respectively.   *(3 marks)*

   (b) **Figure 1** shows an enlarged portion of a graph indicating how the binding energy per nucleon of various nuclides varies with their nucleon number.

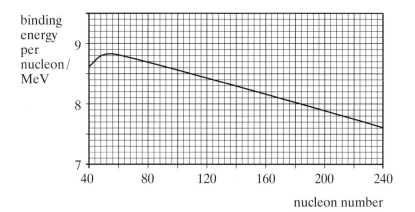

Figure 1

State the value of the nucleon number for the nuclides that are most likely to be stable. Give your reasoning. *(2 marks)*

(c) When fission of uranium-235 takes place, the nucleus splits into two roughly equal parts. Estimate the energy in MeV that will be released during this fission. *(1 mark)*

5   In a nuclear reactor, uranium nuclei undergo *induced fission* by *thermal neutrons*. The reaction is a *self-sustaining chain reaction* which requires *moderation* and has to be *controlled*.

(a) Explain the meaning of the terms
  (i)   induced fission   *(2 marks)*
  (ii) thermal neutrons   *(1 mark)*
  (iii) chain reaction   *(3 marks)*

(b) (i) Describe the process of *moderation* in a nuclear reactor   *(6 marks)*
  (ii) Indicate the physical properties of a suitable moderator and state one typical material used for this purpose. *(3 marks)*

(c) Describe how the rate of fission is controlled in a nuclear reactor. *(4 marks)*

6   A nucleus of plutonium ($^{240}_{94}$Pu) decays to form uranium (U) and an alpha-particle (α).

(a) Complete the equation that describes this decay:
$$^{240}_{94}\text{Pu} \longrightarrow$$
(2 marks)

(b) (i) Show that about 1 pJ of energy is released when one nucleus decays.

  mass of plutonium nucleus $= 3.98626 \times 10^{-25}$ kg
  mass of uranium nucleus $= 3.91970 \times 10^{-25}$ kg
  mass of alpha particle $= 6.64251 \times 10^{-27}$ kg
  speed of electromagnetic radiation $= 2.99792 \times 10^{8}$ m s^{-1} *(3 marks)*

  (ii) The plutonium isotope has a half-life of 2.1×10^{11} s. Show that the decay constant of the plutonium is about 3×10^{-12} s^{-1}. *(3 marks)*

  (iii) A radioactive source in a school laboratory contains 3.2×10^{21} atoms of plutonium. Calculate the energy that will be released in one second by the decay of the plutonium described in part (b)(i). *(3 marks)*

  (iv) Comment on whether the energy release due to the plutonium decay is likely to change by more than 5% during 100 years. Support your answer with a calculation. *(4 marks)*

7   **Figure 2** shows the variation of nuclear binding energy per nucleon with nucleon number for low values of nucleon number.

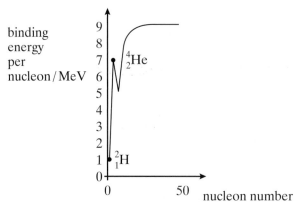

Figure 2

(a) Explain what is meant by the phrase *nuclear binding energy*.   *(2 marks)*

(i) Use the diagram above to explain, in terms of binding energy, why the formation of $^4_2$He (helium) by the fusion of two $^2_1$H (heavy hydrogen) nuclei results in the production of energy.   *(2 marks)*

(ii) Use data from the diagram above to estimate the amount of energy, in J, released when two $^2_1$H nuclei fuse.   *(4 marks)*

8   A water-cooled nuclear reactor has a reactor power output of 550 MW. Two water circuits are used to cool the reactor: a primary circuit that has water flowing in a closed circuit within the reactor, and a secondary circuit in which the primary water is used in a heat exchanger to boil water into steam used to drive turbines.

The temperature of the primary-circuit water is allowed to rise (under pressure) to 315°C in the reactor core and the energy is transferred to the secondary heat exchangers at a temperature of 275°C. The average specific heat capacity of water under these conditions is 5300 J kg^{-1} K^{-1}.

(a) Use the data in the passage to calculate the rate of water flow that will be required in the primary circuit.   *(3 marks)*

(b) Explain why two water circuits are used in this type of reactor.   *(2 marks)*

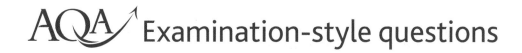
Unit 5 questions: Energy under the microscope

1 (a) State what is meant by an ideal gas. *(3 marks)*

   (b) An ideal gas is pumped into a sealed cylinder of an engine until the pressure
        becomes 2.3 MPa. The internal volume of the cylinder is $0.57 \times 10^{-3}\,m^3$ and the
        temperature of the gas is 37°C.

        Calculate:

        (i)   The number of moles of gas in the cylinder *(3 marks)*

        (ii) The number of gas atoms in the cylinder *(2 marks)*

   (c) Estimate the average separation of the gas atoms. *(3 marks)*

2 (a) The first law of thermodynamics can be written

$$\Delta U = Q + W.$$

        (i)   State the meaning of each term in this equation. *(3 marks)*

        (ii) Explain why, for an isothermal expansion, the first law can be written
              $-W = Q$. *(3 marks)*

   (b) **Figure 1** shows part of an ideal heat engine cycle in which a fixed mass of gas is
        taken through the following processes:

        process A: isothermal compression at low temperature with an input of work of 83 J

        process B: constant volume increase in pressure with an energy input by heating of 200 J

        process C: isothermal expansion at high temperature with work output of 139 J

        process D: constant volume cooling to the original pressure, volume and temperature

        In this cycle, the energy input in process B is the same as the energy rejected in process D.

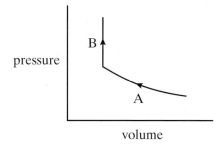

Figure 1

        (i)   Copy Figure 1 and draw in processes C and D to complete the whole cycle. *(2 marks)*

        (ii) Copy and complete the table by applying the first law of thermodynamics to
              each process and to the whole cycle.

process	Q/J	$\Delta U/J$	W/J
A		0	+83
B	+200	+200	
C			-139
D			0
whole cycle			

        (iii) The highest and lowest temperatures of the air during the cycle are 500 K
              and 300 K. Show that the thermal efficiency of the ideal cycle is equal to the
              maximum possible efficiency for any heat engine working between these
              temperature limits.

3 An inventor has designed a gas engine for a small combined heat and power plant which will operate between temperatures of 1400 K and 360 K. The inventor makes two claims about the performance of the engine:

claim 1 When the engine consumes gas at a rate of 9.6 kg h⁻¹, it will deliver a useful mechanical output power of 80 kW. One kilogramme of the gas releases 36 MJ of energy when burnt.

claim 2 At the same time, the engine will also provide energy at the rate of at least 20 kW for heating purposes.

(a) Show that the input power to the engine is approximately 100 kW. *(3 marks)*

(b) Calculate the maximum possible efficiency of any heat engine which operates between temperatures of 1400 K and 360 K. *(3 marks)*

(c) Using the result of your calculation in part (b) and any other necessary calculations, explain whether either or both of the inventor's claims are justified. *(5 marks)*

(d) The water cooling system is designed to remove 30 kW of thermal energy from the engine at 360 K and reject this energy at 300 K. Calculate, in kg s⁻¹, the required flow rate of water through the cooling system.

specific heat capacity of water, $c = 4200$ K kg⁻¹ K⁻¹ *(3 marks)*

4 (a) **Figure 2** shows an electron gun in an evacuated tube. Electrons emitted by *thermionic emission* from the metal filament are attracted to the metal anode which is at a fixed potential, V, relative to the filament. Some of the electrons pass though a small hole in the anode to form a beam which is directed into a uniform magnetic field. *(1 mark)*

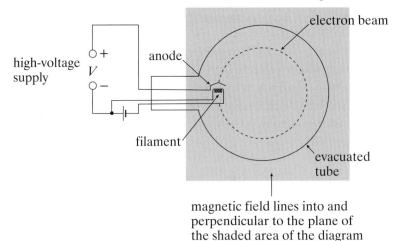

Figure 2

(i) Explain what is meant by thermionic emission *(2 marks)*

(ii) Show that the speed, v, of the electrons in the beam is given by

$$v = \left(\frac{2eV}{m}\right)^{\frac{1}{2}},$$

where m is the mass of the electron and e is the charge of the electron. *(3 marks)*

(b) The beam of electrons travels through the field in a circular path at constant speed

(i) Explain why the electrons travel at constant speed in the magnetic field. *(4 marks)*

(ii) Show that the radius, r, of the circular path of the beam in the field is given by

$$r = \left(\frac{2mV}{B^2e}\right)^{\frac{1}{2}}$$

where B is the magnetic flux density and V is the pd between the anode and the filament. *(3 marks)*

(iii) The arrangement described above was used to measure the specific charge of the electron, e/m. Use the following data to calculate e/m.

$B = 3.1\,\text{mT}$

$r = 25\,\text{mm}$

$V = 530\,\text{V}$ *(4 marks)*

5   (a)   The speed of an object cannot be greater than or equal to the speed of light yet its kinetic energy can be increased without limit. Explain the apparent contradiction that the speed of an object is limited whereas its kinetic energy is not limited. *(3 marks)*

Protons are accelerated from rest through a potential difference of $2.1 \times 10^{10}\,\text{V}$.

       (i)   Show that the kinetic energy of a proton after it has been accelerated from rest through this potential difference is $3.4 \times 10^{-9}\,\text{J}$. *(2 marks)*

       (ii)   Show that the mass of a proton with a kinetic energy value of $3.4 \times 10^{-9}\,\text{J}$ is approximately $23\,m_0$, where m_0 is its rest mass. *(4 marks)*

    (c)   Calculate, in terms of c (the speed of light in vacuum), the speed of a proton which has a mass equal to $23\,m_0$. *(3 marks)*

6   The diagram below shows a number of smoke particles suspended in air. The arrows indicate the directions in which the particles are moving at a particular time.

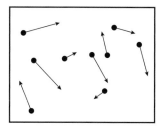

Figure 3

    (a)   (i)   Explain why the smoke particles are observed to move. *(1 mark)*

       (ii)   Smoke particles are observed to move in a random way. State three conclusions about air molecules and their motion resulting from this observation *(3 marks)*

A sample of air has a density of $1.24\,\text{kg}\,\text{m}^{-3}$ at a pressure of $1.01 \times 10^5\,\text{Pa}$ and a temperature of $300\,\text{K}$.

    (b)   (i)   Calculate the mean kinetic energy of an air molecule under these conditions *(2 marks)*

       (ii)   Calculate the root mean square speed for the air molecules. *(3 marks)*

       (iii)   Explain why, when the temperature of the air is increased to $320\,\text{K}$, some of the molecules will have speeds much less than that suggested by the value you calculated in part (b)(ii). *(2 marks)*

7   The diagram below shows part of a linear accelerator, which accelerates ions along the axis of a line of hollow cylindrical electrodes (A–D). Alternate electrodes are connected together and an alternating voltage is applied to them such that the ions are accelerated by the electric field in between each adjacent pair of electrodes.

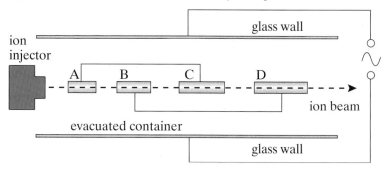

Figure 4

    (a)   Explain how the acceleration of the particles is achieved. Assume that electrode B initially is negative with respect to electrode A. *(5 marks)*

(b) Explain why the speed of an ion does not change whilst they are inside the cylindrical electrodes. *(2 marks)*

(c) The following data relate to an experiment using mercury ions (Hg^+):

accelerating voltage between adjacent pairs of electrodes = 71 kV

frequency of the alternating voltage = 4.0 MHz

charge on a mercury ion = 1.6×10^{-19} C

mass of mercury ion = 3.35×10^{-25} kg

   (i) Show that each mercury ion gains kinetic energy of approximately 1×10^{-14} J as it accelerates between a pair of electrodes. *(3 marks)*

   (ii) Ions are injected into electrode A with an initial velocity of 2.1×10^5 m s^{-1}. Show that the velocity of a mercury ion as it enters electrode B is about 3×10^5 m s^{-1}. *(4 marks)*

   (iii) At each gap ions are accelerated for a time equivalent to 5% of the alternating voltage period. Calculate the force on a mercury ion as it accelerates in the gap between electrodes A and B. *(4 marks)*

   (iv) Calculate the electric field strength across the gap between electrodes A and B. Assume that the electric field is uniform whilst the ion is accelerating *(2 marks)*

   (v) Calculate the length of the gap between electrodes A and B. *(3 marks)*

   (vi) Calculate the length of electrode B. *(3 marks)*

8 (a) A space probe contains a small fission reactor, fuelled by plutonium, which is designed to produce an average of 300 W of useful power for 100 years. If the overall efficiency of the reactor is 10%, calculate the minimum mass of plutonium required.

energy released by the fission of one nucleus of $^{239}_{94}Pu$ = 3.2×10^{-11} J *(8 marks)*

(b) A larger plutonium reactor of similar design is to be used to power a future manned space mission. Outline how the designers might minimise the risk to the astronauts who will spend long periods in the space craft.

Plutonium is a long-lived alpha emitter. *(5 marks)*

9 (a) (i) Complete the equation below which represents the induced fission of a nucleus of uranium $^{235}_{92}U$.

$$^{235}_{92}U + {}^{1}_{0}n \longrightarrow {}^{98}_{38}Cs + {}_{54}Xe + {}^{1}_{0}n$$ *(2 marks)*

   (ii) The graph shows the binding energy per nucleon plotted against nucleon number A.

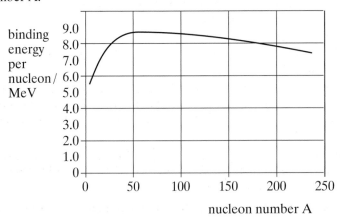

Figure 5

Mark on the graph the position of each of the three nuclei in the equation. *(3 marks)*

   (iii) Use the graph to determine the energy released in the fission process represented by the equation in part (a)(i) *(4 marks)*

(b) (i) Use your answer to part (a)(iii) to estimate the energy released when 1.0 kg of uranium, containing 3% by mass of $^{235}_{92}U$, undergoes fission. *(4 marks)*

(ii) Oil releases approximately 50 MJ of heat per kg when it is burned in air. State and explain one advantage and one disadvantage of using nuclear fuel to produce electricity. *(4 marks)*

10 (a) With reference to the process of nuclear fusion, explain why energy is released when two small nuclei join together, and why it is difficult to make two nuclei come together. *(4 marks)*

(b) A fusion reaction takes place when two deuterium nuclei join, as represented by

$$^2_1H + {}^2_1H \longrightarrow {}^3_1He + {}^1_0n$$

mass of ^2_1H nucleus $= 2.01355\,u$

mass of ^3_2He nucleus $= 3.01493\,u$

mass of neutron $= 1.00867\,u$

(b) (i) Calculate, in kg, the mass difference produced when two deuterium nuclei undergo fusion. *(3 marks)*

(ii) Calculate, in J, the energy released when this reaction occurs. *(3 marks)*

(c) Give an account of the likely benefits to society that may occur if nuclear fusion can be used to generate electrical energy on a commercial scale. *(4 marks)*

11 The diagram below shows a $20\,\mu F$ capacitor used in a medical pacemaker under test. It is connected to a 150 V supply

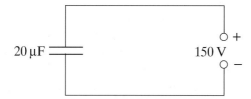

Figure 6

(a) Calculate the charge on the capacitor. *(2 marks)*

(b) (i) Sketch a graph showing how the charge Q on a capacitor varies with V, the potential difference across it. Explain how this graph can be used to calculate the energy stored. *(2 marks)*

(ii) Calculate the maximum energy stored by the capacitor when it has a p.d. of 150 V across it. *(2 marks)*

(c) The fully charged capacitor is removed from the power supply and discharged by connecting a $220\,k\Omega$ resistor across it.

(i) Calculate the maximum discharge current. *(1 mark)*

(ii) Show that the current will have fallen to 10% of its maximum value in a time of approximately 10 s. *(4 marks)*

(d) A pair of identical capacitors are connected across a d.c. power supply and connected (i) in series and (ii) in parallel. The potential difference across the terminals of the power supply is unchanged. State and explain which arrangement stores the greater energy. *(5 marks)*

12 Natural uranium consists of 99.3% $^{238}_{92}U$ and 0.7% $^{235}_{92}U$. In many nuclear reactors, the fuel consists of enriched uranium enclosed in sealed metal containers known as fuel rods.

(a) Explain what is meant by enriched uranium. *(1 mark)*

(b) Why is enriched uranium rather than natural uranium used in many nuclear reactors? *(1 mark)*

(c) By considering the neutrons involved in the fission process, explain how the rate of production of heat in a nuclear reactor is controlled. *(4 marks)*

(d) Explain why all the fuel in a nuclear reactor is not placed in a single fuel rod. *(4 marks)*

Investigative and practical skills

Chapters in this unit

10 **Practical work in A2 physics**

11 **Internal assessment in A2 physics**

12 **Mathematical skills for A2 physics**

■ Moving on from AS level

Practical work is an integral feature of your A2 physics course just as at AS level because it helps you develop your understanding of important concepts and applications as well as learning how scientists work in practice and finding out how important discoveries were made and continue to be made in the subject. A2 practical skills embrace the practical skills you have developed in your AS course and you will develop them further in the context of the more demanding knowledge and understanding of the A2 course. For example, in your studies on radioactivity, you will learn how to use a Geiger counter when you study how to measure the effect of absorbers on different forms of ionising radiation. At AS level you learnt new analytical skills such as using measured data to plot a straight-line graph in order to confirm a theoretical relationship (e.g. load against extension graph for a spring). At A2, such skills are developed further by using them in the context of more complex theoretical relationships (e.g. measuring capacitor discharge and plotting ln V against time to confirm the decay is exponential).

■ Assessment overview

The assessment of A2 investigative and practical skills is undertaken in Unit 6 and carries the same percentage of the total A2 mark as Unit 3 (the corresponding AS Unit) does at AS level. The structure of Unit 6 is similar to that of Unit 3 in that the same two assessment schemes are available, namely scheme T (the PSA/ISA route) and scheme X (the EMPA/PSV route). An outline of each scheme is given below. As at AS, your teacher will decide which scheme you and your fellow students will follow and this may or may not be the same scheme as you followed at AS level. For example, your assessment in Unit 3 might have been through scheme X and your A2 assessment might be through scheme T. Whichever scheme of assessment you follow, they both count for a total of 20% of the A2 mark and the structure and format is the same as at AS level, but the level of complexity is higher at A2 because the A2 topics are more complex and demanding. The differences in demand and complexity between internal assessment at AS and at A2 are explained in more detail in Chapter 10.

Scheme T The ISA/PSA scheme

This assessment scheme is in two parts:

1 **The investigative skills assignments (ISA)** consists of a practical task on a topic in the specification followed by a written test on your ability to analyse data and evaluate results. More details are given about A2 ISAs in Topic 11.1. The written test will ask you about the results of your own task and about given results from a related practical investigation. The practical task and the written test are both set by AQA and are taken under supervision after you have studied the relevant topic. The ISA counts for 41 out of the 50 marks for the Unit.

2 **The practical skills assessment (PSA)** will assess how well you can follow instructions and on how well you can make measurements. The assessment is made by your teacher **towards the end of your course** and is based on your practical work during the course, specifically your ability to follow instructions, your skill in using equipment and how well you can organise yourself and work safely in the laboratory. The PSA assessment counts for 9 out of the 50 marks for the Unit. More details are given about the PSA at A2 in Topic 11.1.

Scheme X The EMPA/PSV scheme

This AQA-marked scheme is in three parts.

Part 1 Practical skills verification
You are required to carry out 5 short practical exercises in normal class time on measuring tasks set by AQA. Your teacher will check that you have carried out each of these tasks satisfactorily. Some of the measuring skills in these tasks will be assessed in the AQA-set practical experiments in part 2.

Parts 2 and 3 Externally-marked practical assessment
These parts consist of practical experiments (part 2) and a written test (part 3) set and marked by AQA. You will need to obtain reliable and accurate results in the experiments as you have to analyse and evaluate them in the written test.

More details about scheme X at A2 are given in Topic 11.2.

10.1 Comparison of physics practical work at A2 and at AS level

The notes that follow apply equally well to either scheme as the skills you need to develop before assessment are the same for both schemes. References below to PSA or ISA features in scheme T apply equally well to the corresponding features in scheme X unless specifically stated.

In any practical assessment at AS or at A2 level, you are assessed on your ability to:

- plan an investigation,
- carry out practical work,
- analyse data from practical experiments and investigations, and
- evaluate the results of practical experiments and investigations.

Planning

In assessment terms, this might be part of the practical task or activities that you have to carry out or it might be part of the written test in which you have to write about how you would improve an investigation or how you would carry out a different investigation in the same topic area. At A2, the topics are more complex than at AS level so you can expect assessment questions on planning to be more demanding than at AS level. For example,

- at AS level, after carrying out a practical task on how you would investigate the rebound height of a ball released from a certain height, you might be asked to say how you would investigate successive rebound heights to find out if there is a pattern.
- at A2, your practical task might involve timing the oscillations of a mass–spring system for different masses. You might then be asked in the written paper to describe how you would investigate the effect of damping on the oscillations of a mass–spring system. Thus the context of the A2 'planning' question is more complex than at AS as you have to describe how you would apply damping to a mass–spring system, how you would vary the degree of damping and how you measure the effect of the damping.

Carrying out practical work

At AS and at A2 you are required to set up apparatus and possibly rearrange it as part of the procedures you have to follow. You also have to make reliable and accurate measurements, selecting and using the appropriate measuring instruments in the process. The difference between what you have done at AS level and what you have to do at A2 lies once again in the more advanced topics in the A2 course and in the level of complexity of some of the instruments and procedures you have to use. For example,

■ At AS level, you might be asked to investigate the electrical characteristics of a circuit in a sealed box by setting up a circuit, given the circuit diagram, and making a set of measurements of current and pd in the forward and reverse directions through the box. In addition, you would be asked to record your measurements in a table and, in this case, to plot a graph of your results.

■ At A2, you might be asked to set up a circuit to charge a capacitor and discharge it through a resistor then make measurements of the capacitor pd at measured times as it charges or discharges. You would have to decide on the number of measurements to be made, the time interval between successive measurements and the exact procedure of how to make the measurements. The timing element in this investigation adds a further level of complexity beyond AS level.

Analysing data

At AS level and at A2 you generally need to process the data (e.g. calculation of mean values) and plot a graph. In many investigations, the graph has to be related to an equation to check a theoretical relationship or to measure a physical property.

■ At AS level, the theoretical equations you meet in the AS course are generally linear equations (e.g. $s = vt$ for a distance–time graph of an object falling in a viscous fluid at terminal speed) or sometimes simple non-linear equations (e.g. $s = \frac{1}{2}gt^2$ for a distance–time^2 graph of an object falling in air).

■ At A2, there may be more variables than at AS level and the processing of the data might be more complicated, for example the calculation of log values. The graph plotting exercise requires the same skills as at AS level but the analysis might be more complicated. For example, you would probably be expected to plot a log graph in a capacitor discharge experiment and use it to determine the time constant RC of the discharge circuit or you might be expected to plot a log–log graph as explained in 12.2 (see Figure 2 in 12.2 and the related text) to establish if two variables x and y relate to each other according to an equation of the form $y = kx^n$.

Evaluating your results

At AS and A2 this involves discussing the strength of your conclusions. From your work at AS level, you should now know how to:

■ distinguish between systematic errors (including zero errors) and random errors,

■ understand in respect of measurements what is meant by accuracy, uncertainty, sensitivity, linearity, reliability, precision and validity,

■ estimate experimental uncertainties for each measured quantity and use them as outlined to estimate the overall percentage uncertainty of a result determined from the measured quantities.

If you are unsure about the meaning of any of the above terms, look them up in the glossary of practical terms at the end of this book.

Using experimental uncertainties

As explained in Topic 15.4 of the AS book,

- if two measurements are added or subtracted, the uncertainty of the result is the sum of the uncertainties of the two measurements,

- if a quantity in a calculation is raised to a power n, the percentage uncertainty is increased n times.

- In addition, at A2, if two or more quantities are multiplied or divided by each other in a calculation, the overall percentage uncertainty in the result is the sum of the uncertainties of each quantity. For example, if the % uncertainty in a resistance R is 5% and in a capacitance C is 4%, the % uncertainty in RC is 9%.

Clearly, the more demanding nature of the A2 topics compared with AS makes the evaluation of a practical investigation more challenging, but the same general features as outlined above still apply. For example,

- at AS level, you might be asked to investigate the motion of an object sliding down a slope by measuring the time taken by the object to slide different measured distances down the slope and plotting a distance–time[2] graph. In your evaluation, you might be asked to use a certain measurement (e.g. the smallest) to estimate the percentage uncertainty in the measurement of the dependent and independent variables so you could compare them and discuss how to improve the investigation.

- at A2, you might be asked to investigate the oscillations of a mass–spring system and to use the measurements to plot a graph of time–period[2] against mass and show the uncertainty in each measurement on the graph, as outlined in *AS Physics* Topic 15.4. This would enable you to draw best-fit straight lines with a maximum and minimum gradient to enable you to determine the uncertainty in the gradient as well as its mean value. In this case, there is clearly more to discuss in terms of the closeness of the best-fit lines to the data than at AS level where only one best-fit line is drawn.

The above examples serve to illustrate the point that at A2, your practical skills build on your AS skills so you need to continue to practise all the practical skills you met at AS level. You need to be aware as you study each A2 topic that the topics are generally harder than at AS level and that consequently the practical work is more demanding, as outlined above.

10.2 More about measurements

At AS level, you should have learnt how to:

- measure lengths using a ruler, a vernier scale, a micrometer and callipers,
- weigh an object and determine its mass using a spring balance or a lever balance or a top pan balance,
- use a protractor to measure an angle and use a set square,
- measure time intervals using clocks, stopwatches and the time base of an oscilloscope,
- measure temperature using a thermometer,
- use ammeters and voltmeters with appropriate scales,
- read analogue and digital displays.

During your A2 course, as outlined in Topic 10.1, in addition to being able to use instruments and techniques that you used at AS level, you are also expected to be able to use instruments that are more complex. Such instruments might include the oscilloscope, the travelling microscope, the data logger, sensors and light gates, the Geiger-Müller tube with a scaler counter or ratemeter, and the spectrometer. In addition, you should know how to time multiple oscillations and how to avoid parallax errors when reading a scale.

Link

If you are unsure about how to use any of the above instruments, see Topic 14.3 in the AS book and consult your teacher.

An oscilloscope

This is used to display waveforms and to measure pds and time intervals. You will have probably used an oscilloscope in Unit 1 of your AS course when you studied music and sound. However, AS practical assessments in Unit 3 do not involve the use of an oscilloscope but your A2 assessment activities may do. In A2 topics such as capacitor discharge, you will use an oscilloscope to measure the pd across a discharging capacitor. When you use an oscilloscope, you should assume that the control dials for its time base and voltage gain are calibrated accurately. However,

- always check if the oscilloscope has a variable control for either the time base or the voltage gain in addition to the fixed settings of each control dial. If so, you need to ensure that the variable control is at the correct setting (e.g. fully clockwise) for the calibration figure for each of the fixed settings to apply.
- make sure if you are measuring direct pds that the oscilloscope input is set for direct pd measurements rather than for ac measurements. Likewise, if you are measuring an ac waveform, you should check the input is set for ac measurements rather than dc measurements.

In addition, when measuring

- an ac waveform, ensure the y-gain is adjusted so the vertical height of the waveform is as large as possible with the full waveform from top to bottom on the screen. When measuring a time period, ensure several cycles are displayed across the screen and that you measure across as many cycles as possible to reduce experimental uncertainty.
- dc potentials, for example in a capacitor discharge experiment, ensure the zero reading is correct for zero input pd and check it has not drifted during the investigation.

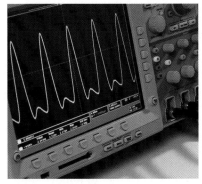

Figure 1 *The oscilloscope*

A travelling microscope

This is a microscope on an adjustable platform that can be moved vertically or horizontally by turning an adjustment screw. The microscope itself can usually be aligned vertically or horizontally, according to whether it is to be used to measure a vertical or a horizontal distance. The platform is fitted with a horizontal and a vertical vernier scale so its horizontal or vertical position can be measured to within ±0.1 mm. A travelling microscope would be used for example to measure the internal diameter of a glass tube (e.g. 1 mm bore) as a micrometer or vernier calipers could not access the internal surface of the tube. Before use, a travelling microscope should be levelled using a spirit level in two perpendicular directions so its platform is horizontal. Otherwise, there could be a systematic error in the measurements.

A data logger

A data logger enables routine or remote measurements to be made as well as measurements over very long or short time scales. Electronic sensors connected to a data logger are necessary to record the variation of a physical property such as temperature. Current and voltage sensors are necessary to measure currents and potential differences.

Data loggers vary considerably in complexity and ease of use. Assuming the data logger and sensors are set up, before using a data logger, you may need to choose:

- the most appropriate time scale for the recording,
- the time interval between successive recordings (or the number of recordings per second/minute/hour),
- the most appropriate range of each sensor.

If a recording is too fast or too long or the sensors are out of range, the recording should be repeated if possible.

Most data loggers will be linked to computers which are loaded with appropriate software for recording, processing and/or plotting graphs of the results. You may need to print a graph out if you intend to use it to measure, for example, the gradient if it is a straight-line graph. However, the computer software may do such measurements for you.

Figure 2 *Using a data logger*

Light gates

These are used with a computer or a data logger or timer to remove some of the random errors associated with personal judgements when a moving object passes a certain position, for example, if you have to time an object to move from rest through a certain distance.

The effect of using light gates should be to reduce the range of the readings for a given measurement. However, light gates may not be suitable for every experiment in which a moving object has to be timed. For example, the time period of an oscillating object that repeatedly moves backwards and forwards through a light gate could only be timed for one half cycle of the object's motion, corresponding to the object moving through the light gate in one direction to start the timing and then in the opposite direction to stop the light gate. The light gate would need to be exactly at the centre of the oscillations otherwise the timing would not be exactly one half cycle. Repeated measurements of one half cycle could be made to give a more reliable mean value and this might give better results than using a stopwatch if the oscillations are too fast to time manually.

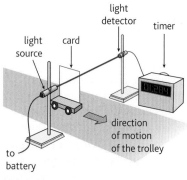

Figure 3 *Using a light gate*

■ The Geiger–Müller tube

This may be used with a **scaler counter** which counts the number of ionising particles that enter the tube or it may be used with a **ratemeter** which gives a read-out of the count rate (i.e. number of counts per unit time) of the particles entering the tube. The tube pd must be set at its operating value which is normally in excess of 300 V. The number of counts in a certain time interval is measured by setting the counter to zero, then starting the counter and stopping it after a certain time.

Figure 4b shows how the count rate varies with the tube pd. The operating pd corresponds to the plateau of the graph sufficiently far from the minimum pd necessary for the tube to operate (i.e. the threshold pd) as to be unaffected by random fluctuations in the tube pd.

■ When using the tube with a scaler counter, the number of counts in a given time (e.g. 100 s) should be measured several times to give a mean value of the count rate (i.e. counts per second). The bigger the total number of counts, the smaller the uncertainty in the measurement. If the time interval is too short, random errors that may occur in starting and stopping the counter could be more significant than if a longer time interval were used. If the time interval is too long, it would be difficult to tell if the activity of the source is decreasing or if an error in starting or stopping the timer has occurred.

■ When using the tube with a ratemeter, ensure the ratemeter is set on the range which gives the largest reading. For example, if the range dial has three positions, 1, 10 and 100 counts per second, the range may need to be set at 1 count per second if the reading is very small on the '10' and '100' positions.

When using either a scaler counter or a ratemeter, remember to measure the background count rate and subtract it from the measurements made when the source is present.

a *a Geiger–Müller tube connected to a scaler counter*

Figure 4 *Using a Geiger–Müller tube*

b *a graph of count rate against tube pd*

■ A spectrometer

This is used to measure the wavelengths of a line emission spectrum or a line absorption spectrum. A spectrometer is fitted with a circular scale to measure the angle of diffraction of the lines of a spectrum. A spectrum analyser is used to obtain an intensity–wavelength (or frequency) display of the light detected by the spectrum analyser detector. Although neither instrument is specified in the AS or A2 unit specifications, you may be asked to use either instrument (given all the necessary instructions) to assess your ability to follow complex instructions.

Internal assessment in A2 physics

11.1 The ISA/PSA scheme at A2 (scheme T)

The structure and format of the ISA/PSA scheme of internal assessment for Unit 6 summarised below is the same as for Unit 3. However, the assessment activities at A2 are based on A2 topics which are in general more demanding than at AS. Consequently, assessment at A2 is more demanding and so the assessment criteria are more demanding at A2 than at AS. The same is true in scheme X, the 'board marked scheme' of internal assessment.

■ Investigative skills assignments

Two A2 physics ISAs are set by AQA each year. You will be assessed using one of these ISAs if you are being assessed through the ISA/PSA scheme. As at AS level, an ISA counts for 41 marks out of the 50 mark total for Unit 3.

The ISA is carried out under supervision and is in two stages.

Stage 1 The practical task

The practical task requires you to carry out practical work using an AQA task sheet which outlines the investigation. The task sheet may be prescriptive, giving precise instructions or it may be more open-ended. Your teacher will tell you in advance when you will carry out the ISA. Also, your teacher will tell you a few weeks before the ISA test the general topic area which the ISA is in.

As at AS level, the task is carried out in the laboratory in a timetabled lesson (or lessons) under supervision and should take no more than about an hour. The task will require you to work on your own and to make measurements and present them in a table of your own design. You will be asked to process the measurement data and to use the data to draw a graph. Remember the demands at A2 are greater than at AS because the topics in the A2 course are more demanding than at AS.

You are not allowed to take work away from the ISA session and all completed work must be handed to your teacher who will assess the work using AQA marking guidelines. Your teacher is not allowed to write any marks or comments on your work as it will be returned to you for use in the written test. The practical task counts for 10 of the 41 marks on the ISA. Candidates are not allowed to redraft or repeat an ISA.

You will be provided with a complete set of practical equipment necessary for the practical task. This equipment should include familiar items that you have used at AS level (e.g. clamps, stands, ammeter, voltmeter, metre ruler, stopwatch, etc.) but it might include an item or materials specific to the task (e.g. conducting paper to investigate a specific electric field configuration). The task sheet will tell you what to do and what measurements to make. Read it carefully to make sure you set up and use the equipment correctly. If you think an item of equipment is not working, ask your teacher to check it.

Stage 2 The written test

You will take the written test in a timetabled lesson under supervision as soon as possible after completion of the practical task. The test is a 1 hour written paper set by AQA and counts for 31 of the 41 ISA marks. Lines to write your answer are provided after each part-question. Your teacher will mark your written test using AQA marking guidelines. In the 'exam room' just before the test begins, you will be provided with the test paper and your completed material from the practical task. The test is in two parts.

a **Section A** will consist of a number of general questions about the practical task. For example, you might be asked about the control variables in the task or about the precision of your measurements. You will not be required to plot a graph here as you will have already done this in the practical task. This section will not have as many marks allocated to it as at AS level although the total for the written paper will still be 31 marks.

b **Section B** will provide a further set of data on the practical task or a closely related task. The questions in this part will ask about methodology, analysis and evaluation of the data. You may be asked in your evaluation to suggest improvements or to discuss further work that could be done, for example to test a prediction. There will be more marks allocated for evaluation and analysis in this section compared with AS as A2 evaluation and analysis questions are more demanding than at AS level because the A2 topics are more demanding.

■ The practical skills assessment

The skills in the PSA are assessed in practical activities that you will do throughout your course. The practical activities will give you opportunities to demonstrate your practical skills. You will be given some instructions when you carry out these activities and you will need to make decisions for yourself about how you organise yourself and how you use the equipment. You will be assessed on your ability to:

■ **demonstrate safe and skilful practical techniques and processes,**

■ **select appropriate methods and equipment,**

■ **make measurements precisely and accurately,**

■ **make and record reliable and valid observations and measurements,**

■ **work with others in experimental activities.**

The paragraphs below shows how your PSA mark at A2 is determined. Note the criteria are more demanding than at AS level and so are worded differently. The three strands are each worth up to 3 marks, giving a total of 9 marks. Your teacher will assess the level you reach by the end of the course in each strand.

Following instructions and group work

■ 3 marks are awarded if you are able to plan and work without guidance, select appropriate techniques, follow complex instructions and participate in group work. **If not, see below.**

■ 2 marks are awarded if you are able plan and work without guidance, select appropriate techniques, follow instructions and participate in group work. **If not, see below.**

■ 1 mark is awarded if you are able to plan and work with some guidance, select appropriate techniques and follow instruction. **If not,** no marks are awarded.

The standard laboratory apparatus you will use to make measurements might include:

■ basic apparatus (metre rule, set square, protractors, stopclock or stopwatch),

■ AS equipment such as electrical meters (analogue or digital), the micrometer, vernier callipers, a top pan electronic balance, measuring cylinders, thermometers and newtonmeters, and

■ more complex instruments as listed in the notes overleaf.

Selection and use of equipment

■ 3 marks are awarded if you can select and use suitable equipment with due regard for precision, including a wide range of at least 6 complex instruments **and** techniques appropriate to the A2 course. **If not, see below.**

■ 2 marks are awarded if you can select and use suitable equipment, including more than 2 complex instruments **and** techniques appropriate to the A2 course. **If not, see below.**

■ 1 mark is awarded if you can select and use suitable equipment, including at least 2 complex instruments **or** techniques appropriate to the A2 course. **If not**, no marks are awarded.

Safety and organisation

■ 3 marks are awarded if you consistently demonstrate safe working practices in the more complex procedures encountered on the A2 course. **If not, see below.**

■ 2 marks are awarded if you demonstrate safe working practices in some of the more complex procedures encountered on the A2 course. **If not, see below.**

■ 1 mark is awarded if you demonstrate safe working practices in using a range of equipment appropriate to the A2 course. **If not**, no marks are awarded.

Notes

1 **Complex instructions** or procedures or techniques refers to instructions or procedures or techniques which are not straightforward and which may involve

   ■ following a set of instructions on the use of a complex instrument where different controls need to be adjusted or used (e.g. a Geiger–Müller tube connected to a scaler counter), or

   ■ changing and measuring physical variables in a sequence while keeping other variables constant (e.g. altering a variable resistor in a capacitor discharge circuit to keep the discharge current constant to see the effect on the capacitor pd), or

   ■ using a technique which involves several stages (e.g. measuring the count rate due to a radioactive source taking account of background radiation).

2 **Complex instruments** include an oscilloscope, a travelling microscope, a Geiger–Müller tube connected to a scaler counter or ratemeter, a data logger, electronic sensors (e.g. temperature, magnetic field, light intensity), light gates, a spectrometer or spectrum analyser.

3 **Safe working practices**: before you carry out a practical task, you should carry out a risk assessment to eliminate (if possible) or minimise any health and safety hazards. A risk assessment requires you to think about the possible hazards in an activity and plan to eliminate or minimise them. Your teacher ought to have made a risk assessment of every practical activity in advance to ensure the practical activities you undertake are safe.

■ Ionising radiation

If you are about to use a Geiger–Müller tube and a radioactive source, you must comply with the safety instructions your teacher will give you, including wearing disposable gloves and using long-handled tongs when you have to transfer the source from its container to a holder. Schools and colleges can only use sealed sources to prevent contamination of the laboratory or people inside the laboratory and you must keep as far from it as reasonably possible. Never look directly into a radioactive source as the eye is not protected by dead skin. You should be provided with eye protection which you should wear. However, you should also carry out your own risk assessment to ensure you use the apparatus you are given safely.

11.2 The EMPA/PSV scheme at A2 (scheme X)

The AQA-marked scheme is the same in structure and format as at AS. However, as with scheme T, the demands at A2 are higher because the A2 topics themselves are more demanding and experiments associated with A2 topics are more demanding than at AS level.

Part 1 (Practical skills verification)

This part is carried out under supervision in the laboratory during normal class time. You will be required to work individually and carry out 5 short practical exercises. The exercises for each year are set by AQA at the start of the year and each one may be carried out at any stage during the year during or after coverage of the relevant topic. Your teacher will tell you in advance when you are to do them. You will not be expected to spend more than 3 hours of laboratory time in total completing these exercises. The exercises will be typical of the normal practical work that would be expected to be covered as part of any A2 course.

In carrying out these exercises, you will be asked to use more complex instruments than at AS level, in addition to standard equipment you used at AS level. Such complex equipment could include an oscilloscope, a travelling microscope, a Geiger–Müller tube connected to a scaler counter or ratemeter, a data logger, electronic sensors (e.g. temperature, magnetic field, light intensity), light gates, a spectrometer or spectrum analyser.

Also, you might be asked to work together at times and you will be expected to follow complex instructions and procedures and to work safely. In addition, you are likely to be asked to make and record accurate measurements and assess the reliability and accuracy of your results.

At the end of each exercise, your results and observations are to be given to the teacher for verification purposes and may be returned to you for use during the remainder of the course. A sample set of part 1 exercises are listed below.

Sample set of part 1 exercises for A2 level	
Exercise	**Measuring equipment used**
1 Measurement of g using a simple pendulum	stopwatch or stopclock, metre ruler
2 Capacitor discharge through a fixed resistor	oscilloscope or digital voltmeter, potential divider, stopwatch or stopclock
3 Measurement of magnetic flux density	top pan balance, U-shaped magnet, thick copper wire, ammeter, variable low voltage power supply
4 Absorption of β radiation by different thicknesses of aluminium foil	Geiger-Müller tube, scaler counter, micrometer, aluminium foil, stopclock or stopwatch
5 Measurement of specific heat capacity or specific latent heat	variable low voltage power supply, low voltage heater, metal block, thermometer, top pan balance, voltmeter, ammeter, stopclock or stopwatch

In Part 2 you will be required to use some of the practical skills from part 1 to undertake assessed practical activities. The measurements and results from these part 2 practical activities will be analysed and evaluated in Part 3, an AQA-set and marked written paper.

Parts 2 and 3 Externally marked practical assessment

Part 2

In this part, you carry out a short practical activity and a longer practical activity, both based on physics from Unit 4 and/or from Unit 5A of the specification. The practical activities will be AQA set and marked. Once completed, you will not be able to attempt part 2 again. You can not carry forward written work from part 1 to these part 2 activities. The two activities will take around $1\frac{1}{2}$ hours in total.

Examples of some A2 longer practical activities for part 2 are listed below.

1   Investigation of the oscillations of a metre ruler as a loaded cantilever (use of stopwatch, metre rule, fiducial mark)
2   Investigation of the effect of varying the resistance in a capacitor charge and discharge circuit (digital voltmeter, capacitor, potential divider, low voltage supply, stopwatch or stopclock)
3   Measurement of the specific latent heat of ice by using ice to cool warm water.

Your teacher will tell you in advance when you are to carry out the part 2 experiment. This will be near the end of the course between March and the end of May. Because the experiment is a skills test like the 'on the road' part of the driving test, the experiment may be used to test other students at other times.

You have to work individually and be supervised throughout. You will be provided with a task sheet with sufficient information and instructions to enable you to obtain reliable measurements which you have to record, process and discuss. In carrying out the activities, you will be expected to:

- manipulate apparatus skilfully and safely,
- make reliable and accurate measurements,
- estimate experimental uncertainties,
- identify anomalous measurements,
- minimise or take account of the effects of random and any systematic error,
- tabulate the results in a well organised and systematic way, taking account of the expected conventions,
- process data,
- graph, or chart, these data as appropriate.

In addition, you will need to show your competence in following more complex procedures than at AS level and in recording and processing more complex data than at AS level.

At the end of the experiment, you have to hand in all your written work (i.e. table of results, calculations, graph, and discussion of errors). This will be returned to you for use in Part 3.

Part 3

This is an AQA-set and marked written paper of duration of 1 hour 15 minutes. Your teacher will arrange when you are to take this test, preferably as soon as possible after part 2. Before you commence the test, your written work from part 2 will be returned to you. At the end of the test, all your written work from parts 2 and 3 will be collected by your teacher who will send it to AQA for marking together with verification forms for part 1.

Some of the questions in the paper will require you to:

■ use your part 2 results and graph to carry out further analysis in order to arrive at a conclusion,

■ assess the overall accuracy of the outcome of the experiment.

In addition, you may be asked to:

■ carry out error calculations on the data from part 2,

■ describe procedures used to overcome errors in part 2,

■ estimate the percentage uncertainty of a result,

■ comment on the reliability of the evidence or procedures used during part 2,

■ discuss all/some of the measurement techniques developed in part 1,

■ make predictions about alternative outcomes,

■ discuss ways of extending the range or reliability of the evidence produced during part 2 of the practical experiment,

■ discuss how you would improve the experiment or how you would carry out a related investigation.

The work you produced in parts 2 and 3 will sent by your teacher to AQA for marking together with your part 1 verification forms.

12.1 Trigonometry

In this chapter, we consider only the A2 mathematical skills that are beyond the requirements for AS level. If you need to check any of the mathematical skills specified for the AS course, you can use Chapter 17 'More on mathematical skills' in the AS book and/or use the on-line exercises that support the AS and A2 books.

▮ Angles and arcs

The radian

The **radian** (rad) is a unit used to express or measure angles. It is defined such that 2π radians = $360°$

When using a calculator to work out sines, cosines, tangents or the corresponding inverse functions, always check that the calculator is in the correct 'angle' mode. This is usually indicated on the display by 'deg' for degrees or 'rad' for radians. Your calculations will be incorrect if you work in one mode when you should be working in the other mode. For example, check for yourself that $\sin 30° = 0.5$ whereas $\sin(30\,\text{rad}) = -0.988$. You also need to know how to change from one mode to the other; read your calculator manual or ask your teacher if you can't do this.

Arcs and segments

Consider an arc of length s on the circumference of a circle of radius r, as shown in Figure 1. The angle θ, in degrees, subtended by the arc to the centre of the circle is given by the equation

$$\theta/\text{degrees} \;=\; \frac{s}{2\pi r} \times 360$$

Because 2π radians = $360°$, applying this conversion factor to the above equation for θ gives

$$\theta/\text{radians} \;=\; \frac{s}{r}$$

Rearranging this equation gives

$$\text{arc length} \;\; s \;=\; r\theta,$$

where θ is the angle subtended in radians.

The small angle approximation

For angle θ less than about $10°$,

$$\sin\theta \approx \tan\theta \approx \theta \text{ in radians, and}$$

$$\cos\theta \approx 1$$

To explain these approximations, consider Figure 1 again. If angle θ is sufficiently small, then the segment OAC will be almost the same as triangle OAB, as shown in Figure 2.

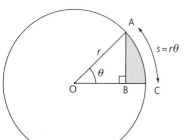

Figure 1 *Arcs and segments*

▮ **Note**

Note that for $s = r$, $\theta = 1\,\text{rad}$

$$\left(= \frac{360}{2\pi} = 57.3°\right)$$

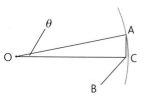

Figure 2 *The small angle approximation*

■ AB ≈ arc length s so $\sin\theta = \dfrac{AB}{OA} \approx \dfrac{s}{r} = \theta$ in radians, ∴ $\sin\theta \approx \theta$ in radians.

■ OB ≈ radius r, so $\tan\theta = \dfrac{AB}{OB} \approx \dfrac{s}{r} = \theta$ in radians, ∴ $\tan\theta \approx \theta$ in radians.

■ Also, $\cos\theta = \dfrac{OB}{OA} \approx \dfrac{r}{r} = 1$, ∴ $\cos\theta \approx 1$

Use a calculator to prove for yourself that for $\sin 10° = 0.1736$, $\tan 10° = 0.1763$ and $10° = 0.1745$ rad. Also, $\cos 10° = 0.9848$. So the small angle approximation is almost 99% accurate up to 10°.

The small angle approximation is used to show that the time period of a simple pendulum of length L is given by the formula $T = 2\pi\sqrt{\dfrac{L}{g}}$, provided the maximum angular displacement of the pendulum from equilibrium is less than about 10°. See Topic 3.1 for more about this equation.

■ Sine and cosine curves

Figure 3 shows how $\sin\theta$ and $\cos\theta$ change as θ increases. Notice that $\sin\theta \approx \theta$ and $\cos\theta \approx 1$ up to about 10°. The general shape of a cosine wave is the same as that of a sine wave so we refer to them both as 'sinusoidal' waveforms. In addition, notice that:

■ the sine wave starts at zero and rises to a maximum from $\theta = 0$ to $\theta = \frac{1}{2}\pi$ rad ($= 90°$) whereas the cosine wave starts at $+1$ and falls to zero from $\theta = 0$ to $\theta = \frac{1}{2}\pi$ rad ($= 90°$).

■ the gradient of the sine wave is zero where the cosine wave is zero (i.e. where it crosses the horizontal axis) and the gradient of the cosine wave is zero where the sine wave is zero.

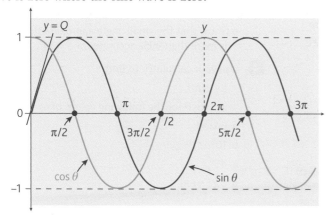

Figure 3 *Sine and cosine curves*

Equations that describe sine waves and cosine waves are often used to calculate, for example, the displacement of an oscillating particle at a certain time or of a wave at a particular position along the wave.

For example, consider the displacement x of a particle on a spring oscillating vertically in simple harmonic motion, as shown in Figure 4a. Let f represent its frequency and A its amplitude. Its displacement varies sinusoidally between a maximum value $+A$ and a minimum value $-A$. Also, suppose $x = +A$ at time $t = 0$. In other words, the object is held above the equilibrium position at displacement $x = +A$ and released at time $t = 0$.

■ Its displacement–time curve will therefore be a cosine wave, as shown in Figure 4b where its time period $T = 1/f$.

■ At time t later, the particle will have gone through ft cycles of oscillation, corresponding to $\theta = 2\pi ft$ radians. Hence its displacement at time t is given by $\boldsymbol{x = A\cos 2\pi ft}$.

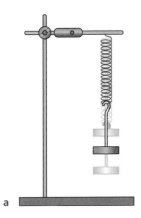

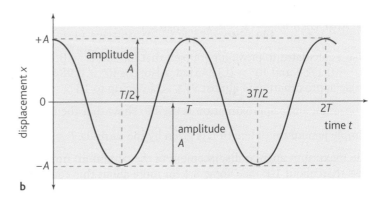

Figure 4 a *An object oscillating on a spring* **b** *Displacement–time curve for x = A cos 2πft*

Summary questions

1 **a** Convert the following angles from degrees into radians and express your answer to one further significant figure than in each question:

i 30°,

ii 50°,

iii 120°,

iv 230°,

v 300°.

b Convert the following angles from radians into degrees and express your answer to one further significant figure than in each question:

i 0.10 rad,

ii 0.50 rad,

iii 1.20 rad,

iv 2.50 rad,

v 6.00 rad.

2 **a** Measure the diameter of a 1p coin to the nearest millimetre. Calculate the angle subtended at your eye, in degrees, by a 1p coin held at a distance of 50 cm from your eye.

b **i** Estimate the angular width of the Moon, in degrees, at your eye by holding a millimetre scale at 50 cm from your eye and measuring the distance on the scale covered by the lunar disc.

ii The diameter of the Moon is 3500 km. The average distance to the Moon from the Earth is 380 000 km. Calculate the angular width of the Moon as seen from the Earth and compare the calculated value with your estimate in **b** **i**.

3 **a** Use the small angle approximation to calculate $\sin\theta$ for $\theta =$

i 2.0°,

ii 8.0°.

b Show that the small angle approximation for $\sin\theta$ is more than 99% accurate for $\theta = 10°$.

4 Use your calculator to find

i $\sin\theta$,

ii $\cos\theta$ for the following values of θ:

a 0.1 rad,

b 10°,

c 45°,

d 0.25π rad.

12.2 Logarithms

Logarithms and powers

Any number can be expressed as any other number raised to a particular power. You can use the y^x key on a calculator to show, for example that $8 = 2^3$ and $9 = 2^{3.17}$. In these examples, 2 is referred to as the base number and is raised to a different power in each case to generate 8 or 9. The power is defined as the **logarithm** of the number generated.

General rules for using logarithms

The rules that apply when using logarithms work for any base but the important ones for this course are the bases 10 and e (2.718) which is the base for natural logarithms.

The following discussion of the general rules for using logarithms are shown using the base 10 but they work equally well for base e (2.718).

Suppose a number $n = 10^p$. The base is 10 and $p = \log_{10} n$.

We say that p is the logarithm of n to the base 10.

Note $\log_{10}(10^p) = p$ since $10^p = n$ and $\log_{10} n = p$.

1 **For any two numbers m and n,**

$\log_{10}(nm) = \log_{10} n + \log_{10} m$

This is shown as follows:

Let $p = \log_{10} n$ and let $q = \log_{10} m$

$n = 10^p$ and $m = 10^q$

$nm = 10^p \times 10^q = 10^{p+q}$ so $\log_{10}(nm) = p + q = \log_{10} m + \log_{10} n$

2 **For any two numbers m and n,**

$\log_{10}\dfrac{n}{m} = \log_{10} n - \log_{10} m$

This is shown as follows:

Let $p = \log_{10} n$ and let $q = \log_{10} m$

$n = 10^p$ and $m = 10^q$.

So $\dfrac{1}{m} = \dfrac{1}{10^q} = 10^{-q}$

$\dfrac{n}{m} = 10^p \times 10^{-q} = 10^{p-q}$ so $\log_{10}\left(\dfrac{n}{m}\right) = p - q = \log_{10} n - \log_{10} m$

3 **For any number m raised to a power p,**

$\log_{10}(m^p) = p\log_{10} m$

This is because $m^p = m$ multiplied by itself p times.

$= m \times m \times m \times \ldots$ for p terms

$\xleftarrow{\hspace{2cm}} p \text{ terms} \xrightarrow{\hspace{2cm}}$

Therefore $\log_{10} m^p = \{\log_{10} m + \log_{10} m + \ldots + \log_{10} m\} = p\log_{10} m$

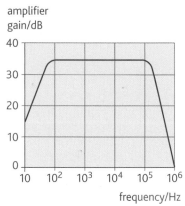

Figure 1 *Logarithmic scales*

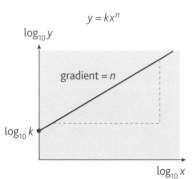

Figure 2 *Using logs to test y = kxⁿ*

> ■ **Hint**
>
> Note that natural logs could be used here instead of base 10 logs; the gradient would still be n but the y-intercept would be $\ln k$.

> ■ **Hint**
>
> The Richter scale for earthquakes is another example. A 'Richter scale 8' earthquake is ten times as powerful as a 'Richter scale 7' earthquake.

More on base 10 logarithms

Base 10 logs are written as $\log_{10}$ or lg (or sometimes incorrectly as log).

For example,

- $100 = 10^2$ so $\log_{10} 100 = 2$
- $50 = 10^{1.699}$ so $\log_{10} 50 = 1.699$
- $10 = 10^1$ so $\log_{10} 10 = 1$
- $5 = 10^{0.699}$ so $\log_{10} 5 = 0.699$

The above examples illustrate the product rule for logs

$$(\text{i.e. } \log_{10} nm = \log_{10} n + \log_{10} m)$$

since $\log_{10} 50 = \log_{10} 5 + \log_{10} 10$

$\log_{10} (5 \times 10) = 0.699 + 1 = 1.699$, which is $\log_{10} 50$.

Uses of base 10 logs

In graphs where a **logarithmic scale** is necessary to show the full range of a variable that covers a very wide range, as shown in Figure 1. Notice in Figure 1 that the frequency increases by ×10 in equal intervals along the horizontal axis.

In data analysis where a relationship between two variables may have of the form $y = kx^n$ and k with and n as unknown constants.

This equation can be converted into the following log equation:

$$\log_{10} y = \log_{10} k + \log_{10} x^n$$

$$\text{so } \log_{10} y = \log_{10} k + n \log_{10} x \text{ or } \log_{10} y = n \log_{10} x + \log_{10} k$$

Comparing this final equation with the general formula for a straight line graph, $y = mx + c$, a graph of $\log_{10} y$ (on the vertical axis) against $\log_{10} x$ is a straight line of gradient n with an intercept on the y axis equal to $\log k$.

In certain formulae where a ×10 scale is used. For example, the gain of an amplifier in decibels (dB) is a ×10 scale defined by the formula

$$\text{voltage gain/dB} = 10 \log_{10} \left| \frac{V_{\text{out}}}{V_{\text{in}}} \right|$$

where V_{out} and V_{in} are the output and input voltages respectively. If $V_{\text{out}} = 50 V_{\text{in}}$, the gain of the amplifier is $17\,\text{dB}$ $(= 10 \log_{10} 50)$.

■ Natural logarithms

Natural logs are written as $\log_{e}$ or ln, where e is the exponential number used as the base of natural logarithms and is equal to 2.718. For example,

- $2.718 = e^1$ so $\ln 2.718 = 1$
- $7.389 = e^2$ so $\ln 7.389 = 2$
- $20.009 = e^3$ so $\ln 20.009 = 3$
- In general, for any number n, if p is such that $n = e^p$, then $\ln n = p$.

Uses of natural logarithms

Natural logs are used in the equations for radioactive decay (Topic 8.3) and capacitor discharge (Topic 8.6) or any other process where the rate of change of a quantity is proportional to the quantity itself. For example, the rate of decrease of pd across a capacitor discharging through a resistor is proportional to the pd across the capacitor. This type of change is described as an exponential decrease because the quantity decreases by the same factor in equal intervals of time.

Using the rules described above, the equation $x = x_0 e^{-\lambda t}$ can be converted to the form

$$\ln x = \ln x_0 - \lambda t \quad or \quad \ln x = -\lambda t + \ln x_0$$

Therefore, comparing this with the general equation for a straight line graph, $y = mx + c$, a graph of $\ln x$ (on the vertical axis) against t (on the horizontal axis) is a straight line with a gradient equal to $-\lambda$ and a y-intercept equal to $\ln x_0$.

Comparing the equation for capacitor discharge $Q = Q_0 e^{-t/RC}$ with the radioactive decay equation $N = N_0 e^{-\lambda t}$,

- for capacitor discharge, $\ln Q = \ln Q_0 - t/RC$ so a graph of $\ln Q$ (on the vertical axis) against t is a straight line which has a gradient $-1/RC$ and $\ln Q_0$ as its y-intercept

- for radioactive decay, $\ln N = \ln N_0 - \lambda t$ so a graph of $\ln N$ (on the vertical axis) against t is a straight line which has a gradient $-\lambda$ and $\ln N_0$ as its y-intercept.

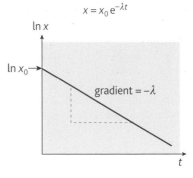

Figure 3 *Using logs to test* $x = x_0 e^{-\lambda t}$

Summary questions

1 **a** Use your calculator to work out

 i $\log_{10} 3$

 ii $\log_{10} 15$

 b Use your answers in **a** to work out

 i $\log_{10} 45$

 ii $\log_{10} 5$

2 The gain of an amplifier, in decibels, is given by the formula $10 \log_{10} \left(\dfrac{V_{out}}{V_{in}} \right)$.

 a Calculate the gain, in decibels (dB), for

 i $V_{out} = 12V_{in}$

 ii $V_{out} = 5V_{in}$

 b Show that the gain, in decibels, of an amplifier for which $V_{out} = 60V_{in}$ is equal to the sum of the gain in **a i** and the gain in **a ii** above.

3 Write down the gradient and the y-intercept of a line on a graph representing the equation $\log_{10} y = n \log_{10} x + \log_{10} k$ for

 a $y = 3x^5$

 b $y = \frac{1}{2}x^3$

 c $y = x^2$

4 **a** Use your calculator to work out

 i $\ln 3$

 ii $\ln 15$

 b Use your answers in **a** to work out

 i $\ln 45$

 ii $\ln 5$

13 Extension mathematics

13.1 Simultaneous and quadratic equations

■ Introduction

There are some mathematical tools that are not needed for the AS or A2 physics course but which are very useful tools in physics and other scientific disciplines. These tools make it easier to analyse data and derive useful relationships between physical quantities. The techniques for solving simultaneous equations and quadratics and the processes of differentiation and integration are discussed. They are included to help interested students to understand the basis for the techniques and appreciate how these are applied to some of the topics covered in the course.

You will not be tested on these nor will you be required to use the techniques in the examination.

■ Linear simultaneous equations

Two linear equations with two variable quantities, x and y, in each can be solved to find the values of x and y. Such a pair of equations are referred to as **simultaneous equations** because they have the same solution. They are described as **linear** because they contain terms in x and y and do not contain any higher order terms such as x^2 or y^2.

The general equation for a straight-line graph is $y = mx + c$, as explained in Topic 17.4 of the AS book. Two straight lines on a graph can be represented by two such equations. Provided the two lines are not parallel to one another, they cross each other at a single point. The coordinates of this point are the values of x and y that fit both equations. In other words, these coordinates are the solution of a pair of simultaneous equations representing the two straight lines. See Topic 17.4 in the AS book.

The graph approach to finding the solution of a pair of simultaneous equations is shown in Figure 1 and is described in Topic 17.4 in the AS book. However, plotting graphs takes time and is not as accurate as a systematic algebraic method. This method can best be explained by considering an example, as follows

$$2x - y = 2 \qquad \text{(equation 1)}$$
$$x + y = 4 \qquad \text{(equation 2)}$$

Make the coefficient of x the same in both equations by multiplying one or both equations by a suitable number. In the above equation, this is most easily achieved by multiplying equation 2 throughout by 2 to give $2x + 2y = 8$.

The two equations to be solved are now

$$2x - y = 2 \qquad \text{(equation 1)}$$
$$2x + 2y = 8 \qquad \text{(modified equation 2)}$$

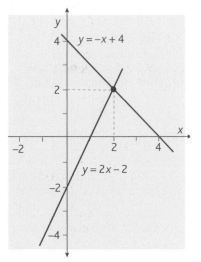

Figure 1 *A graphical solution*

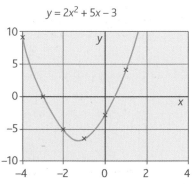

Figure 2 $y = 2x^2 + 5x - 3$

Subtracting modified equation 2 from equation 1 gives

$$(2x - y) - (2x + 2y) = 2 - 8$$

$$\therefore -y - 2y = -6$$

$$-3y = -6$$

$$y = \frac{-6}{-3} = 2$$

Substituting this value into equation 1 or equation 2 enables the value of x to be determined. Using equation 2 for this purpose gives $x + 2 = 4$, hence $x = 4 - 2 = 2$.

The solution of the two equations is therefore $x = 2, y = 2$.

Linear simultaneous equations with two unknown quantities can arise in several parts of the A level physics course, for example

■ $v = u + at$ in kinematics (see AS Topic 7.2)

■ $V = \varepsilon - Ir$ in electricity (see AS Topic 12.6)

■ $E_{Kmax} = hf - \phi$ (see AS Topic 4.1).

■ The quadratic equation

Any quadratic equation can be written in the form $ax^2 + bx + c = 0$, where a, b and c are constants. The general solution of the quadratic equation $ax^2 + bx + c = 0$ is

$$x = \frac{-b \pm \sqrt{(b^2 - 4ac)}}{2a}$$

Note that every quadratic equation has two solutions, one given by the $+$ sign before the square root sign in the above expression, and the other given by the $-$ sign. For example, consider the solution of the equation $2x^2 + 5x - 3 = 0$.

As $a = 2$, $b = 5$ and $c = -3$, then the solution is

$$x = \frac{-5 \pm \sqrt{(5^2 - (4 \times 2 \times -3))}}{2 \times 2} = \frac{-5 \pm \sqrt{49}}{4} = \frac{-5 \pm 7}{4} = +0.5 \text{ or } -3$$

A graph of $y = 2x^2 + 5x - 3$ is shown in Figure 2. Note that the two solutions above are the values of the x-intercepts, which is where $y = 0$.

Quadratic equations occur in A level physics where a formula contains the square of a variable. The equation $s = ut + \frac{1}{2}at^2$ for displacement at constant acceleration is a direct example. Other examples can arise indirectly. For example, suppose the pd across a certain type of component varies with current I according to the equation $V = kI^2$. In a circuit with a battery of negligible internal resistance and a resistor of resistance R, the battery pd, $V_0 = IR + kI^2$. Given values of R, k and V_0, the current could be calculated using the solution for the quadratic equation with $a = k$, $b = R$ and $c = -V_0$.

■ Hint

You can check this using equation 2 (i.e. $x = 2$, $y = 2$ is also a solution for $x + y = 4$).

■ Summary questions

1 Solve each of the following pairs of simultaneous equations.

a $3x + y = 6$; $2y = 5x + 1$

b $3a - 2b = 8$; $a + b = 2$

c $5p + 2q = 18$; $q = 2p$

2 Use the data and the given equation to write down a pair of simultaneous equations and so determine the unknown quantities in each case:

a For $v = u + at$, when $t = 3.0\,\text{s}$, $v = 8.0\,\text{m s}^{-1}$ and when $t = 6.0\,\text{s}$, $v = 2.0\,\text{m s}^{-1}$. Determine the values of u and a.

b For $\varepsilon = IR + Ir$, when $R = 5.0\,\Omega$, $I = 1.5\,\text{A}$ and when $R = 9.0\,\Omega$, $I = 0.9\,\text{A}$. Determine the values of ε and r.

3 Solve each of the following quadratic equations.

a $2x^2 + 5x - 3 = 0$

b $x^2 - 7x + 8 = 0$

c $3x^2 + 2x - 5 = 0$

4 Use the data and the given equation to write down a quadratic equation and so determine the unknown quantity in each case:

a $s = ut + \frac{1}{2}at^2$, where $s = 20\,\text{m}$, $u = 4\,\text{m s}^{-1}$ and $a = 6\,\text{m s}^{-2}$; find t.

b $P = \dfrac{V^2R}{(R + r)^2}$, where $P = 16\,\text{W}$, $V = 12\,\text{V}$, $r = 2.0\,\Omega$; find R.

13.2 Differentiation and the exponential change

Differentiation and rates of change

Figure 1 shows how a variable quantity y changes with respect to a second quantity x. The gradient of the curve at any point is the rate of change of y with respect to x at that point. This can be worked out from the graph by drawing a tangent to the curve at that point and measuring the gradient of the tangent. Figure 1 shows the idea. The rate of change of y with respect to x at point P, $\dfrac{\Delta y}{\Delta x}$, is equal to the gradient of the tangent to the curve at P.

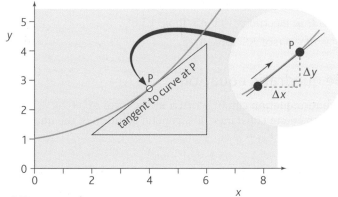

Figure 1 *Tangents and curves*

The rate of change of y with respect to x can be worked out algebraically if the equation relating y and x is known. This process is known as **differentiation.** For example,

- for $y = x^2$, then increasing x to $(x + \Delta x)$ increases y to $(y + \Delta y)$ where $y + \Delta y = (x + \Delta x)^2$

  Multiplying out $(x + \Delta x)^2$ gives $(y + \Delta y) = x^2 + 2\Delta x + \Delta x^2$

  Subtracting $y = x^2$ from this equation gives $\Delta y = 2\Delta x + \Delta x^2$

  Dividing by Δx therefore gives $\dfrac{\Delta y}{\Delta x} = \dfrac{2\Delta x + \Delta x^2}{\Delta x} = 2x + \Delta x$

  Therefore, if the change Δx is negligibly small and tending to zero $\Delta x \longrightarrow 0$, $\dfrac{\Delta y}{\Delta x} = 2x$ which is therefore the formula for the gradient at x.

  This is written $\dfrac{dy}{dx} = 2x$, where $\dfrac{dy}{dx}$ is the mathematical expression for the rate of change of y with respect to x.

- for the general expression $y = x^n$, it can be shown that $\dfrac{dy}{dx} = nx^{n-1}$

For example, if $y = 3x^5$, then $\dfrac{dy}{dx} = 15x^4$

In physics, the rate of change is very often the variation of a quantity with respect to time, as when analysing motion or the charge on a capacitor. Rate of change with distance occurs, for example when intensity of radiation varies with distance travelled through an absorbing medium.

Differentiation of a sine function

In the study of simple harmonic motion a graph of $\sin x$ against time t shows how displacement of an object varies with time when at $t = 0$, the displacement is zero and increasing. The variation in the gradient of the displacement–time graph shows how the velocity changes with time. From your studies of simple harmonic motion in Topic 3.1 you should know that the shape of this variation is the shape of a cosine graph.

In other words, the gradient of $\sin x$ is $\cos x$. so differentiating $\sin x$ gives $\cos x$ and differentiating $\cos x$ gives $-\sin x$.

■ Exponential change

Exponential change occurs when the change of a quantity is proportional to the quantity itself. Such a change can be an increase (i.e. exponential growth) or a decrease (i.e. exponential decay).

In both cases, the quantity changes by a fixed proportion in equal intervals of time. As the A2 specification requires knowledge and understanding of the equations and graphs for exponential decrease and of graphs only for exponential growth this analysis will concentrate on exponential decrease.

For an exponential decrease, the rate of change is negative and is proportional to x, therefore $\dfrac{dx}{dt} = -\lambda x$, where λ is referred to as the decay constant.

Let's consider why the equation $\dfrac{dx}{dt} = -\lambda x$ represents an exponential decrease.

The equation above describes a change where the rate of change of the variable quantity x decreases with time at a rate in proportion to the value of quantity x..

If x decreases by Δx in time Δt, the rate of change is $\dfrac{\Delta x}{\Delta t}$.

This is written as $\dfrac{dx}{dt}$ in the limit $\Delta t \longrightarrow 0$.

Now consider why the solution of this equation is $x = x_0 e^{-\lambda t}$, where x_0 is a constant.

Look at this equation:

$$x = x_0\left(1 + t + \frac{t^2}{2 \times 1} + \frac{t^3}{3 \times 2 \times 1} + \frac{t^4}{4 \times 3 \times 2 \times 1}\right.$$
$$\left. + \text{ similar higher order terms}\right) \ldots$$

Applying the rules of differentiation to it gives:

$$\frac{dx}{dt} = x_0\left(0 + 1 + t + \frac{t^2}{2 \times 1} + \frac{t^3}{3 \times 2 \times 1}\right.$$
$$\left. + \text{ similar higher order terms}\right) \ldots \text{ which is the same as } x.$$

So $\dfrac{dx}{dt} = x$ if x is the above function.

It can be shown that the function in brackets above may be written as n^t, where n is a specific number which is referred to as the exponential number e.

Therefore, $e^t = 1 + t + \dfrac{t^2}{2 \times 1} + \dfrac{t^3}{3 \times 2 \times 1} + \dfrac{t^4}{4 \times 3 \times 2 \times 1}$

$+ \text{ similar higher order terms}$

■ Note

In your studies of capacitor discharge (Topic 8.6) and of radioactive decay (Topic 8.3) , you will have met and used the equation $\dfrac{dN}{dt} = -\lambda N$ and the solution of this equation $N = N_0 e^{-\lambda t}$. You will therefore know that the discharge is exponential.

The value of e, the exponential number, can be worked out by substituting $t = 1$ in the above expression for e^t, giving $e = 1 + 1 + \frac{1}{2} + \frac{1}{6}$ + etc. $= 2.718$ to 4 significant figures.

If $\frac{dx}{dt} = -\lambda x$ then dividing both sides of the equation by $-\lambda$ gives $-\frac{1}{\lambda}\frac{dx}{dt} = x$

Substituting z for $-\lambda t$ therefore gives $\frac{dx}{dz} = x$ which has the solution

$$x = x_0 e^z = x_0 e^{-\lambda t}$$

The half-life $T_{\frac{1}{2}}$ of an exponential decrease is the time taken for x to decrease from x_0 to $\frac{1}{2}x_0$.

Substituting $x = \frac{1}{2}x_0$ and $t = T_{\frac{1}{2}}$ into $x = x_0 e^{-\lambda t}$ gives $\frac{x_0}{2} = x_0 e^{-\lambda T_{\frac{1}{2}}}$

Applying logs to both sides gives $\ln x_0 - \ln 2 = \ln x_0 - \lambda T_{\frac{1}{2}}$

which simplifies to $\lambda T_{\frac{1}{2}} = \ln 2$

$$\therefore T_{\frac{1}{2}} = \ln\frac{2}{\lambda} = \frac{0.693}{\lambda}$$

The time constant τ of an exponential decrease is the time taken for x to decrease from x_0 to $\frac{x_0}{e}$ $(= 0.368 x_0$ as $\frac{1}{e} = 0.368)$.

Substituting $x = \frac{x_0}{e}$ and $t = \tau$ into $x = x_0 e^{-\lambda t}$ gives $\frac{x_0}{e} = x_0 e^{-\lambda t}$

Applying natural logs to both sides gives $\ln x_0 - \ln e = \ln x_0 - \lambda \tau$

which simplifies to $\tau = \frac{1}{\lambda}$ as $\ln e = 1$

For capacitor discharge, $\lambda = \frac{1}{CR}$ therefore $\tau = \frac{1}{\lambda} = CR$.

Testing exponential decrease

As explained in Topic 12.2, $\ln\left(e^{-\lambda t}\right) = -\lambda t$

Therefore, $\ln x = \ln\left(x_0 e^{-\lambda t}\right) = \ln x_0 + \ln\left(e^{-\lambda t}\right) = \ln x_0 - \lambda t$

Suppose two physical variables x and t are thought to relate to each other through an equation of the form $x = x_0 e^{-\lambda t}$. If so, a graph of $\ln x$ on the y–axis against t on the x-axis would be a straight line in accordance with the equation $\ln x = \ln x_0 - \lambda t$ where the gradient is $-\lambda$ and the y-intercept is $\ln x_0$.

Summary questions

1 a For each exponential decrease equation, write down the initial value at $t = 0$ and the decay constant:

   i $x = 2e^{-3t}$

   ii $x = 12e^{-t/5}$

   iii $x = 4e^{-0.02t}$

   b For each exponential decrease equation above, work out the half-life.

2 A radioactive isotope has a half-life of 720 s and it decays to form a stable product. A sample of the isotope is prepared with an initial activity of 12.0 kBq. Calculate the activity of the sample after:

   a 1 min,

   b 5 min,

   c 1 h.

3 A capacitor of capacitance 22 µF discharged from a pd of 12.0 V through a 100 kΩ resistor.

   a Calculate:

   i   the time constant of the discharge circuit,

   ii the half-life of the exponential decrease.

   b Calculate the capacitor pd

   i   2.0 s, and

   ii 5.0 s after the discharge started.

4 A certain exponential decrease process is represented by the equation

   $x = 1000e^{-5t}$

   a i Calculate the half-life of the process.

   ii Calculate x when $t = 0.5$ s.

   b Show that the above equation can be rearranged as an equation of the form $\ln x = a + bt$ and determine the values of a and b.

13.3 Areas and integration

From the AS course, you should recall that the area under a line on a graph can give useful information if the product of the y-variable and the x-variable represents another physical variable. For example, the tension against extension graph for a spring is a straight line through the origin and the area under the line represents the work done to stretch the spring. See *AS Physics* Topic 9.1.

Table 1 gives some further examples where the area under a graph has physical significance

Table 1 *Areas in graphs*

examples (y-variable first)	area between the line and the x-axis	equation	units
power against time	energy transferred	energy transferred = power × time	$1\,W = 1\,J\,s^{-1}$
potential difference against charge (or stored)	electrical energy transferred	electrical energy transferred = pd × charge	$1\,V = 1\,J\,C^{-1}$
current against time	charge transferred	charge = current × time	$1\,C = 1\,A\,s$
force against time	change of momentum (or impulse)	change of momentum = force × time	$1\,kg\,m\,s^{-1} = 1\,N\,s$
force against distance	work done	work done = force × distance	$1\,J = 1\,N\,m$

To find the area under the line, we can either:

- count the squares of the grid under the line and multiply the number of squares by the amount of the physical variable that one square of area represents, or
- use the mathematical process known as **integration** as outlined below.

The first of these techniques is expected in the AS and A2 course .

The following notes relate to the mathematical process of integration and are not an A2 requirement but are intended to give a deeper understanding of how areas under curves can be calculated.

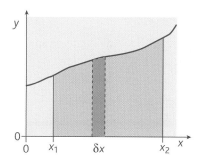

Figure 1 *Integration*

Figure 1 shows how a y-variable changes as the x-variable changes.

A small increase of the x-variable, δx (δ for small) gives little or no change of the y-variable. The area under that section of the curve, $\delta A = y\,\delta x$ as it is a strip of width δx and height y. Note that rearranging

$\delta A = y\,\delta x$ gives $y = \dfrac{\delta A}{\delta x}$.

Hence the total area under the line from x_1 to x_2 in Figure 1 is equal to the area of all the strips, each of width δx, from x_1 to x_2. The process of adding the individual strip areas together to give the total area is called **integration.**

In mathematical terms,

Total area $A = \int_{x_1}^{x_2} \delta A = \int_{x_1}^{x_2} y\, \delta x$, where $\int$ is the mathematical symbol for integration.

As $y = \dfrac{\delta A}{\delta x}$, then differentiating A in terms of x gives y. If we know the formula for y in terms of x, we can find the formula for A in terms of x by using the differentiation formula in Topic 13.2 in reverse.

For example, if $y = 2x$, then using the process of reverse differentiation gives $A = x^2$.

Force-field curves, such as the inverse square law of force between two point charges, give areas that represent potential energy. We can use the ideas outlined above to obtain an exact formula for the potential energy of two point charges at a certain distance apart.

Consider the two point charges q_1 and q_2 at distance apart r. The force F between the charges is given by Coulomb's law

$$F = \frac{q_1 q_2}{4\pi\varepsilon_0} \times \frac{1}{r^2}$$

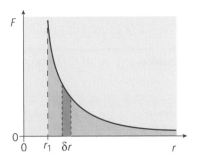

Figure 2 *The inverse square law of force*

If the charges move so their distance apart changes by δr, the work they do in this movement $= F\delta r$. This is represented on Figure 2 by the narrow strip of width δr.

Since the work they do reduces their potential energy, their change of potential energy $\delta E_p = -F\delta r$

When the distance apart decreases to r_1 from infinite separation, the potential energy changes from zero at infinite separation to E_p at distance apart r_1. Since E_p is represented by the total area under the line from $r =$ infinity to $r = r_1$

$$E_p = \int_{\text{infinity}}^{r} \delta E_p = \int_{\text{infinity}}^{r} -F\delta r$$

Because the force is given by the inverse square law above,

$$E_p = \int_{\text{infinity}}^{r} \frac{-k}{r^2} \delta r$$

where $k = -\dfrac{q_1 q_2}{4\pi\varepsilon_0}$

Therefore, $E_p = \dfrac{k}{r}$ because differentiating $\dfrac{-1}{r}$ gives $\dfrac{1}{r^2}$.

See Topic 13.2 if necessary.

Hence their potential energy at distance r_1 apart, $E_p = \dfrac{q_1 q_2}{4\pi\varepsilon_0 r_1}$ as the potential energy at infinity is zero.

> ### Note
>
> The inverse square law also applies to the gravitational force $F = \dfrac{GMm}{r^2}$ between two point masses M and m. The constant k is written as $-GMm$.
>
> Therefore, for a small mass m at distance r from the centre of a spherical planet of mass M at or beyond its surface, the gravitational potential energy $E_p = -\dfrac{GMm}{r}$

Summary questions

1 For a velocity–time graph, what physical variable is represented by:

a the gradient,

b the area under the line?

2 What physical variable is represented by:

a the area under a graph of acceleration against time,

b the area under a graph of current against time,

c What physical variable is represented by the area under a graph of pressure against volume for a gas?

d State the unit of

  i pressure,

  ii volume,

  iii pressure × volume.

3 For the electric field near a point charge, what physical variable is represented by

a the area under the graph of electric field strength E against distance r in Figure 3a?

b the gradient of the graph of electric potential V against distance r in Figure 3b?

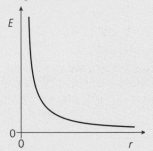

Figure 3a   **Figure 3b**

4 a For the gravitational field strength near a spherical object, what physical variable is represented by

  i the area under the graph of gravitational field strength g against distance r in Figure 4a?

  ii the gradient of the graph of gravitational potential V_{grav} against distance r in Figure 4b?

b Which of the graphs shown in Figures 3 and 4 are inverse square curves?

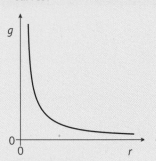
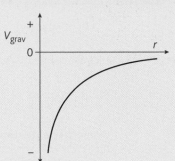

Figure 4a   **Figure 4b**

Useful data for AS Physics (Specification B)

Fundamental constants and other numerical data

Quality	Symbol	Value	Units
speed of light in vacuo	c	3.00×10^8	$\mathrm{m\,s^{-1}}$
Planck constant	h	6.63×10^{-34}	$\mathrm{J\,s}$
gravitational constant	G	6.67×10^{-11}	$\mathrm{N\,m^2\,kg^{-2}}$
gravitational field strength	g	9.81	$\mathrm{N\,kg^{-1}}$
acceleration due to gravity	g	9.81	$\mathrm{m\,s^{-2}}$
electron rest mass	m_e	$9.11 \times 10^{-31}\,\mathrm{kg}$ $5.5 \times 10^{-4}\,\mathrm{u}$	kg
electron charge	e	-1.60×10^{-19}	C
proton rest mass	m_p	$1.67(3) \times 10^{-27}\,\mathrm{kg}$ $1.00728\,\mathrm{u}$	kg
neutron rest mass	m_n	$1.67(5) \times 10^{-27}\,\mathrm{kg}$ $1.00867\,\mathrm{u}$	kg
permittivity of free space	ε_0	8.85×10^{-12}	$\mathrm{F\,m^{-1}}$
molar gas constant	R	8.31	$\mathrm{J\,K^{-1}\,mol^{-1}}$
Boltzmann constant	k	1.38×10^{-23}	$\mathrm{J\,K^{-1}}$
Avogadro constant	N_A	6.02×10^{23}	$\mathrm{mol^{-1}}$
Wein constant	α	2.90×10^{-3}	$\mathrm{m\,K}$

Geometrical equations

arc length	$r\theta$
circumference of circle	$2\pi r$
area of circle	πr^2
surface area of sphere	$4\pi r^2$
volume of sphere	$\frac{4}{3}\pi r^3$
surface area of cylinder	$2\pi rh$
volume of cylinder	$\pi r^2 h$

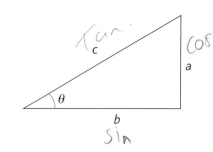

$$\sin\theta \quad \frac{a}{c}$$
$$\cos\theta \quad \frac{b}{c}$$
$$\tan\theta \quad \frac{a}{b}$$

$$c^2 = a^2 + b^2$$

Unit conversions

1 atomic mass unit (u)	$1.661 \times 10^{-27}\,\mathrm{kg}$
1 year (y)	$3.15 \times 10^7\,\mathrm{s}$
1 parsec (pc)	$3.08 \times 10^{16}\,\mathrm{m}$ $3.26\,\mathrm{ly}$
1 light year (ly)	$9.45 \times 10^{15}\,\mathrm{m}$

Particle properties

Properties of quarks
Antiparticles have opposite signs

type	charge	baryon number	strangeness
u	$+\frac{2}{3}e$	$+\frac{1}{3}$	0
d	$-\frac{1}{3}e$	$+\frac{1}{3}$	0
s	$-\frac{1}{3}e$	$+\frac{1}{3}$	-1

Properties of leptons

lepton	lepton number
particles: $e^-, \nu_e ; \mu^-, \nu_\mu ; \tau^-, \nu_\tau$	$+1$
antiparticles: $e^+, \bar{\nu}_e ; \mu^+, \bar{\nu}_\mu ; \tau^+, \bar{\nu}_\tau$	-1

AS formulae

Waves

wave speed	$c = f\lambda$
period	$T = \dfrac{1}{f}$
intensity	$I = \dfrac{P}{A}$
stretched string frequency	$f = \dfrac{1}{2l}\sqrt{\dfrac{T}{\mu}}$
beat frequency	$f = f_1 - f_2$
fringe spacing	$w = \dfrac{\lambda D}{s}$
diffraction grating	$n\lambda = d\sin\theta$
half beam width	$\sin\theta = \dfrac{\lambda}{a}$
refractive index of a substance s,	$n_s = \dfrac{c}{c_s}$

For two different substances of refractive indices n_1 and n_2,

law of refraction	$n_1\sin\theta_1 = n_2\sin\theta_2$
critical angle	$\sin\theta_c = \dfrac{n_2}{n_1}$ for $n_1 > n_2$

Mechanics

speed or velocity	$v = \dfrac{\Delta s}{\Delta t}$
acceleration	$a = \dfrac{\Delta v}{\Delta t}$
equations of motion	$v = u + at$
	$s = \dfrac{(u+v)}{2}t$
	$v^2 = u^2 + 2as$
	$s = ut + \frac{1}{2}at^2$
force	$F = ma$
change in potential energy	$\Delta E_p = mg\,\Delta h$
kinetic energy	$E_k = \frac{1}{2}mv^2$
momentum	$p = mv$
impulse	$F\,\Delta t = \Delta(mv)$
spring stiffness	$k = \dfrac{F}{\Delta L}$
energy stored for $F \propto L$	$E = \frac{1}{2}F\Delta L$
work	$W = Fs$

power	$P = \dfrac{\Delta W}{\Delta t} = Fv$
density	$\rho = \dfrac{m}{V}$

Quantum physics and astrophysics

photon energy	$E = hf$
Einstein equation	$hf = \varphi + E_{Kmax}$
line spectrum equation	$hf = E_1 - E_2$
de Broglie wavelength	$\lambda = \dfrac{h}{p} = \dfrac{h}{mv}$
Doppler shift for $v \ll c$	$\dfrac{\Delta f}{f} = -\dfrac{\Delta\lambda}{\lambda} = \dfrac{v}{c}$
Wien's law	$\lambda_{max}T = 0.0029\,\text{m K}$
Hubble law	$v = Hd$
intensity for a point source	$I = \dfrac{P}{4\pi r^2}$

Electricity

current	$I = \dfrac{\Delta Q}{\Delta t}$
electromotive force (emf)	$\varepsilon = \dfrac{E}{Q}$
	$\varepsilon = IR + Ir$
resistance	$R = \dfrac{V}{I}$
resistors in series	$R = R_1 + R_2 + R_3 + \dots$
resistors in parallel	$\dfrac{1}{R} = \dfrac{1}{R_1} + \dfrac{1}{R_2} + \dfrac{1}{R_3} + \dots$
resistivity	$\rho = \dfrac{RA}{L}$
power	$P = VI = I^2R = \dfrac{V^2}{R}$
potential divider formula	$V_0 = \left(\dfrac{R_1}{R_1 + R_2}\right) \times V_i$
energy	$E = VIt$
efficiency	$\dfrac{\text{useful output power}}{\text{input power}}$

Energy production and transmission

rate of heat transfer by conduction $= UA\,\Delta\theta$

maximum energy for a wind turbine $= \frac{1}{2}\pi r^2\rho v^3$

Useful data for A2 Physics (Specification B)

A2 Formulae

Gravitational fields and mechanics

magnitude of gravitational force $\quad F = \dfrac{GMm}{r^2}$

magnitude of field strength $\quad g = \dfrac{F}{m}$

$\quad g = \dfrac{GM}{r^2}$

for point masses $\quad \Delta E_p = GMm\left(\dfrac{1}{r_1} - \dfrac{1}{r_2}\right)$

$\quad V = -\dfrac{GM}{r}$

potential escape velocity $\quad v_{esc} = \sqrt{\dfrac{2GM}{R}}$

rocket equation $\quad v_f = v_e \ln\left(\dfrac{m_0}{m_f}\right)$

Stokes' law $\quad F = 6\pi\eta rv$

Electric fields

field strength for uniform field $\quad E = \dfrac{V}{d}$

force on a charge $\quad F = EQ$

field strength for radial field $\quad E = \dfrac{Q}{4\pi\varepsilon_0 r^2}$

for point charges $\quad F = \dfrac{Qq}{4\pi\varepsilon_0 r^2}$

electric potential $\quad V = \dfrac{Q}{4\pi\varepsilon_0 r}$

electron gun equation $\quad eV = \frac{1}{2}mv^2$

Magnetic fields

force on current-carrying conductor $\quad F = BIl$

force on moving charge $\quad F = BQv$

magnetic flux $\quad \Phi = BA$

magnetic flux linkage $\quad = BAN$

$\quad = N\Phi$

induced emf $\quad \varepsilon = -N\dfrac{\Delta\Phi}{\Delta t}$

Capacitors

capacitance $\quad C = \dfrac{Q}{V}$

energy stored $\quad E = \frac{1}{2}QV$

decay of charge $\quad Q = Q_0 e^{-t/RC}$

time constant $\quad RC$

time to halve $\quad RC\ln 2$

Relativity

mass increase $\quad m = \dfrac{m_0}{\sqrt{\left(1 - \dfrac{v^2}{c^2}\right)}}$

time dilation $\quad t = \dfrac{t_0}{\sqrt{\left(1 - \dfrac{v^2}{c^2}\right)}}$

Circular motion

angular velocity	$\omega = \dfrac{v}{r}$
angular acceleration	$\alpha = \dfrac{\Delta\omega}{\Delta t}$
angular frequency	$\omega = 2\pi f$
centripetal force	$F = \dfrac{mv^2}{r} = mr\omega^2$
centripetal acceleration	$a = \dfrac{v^2}{r} = r\omega^2$
angular momentum	$L = I\omega$
angular kinetic energy	$E_k = \frac{1}{2}I\omega^2$
moment of inertia	$I = \dfrac{T}{\alpha}$
torque	$T = Fd$
equations of angular motion	$\omega_2 = \omega_1 + \alpha t$
	$\omega_2^2 = \omega_1^2 + 2\alpha s$
	$\theta = \dfrac{(\omega_1 + \omega_2)}{2}t$
	$\theta = \omega_1 t + \frac{1}{2}\alpha t^2$
power	$P = T\omega$

Oscillations

acceleration	$a = -(2\pi f)^2 x$
displacement	$x = A\cos(2\pi ft)$
maximum speed	$v_{max} = 2\pi fA$
maximum acceleration	$a_{max} = (2\pi f)^2 A$
for a mass–spring system	$T = 2\pi\sqrt{\dfrac{m}{k}}$
for a simple pendulum	$T = 2\pi\sqrt{\dfrac{l}{g}}$

Gases and thermal physics

pressure	$p = \dfrac{F}{A}$
gas law (N is number of atoms)	$pV = NkT$
gas law (n is quantity in mol)	$pV = nRT$
kinetic theory model	$pV = \frac{1}{3}Nm<c^2>$
kinetic energy of gas molecule	$\frac{1}{2}mc_{rms}^2 = \frac{3}{2}kT$
root mean square speed of molecules	$c_{rms} = \sqrt{<c^2>}$
energy to change temperature	$Q = mc\Delta\theta$
first law of thermodynamics	$\Delta U = Q + W$
	W = work done on the system
entropy change	$\Delta S = \dfrac{Q}{T}$
maximum thermal efficiency	$\eta = \dfrac{T_H - T_C}{T_H}$
work done	$W = p\Delta V$

Radioactivity and nuclear physics

absorption of radiation	$I = I_0 e^{-\mu x}$
radioactive decay	$N = N_0 e^{-\lambda t}$
half-life	$T_{\frac{1}{2}} = \dfrac{\ln 2}{\lambda}$
activity	$A = \lambda N$
mass–energy equivalence	$\Delta E = \Delta mc^2$

Glossary (A2 only)

A glossary of practical terms is given on p245.

A

absolute zero: the lowest possible temperature, the temperature at which an object has minimum internal energy.

absolute temperature: T, in kelvin = temperature in °C + 273(.15).

absorption: the process by which the intensity of radiation is reduced as it passes through a material medium due to energy transfer to the medium: e.g. by ionisation or excitation of atoms in the medium.

absorption cross-section: a measure of the probability of a particle being absorbed by another in an interaction. It is defined by the area through which a colliding particle must pass for an interaction to occur. It is measured in 'barn' where 1 barn = $1 \times 10^{-28}\,m^2$.

activity, A, of a radioactive isotope: the number of nuclei of the isotope that disintegrate per second. The unit of activity is the becquerel (Bq), equal to 1 disintegration per second.

adiabatic change: this occurs when no heat enters or leaves the system when a change in internal energy takes place ($Q = 0$). Such changes take place quickly so that there is no time for heat transfer to take place and/or when gases are in well insulated containers.

alpha radiation: particles that are each composed of two protons and two neutrons. An alpha (α) particle is emitted by a heavy unstable nucleus which is then less unstable as a result. Alpha radiation is easily absorbed by paper, has a range in air of no more than a few centimetres and is more ionising than beta (β) or gamma (γ) radiation.

amplitude of oscillations of an oscillating object: the maximum displacement from equilibrium.

angular displacement (angle), θ: the angle an object in circular motion turns through. If its time period is T and its frequency is f, its angular displacement in time t, in radians $= 2\pi ft = \dfrac{2\pi t}{T}$.

angular velocity/speed: the rate of change of angular displacement of an object in circular (or orbital or spinning) motion.

anomaly: a reading that deviates from the expected reading. In geophysics it is a measurement of a quantity that differs significantly from the same measurements in the surrounding area.

attenuation coefficient, μ: a measure of the ability of a substance to reduce the intensity of radiation by absorption or diffusion.

atomic mass unit, u (correctly referred to as the unified atomic mass constant): $\frac{1}{12}$th of the mass of an atom of the carbon isotope $^{12}_{6}C$, equal to $1.661 \times 10^{-27}\,kg$.

atomic number, Z of an atom of an element: the number of protons in the nucleus of the atom.

Avogadro constant, N_A: the number of atoms in 12 g of the carbon isotope $^{12}_{6}C$. N_A is used to define the mole. Its value is $6.02 \times 10^{23}\,mol^{-1}$.

B

background radiation: radiation due to naturally occurring radioactive substances in the environment (e.g. in the ground or in building materials or elsewhere in the environment). Background radiation is also caused by cosmic radiation.

becquerel: the activity of a radioactive source when one disintegration occurs per second.

beta-minus (β^-) radiation: electrons (β^-) emitted by unstable neutron-rich nuclei (i.e. nuclei with a neutron/proton ratio greater than for stable nuclei). β^- radiation is easily absorbed by paper, has a range in air of no more than a few centimetres and is less ionising than alpha (α) radiation and more ionising than gamma (γ) radiation.

beta-plus (β^+) radiation: positrons (β^+) emitted by unstable proton-rich nuclei (i.e. nuclei with a neutron/proton ratio smaller than for stable nuclei). Positrons emitted in solids or liquids travel no further than about 2 mm before they are annihilated.

binding energy of a nucleus: the work that must be done on a nucleus (or energy input needed) to separate a nucleus into its constituent neutrons and protons.
- binding energy = mass defect $\times c^2$.
- binding energy in MeV = mass defect in u $\times$ 931.3

binding energy per nucleon: The work done per nucleon (or energy input needed) to separate a nucleus into its constituent parts.
- the binding energy per nucleon of a nucleus = $\dfrac{\text{the binding energy of a nucleus}}{\text{nucleon number } A}$.
- the binding energy per nucleon is greatest for iron nuclei of mass number about 56.
- the binding energy curve is a graph of binding energy per nucleon against mass number A.

biological half-life: the time taken for half of the atoms of an element to be lost by the (human) body.

Boltzmann constant k: the molar gas constant divided by the Avogadro number (i.e. R/N_A). See kinetic energy of the molecules of an ideal gas

Brownian motion: the random and unpredictable motion of a particle such as a smoke particle caused by molecules of the surrounding substance colliding at random with the particle.

C

capacitance of a capacitor: the charge stored per unit pd. The unit of capacitance is the farad (F), equal to 1 coulomb per volt.

For a capacitor of capacitance C at pd V, the charge stored, $Q = CV$.

capacitor energy: energy stored by the capacitor, $E = \frac{1}{2}QV = \frac{1}{2}CV^2 = \frac{1}{2}Q^2/C$

capacitor discharge through a fixed resistor of resistance R,
1. time constant $= RC$
2. exponential decrease equation for current I, charge Q or pd V given by $x = x_0 e^{-t/RC}$ where x represents I, Q or V.

centripetal acceleration: the acceleration of an object when moving in a circular path.
1. for an object moving at speed v (or angular speed ω) in uniform circular motion, its centripetal acceleration $a = v^2/r = \omega^2 r$ towards the centre of the circle.
2. for a satellite in a circular orbit, its centripetal acceleration $v^2/r = g$.

centripetal force: the resultant force on an object that moves along a circular path. For an object of mass m moving at speed v along a circular path of radius r, the centripetal force $= \dfrac{mv^2}{r}$ towards the centre of the circle.

chain reaction: a series of reactions in which each reaction causes a further reaction. In a nuclear reactor, each fission event is due to a neutron colliding with a $^{235}_{92}\text{U}$ nucleus which splits and releases two or three further neutrons which can go on to produce further fission. A steady chain reaction occurs when one fission neutron on average from each fission event produces a further fission event.

characteristic X-rays: short wave radiation of specific frequencies that depend on the element forming the target for the electrons in an X-ray tube.

coherent bundle: A bundle of optical fibres that retain the same spatial configuration so that they transmit a true image.

collisions: an elastic collision is one in which the total kinetic energy after the collision is the same as before the collision. In an inelastic collision some of the kinetic energy is transferred to other forms of energy. In an explosive collision other forms of energy are transferred to kinetic energy.

conductivity: measure of the ability of a material to conduct electricity; reciprocal of resistivity.

conservation of energy: this states that in any change, the total amount of energy after the change is always equal to the total amount of energy before the change.

conservation of momentum: for a system of interacting objects, the total momentum of the objects remains constant provided no external resultant force acts on the system.

continuous spectrum: a spectrum in which all possible wavelengths are present, i.e. there are no frequencies missing within the frequency range of the spectrum.

contrast medium: a substance swallowed by a patient to improve the definition of images produced using X-rays or other scanning methods.

control rods: rods made of a neutron-absorbing substance such as cadmium or boron that are moved in or out of the core of a nuclear reactor to control the rate of fission events in the reactor.

coolant: a gas or liquid used in a reactor to transfer the energy released in the fission process to a heat exchanger

Coulomb's law of force: for two point charges Q_1 and Q_2 at distance apart r, the force F between the two charges is given by the equation $F = \dfrac{Q_1 Q_2}{4\pi\varepsilon_0 r^2}$, where ε_0 is the permittivity of free space.

count rate: the number of counts per unit time detected by a Geiger tube. Count rates should always be corrected by measuring and subtracting the background count rate (i.e. the count rate with no radioactive source present).

critical angle: the angle between the incident ray and the normal at an interface that produces an angle of refraction of 90°. At greater angles of incidence the light is totally reflected. This can occur when light travels into a medium with a lower refractive index.

cyclotron: a particle accelerator in which charged particles are accelerated in a spiral path inside a pair of evacuated 'dees'. The acceleration is produced by a combination of electric and magnetic fields.

D

damped oscillations: oscillations that reduce in amplitude due to the presence of resistive forces such as friction and drag.
- for a lightly-damped system, the amplitude of oscillations decreases gradually.
- for a heavily damped system displaced from equilibrium then released, the system slowly returns to equilibrium without oscillating.
- for a critically-damped system, the system returns to equilibrium in the least possible time without oscillating.

daughter nucleus: the nucleus that is formed following the radioactive decay of a (parent) nucleus.

de Broglie wavelength: a particle of matter has a wave-like nature which means that it can behave as a wave. For example, electrons directed at a thin crystal are diffracted by the crystal. The de Broglie wavelength, λ, of a matter particle depends on its momentum, p, in accordance with de Broglie's equation $\lambda = \dfrac{h}{p} = \dfrac{h}{mv}$.

decay constant λ: the probability of an individual nucleus decaying per second.

density: mass of an object divided by its volume $\rho = \dfrac{M}{V}$.

deuteron: the nucleus of 'heavy' hydrogen consisting of a proton and a neutron.

diffraction: the spreading of waves when they pass through a gap or round an obstacle. X-ray diffraction is used to determine the structure of crystals, metals and long molecules. Electron diffraction is used to probe the structure of materials. High energy electron scattering is used to determine the diameter of the nucleus.

Doppler effect: the apparent change in frequency of sound or electromagnetic radiation observed when a source and observer move toward or away form each other.

E

eddy currents: induced currents that circulate in closed loops within electrical conductors when subjected to a changing magnetic field.

elastic collision: a perfectly elastic collision is one in which the total kinetic energy after the collision is equal to the total kinetic energy before the collision.

elasticity: the property of a body by which it tends to return to its original size and shape after being deformed.

electric field: a region in which a charged particle experiences a force due to its charge.

electric field strength, E, at a point in an electric field: the force per unit charge on a small positively charged object at that point in the field.

electric potential, V, at a point in an electric field: the work done per unit charge on a small positively charged object to move it from infinity to that point in the field.

electrical potential energy: energy that a charged particle has due to its position in an electric field. The change in electrical potential energy when it moved through a potential difference of V is given by VQ.

electromagnetic induction: the generation of an emf when the magnetic flux linkage through a coil changes or a conductor cuts across magnetic field lines.

electromagnetic radiation: these are transverse waves that consist of electric and magnetic fields that oscillate at right angles to each other and at right angles to the direction of propagation of the energy of the wave.

electron-volt: energy equivalent to 1.6×10^{-19} J. The energy gained by an electron when accelerated through a pd of 1 volt.

energy density: the energy per unit volume of an energy source, e.g. a battery.

energy levels: the well-defined energies that an electron can occupy in an atom or molecule.

entropy: a measure of the disorder in a system. In any practical change that takes place in a closed system the disorder increases and therefore the total entropy increases.
The change in entropy of any system is equal to the heat transferred divided by temperature; where Q is the heat supplied to the system and T is the absolute temperature of the system.

equipotential: a line or surface in a field along which the electric or gravitational potential is constant.

excite: to excite means to move electrons or atoms from a low energy state to a higher energy state.

excited state: states that an electron can occupy that have higher energies than the lowest that an electron can occupy in an atom (the ground state).

explosion: in an explosion where two objects fly apart, the two objects carry away equal and opposite momentum.

exponential decrease: exponential change happens when the rate of change of a quantity is proportional to the quantity itself. For an exponential decrease of a quantity x, $\frac{dx}{dt} = -\lambda x$ where λ is referred to as the decay constant. The solution of this equation is $x = x_0 e^{-\lambda t}$ where x_0 is an initial value of x.

F

farad: unit of capacitance equal to one coulomb per volt.

Faraday's law of electromagnetic induction: the induced emf in a circuit is equal to the rate of change of magnetic flux linkage through the circuit.
For a changing magnetic field in a fixed coil of area A and N turns, the induced emf $= NA\frac{\Delta B}{\Delta t}$.

field of view: the angle within which an image is obtained. This may be an image visible to the eye or another image forming device such as a camera. To be visible the object must be within this angle.

fission: the splitting of a $^{235}_{92}$U nucleus or a $^{239}_{94}$Pu nucleus into two approximately equal fragments. Induced fission is fission caused by an incoming neutron colliding with a $^{235}_{92}$U nucleus or a $^{234}_{94}$Pu nucleus .

flux linkage: see magnetic flux linkage.

force = rate of change of momentum
$= \dfrac{\text{change of momentum}}{\text{time taken}}$
= mass × acceleration

free oscillations: oscillations where there is no damping and no periodic force acting on the system so the amplitude of the oscillations is constant.

forced oscillations: oscillations of a system that is subjected to an external periodic force.

frequency of an oscillating object: the number of cycles of oscillation per second.

fuel rods: rods that contain the uranium or plutonium in a fission reactor.

fusion (nuclear): the fusing together of light nuclei to form a heavier nucleus.

fusion (thermal): the fusing together of metals by melting them together.

G

gal: a unit for gravitational field strength used in geophysics; equivalent to $0.01\,\text{N kg}^{-1}$.

gamma: a unit for magnetic flux density used in geophysics and archaeological surveying; equivalent to 10^{-9} T.

gamma radiation: electromagnetic radiation emitted by an unstable nucleus when it becomes more stable.

geostationary satellite: a satellite that stays above the same point on the Earth's equator as it orbits the Earth because its orbit is in the same plane as the equator, its period is exactly 24 h and it orbits in the same direction as the Earth's direction of rotation.

gold leaf electroscope: a device used to detect electric charge.

gradient fields: computer-controlled magnetic fields of variable strength used in MRI scanners.

gravitational constant, G: the constant of proportionality in Newton's law of gravitation.

gravitational potential, V, at a point in a gravitational field: the work done per unit mass to move a small object from infinity to that point. At distance r from the centre of a spherical object of mass M, $V = -\dfrac{GM}{r}$.

gravitational potential energy: at a point in a gravitational field, this is the work done to move a small object from infinity to that point. The change of gravitational potential energy of a mass m moved through height h near the Earth's surface, $\Delta E_p = mg\Delta h$.

gravitational field strength, g: the force per unit mass on a small mass placed in the field.

- $g = \dfrac{F}{m}$, where F is the gravitational force on a small mass m.
- at distance r from a point mass M, $g = \dfrac{GM}{r^2}$
- at or beyond the surface of a sphere of mass M, $g = \dfrac{GM}{r^2}$, where r is the distance to the centre.
- at the surface of a sphere of mass M and radius R, $g_s = \dfrac{GM}{r^2}$

half-life, $T_{1/2}$ of a radioactive isotope: the time taken for the mass of the isotope to decrease to half the initial mass or for its activity to halve. This is the same as the time taken for the number of nuclei of the isotope to decrease to half the initial number.

half-thickness or half-value thickness: the thickness of an absorber that reduces the intensity of gamma radiation to half the original value.

Hall effect: the establishment of a pd at right angles to the direction of the flow of charge when a magnetic field is applied perpendicular to a conductor.

Hall probe: a device used to measure magnetic flux density.

heat: energy transfer due to a difference of temperature. The symbol Q is used for heat.

heat capacity: the energy needed to change the temperature of an object by 1 K.

heat engine: a heat engine uses heat to do work and then rejects to the surroundings any heat which cannot be used to do work.

I

ideal gas law: $pV = nRT$, where p is the gas pressure, V is the gas volume, n is the number of moles of gas, T is the absolute temperature and R is the molar gas constant.

impulse of a force acting on an object; force × time for which the force acts.

incoherent bundle: a bundle of fibres which are used to illuminate objects (e.g. inside the body) and for which spatial configuration of the individual fibres is not important.

induced emf: see electromagnetic induction

induced fission: see fission

integration: mathematic process of finding the area under a curve from its mathematical equation.

intensity: the intensity of γ-radiation from a point source varies with the inverse of the square of the distance from the source. The same rule applies to radiation from any point source that spreads out equally in all directions and is not absorbed.

intensity of radiation at a surface. The radiation energy per second per unit area at normal incidence to the surface. The unit of intensity is $J\,s^{-1}\,m^{-2}$ or $W\,m^{-2}$.

internal energy of an object: the sum of the random distribution of the kinetic and potential energies of its molecules,

internal resistance: the resistance inside a supply due to the chemicals or electrical components from which it is made. The internal resistance is in series with any external resistance. It dissipates energy and limits the maximum current available from the supply.

ionise: to ionise means to add or remove an electron from an atom or molecule leaving it with an overall charge.

ionising radiation: radiation that produces ions in substances it passes through. It destroys cell membranes and damages vital molecules such as DNA directly or indirectly by creating 'free radical' ions which react with vital molecules.

ions: the charged particles that result following the addition or removal of electrons from an atom or molecule.

isothermal change: this occurs when a change takes place at constant temperature. This means that there is no change in internal energy so $\Delta U = 0$. Any work done on the system is equal to the heat transfer that takes place to the surroundings during the change or vice versa.

isotopes of an element: atoms which have the same number of protons in each nucleus but different numbers of neutrons.

inverse square laws: laws in which one physical quantity (e.g. force) is inversely proportional to the square of another quantity (e.g. distance between particles) such as occurs in Newton's law of gravitation and Coulomb's law of force between charges.

K

kinetic energy: the energy of a moving object due to its motion. For an object of mass m moving at speed v, its kinetic energy $E_K = \frac{1}{2}mv^2$, provided $v \ll c$ (where c is the speed of light in free space).

kinetic energy of the molecules of an ideal gas: the mean kinetic energy of a molecule of an ideal gas $= \frac{3}{2}kT$, where the Boltzmann constant $k = \dfrac{R}{N_A}$.

The total kinetic energy of n moles of an ideal gas $= \frac{3}{2}RT$.

kinetic theory of a gas: a theory that assumes a gas to consist of identical point molecules which do not attract one another and which are in continual random motion colliding elastically with each other and with the container. Using the theory the pressure p of N molecules of such a gas in a container of volume V is given by $pV = \frac{1}{3}Nm\langle c^2\rangle$, where m is the mass of each molecule and $\langle c^2\rangle$ is the mean square speed of the gas molecules.

Assuming that the mean kinetic energy of a gas molecule $\frac{1}{2}m <c^2> = \frac{3}{2}kT$, where $k = \frac{R}{N_A}$, it can be shown from $pV = \frac{1}{3}Nm <c^2>$ that $pV = nRT$ which is the Ideal Gas Law.

Kepler's 3rd law: for any planet, the cube of its mean radius of orbit r is directly proportional to the square of its time period T. Using Newton's law of gravitation, it can be shown that $\frac{r^3}{T^2} = \frac{GM}{4\pi^2}$.

L

Lenz's law states that when a current is induced by electromagnetic induction, the direction of the induced current is always such as to oppose the change that causes the current.

line of force or a field line: a line followed by a small mass in a gravitational field (or a small positively-charged object in an electric field or a free north pole in a magnetic field) acted on by no other forces other than the force due to the field.

linear accelerators (or 'linacs'): particle accelerators in which charged particles are accelerated by the electric fields between pairs of 'drift tubes' arranged in a straight line.

line spectrum: a spectrum which consists of radiation of specific frequencies. They are produced by electron transitions between the well-defined energy levels in atoms.

longitudinal waves: mechanical waves in which the oscillation of particles that transmit the wave are in the direction of propagation of the wave energy, e.g. sound.

M

magnetic field strength: see magnetic flux density

magnetic flux density, B: this is the magnetic force per unit length per unit current on a current carrying conductor at right angles to the field lines. The unit of magnetic flux density is the tesla (T). B is sometimes referred to as the magnetic field strength. $F = BIl\sin\theta$ gives the magnitude of the force F on a length l of wire carrying a current I in a uniform magnetic field B at angle θ to the field direction.

$F = BQv\sin\theta$ gives the force F on a particle of charge Q moving through a uniform magnetic field B at speed v in a direction at angle θ to the field . If the velocity of the charged particle is perpendicular to the field, $F = BQv$.

magnetic flux $N\Phi = BA$ for a uniform magnetic field of flux density B that is perpendicular to an area A.

magnetic flux linkage $N\Phi = NBA$ where N is the number of turns on a coil having flux density B perpendicular to area A. The unit of magnetic flux and of flux linkage is the weber (Wb), equal to $1\,T\,m^2$ or $1\,V\,s$.

mass defect of a nucleus: the difference between the mass of the separated nucleons (i.e. protons and neutrons from which the nucleus is composed) and the nucleus.

mass number: see nucleon number

mass spectrometer: a device used to measure the mass-to-charge ratio of charged particles (usually ions) by deflecting them by a magnetic field.

mean kinetic energy: for a molecule in a gas at absolute temperature T, its mean kinetic energy $= \frac{3}{2}kT$, where k is the Boltzmann constant $(= R/N_A)$.

metastable state: an excited state of the nuclei of an isotope that lasts long enough after α or β-emission for the isotope to be separated from the parent isotope (e.g. technetium $^{99m}_{43}Tc$).

moderator: substance in a thermal nuclear reactor that slows the fission neutrons down so they can go on to produce further fission.

mole: one mole of a substance consisting of identical particles is the quantity of substance that contains N_A particles of the substance. The molar mass of a substance is the mass of one mole.

molar gas constant R: see the ideal gas law.

momentum: mass × velocity. The unit of momentum is $kg\,m\,s^{-1}$.

multipath dispersion: the dispersion that occurs in optical fibres due to the light taking paths of different total length along the fibre.

N

natural frequency: the frequency of free oscillations of an oscillating system.

Newton's law of gravitation or Newton's gravitational law: the gravitational force F between two point masses m_1 and m_2 at distance r apart is given by $F = -\frac{Gm_1m_2}{r^2}$ where the minus sign indicates the force is an attractive force.

Newton's laws of motion

- **1st law:** an object continues at rest or in uniform motion unless it is acted on by a resultant force.
- **2nd law:** the rate of change of momentum of an object is proportional to the resultant force on it. Since $\Delta p = m\Delta v$, so $F = ma$.
- **3rd law:** when two objects interact, they exert equal and opposite forces on one another.

nucleon: a neutron or a proton in the nucleus.

nucleon number: the total number of protons and neutrons (number of nucleons) in the nucleus.

nuclide ^A_ZX: a nucleus composed of Z protons and $(A–Z)$ neutrons, where Z is the proton number (and also the atomic number of element X) and A is the nucleon number.

P

particle accelerators: devices such as cyclotrons and synchrotrons in which charged particles are accelerated to very high velocities and kinetic energies.

permeability of free space: a constant of value $4\pi \times 10^{-7}\,H\,m^{-1}$. Higher magnetic flux densities are produced in materials with higher permeability when placed in the same inducing field.

phase difference in radians: for two objects oscillating with the same time period, T, the phase difference, $= \frac{2\pi\Delta t}{T}$, where Δt is the time between successive instants when the two objects are at maximum displacement in the same direction.

photodiode: a diode that has the ability to store the charge that is generated when photons of a suitable energy are incident on it. The charge may be stored as in a CCD device or used to generate small currents in a circuit.

photon: electromagnetic radiation consists of photons. Each photon is a wave packet of electromagnetic radiation. The energy of a photon, $E = hf$, where f is the frequency of the radiation and h is the Planck constant.

pixel: a small element that forms part of a graphic image which contains many such elements. The greater the concentration of the pixels the better the quality of the image.

plasma: a state of matter in which gaseous matter exists in the form of positive ions and electrons; at very high temperatures a plasma consists of atomic nuclei and electrons.

positron: a particle of antimatter that is the antiparticle of the electron.

potential: see electrical potential and gravitational potential

potential difference: this is equal to the work done (energy transferred) when a charge of one coulomb moves between two points that are at a different potential.

potential gradient at a point in a field: the change of potential per unit change of distance along the field line at that point. The potential gradient = – the field strength at any point.

power: rate of transfer of energy = $\dfrac{\text{energy transferred}}{\text{time taken}}$.

precession: when a spinning top spins it moves around a vertical axis through the point of contact with the ground and it is said to undergo precession. A spinning proton undergoes similar motion in a magnetic field.

pulse length: when the voltage or current output of an electrical circuit rises above its normal base state of 0 for a relatively short period, the output is said to be a voltage pulse or a current pulse. The time for which the voltage or current output lasts is called the pulse length (or pulse width).

Q

quantum efficiency: the percentage of photons that fall on a photosensitive area that are used to generate an image.

R

radial field: a field in which the field lines are straight and converge or diverge as if from a single point.

radian: 1 radian = $\dfrac{360}{2\pi}$ degrees

reflect: waves are said to reflect when they are incident on a reflective surface so that the direction of propagation of energy is partially or totally deviated so that it travels back into the original medium.

refraction: waves are said to undergo refraction at an interface between two media when the direction of propagation of the energy in the new medium is different from that in the original medium.

refractive index: $\dfrac{\sin i}{\sin r}$ = a constant; where i is the angle between the incident ray and the normal, r is the angle between the refracted ray and the normal, and the constant is called the refractive index n.

renewable energy: this is energy from a source that is continually renewed. Examples include hydroelectricity, tidal power, geothermal power, solar power, wave power and wind power.

resistance R: the property that describes the ability of a component to restrict the rate of flow of charge through it.

$$R = \dfrac{V}{I} = \dfrac{\text{pd}}{\text{current}}$$

resistivity: resistance per unit length × area of cross-section

resonance: the amplitude of vibration of an oscillating system subjected to a periodic force is largest when the periodic force has the same frequency as the resonant frequency of the system. For a lightly damped system, the frequency of the periodic force = natural frequency of the oscillating system.

resonant frequency: the frequency of an oscillating system in resonance.

S

scattered: when energy from radiation is dispersed in different directions as it passes through matter it is said to be scattered. The process reduces the energy of the transmitted beam.

seismometer: a device for recording and measuring movement of the ground due to earthquakes or explosions.

simple harmonic motion: an object oscillates in simple harmonic motion if its acceleration is proportional to the displacement of the object from equilibrium and is always directed towards the equilibrium position.

simple harmonic motion applications
1. for a simple pendulum of length L, its time period $T = 2\pi(L/g)^{1/2}$
2. for an oscillating mass m on the end of a vertical spring, its time period $T = 2\pi(m/k)^{1/2}$, where k is the spring constant.

sinusoidal curve: any curve with the same shape as a sine wave (e.g. a cosine curve).

specific charge: this is the charge per unit mass of a particle; specific charge = $\dfrac{\text{charge carried by the particle}}{\text{mass of the particle}}$ $\left(= \dfrac{e}{m} \text{ for an electron}\right)$.

specific heat capacity, c, of a substance: the energy needed to raise the temperature of 1 kg of the substance by 1 K without change of state. To raise the temperature of mass m of a substance from T_1 to T_2, the energy needed, $Q = mc(T_2 - T_1)$, where c is the specific heat capacity of the substance.

superconducting: a conductor that has zero resistance at temperatures above absolute zero is said to be superconducting. The resistance drops to zero when a transition temperature is reached.

synchrotrons: particle accelerators, such as CERN's LHC and LEP, in which particles are accelerated through an evacuated chamber in a circular path of fixed radius using synchronised electric and magnetic fields that increase in strength as the particles get faster.

T

temperature: the degree of hotness of an object. Heat flow occurs from the body that is at the higher temperature.

tesla, T,: measure of magnetic flux density. When a force of 1 N is exerted on a conductor of length 1 m and which carries a current of 1 A, the magnetic flux density perpendicular to the conductor is 1 T.

thermal energy: the internal energy of an object due to temperature.

thermal equilibrium: two objects at the same temperature are in thermal equilibrium so no overall heat transfer occurs between them.

thermal nuclear reactor: nuclear reactor which has a moderator in the core.

thermionic emission: the emission of electrons produced by raising a surface to a high temperature.

thermocouple: a temperature-sensing element that converts thermal energy directly into electrical energy.

time constant: the time taken for the pd across a capacitor to fall to $1/e$ (37%) of its initial value current when discharging through a resistor; time constant $= RC$. The pd halves in time $0.69 \times$ time constant.

time period (or period) is the time taken for one complete cycle of oscillations.

torque: a torque(or moment) produces a turning effect. The magnitude is calculated from force $\times$ perpendicular distance of the force from the axis of rotation. A resultant torque produces an angular acceleration.

transverse waves: for transverse mechanical waves the oscillations of particles in the transmitting medium are perpendicular to the direction of propagation of the energy. (see also electromagnetic waves)

U

uniform field: a region where the field strength is the same in magnitude and direction at every point in the field.
- The electric field between two oppositely charged parallel plates is uniform. The electric field strength $E = V/d$, where V is the pd between the plates and d is the perpendicular distance between the plates.
- The gravitational field of the Earth is uniform over a region which is small compared to the scale of the Earth.
- The magnetic field inside a solenoid carrying a constant current is uniform along and near the axis.

van de Graaff generator: an electrostatic machine which uses a moving belt to accumulate very high voltages on a hollow metal sphere. Often used to accelerate charged particles before they are fed into a particle accelerator.

W

weber: unit of magnetic flux, $1\,Wb = 1\,T\,m^2$

work done: work is energy transferred by means of a force. The work done W by a force F when its point of application moves through displacement s at angle θ to the direction of the force is given by $W = Fs\cos\theta$.

work function: the minimum energy needed by an electron to escape from a metal surface.

X

X-rays: electromagnetic radiation of wavelength less than about 1 nm. X-rays are emitted when fast moving electrons are decelerated rapidly on impact with a metal surface. X-rays are ionising and highly penetrating.

Glossary of practical terms

accepted value: the value of the most accurate measurement available, sometimes referred to as the 'true value'

accuracy: a measure of confidence in a measurement, often expressed as the uncertainty or probable error of the measurement.

dependent variable: a physical quantity whose value depends on the value of another physical variable

independent variable: physical quantities whose values are selected or controlled by the experimenter.

linearity: an instrument that gives readings that are directly proportional to the magnitude of the quantity being measured.

mean value of a set of readings: this is the sum of the readings divided by the number of readings.

percentage uncertainty:
$$\frac{\text{uncertainty}}{\text{mean value}} \times 100\%$$

precision of a measurement: the degree of exactness of a measurement, usually expressed as the uncertainty of the readings used to obtain the measurement.

precision of an instrument: the smallest non-zero reading that can be measured using the instrument.

random errors: errors that vary in an unpredictable manner with no recognisable pattern or trend or bias.

range of a set of readings: the difference between the largest and the smallest reading.

reliable measurement: a measurement is reliable if a consistent value is obtained each time the same measurement is repeated.

sensitivity of an instrument: the output response per unit input quantity.

systematic errors: errors that show a pattern or a bias or a trend; e.g. due to zero errors in meters.

uncertainty of a measurement: an expression of the spread of values which are likely to include the accepted value. Given by half the range of the readings used to obtain the measurement.

valid measurement: measurements that give the required information by an acceptable method.

zero error of an instrument: a systematic error due to a non-zero reading when the true value of the quantity being measured is zero.

Answers

1.1
3 1570 N when acceleration upwards, 220 N when accelerating downwards

1.2
3 $5.87\,\text{m}\,\text{s}^{-1}$

1.3
2 66.5 N
3 $7.9 \times 10^6\,\text{m}$

1.4
1 270 km
2 $1.88 \times 10^{23}\,\text{kg}$
4 $T_P : T_Q = 8.14 : 1$

2.1
1 a $9.8 \times 10^4\,\text{J}$
  b $9.7 \times 10^4\,\text{J}$
2 Approx. $5.8\,\text{km}\,\text{s}^{-1}$

2.2
4 $1.12 \times 10^4\,\text{m}\,\text{s}^{-1}$

2.3
3 $0.51\,\text{m}\,\text{s}^{-1}$ in the opposite direction to the panel
4 a $0.0192\,\text{kg}\,\text{s}^{-1}$
  b $0.022\,\text{m}\,\text{s}^{-2}$

2.4
1 $11\,\text{m}\,\text{s}^{-1}$
3 0.027, 0.135

2.5
3 a 313 K
  b 273 K

3.1
3 8.97 s
4 $1.27 \times 10^{-2}\,\text{m}$
5 $15\,\text{m}\,\text{s}^{-1}$; 630 kJ

3.2
2 580 N

3.3
2 0.51 s, $18\,\text{m}\,\text{s}^{-1}$

3.4
1 $592\,\text{N}\,\text{m}^{-1}$
2 $42\,\text{m}\,\text{s}^{-1}$

3.5
1 58.7 N
2 a 608 N
  b 1.61 m
4 22.8°

3.6
3 a $9.6 \times 10^2\,\text{kg}\,\text{m}^2\,\text{rad}\,\text{s}^{-1}$
  b $2.1\,\text{rad}\,\text{s}^{-1}$
4 $2.78 \times 10^6\,\text{kg}\,\text{m}^2$

4.2
1 $1.6 \times 10^{14} : 1$
2 977.4 gal
3 $0.01\,\text{N}\,\text{kg}^{-1}$

4.4
1 $3.2 \times 10^{-4}\,\text{N}$
3 0.046 T

4.5
1 $\text{T}\,\text{m}^2$; T
2 0.030 V

4.8
2 No. The additional time taken is 0.05 ms.
3 36°

5.1
4 0.049 m

5.2
3 $2.5 \times 10^{-11}\,\text{m}$

5.3
3 1.25 mm
4 $0.22\,\text{m}\,\text{s}^{-1}$

5.4
3 10.6 MHz

5.5
4 25.2°

6.1

1 a 1.6×10^7 Pa b 3.2×10^5 Pa
3 4.00×10^4 m^2 s^{-2}
4 2.42×10^5 m^2 s^{-2}

6.2

1 a 6.21×10^{-21} J b 2.65×10^5 m^2 s^{-2} c 515 m s^{-1}
2 3.74×10^6 m^2 s^{-2}

6.3

2 b 25%
3 b 230 J

6.4

2 1.84 MJ
3 3.37 K

6.5

2 a 25%
  b i 6.0 kJ ii -20 J K^{-1} iii $+20$ J K^{-1} iv 0

7.1

2 3.19×10^{-10} N
3 3.01×10^5 V m^{-1}
4 5.9×10^7 m s^{-1}

7.2

2 a 2.63×10^{13} m s^{-2} b 4.44×10^{-8} s c 0.259 m
4 b 1.59 cm

7.3

3 16.6 cm, 17.2 cm, 17.5 cm

7.4

3 a 9.06×10^{-5} m b 6.42×10^{-4} m

7.5

1 1.08 MeV
2 b 33 ns c 15.2 MHz d 3.2×10^{-16} J e 522

8.1

1 93 protons; 144 neutrons
2 proton number = 10; nucleon number = 21; electron neutrino
3 2 alpha particles and 4 beta particles
4 8.0×10^{-13} J; 1.5×10^7 m s^{-1}

8.2

1 1.1×10^5 ions
3 13.9 s^{-1}

8.3

1 9.1×10^{-13} s^{-1}
2 i 3.8×10^{13} atoms ii 2.0×10^{-9} g
4 187 years

8.4

3 a 40 kBq b 5.1 kBq

8.5

2 2.2×10^{-6} W (2.2 µW)
3 3.0×10^6 Bq
4 3.6 mg

8.6

1 1.65 µC; 2.9 µJ
2 370 V
3 a 2.84 s b 43.5 s

9.1

1 4.2×10^{-13} kg
2 3.65×10^{-10} kg
4 6300 Bq

9.2

1 7.06 MeV
2 20.58 MeV
3 1.3×10^6 J

9.3

3 $^{135}_{50}$Sn (tin -135)
4 0.181 u ; 2.70×10^{-11} J; 169 MeV

9.4

1 Binding energy falls by 0.093 MeV so no energy released.
2 6.8×10^{11} J

12.1

1 a i 0.524 rad ii 0.873 rad
    iii 2.094 rad iv 4.014 rad v 5.236 rad
  b i 5.73° ii 28.7° iii 68.8°
    iv 143.2° v 343.8°
2 a 20 mm, 2.3° b ii 0.5°
3 a i 0.035 ii 0.140
4 a i 0.0998 ii 0.995
  b i 0.1736 ii 0.9848
  c i 0.7071 ii 0.7071
  d i 0.7071 ii 0.7071

12.2

1 a i 0.477 ii 1.176 b i 1.653 ii 0.699
2 a i 10.8 dB ii 7.0 dB b 17.8 dB
3 a $n = 5, k = 3$ b $n = 3, k = \frac{1}{2}$ c $n = 2, k = 1$
4 a i 1.10 ii 2.71 b i 3.81 ii 1.61

13.1

1 a $x = 1, y = 3$ b $a = 2.4, b = -0.4$ c $p = 2, q = 4$

2 a $u = 14\,\text{m s}^{-1}, a = -2.0\,\text{m s}^{-2}$ b $r = 1.0\,\Omega, \varepsilon = 9.0\,\text{V}$

3 a 0.5 or −3   b 1.4 or 5.6

   c $-\frac{10}{6} = -1.67$ (to 3 sig. figs) or 1

4 a $t = -\frac{20}{6} = -3.33$ (to 3 sig. figs) or 2 s   b $R = 1$ or $4\,\Omega$

13.2

1 a i 2, 3   ii 12, 0.2   iii 4, 0.02

   b i 0.23 s   ii 3.5 s   iii 35 s

2 a 11.3 kBq   b 9.0 kBq   c 0.38 kBq

3 a i 2.20 s   ii 1.52 s   b i 4.83 V   ii 1.24 V

4 a i 0.14 s   ii 82   b $a = 6.9, b = -5$

13.3

2 d i Pa or N m^{-2} ii m^3 iii J

Index

A

ablation 7
absolute temperature 115
absolute zero 114
absorption
    beta particles 157, 158
    gamma rays 158
absorption cross-section 188–9
acceleration graph, water rocket 28
activity 161
    radioactive 160
adiabatic changes 116
adiabatic explosions 30
Advanced Gas-Cooled Reactor (AGR) 189
alpha radiation 155
    ionising and penetrating properties 157
amplitude 34
analysing data 209
angle of dip 64
angular displacement (angle) 50
angular momentum 51
angular velocity 11
anomalies 60
    resistivity surveying 78–9
antineutrino 155
archaeology 59, 78
arcs and arc segments 220
areas in graphs 231; see also integration
AS level, compared with A2 level 208–10
atmospheric drag 7
atomic battery 166–8
atomic mass unit 178
atomic nucleus see nucleus
atomic number, and neutrons 179–80
attenuation coefficient 86
Aurora Borealis 193
Avogadro constant 161

B

background radiation 158–9
Bainbridge, Kenneth 137
barium meal 87
Barton's pendulum 45
Becquerel, Henri 154
becquerel (unit) 160
BEPN (binding energy per nucleon) 183

beta radiation 156
    ionising and penetrating properties 157
beta-voltaic cell 168
binding energy 182–4
biological half-life 165
blood flow 94
Boltzmann constant 113
bremsstrahlung 89
Brownian motion 110
bubble chamber 145
building materials 58
bungee, reverse 44
bungee jumping 41–3

C

caesium-137 167
cancer 154
capacitance 169
capacitor energy 170
capacitors 169–73
    electrolytic 171
    as timers 171–2
carbon dating 139, 181
Carnot cycle 117
CCD 97
centripetal force 11, 12, 47–9
chain reaction 188
characteristic X-rays 90–1
charge-coupled device (CCD) 97, 99–100
    coloured images 100
circular motion 11–12
COBE satellite 114
coefficient of viscosity 6
cogeneration 126
coherent bundle 98
cold fusion 192
cold gas rocket propulsion 31
collisions 22–3
combined heat and power (CHP) plants 126
Compact Linear Collider (CLIC) 148
complex instructions 216
complex instruments 216
Compton scattering 91
conservation of energy 21, 178–9
conservation rules 21–4
continuous flow cooling 122–3
continuous spectrum 89
contrast medium 86–7
control rods 188
cooling systems 121–3
    fission reactors 189

corkscrew rule 65
cosine curves 221–2
cosmic background radiation 114
cosmic rays 142
Coulomb's law 130
count rate 161
critical angle 81–2
critical mass 188
CT scanning 87
Culham Science Centre 192
Curie, Marie 154
curium-234 167
current-balances 68
cyclotron 144–5

D

damping factor 42
data logger 212
daughter nucleus 180
decay constant 160
decay series 156
defibrillators 170
deuteron 190, 191–2
Diamond synchrotron 17
differentiation 228
displacement graph, water rocket 28
Doppler effect 94

E

Earth
    gravitational field 8–9
    magnetic field 65
    retention of atmosphere 20
    rotation 12
eddy currents, magnetic fields 74–6
elastic collisions 22–3
elasticity 41
electric fields
    deflection of particles 133
    and gravitational fields 130–1
    uniform 131
electrolytic capacitor 171
electromagnetic fields
    direction 72
    induced 71–3
electromagnetic induction 71–3
electromagnetic radiation 89
electron beam welding 132
electron gun 132
electron volt (eV) 89, 132
electrons
    specific charge 132
    thermionic effect 131–2
endoscopy 97–8

energy
  binding 182–4
  conservation 21, 178–9
  equivalence with mass 178–81
  internal 29, 113, 121–3
  kinetic 40, 51, 113
energy density of a capacitor 168
entropy 114, 124
equipotential surfaces 16–17
  and field lines 18
escape velocity 19
excitation, protons 95
explosive collisions 23
exponential change 229–30
exponential decrease 229–30
extra high tension (EHT) power
    supplies 136

F

farad 169
Faraday's laws 71
Fermi, Enrico 185
Fermilab 148
fibre optics 97, 98
field of view 98
fields *see* electric fields; gravity;
    magnetic fields
fine-beam tube 134
fission 185–9
  coolant 189
  moderator 188
  problems 186
Fleming's left-hand rule 67, 133
fluids 6
fluorine-18 164
flux *see* magnetic flux
force-field curves 232
four stroke engine 118
frequency 34
fuel rods 188

G

g-forces 4–5
  on pendulum rides 39
gal 61
gamma radiation 156
  inverse-square law 159
  ionising and penetrating
    properties 158
gamma (unit) 68
gases
  in cylinder 112
  internal energy 113
  isothermal changes 116
  kinetic theory 110–11
Geiger–Müller tube 157, 213
geophone 73
geophysics 58–0
  seismology 80–2
  soil resistivity 77–9

geostationary orbit 12
geosynchronous orbit 12
gradient field 95
graphs
  area under curve 231
  logarithmic scale 224
gravimeter 62–3
gravitational constant 8
gravitational field strength 4, 9, 61
gravitational potential 16–18
gravitational potential energy 16
gravitron 47
gravity 8–10
  field lines 18
  field strength 4, 9, 61
  gravitational constant 8
  potential 16–18
  potential energy 16
gravity surveying 61–3

H

half-life 162, 230
  biological 165
  measurement 163
half-thickness 158
Hall effect 68
Hall probe 69
harmonics 45
heat 29
  equivalence to work 121
heat engines 116–17, 125–6
Helmholtz coils 135
Higgs boson 143
Hounsfield, Sir Godfrey 87

I

ideal gas equation 30
impulse 21
incoherent bundle 98
induced current 72
induced fission *see* fission
inelastic collisions 23
inertia 50–3
integration 231–2
internal combustion engine 118–
    19, 121–2
  internal energy 121–3
internal energy 29
  of gas 113
  internal combustion engine
    121–3
International Linear Collider (ILC)
    143, 148
inverse-square law 8, 159, 232
investigative skills assessment (ISA)
    207, 214–15
iodine 155, 161, 180
ion detector, mass spectrometer 138
ion propulsion 31
ionisation 157–8

ionising radiation 88
  safety 216
ions 75–6
isothermal changes 116
isotopes 154

J

Joint European Torus (JET) reactor
    192–3

K

Ketterle, Wolfgang 114
kinetic energy
  gases 113
  rotational 51
  in simple harmonic motion 40
kinetic theory of gases 110–11
  and molecular energy 113

L

Lamor frequency 70
  protons in magnetic resonance
    imaging 95–6
Large Electron Positron (LEP)
    collider 146
Large Hadron Collider (LHC) 143,
    147
Lawrence, E. O. 144
Lenz's law 72–3
light gates 212
linear accelerator (linac) 140–3
linear simultaneous equations 226
liquid cooling 122
logarithms 223–5
London Eye 47, 48
longitudinal waves 92

M

magnetic field surveying 64–5
magnetic fields
  definition 64
  eddy currents 74–6
  effects on charged particles 133–4
  flux 67
  change without movement 74–5
  flux cutting 71–2
  flux density 68–0
  flux linkage 72
  producing 66
  strength 65
magnetic resonance imaging 95–6
  disadvantages 96
Magnox reactor 189
mass 4
  equivalence to energy 178–1
  of Sun 13
mass absorption coefficient 87
mass defect 183
mass number 182
mass spectrometer 137–8

mean kinetic energy, gases **113**
medicine **164–5**
  risk **196**
metal detectors **76**
metals, work function **131**
metastable isotopes **165**
microscope
  scanning electron **132**
  travelling **212**
Millennium Bridge **46**
moderator, fission **188**
molar gas constant *see* ideal gas law
mole (unit) **161**
momentum **21**
  on Earth **24**
  in space **23**
momentum selector, mass
  spectrometer **138**
MOS capacitor **99**
motion sickness **40**
MRI **95–6**
multipath dispersion **98**
muons **142**

N

National Radiological Protection
  Board (NRPB) **195**
natural logarithms **224–5**
neutrons, and atomic number
  179–80
Newton, Isaac **8**
Newton's cradle **22**
Newton's third law **22**
non-intrusive exploration **58–60**
nuclear decay, energy released **179**
nuclear fission **185–9**
nuclear fusion **190–3**
nuclear power
  fission **185–9**
  fusion **190–3**
  risks **197**
nuclear radiation, types **154–6**
nucleus
  binding energy **182–4**
  nuclides **154**
  stability **179–81**
  see also nuclear fission; nuclear
    fusion
nuclides **154**

O

orbital velocity **20**
ores **58**
oscillations
  damped **43**
  damping **44–5**
  decay **44, 44–5**
  resonance **45–6**
  time period **11–12, 34**
  see also simple harmonic motion

oscilloscope **211**
Otto cycle **118, 119**

P

P waves **80**
pacemakers **166, 166–7, 169,
  170–1**
particle accelerators
  cyclotron **144–5**
  linear **140–3**
  synchrotron **146–9**
particles
  charged
    deflection by magnetic field
      133–5
    deflection by uniform electric
      field **133**
pendulum **34, 36**
  compound **52–3**
  g-forces **39–40**
period **11–12, 34**
permeability of free space **96**
permittivity of free space **130**
PET scanners **164**
Petronas Towers **58**
photodiode **99**
photons, and CCDs **99**
pixel **99**
plasmas, in JET reactor **192–3**
plutonium **167, 185–9**
pollution **123**
polonium **154, 167**
positron **191**
potential difference **77**
potential well **17**
practical skills assessment (PSA)
  207
practical skills verification (PSV)
  217–18
practical tasks **214**
practical work **208–10**
precession **95**
pressure **110–12, 112**
pressurised water reactor
  (PWR) **187**
protactinium-234 **163**
proton magnetometer **69**
protons, and magnetic resonance
  imaging **95–6**
pulse length, pacemakers **169**

Q

quadratic equations **227**
quantum efficiency **99–100**

R

radian **220**
radiation
  electromagnetic **89**
  background **114, 158–9**

nuclear **154–6, 157**
  in medicine **164–5**
  risk and protection **196–7**
radioactive decay **154–6, 160–3**
  decay series **156**
  half-life **162**
radiocarbon dating **139, 181**
radioisotope thermoelectric
  generator (RTG) **168**
radium **154**
reflection, seismic waves **81**
refraction, seismic waves **81, 82**
resistance, of soil **78**
resistivity **77–9**
resistivity surveying **77–80**
resonance **44–5**
restoring force **41**
reverse bungee **44**
Richter scale **81, 224**
risk **194–7**
rocket equation **26–7**
rockets
  and escape velocity **20**
  forces acting on **25**
  fuel types **30–1**
  launching **25–6**
  loss of mass **26**
  propulsion **25–6**
  thermodynamics **30**
  water rockets **27–8**
  working fluid **29**
Roentgen, Wilhelm Conrad **86**
roller coasters **38**
rotation **47–9, 50–3**
rotor **47**

S

S waves **80–1**
safety **216**
  water rockets **28**
  see also risk
Sankey diagram **125**
satellites **12**
  energy in orbit **20**
scanning electron microscope **132**
scattering **91**
scheme T **207**
scheme X **207, 217–19**
Schwarzschild radius **19–20**
search coil **75**
seismic waves **80–1**
seismology **80–2**
seismometer **80–1**
sign convention **30**
simple harmonic motion **35–8**
  kinetic energy **40**
simultaneous equations **226–7**
sine functions **35–7, 221–2**
  differentiation **229**
sinusoidal waveforms **35–7, 221–2**

small angle approximation **220–1**
soil conductivity **75–6**
soil conductivity meter **75–6**
solid rocket fuel **31**
Space Shuttle **7**
Special Theory of Relativity **20,**
 141, 142
specific heat capacity **120**
spectrometer **213**
spectrum, continuous **89**
springs, loaded **41–2**
Stanford Linear Accelerator in
 California (SLAC) **140–3**
Stokes' law **6**
streamline flow **6**
strontium-90 **167**
Sun
 mass **13**
 nuclear fusion **190–3**
swing carousel **49**
synchrotron **146–9**
synchrotron radiation **146–7, 148**

Tacoma Narrows bridge **46**
Tara ore body **59**
technetium-99m **164–5**
temperature **120**
terminal velocity **6**
tesla **67**
thermal efficiency, heat engine **123,**
 125

thermionic effect **131–2**
thermionic emission **89, 131**
thermocouple **168**
thermodynamics
 zeroth law **120**
 first law **29–30, 113–14, 116–17**
 second law **124–6**
thermopile **168**
Thompson, J. J. **135–6**
thrust **25**
time constant **172, 230**
time dilation **141–2**
time period **11–12, 34**
time's arrow **124**
torque **50**
transformers **74–5**
travelling microscope **212**
trigonometry **220–2**
turbulent flow **6**

ultrasound **92–4**
 compared with X-ray imaging **94**
uranium-235 **185**

velocity graph, water rocket **28**
velocity selector, mass spectrometer
 138
velodromes **49**
viscosity **6**

water rockets **27–8**
weber (unit) **67**
weight **4**
 and Earth's rotation **12**
weightlessness **4–5**
White, Edward **23**
work **29**
 equivalence to heat **121**
work function **131**
written test **215**

X-rays
 beam production **89**
 characteristic **90–1**
 dangers **88**
 discovery **86**
 imaging **86–7, 94**
 interactions with matter **91**
 properties **89**

Acknowledgements

Photograph Acknowledgements

The authors and publisher are grateful to the following for permission to reproduce photographs and other copyright material in this book.

Alamy: p 197; **Alamy/AEP:** p 59(right); **Alamy/Andrew Warburton:** p 44; **Alamy/David Ball:** p 48; **Alamy/Design Pics Inc.:** p 58(right); **Alamy/Henry George Beeker:** p 3; **Alamy/Ivo Roospold:** p 52(bottom); **Alamy/JTB Photo Communications, Inc.:** p 15; **Alamy/T. Lehne/Lotuseaters:** p 74; **Alamy/Leslie Garland Picture Library:** p 171; **Alamy/Lightworks Media:** p 52(top); **Alamy/Medical-on-Line:** p 95(top), 97(top); **Alamy/Paul Cox:** p 49; **Alamy/Phototake Inc.:** p 88; **Alamy/Rolf Richardson:** p 58(left), 182(left); **Alamy/sciencephotos:** p 134, 213; **Alamy/Skyscan Photolibrary:** p 185(bottom); **Alamy/Springfield Photography:** p 55; **Alamy/Trevor Smith:** p 93; **Ann Ronan Picture Library:** p 154; **Arco Images/Frank, R.:** p 42; **Carsten Reisinger:** p 196(top); **Corbis/David Batterbury:** p 34; **EFDA:** p 192(right), 193; **Eye Ubiquitous:** p 34; **Dorling Kindersley/Andy Crawford:** p 110; **Fotolia.com/Photoma:** p 124; **Martyn Chillmaid:** p 68; **NASA:** p 23; **Science Photo Library:** p 145; **Science Photo Library/Andrew Lambert Photography:** p 212; **Science Photo Library/Argonne National Laboratory:** p 185 (top); **Science Photo Library/CERN:** p 109, 146; **Science Photo Library/David M. Martin:** p 97(bottom); **Science Photo Library/David Parker:** p 99, 165; **Science Photo Library/Edward Kinsman:** p 27, 31; **Science Photo Library/Gary Hincks:** p 13; **Science Photo Library/GIPHOTOSTOCK:** 211; **Science Photo Library/Gustoimages:** p 95(bottom); **Science Photo Library/Mehau Kulyk:** p viii; **Science Photo Library/Martyn F. Chillmaid:** 22; **Science Photo Library/NASA/ESA/STSCI/A.Wilson, UMD, et al.:** p 20; **Science Photo Library/Pascal Goetgheluck:** p 76; **Science Photo Library/Stanford Linear Accelerator Center:** p 140; **Science Photo Library/Volker Steger:** p 114; **Science Photo Library/Zephyr:** p 86; **Stratascan:** p 60; **UKAEA, courtesy of Emilio Segre Visual Archives:** p 196(bottom).

Every effort has been made to trace and contact all copyright holders and we apologise if any have been overlooked. The publisher will be pleased to make the necessary arrangements at the first opportunity.

Authors' Acknowledgements

In addition to my thanks for the encouragement and consistent advice offered by Ken, I would like to thank my students past and present and my colleagues in both the Bromsgrove School Physics Department and the AQA Physics B teams: Andy Burton, Michael Thompson, Emma Rein and David Wilson and John Avison, David Homer, Gerard Kelly, Barrie Lancaster and Roger Oakley; each of you has influenced my views of physics in subtle and sometimes less subtle ways. Above all I would like to thank my wife, Adele, for always keeping my feet on the ground and putting working on this book into perspective.

Mike Bowen-Jones

I, too, would like to thank those colleagues from AQA who Mike has already mentioned and also all those teaching and examining colleagues with whom I have had the pleasure to work over the years. The influence of the many hours of discussion with them in formulating my views on the teaching, learning and examining of physics is immeasurable. My thanks too to all those students whose questions and enthusiasm for the physics have stimulated my own exploration of the subject. Finally, and most of all, I would like to thank my wife, Lynette, for her tireless support and encouragement throughout the project.

Ken Price

The authors also wish to thank the publishing team at Nelson Thornes, in particular Carol Usher and Eleanor O'Byrne for their highly professional support throughout the project. Thanks also to the development editors, Ros and Chris Davies for their invaluable work on the drafts and suggestions for improvements.